Crossing the Borders

New Methods and Techniques in the Study of Archaeological Materials from the Caribbean

Edited by
Corinne L. Hofman, Menno L. P. Hoogland, and
Annelou L. van Gijn

THE UNIVERSITY OF ALABAMA PRESS
Tuscaloosa

Copyright © 2008
The University of Alabama Press
Tuscaloosa, Alabama 35487-0380
All rights reserved
Manufactured in the United States of America

Typeface: Minion and Stone Sans

∞

The paper on which this book is printed meets the minimum requirements of American
National Standard for Information Sciences-Permanence of Paper for Printed Library
Materials, ANSI Z39.48-1984.

Library of Congress Cataloging-in-Publication Data

Crossing the borders : new methods and techniques in the study of archaeological
materials from the Caribbean / edited by Corinne L. Hofman, Menno L. P. Hoogland,
and Annelou L. van Gijn.
p. cm. — (Caribbean archaeology and ethnohistory)
Outcome of a symposium held at the 71st Meeting of the Society for American
Archaeology in Puerto Rico in April 2006.
Includes bibliographical references and index.
ISBN-13: 978-0-8173-1585-6 (cloth : alk. paper)
ISBN-10: 0-8173-1585-3 (alk. paper)
ISBN-13: 978-0-8173-5453-4 (pbk. : alk. paper)
ISBN-10: 0-8173-5453-0 (alk. paper)
1. Indians of the West Indies—Antiquities—Congresses. 2. Excavations (Archaeology)—
West Indies—Congresses. 3. Archaeology—West Indies—Methodology—Congresses.
4. West Indies—Antiquities—Congresses. I. Hofman, Corinne Lisette, 1959– II. Hoogland,
Menno Lambertus Pieter, 1954– III. Gijn, Annelou L. van, 1954– IV. Society for American
Archaeology. Meeting (71st : 2006 : Puerto Rico)
F1619.C76 2008
972.9′01072—dc22

2007025952

Contents

Contents / vii

List of Illustrations

TABLES

Crossing the Borders

1

Crossing Disciplinary Boundaries and National Borders

New Methods and Techniques in the Study of Archaeological Materials from the Caribbean

Corinne L. Hofman, Menno L. P. Hoogland, and Annelou L. van Gijn

Introduction

During the past decades, Caribbean scholars have increasingly employed and developed new methods and techniques for the study of archaeological materials. While the aim of earlier research in the Caribbean was mainly to define typologies on the basis of pottery and lithic assemblages leading to the establishment of chronological charts for the region, it was not until the 1980s that the use of technological and functional analyses of artifacts gained interest. The 1990s saw a veritable boom in this field, introducing innovative methods and techniques for analyzing artifacts and human skeletal remains. Innovative approaches that were introduced included microscopic use-wear analysis, starch residue and phytolith analysis, stable isotope analysis, experimental research, ethnoarchaeological studies, geochemical analyses, and aDNA studies. Such studies benefited from a diverse array of experience related to the international background of the researchers constituting the archaeological community of the Caribbean. Most of these methods and techniques have long proven to be very successful in the study of archaeological materials elsewhere in the world, but in the Caribbean were less common and had not been applied systematically. The application of these approaches has shown their intrinsic value for the interpretation of the archaeological data of recently excavated sites throughout the Caribbean region and have provided new insights into the interpretation of the precolonial societies of the Caribbean, specifically regarding artifact manufacturing processes, technological systems, resource exploitation, diet, mobility, exchange, social organization, continuity, and cultural change.

The present volume forms an outcome of the symposium titled "New Methods and Techniques in the Study of Material Culture in the Caribbean," held at the 71st Meeting of the Society for American Archaeology in Puerto Rico in April 2006. The symposium was organized by Corinne Hofman and Annelou van Gijn, both of the Faculty of Archaeology at Leiden University, as a product of collaborative research between its Caribbean Research Group and the Laboratory of Artifacts initiated 15 years ago.

The purpose of this volume is to bring together new methods and techniques in the study of archaeological materials from the Caribbean and to assess possible avenues of mutual benefit and integration. The introduction of innovative approaches has generated new research questions for the archaeology of the Caribbean in general over the past years. The current volume comprehensively explores the advantages and disadvantages in the application of a selected number of newly emerging methods and techniques.

Each of these approaches is illustrated by a case study. A background to the study of archaeological materials in the Caribbean since the 1930s is provided in order to contextualize the latest developments in this field.

Background to the Study of Archaeological Materials in the Caribbean

The Initiators: 1930s–1980s

Typo-chronological studies have been the driving force in Caribbean archaeology since the early 1930s. Such studies were used to describe the cultural development in the Caribbean on the basis of pottery, because pottery represents a very important part of the material culture of Amerindian communities, besides artifacts made of shell, coral, and stone, and perishable materials such as wood, calabash, fibers, cotton, and feathers. The actual ratio of perishable vs. nonperishable materials in the original artifact assemblages of the Amerindian communities in the Caribbean is unknown, although it is most likely that perishable materials accounted for more than half of the material culture assemblage.

In order to establish a typo-chronological framework for the Caribbean, Irving Rouse (1972) employed the multivariate "modal" approach and advocated the classification of pottery styles as the basis for delimiting a material culture and the people behind that culture. In his view, recurrent artifact assemblages or "cultures" can be ascribed to one people and the cultural development of that people can be described on the basis of the development of style. Rouse, who followed the Midwestern Taxonomic System developed by McKern (Lyman and O'Brien 2002), defined a pottery style or complex as the entire pottery repertoire of a people during one single cultural period. This hierarchical scheme was conceived of as analogous to the biological classification system created by the eighteenth-century Swedish naturalist, Carolus Linnaeus.

Rouse emphasized each pottery style as defined by a unique set of material, shape, and/or decorative attributes, which may also be used to identify the area and period, and the people and culture responsible for its manufacture (Rouse 1972, 1989:385). Continuities and changes in modes were traced from style to style within a series or subseries in order to define and determine its origin (Rouse 1964, 1982). Style, series, and subseries names are derived from the site at which the characteristic modes were first identified. Rouse's method was subsequently adopted by McKusick (1960), Allaire (1977), Boomert (1980), and many others in the course of time. More recently, Rouse added the concept of wares to the notion of pottery styles. A ware is characterized by a set of modes for material, technology, shape, and decoration and can represent or be part of a pottery style (Rouse 1992: 81, 185).

Meanwhile, other Caribbean scholars developed alternative classification schemes. These were introduced into Caribbean archaeology by French, Spanish, North American, Antillean, and later also Dutch researchers (e.g., Barbotin 1974; Bullen 1964; Bullen and Bullen 1968; Gauthier 1973; Hoffman 1967; Mattioni and Bullen 1970; Petitjean Roget 1963, 1968, 1970; Pinchon 1952; Rainey 1940; Sears and Sullivan 1978; Winter 1978).

The French priest Père Pinchon (1952) for example, divided partial to complete vessels into domestic (plain, simple decoration) and ritual (elaborate decoration) earthenware and assigned functions to them based on ethnographic examples. Jacques Petitjean Roget (1970) classified vessel types on the basis of decoration, shape, and size. Scholars of the Spanish-speaking islands and Venezuela such as Veloz Maggiolo, Sanoja, and Vargas Arenas (Sanoja 1979; Vargas Arenas 1979a, 1979b) classified ceramic assemblages from the Guianas, Dominican Republic, and Venezuela on the basis of ware and decoration, vessel shape, and size in order to create profiles corresponding to "phases." In this same vein, scholars of the American school like Bullen (1964), Hoffman (1979), and Sears and Sullivan (1978) used the Southeastern System (Ford 1954) to identify types (types, local sequences, and specimens). This approach, also called the type-variety method, was introduced into the Caribbean by Evans and Meggers (1960). Bullen (1962, 1964) used the method to classify pottery on the Windward Islands (Grenada) and the Virgin Islands (St. Thomas), Hoffman (1967, 1979) for the classification of materials from the Bahamas and Antigua, while Sears and Sullivan (1978) classified pottery from the Bahamas using this method. In order to define a type they used the name of a site in combination with the name of the style variety (for example, Pearls Incised or Palmetto Punctate).

Some of the studies made use of data from ethnohistory or ethnography in order to arrive at interpretations of vessel function (e.g., Barbotin 1974; Petitjean Roget 1963). Jacques Petitjean Roget (1963) and later Maurice Barbotin (1974:Plates V–VIII) exploited information from the Carib-French and French-Carib dictionaries by Père Raymond Breton for his descriptions of the Island Carib pottery. These scholars made attempts to assign functions to specific vessel shapes on the basis of Breton's description of their use. Barbotin (1974) describes among others the *chamacou* and the *taoloüa*, which are large wide-mouthed pots serving as containers or drinking bowls, the *tourare*, equally large but higher and used as a cooking pot for vegetables, fish, and meat; the *ialigali*, a bottomless pot for grilling fish; and the *boutalli*, the griddle. Numerous others later took up this kind of research. Ethnohistoric sources also formed the basis to discuss the use, availability, and role of metals among the indigenous peoples of the Caribbean (Alegría 1974; Guarch 1978; Oliver 2000; Szaszdi Nagy 1984).

In addition to this focus on pottery, research into lithic technology and function was also initiated (e.g., Alegría et al. 1955; Barbotin 1973; Boomert and Kroonenberg 1977; Haag 1970; Pantel 1976; Petitjean Roget 1974, 1978; Pike and Pantel 1974; Pinchon 1961; Roobol and Lee 1976; Rouse 1941; Veloz Maggiolo and Ortega 1973), besides that of shell implements and ornaments as well as coral tools (Alcolado 1976; Armstrong 1979; Bullen 1964; Clerc 1974; Coomans 1965; Goodwin and Walker 1975; Goodwin et al. 1979; Sickler Robinson 1978; Sutty 1978). This category of studies resulted in descriptions of the technological and morphological aspects of lithic, shell, and coral artifacts, which were considered supplementary to the frameworks established on the basis of pottery. Apart from establishing typologies and sequences of production, typo-technological studies were used as a relative dating method and to make inferences about exchange items (e.g., Barbotin 1970; Bullen and Bullen 1967, 1970; Harris 1978; Mattioni 1970, 1971; Mattioni and Bullen 1970; Petitjean Roget 1970; Vescelius and Robinson 1979). Finally, there are the first archaeo-metallurgical studies of Krieger, and colleagues summarized in Vega (1979), employing basic wet chemistry techniques to identify approximate chemical compositions of metal artifacts excavated from sites in Cuba and the Dominican Republic. Vega himself was the first to then develop the application of archaeometric techniques using atomic absorption spectrophotometry (AAS) for chemical analysis. He focused on a study of metal artifacts recovered from archaeological sites in Haiti and the Dominican Republic. His analyses revealed the presence of European brass in an indigenous context for the first time, citing the high zinc content of a metal sample with 84.95 percent copper and 13.13 percent zinc (Vega 1979). Vega argues that the Taíno were exploiting and working locally available gold and copper into ornaments before European contact. This metalworking tradition then adopted the use of European brass as it became available in the fifteenth and sixteenth centuries.

Chanlatte Baik investigated a metal object discovered during excavations of an indigenous burial in Guayanilla, Puerto Rico (Chanlatte Baik 1977). Chanlatte Baik then discovered a modern source of riverine gold nuggets found in the local Rio Congo by José Rodriguez, a local resident. He consequently argued that local gold resources were being exploited and worked by basic hammering and annealing.

The New Generation: 1980s–Early Twenty-First Century

From the 1980s onward, the number of studies focusing on technological aspects of archaeological materials in the Caribbean rapidly increased. Scholars gradually initiated new approaches involving archaeometric techniques, often already tested and in use in other parts of the world, next to applying conventional technological research. With the introduction of these new approaches the typological studies of artifacts initiated during the past few decades were systematically elaborated and complemented. A wide array of characterization studies, studies on manufacturing techniques, production sequences, and functional studies, have seen light in Caribbean archaeological research during the past two decades.

Technological Studies. Technological studies of artifacts have been undertaken to document production sequences, manufacturing techniques, and use. These studies not only include the analysis of pottery and lithics but to an increasing extent also that of shell and coral tools. Evidently, the diversity in classification methods described above was also pertinent in the way technology was approached. In this respect, mention should be made of the impact of the French school of André Leroi-Gourhan (1943) and his concept of the *chaîne opératoire* for the study of materials, which was introduced into Caribbean archaeology by archaeologists working on the French Islands (e.g., Allaire 1985; Bérard 2001; Rostain and Dacal Moure 1997; Serrand 2002). The principle of studying all sequences of the process of tool production and the pottery manufacture process, including the sourcing of the raw materials, processing, shaping, and finishing of the final product, emphasized the importance of incorporating technology into the study of Caribbean archaeological materials otherwise mainly focused on the classification of stylistic and morphological characteristics.

Other noteworthy frameworks in use in the Caribbean were based on differences between archaeological assemblages (Chanlatte Baik 1981); ecology and cultural lifeways (Goodwin 1979); or on more Marxist approaches like those by Dominican (Veloz Maggiolo 1991) and Cuban (Dacal Moure and Rivero de la Calle 1984) archaeologists. The Dominican/Cuban scheme was based on five stages of *modo de vida*, or ways of life, in which an evolutionary stage was related to a "mode of production."

Following in the footsteps of the earlier generation of researchers, ethnohistoric and ethnographic research continued to be incorporated into technological studies in several instances in order to get grips on the relation between vessel form and function (e.g., Bloo 1997; Boomert 1986; Harris 1995; Hofman and Bright 2004; Petitjean Roget 1995; Roe 1989; Rostain 1991; Rouse 1992). Boomert (1986), for example, made extensive use of various ethnohistoric sources in addition to ethno-graphic data from the Kari'na of the South American mainland in his discussion of the Cayo complex of St. Vincent. Harris (1995) used the same ethnohistoric in-formation but also ethnographic data from the Shipibo-Conibo and the eastern Tukanoan people of the Peruvian Amazon in order to establish an ethnotypology for Antillean pottery (see below).

The study of the manufacturing process and function of pottery has revealed a wide range of techniques employed in the production of Caribbean pottery (Bloo 1997; Curet 1997; Harris 1995; Hofman et al. 1993, this volume; Jacobson 2002; Jouravleva and La Roza Corzo 2003; Roe 1989). Systematic insights were obtained in the fabrication sequences and ways of vessel shaping, decorating, and firing. In some cases it has been evidenced that several techniques were combined in the shaping of one vessel. This kind of research also enabled differentiation between pottery assemblages on the basis of technological parameters (Bonnissent 1995; Hofman 1993; Hofman, Hoogland, and Delpuech et al. 2003), rather than on exclu-sively stylistic and/or morphological attributes. As such, it was established that the Caribbean ceramics from the Early Ceramic Age can be clearly divided into classes in terms of fabric, shaping, decoration, and firing techniques (Hofman and Jacobs 2000/2001; Hofman et al. 2003). Roe and Harris both focused on complete vessels instead of pottery sherds in their approaches to pottery interpretation (see also Espenshade 2000). Roe (1989) adopted a "generative grammatical" approach that views the potter as selecting among pastes, decorative and functional elements, and motifs in designing and making a unique vessel. Roe built upon Rouse's modal analytic framework and aimed at reconstructing both stereotyping and innova-tion in archaeological pottery complexes. Harris (1995, 2001) introduced the no-tion of ethnotypology, focused on ethnographic reality, classifying pottery spe-cifically by vessel types, defining Hypothetical-Vessel-Functions and Codes (ware, iconography, and form).

An interesting feature is that basketry was accidentally or purposefully used as a base for pottery manufacture as evidenced by textile impressions on ceramic sherds from Caribbean sites. As a result various weaving techniques could be docu-mented that provide insight into Amerindian fiber work (Berman and Hutcheson 1997, 2000, 2001a, and 2001b; Hutcheson 2001, this volume; Petersen et al. 1999). The rare occurrence of basketry impressions on ceramics encountered at archaeo-logical sites suggests that the Amerindian populations across the Caribbean re-gion in general seem to have been making their ceramics on fiber mats only oc-casionally, whereas this appears to have been a common practice in the Bahamas (e.g., Chanlatte Baik 1984; Granberry and Winter 1995; Hoffman 1970; Hofman et al. 2001; Rouse and Cruxent 1963). Petersen and colleagues (1999) identified the techniques of coiling, plaiting, and twining as shown by textile impressions on ce-ramic sherds from Antigua and Montserrat. Twill plaiting predominates, a technique also employed most frequently in the Bahamas (Berman and Hutcheson 1997). Petersen and colleagues (1999) tentatively conclude that in the Northern Lesser Antilles at least, basketry may have been used as a base for ceramic manufacture largely, or solely, during the Early Ceramic Age.

The lithic technology of the precolonial peoples of the Caribbean has not been extensively studied to date. Research has predominantly been oriented toward tool and flake production and use, generating a panoply of descriptive texts on lithic reductive technology, morphology, and style (e.g., Allaire 1985; Bartone and Crock 1991; Bérard 1999a, 2001, this volume; Davis 2000, 2002; De Waal 1999a; Febles and Baena 1995; Febles et al. 1995; Harris 1983, 1991; Haviser 1999; Jérémie 1995; Knippenberg 1999a; Lewenstein 1980; Ortega and Guerrero 1985; Pantel 1991; Rodríguez Ramos 1999, 2001a, 2003; Roe et al. 1990; Rostain 1995; Stevens 2002; Vialon 2001; Walker 1980a). Many of these studies on lithic technology were aimed at detecting typo-chronological variants. Initially, the typology of Caribbean flint tools was based on the form and size of the tool in relation to similar tools in Europe and North America. The function of these tools was also transferred onto the implements found in Caribbean sites. Gus Pantel (1991:159) proposed an alternative approach emphasizing technological aspects of the Caribbean flaked stone tools based on a paradigmatic classificatory system in which dimensions and modes are described. The dimension refers to major axe variation in flaked stone assemblages, while modes represent specific individual variants. With his classification model he addressed more fundamental questions as to why cultural differences exist. Pantel is concerned with the lithic resources available to peoples in individual island biospheres and the acquisition and/or development of the technological skills necessary to exploit these environments.

Besides aiming at a better understanding of prehistoric technologies and the function of lithic tools, questions concerning typo-chronology and diachronic change within island assemblages were also addressed. Some of the Caribbean technological studies focused more specifically on axe-adze production and axe use (Berman et al. 1999; Chancerel 2003; Harris 1983; Mattioni 1990; Rostain 1994, 1995; Rostain and Wack 1987). Harris's (1983) classification, which served as a good temporal/chronological framework for axe/adzes, is based upon the shape of butts and blades. Their framework was derived from the analysis of more than 500 axes and adzes from all over the Lesser Antilles.

Another important category encompasses lapidary objects such as beads and pendants. Bead production evidences a highly refined lithic technology (e.g., Bartone and Crock 1991; Crock and Bartone 1998; De Mille 1996; De Mille et al. 1999; Haviser 1990a; Murphy et al. 2000; Watters and Scaglion 1994). While studies on the technological aspects of bead manufacture and source identification are still ongoing, most of the bead research has been focused on spatial and temporal distributions, identifying variability, and verifying centers for bead manufacture in the islands (Boomert 1987a, 1987b, 2000:439; Cody 1991; Haviser 1999; Narganes Storde 1995a, 1995b; Rodríguez López 1991b; Watters 1997a:8, 1997b).

Typo-technological studies of shell and coral tools have been recently added to the array. Functional categories of shell tools were established on the basis of morphology, modification, and macroscopic use-wear traces, in some cases complemented with experiments (e.g., Alegría et al. 1981; Brokke 1999; Carlson 1995; Cartwright et al. 1991; Dacal Moure 1978, 1997; Dacal Moure and Croes 2001, 2004; Haviser 1990a; Izquierdo Diaz 1988, 1991; Jones O'Day and Keegan 2001; Keegan 1981, 1984; Lammers-Keijsers 2001; Lundberg 1985; Serrand 1995, 1997, 2001, 2002; Serrand et al. 1997; Van der Steen 1992; Vargas Arenas et al. 1993). Research goals involved investigation of *Strombus* axe/adze manufacture and use (Antczak 1998; Keegan 1984; Serrand 2001) and shell bead production (e.g., Carlson 1995; Dacal Moure 1989; Linville 2004; Littman and Keegan 1991). Methods for classifying shell artifacts have been presented by Dacal Moure (1978:22) and in a similar way defined by Keegan (1981:82), as departing from the fact that the morphology of the shell is the primary factor that describes tool form. Dacal Moure (1997:159) adapted his method while studying the shell artifacts of the Tanki Flip site on Aruba and put more emphasis on the relationship between artifacts and raw materials with the intention to better understand Amerindian activities. He made a division between recurrent forms, the more elaborate or highly modified (often polished) artifacts including beads and bead-blanks, and other shell material. Littmann and Keegan (1991:150) describe bead manufacture on the basis of broken beads and bead blanks from the site of Grand Turk. They distinguished two steps in bead manufacture involving flaking, chipping, and/or cutting the shell into a rounded bead blank with flat sides. According to Littman and Keegan, this was obviously the stage at which they were drilled.

Studies on the technology and function of coral tools of Caribbean sites have also continued to expand (e.g., De Waal 2002; Rostain 1997; Sipe et al. 1980; Steenvoorden 1992). Steenvoorden (1992:124–138) macroscopically identified use-wear on coral implements for the Saladoid site of Golden Rock on St. Eustatius and interpreted the fragments as grinders, polishing/rubbing tools, scalers, and bores or gimlets on the basis of their wear patterns, shapes, and worked edges in a similar way to Goodwin and Walker (1975:49), who described tools made of coral from Villa Taina in Puerto Rico.

Microscopic Use-Wear Analysis. Although there have been general attempts to relate artifact technology, morphology, and function, only very few older studies applied microscopic use-wear analysis in order to confirm hypotheses about tool function and to improve our understanding of the way artifacts were handled in the domestic activities carried out. Since the mid-1970s microscopic use-wear analysis has been a well-known method in European archaeology and elsewhere

(Van Gijn 1990), but unfortunately it has been applied only in rare cases in Caribbean archaeology (Bartone and Crock 1991; Lundberg 1985; Sears and Sullivan 1978; Walker 1980a).

In 1980 Walker was the first to apply the Low Power microscopic approach to a Ceramic Age flint assemblage, that from Sugar Factory Pier on St. Kitts (Walker 1980a, 1980b, 1983). During the last couple of years, Low Power techniques have been supplemented by the High Power approach, and both have been increasingly applied to flint assemblages from the Caribbean (Briels 2004; Lammers-Keijsers 2007). Until about five years ago the majority of use-wear research worldwide was directed at flint tools. Recently, tools made of pottery, shell, bone, antler, or coral have been examined as well (i.e., Barton and White 1993; López Varela et al. 2002; Maigrot 1997, 2001; Oversteegen et al. 2001; Van Gijn 2005; Van Gijn and Hofman in press). Some of these studies were done on Caribbean artifacts (Kelly 2001, 2003, 2004; Kelly and Van Gijn this volume; Lammers-Keijsers 1999; Van Gijn et al. this volume).

In a similar vein, Christy de Mille and Tamara Varney (2003, this volume) used scanning electron microscopy (SEM) on molds of stone beads from Saladoid sites on Antigua to examine traces of manufacture. This research addresses questions as to the manufacturing techniques, organization of production, and intra- and intersite variability in order to get a better understanding of Saladoid lapidary technology as a whole, in which technology is viewed as socially meaningful and mediated.

In the process, use-wear analysis has also provided information on organic materials worked by the Caribbean Amerindians, otherwise lost in the archaeological matrix but which play a crucial role in comprehending past subsistence and craft activities (Briels 2004; Kelly 2003, 2004; Lammers-Keijsers 2007; Nieuwenhuis 2002; Van Gijn et al. this volume).

Recently, starch and phytolith analysis on stone tools and ceramics has proven to be a potentially valuable source of information on what plant species were processed with these tools in Caribbean archaeological sites (Lundberg 1989; Nieuwenhuis this volume; Pagán Jiménez and Oliver this volume; Pagán Jiménez et al. 2005; Rodríguez Suárez 2004; Rodríguez Suárez and Pagán Jiménez this volume). This kind of research may also be an aid to paleobotanical investigation in defining plant species (Newsom this volume; Newsom and Wing 2004; Pagán Jiménez and Oliver this volume; Pagán Jiménez et al. 2005).

Only in rare cases has the entire toolkit of Caribbean sites been studied, involving the technological and functional analysis of shell, coral, and stone tools and the interaction of these tools in particular activities (Kelly 2004; Rostain 2001; Rostain and Dacal Moure 1997; Van Gijn et al. this volume). This type of research starts from the premise that technology is a cultural phenomenon that plays an active role in the reproduction of society and in processes of change (Appadurai

1986; Dobres and Hoffman 1994; Lemonnier 1986, 1993a, 1993b; Van Gijn in press). People make choices that are in harmony with the existing technological system. Microscopic use-wear analysis makes it possible to track the more hidden technological choices. Central to this research is the comparison of the function of each tool category and the determination of the choice of raw materials for specific activities. Were these choices related to cultural or technological parameters and does the picture change through time?

Rostain and Dacal Moure's (1997:265–278) study focused on shell, coral, stone, and bone implements from the Tanki Flip site on Aruba. In order to compare tools made of different raw materials they focused on the manner in which these materials had been modified by the Amerindians using the classification scheme of Leroi-Gourhan (1943) based on type of modification (type of movement and working edge). They distinguished between three types of movement (impact, pressure, and pressure with hammer) and three types of working edges (cutting edge, point, and flat side). Rostain and Dacal Moure conclude that the manufacturing techniques for stone, shell, coral, and bone comprised flaking (freehand and bipolar percussion), hammering, pecking, abrading, polishing, incising, and drilling and concluded that the Amerindians at Tanki Flip had the ability to apply the majority of the techniques to various hard raw materials, without striving to an aesthetically high level, however.

Experimental Archaeological Analysis and Ethnoarchaeology. Technological and functional studies of archaeological materials in the Caribbean have benefited from experimental archaeology and ethnoarchaeology. Replicas have been made to enhance the understanding of certain techniques, and experiments have been used to carry out specific activities (e.g., Bérard 2001; Bonnissent 1995; Briels 2004; Dacal Moure et al. 2004; Hofman and Jacobs 2000/2001, 2004; Hofman et al. 1993, this volume; Keegan 1981; Kelly 2001, 2003, 2004; Lammers-Keijsers 1999, 2001; Lundberg 1985; Petitjean Roget 1990; Rostain 1991; Van der Steen 1992; Vialon 2001; Walker 1980a). Jeff Walker (1980a) studied the manufacturing techniques and functions of the lithic artifacts found at the Sugar Factory Pier site on St. Kitts by incorporating data from ethnography and experimental archaeology into his archaeological analysis. Walker replicated flint tools and employed them for peeling and grating tubers, sawing, whittling and planting wood, and engraving shell. He also used data from ethnography and ethnohistory, which provided additional data on the use of stone tools. The combination of the different data sets has generated new insights in site activities, subsistence patterns, and potential trade networks (Walker 1980a:73).

Ethnoarchaeological studies from northern South America have also enhanced our understanding of the various sequences of the manufacturing process and use of artifacts in precolonial Caribbean assemblages as well as that of the sociocultural parameters and choices involved in the actions (e.g., Cornette 1991, 1992; Duin 2000/2001; Hofman and Jacobs 2000/2001; Van den Bel 1995; Vredenbregt 2004). In recent years, a number of anthropologists and archaeologists worldwide have made clear that technological behavior is social, political, and symbolic/cognitive, and as such it is embedded in the behavior, ideas, and value systems of a society (Lemonnier 1993a; Stark 1998).

Most of the Caribbean ethnoarchaeological studies deal with the manufacturing process of pottery. Cornette (1991, 1992) adopted a morpho-stylistical and technological approach to the pottery of the Galibi (Kari'na) of coastal French Guiana. He used archaeological and ethnographic data and conducted research among the Galibi on the fabrication process. His study resulted in a very useful overview of the rapidly disappearing Kari'na pottery tradition. Vredenbregt (2004) similarly made a study of the closely related pottery manufacturing traditions of the Kari'na of the lower Maroni River in Suriname. She studied the raw materials, manufacturing process, and function of the pottery vessels with the notion that it was permeated with the animistic and mythological worldview of the people who produced the ceramics.

Petrographic Analysis. Low-tech microscopic analysis of the fabrics and high-tech petrographic analysis has been used to explore the source of origin(s) of clay and nonplastic inclusions (temper). The outcome of these studies on pottery provided insight into the differential use of clay sources through time and between pottery styles (Curet 1997; Faupl 1986; Goodwin 1979; Goodwin and Thall 1983; Hofman and Jacobs 2000/2001, 2004; Hofman et al. this volume; Mann 1986; Walter 1991:13, 45); the procurement at local sources if the needed raw materials were available (Arts 1999; Bloo 1997; Van As and Jacobs 1992); the subsequent use of different clay sources on one island (Belhache et al. 1991; Cox O'Connor and Smith 2001); the selective choice of clay sources and within clay sources (Hofman et al. 1993); and the procurement of raw materials or finished pottery products on neighboring islands or on the mainland of South America (Boomert 1986; Crock 2000; Donahue et al. 1990:229; Fuess 2000; Fuess et al. 1991; Hofman et al. 2005; Petersen and Watters 1991b:355). As such, it was evidenced that in the Leeward Islands of the Lesser Antilles, the islands of volcanic origin served as sources for raw materials of finished ceramic products for the limestone islands of Barbuda and Anguilla (Crock 2000; Donahue et al. 1990:229; Petersen and Watters 1991b:355). In the southern Lesser Antilles, on St. Vincent, part of the Cayo pottery assemblage was found to be tempered with *caraipé*, the burned bark of the *kwepi* tree of the *Licania* genus. This is not a species indigenous to these islands and must have come from the mainland of South America or Trinidad where this tree species is endemic (Boomert 1986). Contacts between the islands and the South American mainland during the Late Ceramic Age have therefore been postulated.

Similarly, petrographic analysis has been used to identify the nature of greenstone artifacts found at the site of Hope Estate, St. Martin, and to establish the source area of this material (Van Tooren and Haviser 1995). It was identified as radiolarite or tephrite and its local origin at Hope Hill was confirmed. The identification of this source area presented important opportunities for later research on inter-island contacts (Crock 2000; Crock and Petersen 2004; Knippenberg 2004, 2006). Rock types from the site of Tanki Flip, Aruba, were identified by petrographic analysis in order to discriminate foreign origins (Rostain 1995, 1997a). As no chert deposits occur on Aruba, the Tanki Flip occupants would have traveled to quarries on other islands or the mainland, either to exchange the chert with people living near these quarries or people having access to them.

Archaeometric Techniques. Neutron Activation Analysis (NAA), neutron radiography, X-ray fluorescence (XRF), infrared absorption, emission spectrophotometry, trace element analysis using Inductively Coupled Plasma Atomic Emission Spectroscopy (ICAPAES), and Thermal Ionization Mass Spectrography (TIMS), among others have been gradually added to the array of conventional archaeometric methods and techniques and have been employed in conjunction with them in order to determine the chemical composition of the mineral constituents of pottery or lithics and the geological signature of raw materials. The introduction of these innovative methods and techniques to the study of Caribbean pottery and lithic assemblages has yielded fruitful results over the past few years.

From the late 1980s onward, these techniques have been used in addition to petrographic analysis to determine variations in chemical composition of pottery to infer chronological variation or continuity in ceramic production processes and/or to determine local or exotic provenance (e.g., Carini 1991; Cox O'Connor 1997; Cox O'Connor and Smith 2001, 2003; Gustave et al. 1991; Lundberg et al. 2002; Ortiz 1996; Walter 1991; Winter and Gilstrap 1991).

Over the years these techniques have been refined to enable more precise pinpointing of the source areas of pottery, lithic, and also metal raw materials. They also permitted new inferences on the distribution patterns of certain raw materials across the Caribbean islands (Fandrich 1991; Hofman et al. 2005, this volume; Isendoorn et al. 2005; Knippenberg 2004, 2006, this volume). Reg Murphy and others (2000) conducted an exceptionally interesting study on the identification of sources for semiprecious raw materials used for the manufacture of the gems and ornamental materials from Early Ceramic Age Antigua combining typo-technological analysis with archaeometric techniques.

Murphy and colleagues studied the morphological and physical properties of the shell and rock specimens and categorized them as finished products, blanks, three-pointed stones, or raw materials. Representative samples were selected from each category for detailed mineralogical and petrographic analysis. These analyses included microscopic examination, measurement of gravity by the hydrostatic method, and qualitative analysis of the chemical composition for sodium and heavier elements by energy-dispersive X-ray spectrometry using a Cambridge Model 250 scanning electronic microscope (SEM-EDS) and Laser Raman microspectrometry (Murphy et al. 2000:238). In addition, a number of samples were submitted to X-ray diffraction (XRD), and thin sections to petrographic analysis. From these analyses they conclude that only 2 percent of the specimens are of non-local origin, and these concern only finished objects (Murphy et al. 2000:242).

New methods and techniques in archaeometallurgical studies have been recently applied in South and Central America (Gordus and Shimada 1995; La Niece and Meeks 2000; Lechtman 1988; Merkel et al. 1995; Siegel and Severin 1993; Whitehead 1990). Bray (1993, 1997, 2003) has worked extensively with assemblages from Colombia using XRF techniques to study surface enrichment processes. These studies have acted as a useful example of how microanalytical techniques can be used to enable better interpretation of metal assemblages from indigenous contexts in the Caribbean. Siegel and Severin used energy dispersive spectrometry on a microprobe to analyze the chemical composition of one gold artifact excavated from the Maisabel site in Puerto Rico (Siegel and Severin 1993). This study was restricted to the surface of the object only. They dated the archaeological context to A.D. 70–374 leading to the conclusion that *guanín* had a long history of use among the indigenous peoples of the Caribbean before European arrival and that this was the earliest gold/copper alloy to be reported from an archaeological context in the West Indies (Siegel and Severin 1993).

Most recently, archaeometric methods and techniques have been introduced to the study of human skeletal remains of precolonial populations in the Caribbean. These studies have enabled the formulation of new questions about Amerindian mobility, marital rules, as well as life and health conditions. These questions can now be tackled by state-of-the-art methods and techniques such as stable isotopes used for exploring the contribution of different types of resources to the diet of precolonial populations (Keegan and DeNiro 1988; Norr 2002; Stokes 1995, 1998, 2005; Van Klinken 1991). After Keegan and DeNiro (1988:326) had mapped the distribution of nitrogen and stable carbon isotopes in the food chains in the Bahamian archipelago, they were able to reconstruct two trends in the diet of a sample of 17 Lucayan Taíno individuals. The marine component of the diet varied from predominantly mollusk oriented to more pelagic fish oriented. For other individuals a distinction could be made between sea grass and shallow water reef environments and other oceanic environments. Stokes (1998) determined carbon and nitrogen isotope signatures of bone collagen and apatite carbonate of 102 human bone samples from 19 sites located in the Greater Antilles and the Leeward islands of the Lesser Antilles. The combination of bone collagen being a sign of the source of protein and the apatite reflecting the source of protein and carbohydrates provide detailed insight in the diets in relation to the different environmental settings during Saladoid and Ostionoid times.

During a recent project on Puerto Rican burial assemblages, stable isotope analysis was combined with trace element analysis (Curet personal communication 2005), intended to show human migration in the region. Trace element analysis was also performed on skeletal remains from the Tutu site on St. Thomas (Farnum and Sandford 2002). Strontium isotopic analysis, another method to determine provenance, was recently employed on human skeletal remains from Saba and Guadeloupe (Booden et al. this volume; De Jong 2003; Hoogland and Hofman in press). Such analyses have been successfully applied in other parts of the world to trace migration and mobility patterns (e.g., Price et al. 2002; Wright 2005).

Finally, analysis of mitochondrial aDNA has been carried out and is ongoing on precolonial populations from several islands of the Greater Antilles. This research is aimed at determining place of origin, affiliation, and migratory routes of people and more generally to identify the ancestors of the Taínos and other indigenous Caribbean peoples, as well as their routes of migration and settlement (Curet personal communication 2005; Lalueza-Fox et al. 2001, 2003; Luna Calderón 2002; Martinez-Cruzado et al. 2001). Important results in this field indicate that the Taínos from the site of La Caleta in the southeastern Dominican Republic had a substantially reduced mtDNA diversity, which is indicative of an important founder effect during the colonization of the Caribbean Islands. This is assumed to have been a linear migratory movement from mainland South America following the chain configuration of the Antilles (Lalueza-Fox et al. 2001). In this same light, migration studies have also focused on DNA of the present-day population. Martinez-Cruzado and colleagues (2001) drew a genetic portrait of the present-day population of Puerto Rico to obtain information about the history and origins of its present population.

Outline of the Volume

This volume is divided into three parts, encompassing (1) provenance studies, (2) functional analysis, and (3) new trends and new directions in paleobotanical and paleo-osteological studies.

The first section includes provenance studies examining pottery, metal, and lithics using conventional archaeological and archaeometric techniques. The chapters on the functional analysis of artifacts involve typo-technological and microscopic approaches, while the studies on paleoethnobotany and paleo-osteology also display the use of a diverse array of new methods and techniques.

Provenance Studies

During the past few years, provenance studies have revealed new information using archaeometric techniques and interdisciplinary research. Recently, two major projects have been initiated for the provenance study of pottery in the Caribbean. One of these is the program directed by Christophe Descantes and was the main focus of the SAA symposium, titled "An Exploratory Study into Chemical Characterization of Caribbean Ceramics. In Memory of J. B. Petersen."

The second project, also presented at the aforementioned symposium, represents the one initiated at Leiden University, The Netherlands, in which both pottery sherds and clay samples from the different islands along the Antillean chain have been submitted to a combination of archaeometric techniques encompassing conventional archaeological methods and geochemical analysis. In addition, ethnoarchaeological research is used to contextualize clay-sourcing practices in traditional Amerindian communities in northern South America in order to get a better understanding of clay procurement strategies. Corinne Hofman, Daan Isendoorn, Mathijs Booden, and Loe Jacobs present their combined approach in Chapter 2 and illustrate it with a case study from the island of Saba in the northern Lesser Antilles.

Jago Cooper, Marcos Martinón-Torres, and Roberto Valcárcel Rojas present an archaeometallurgical study for tracing the provenance of metal ornaments from the cemetery of El Chorro de Maíta and some nearby sites in Cuba (Chapter 3). The methods used are ED-XRF, optical microscopy, and SEM-EDS. Emphasis is put on the manufacture, composition, and origin of the different alloys identified. The results of this study offer insights into the relationships between the Europeans and the indigenous populations, their trade systems, and the influence by the colonizers on local customs and values.

In Chapter 4 Sebastiaan Knippenberg and Hans Zijlstra present a case study on the methodologies employed in the characterization of flint and chert sources in the northern Lesser Antilles with the aim of provenancing artifacts. Using multiple approaches, this study does not only aim at characterizing sources, but also at explaining the differences between the sources. Trace element composition is being discussed as well as the effects of chemical weathering.

Functional Studies of Artifacts

Functional studies of artifacts concentrate on organic and inorganic materials using macroscopic and microscopic techniques.

Charlene Dixon Hutcheson discusses a new method for studying past weaving techniques using dental alginate molds on ceramics from the Bahamas (Chapter 5).

Christy de Mille, Tamara Varney, and Michael Turney present new methods for investigating stone bead drilling techniques using molds and scanning electron microscopy in Chapter 6. They illustrate their case with beads from Saladoid sites on Antigua.

In Chapter 7, Benoît Bérard, who has built up his experience in the European Paleolithic, stresses the importance of studying lithic technology for the understanding of Caribbean cultural traditions and change. He illustrates his case by comparing the *chaîne opératoire* of lithic *débitage* of two sites on Guadeloupe and Martinique belonging to the Huecan and Cedrosan Saladoid subseries.

Microscopic analysis of tools has led to a better understanding of the way tools were manufactured and used during prehistory and provides insight into the domestic activities carried out at a given site. Annelou van Gijn, Yvonne Lammers-Keijsers, and Iris Briels (Chapter 8) stress the importance of studying use-wear analysis on different categories of artifacts, including ceramic and lithic, shell and coral artifacts, in order to reconstruct the technological system of a site. In this chapter the authors focus on the technical and functional relationships among these materials in a study of artifacts from the sites of Plum Piece on Saba and Morel and Anse à la Gourde on Guadeloupe.

Together with Harold Kelly, Annelou van Gijn tackles the study of coral tools from the site of Anse à la Gourde combining use-wear analysis and experimental archaeology in Chapter 9. The coral tools are categorized as tools on the basis of their modified shapes, residue, and use-wear traces. Experiments with replicated coral tools were carried out with shell, clay, bone, wood, seeds, and plant materials.

Phytolith and starch residue analysis has lately received new impetus in the Caribbean. They yield detailed information on the function of specific tools and pottery and the importance of plant processing for dietary purposes. Channah Nieuwenhuis stresses the significance of phytolith and starch residue analysis in combination with use-wear analysis illustrating her case with Archaic Age stone tools from the island of Saba (Chapter 10).

Jaime Pagán Jiménez and José Oliver present a case study of starch residue analysis on seven lithic artifacts from two sites on Puerto Rico, namely Cueva de Los Muertos and Vega de Nelo Vargas (Chapter 11). The information obtained reveals that phyto-cultural dynamics in central Puerto Rico are sufficiently varied to suggest the presence of different agricultural production scenarios coexisting in the intra- and interisland spectra.

Roberto Rodríguez and Jaime Pagán Jiménez show the importance of starch residue analysis in the interpretation of the use of ceramic griddles from the site of Macambo II in Cuba in Chapter 12. A multifunctional use for these griddles is put forward.

New Trends in Paleobotanical and Paleo-Osteological Research

After more than two decades of established paleobotanical research in the Caribbean, Lee Newsom explores new methods and techniques in the study of plant macroremains, including utilizing wood collections for their dendrochronological records, efforts to recover information on plant use through chemical residues, the potential of wetland sites, and the significance of ancient germplasm collections as a record of biodiversity and species dynamics (Chapter 13).

Paleo-osteological research presented in this volume concentrates on analysis carried out recently on the human skeletal assemblages from the Lesser and Greater Antilles. Alfredo Coppa and colleagues investigate biological relationships, using dental morphology to explain migration dynamics (Chapter 14). Their results demonstrate that the biological data from dental morphology support the hypothesis of at least two migratory waves in the peopling of the Caribbean islands.

Mathijs Booden, Raphaël Panhuysen, Menno Hoogland, Hylke de Jong, Gareth Davies, and Corinne Hofman use $^{87}Sr/^{86}Sr$ on teeth and bone samples to determine the origin of the population at the Troumassoid site of Anse à la Gourde on Guadeloupe (Chapter 15).

The volume is concluded by an epilogue by William Keegan (Chapter 16) in which he discusses the new insights that can be obtained by means of the innovative methods and techniques illustrated in the previous chapters.

Acknowledgments

The editors of the volume would like to acknowledge William Keegan for moderating the session at the SAA in Puerto Rico. We would like to thank Corne van Woerdekom for all the hours he has spent in editing the extensive list of references. We also thank Eric Mulder for checking references and Medy Oberendorff and Alistair Bright for their help with the figures.

I
PROVENANCE STUDIES

2
In Tuneful Threefold

Combining Conventional Archaeological Methods, Archaeometric Techniques, and Ethnoarchaeological Research in the Study of Precolonial Pottery of the Caribbean

Corinne L. Hofman, A. J. Daan Isendoorn, Mathijs A. Booden, and Loe F. H. C. Jacobs

Introduction: Complementary Methods

Studies that compare clays, temper materials, and potsherds have proved to be essential when studying the provenance, procurement strategies, manufacturing techniques, and distribution patterns of precolonial pottery in the insular Caribbean (Hofman et al. 2005). In the present study conventional archaeological methods, that is, workability tests, technological experiments, thin sectioning, and microscopic fabric analyses, are combined with geochemical analysis such as X-ray fluorescence spectrometry and ethnoarchaeological research to determine and conceptualize the provenance of pottery of a number of archaeological sites on the island of Saba in the northern Lesser Antilles.

Conventional approaches have proved on the one hand to be very suitable for large sample sizes and provide information on texture, temper, and production techniques. Geochemical analyses on the other hand complement these data with more precise characterization of the mineral constituents of the raw clay materials and the pottery enhancing provenance identification.

Ethnoarchaeological research has been found to be essential in understanding and interpreting the pottery procurement strategies and manufacturing traditions of precolonial Caribbean communities (see also Bishop et al. 1982; Lemonnier 1993b; Stark 1998).

Conventional Archaeological Methods

Workability tests and technological experiments were used to evaluate the suitability of the clays for manufacturing techniques such as coiling, molding, pinching, flattening, and smoothening and drying as well as to test firing and post-

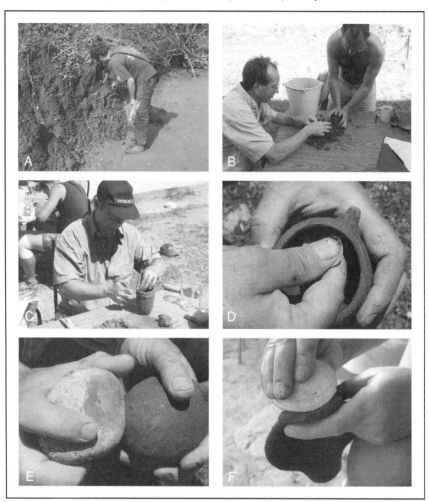

Figure 2.1. Workability tests. A: clay source; B: kneading of the clay; C: coil building of a test vessel; D–F: surface finishing of the test vessel with stone and shell.

firing behaviors of the clays. Experiments and ethnoarchaeological observations evidenced that traditional potters on the mainland used similar techniques (Duin 2000/2001; Hofman and Jacobs 2000/2001; Hofman et al. 1993; Van den Bel 1995; Vredenbregt 2004).

After kneading and pounding the clay, attempts were made to coil the clay and build up small pots (Figure 2.1). The specimens that survived the shaping test successfully (without cracks) were further tested for smoothening and drying.

This was done with shell and calabash tools as similar materials were found to have been employed by the precolonial potters to finish their wares (Van Gijn and

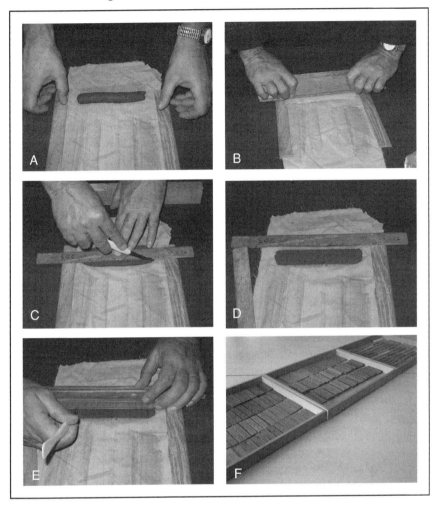

Figure 2.2. Test bars. A: coiling of the clay; B–E: preparation of the test bar; F: complete set of workable test bars after firing.

Hofman in press). For the firing tests, test bars were fired at various temperatures and varying lengths of time and then measured for the degree of linear shrinkage (Figure 2.2). The combination of the degree of plasticity, the possibility to make and pile up coils, and the degree of shrinkage ultimately determined whether the clays were considered suitable or not.

Stereomicroscopic fabric analysis was used for the identification of the mineral and nonmineral constituents in the clays and potsherds. In this context fabric encompasses the composition and structure of fired pottery (i.e., the total appearance of the matrix and inclusions). It includes the texture, color, hardness, and type of nonplastics, their shape, size, and quality as well as the presence and shape of pores and cracks. Potsherds were cut with a diamond saw and treated with fine sandpaper to obtain a smooth fraction surface. The sherds were fired in an oxidizing oven at a temperature of 750°C for 30 minutes. The refiring removes organic impurities and improves the visibility of the inclusions and the paste color. This is because all carbon is burned and volatilized in the oxidizing refiring atmosphere. Refiring also implies a standardization in circumstances and temperatures and therefore makes the comparison of the samples more reliable.

Geochemical Analysis

X-ray fluorescence spectrometry (XRF) was carried out at the Free University Amsterdam to identify and compare the bulk chemical composition of raw clay materials and the precolonial potsherds (see also Hooijkaas and Booden 2004). Element abundance ratios in the clays and potsherds showed several distinct groups, each geographically related. Since most potsherds can be geographically linked to their clay source, it was possible to identify exotic potsherds in the sample set.

XRF was carried out to determine the concentrations of over 30 elements in each sample of clay and potsherds. In order to prepare the samples for analysis, they were oven dried, then crushed in a jaw crusher, homogenized, and finally pulverized in an agate planetary ball mill. The powdered samples were then pressed into pellets after mixing them with 10 percent binding powder (Emu) and homogenizing the mixture in an agate ball shaker. These pellets were then loaded into the XRF-spectrometer to perform a quantitative analysis of the elemental composition. The resulting data were analyzed graphically and through multivariate statistical analysis.

Ethnoarchaeological Research

Ethnoarchaeological studies among Palikur, Wayana, and Kari'na potters in Surinam and French Guiana has been carried out by a number of graduate students from Leiden over the past 10 years. The data collected during their fieldwork in combination with the results obtained from the technological and geochemical analyses have proved to be very helpful in understanding the sociocultural parameters involved in the modes of clay procurement and the selection of clay and temper materials in traditional Amerindian society (Duin 2000/2001; Hagen 1991; Hofman and Jacobs 2000/2001; Jacobs and Van den Bel 1995:125–130; Van den Bel et al. 1995; Vredenbregt 2004).

Searching for the Source:
Provenance of the Pottery from Saba

Archaeological research of Ceramic Age sites on Saba has been carried out between 1987 and 2002 (Hofman 1993; Hoogland 1996) (Figure 2.3). Studies of the

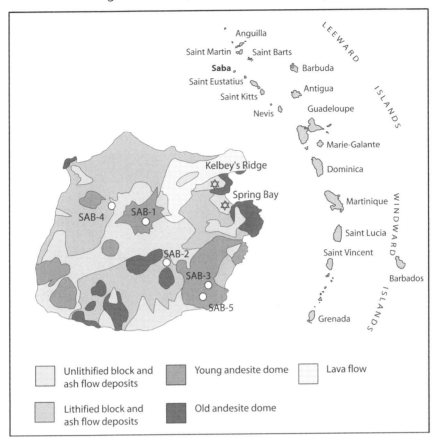

Figure 2.3. A simplified geological map of Saba with locations of clay sampling sites and archaeological sites indicated. Modified after Roobol and Smith (2004).

pottery consisted of a stylistic, morphological, and technological analysis of Cedrosan Saladoid, Mamoran Troumassoid, and Chican Ostionoid ceramics from the sites of Spring Bay, The Bottom, and Kelbey's Ridge dated between A.D. 600 and 1350 (Hofman 1993).

The technological analysis included workability tests and experiments with four clay samples from Saba, stereomicroscopic fabric analysis of the clays and 700 potsherds, and geochemical analysis on 37 potsherds and 19 clays. In addition to the four Saban clays, clays that came from St. Eustatius, St. Martin, and Anguilla, have been added to the fabric and geochemical analyses for comparative reasons.

The Saban clays have been collected in 1989 and 2005 from Rendezvous Bay, Mount Scenery, Booby Hill, and Plum Piece. On St. Eustatius two clays have been collected at Gilboa Hill and Tumble Down Dick Bay. On St. Martin nine clays have been collected from Fort Amsterdam Cape, coast south of Guana Bay, near the French border, above the valley north of Bel Air, roadside outcrop in the Mornes Rouge on the west side of St. Martin, Anse des Pères, small riverbed running to Anse des Pères, southern shore of Saline d'Orient, and hill south of Étang des Poissons. Finally, on Anguilla, four clay samples have been collected from Crocus Bay, Sandy Ground, and Bad Cox Pond (Booden and Isendoorn 2005; Hofman et al. 1993; Van Olst and Hoogland 1996). The sample of potsherds comprised an equal amount of griddle sherds, decorated sherds, red slipped sherds, as well as undecorated rim and body sherds next to bases from the sites of Spring Bay 1 (a, b, c), The Bottom, and Kelbey's Ridge 2 on Saba as well as some potsherds from the site of Golden Rock on St. Eustatius.

Conventional Archaeological Methods

Workability Tests. Workability tests showed that two of the four Saban clays can be regarded as suitable for making pottery. The workability properties of the clays were tested, as was the suitability of the clay mixtures for coiling and molding. The clays were experimentally fired to test the firing and postfiring behaviors of the mixtures and for comparison with the precolonial potsherds.

Fabric analysis included macroscopic and microscopic observation. Fired sections of the clays were compared with those of the potsherds and provided insights into the microscopic and textural composition. This also provided information on the potential source areas on Saba (see also Hofman 1993).

Of the Saban clays, the tests showed that those from Rendezvous Bay (Sab-02) and Booby Hill (Sab-03) can be regarded as suitable for making pottery, whereas the clays from Mount Scenery and Plum Piece are not. On St. Eustatius, Gilboa Hill (STE-02) produced the best suitable clay. The one from Tumble Down Dick (STE-01) seems best for making red slip. The clays collected on Anguilla and St. Martin are all suitable.

Technological Experiments. Experiments with the manufacturing techniques showed that much of the pottery produced with the Saban clays consists of a rather friable material. This is caused by the presence of many nonplastic grains of several types in the matrix (mainly silicates like quartz and feldspars, but also in lower quantities pyroxenes, amphiboles, siltstones, and rock fragments). In general, the actual clay content of the substances used for the pottery is low. Also, the original firing temperature of the fabric was relatively low: between 650°C and 800°C. This has been deduced from comparison of the original sample by a step-by-step refiring of parts of the sample. These factors result in a fragile pottery that cracks easily, suggesting that the life span of the products made from this friable material was relatively short.

Noteworthy also is the fact that despite the presence of many nonplastic grains that appear in the clay naturally, part of these mixtures seem to shrink a lot, especially during the first periods of drying from soft to leather-hard. This is illustrated by the high water content of the clay samples that were tested. These have equally high rates of linear shrinkage. Although there is good reason to believe that the precolonial potters made a better selection of clay types than we can, it is likely that high shrinkage was a general problem with the types found on Saba. It is possible that careful selection in terms of clay workability took place at the source (Hofman 1993). When high shrinkage and a lack in cohesive strength occur together, this indicates a high content of fine material in the mixture but a low content of the real clay mineral. Therefore, from a technological point of view, the potters had to make some concessions. To avoid the formation of cracks during drying, they had to dry their products slowly at least.

Shaping techniques were highly tolerant. This is not only true for the coiling technique, but especially so for molding and flattening out of clay slabs. Such techniques can still be used when working with rather poor clays. When these techniques are used, the exact content of nonplastic grains is not an important factor. However, the potters had to reduce the shrinkage of their clays and dry their products slowly and for all evenly. If not, cracks formed during the drying process would destroy their wares even before firing. This would explain why, despite the natural presence of nonplastic grains in the clay, the potters still added temper to their mixtures. Noteworthy, though, is the absence of vegetable fibers in the potsherds, which could have served to strengthen the texture of the fabric and improve the local clays. Addition of fibrous material to the clay reduces shrinkage and improves the cohesion of the mass. This is important during shaping and it prevents drying cracks (Skibo et al. 1989:23).

Microscopic Fabric Analysis. The majority of the Saban potsherds show mineral assemblages characteristic of volcanic islands in the region in general with basaltic hornblende, feldspar (plagioclase), and quartz as the dominant mineral types (see also Bullen 1964; Bullen and Bullen 1972; Donahue et al. 1990; Gauthier 1974; Goodwin 1979; Hoffman 1979; Hofman 1993; Mattioni 1982; Petersen and Watters 1991b; Schroever et al. 1985; Van As and Jacobs 1992; Westermann and Kiel 1961).

Both potsherds and clays show little variation in mineral content. Of the nonopaque minerals, eight different types were identified. In the potsherds, enstatie, epidote, amphiboles (hornblende), and pyroxenes (augite and hypersthene) prevail. Other minerals characteristic of volcanic regions (volcanic rock fragments), appear in varying quantities in both the pottery and the clay samples (Hofman 1993). The majority of the potsherds have a fabric comparable to the clays collected from Saba, but several sherds evidently show a nonlocal fabric (Figure 2.4). One of the Mamoran Troumassoid potsherds from The Bottom (BOT-242), for example, developed a light firing color after refiring at 750°C under oxidizing conditions, in

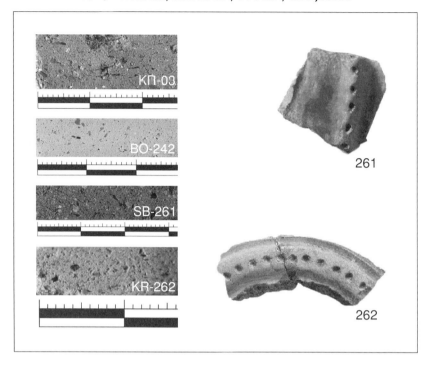

Figure 2.4. Cross sections of four sherds from Saba (Kelbey's Ridge 2, The Bottom, and Spring Bay 3). Two decorated sherds from Spring Bay 3 and Kelbey's Ridge 2.

contrast to the clays from Saba. This fabric appeared to have a fabric very similar to one of the clays from a neighboring limestone island, possibly Anguilla, Long Island, or the northern region of Antigua.

Another example is a sherd from Kelbey's Ridge 2 (KR-262), which shows stylistic affiliations with the Chican pottery from Hispaniola. The sherd shows a non-local fabric, however, not typical of limestone islands either. It is most likely a sedimentary clay from one of the larger islands. Similar observations were made for a Mamoran sherd from Spring Bay 3 (SB-261). The sherd has a decoration of notched fillets, typical of Ostionan ceramics.

Geochemical Analysis

A total of 37 sherds have been selected at random from the bulk sample of the various Saban assemblages and were analyzed using XRF and subsequently compared to clay samples from Saba, St. Eustatius, St. Martin, and Anguilla. Major elements and trace elements in both clays and potsherds were examined (Figure 2.5 and Table 2.1).

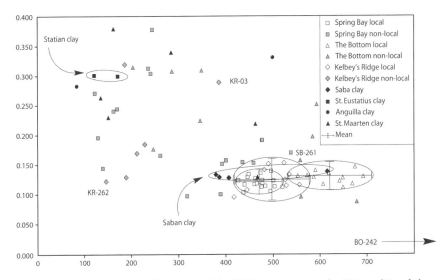

Figure 2.5. Diagram showing the results of the XRF measurements for Y/Zr and Ba of clay samples from Saba, St. Eustatius, St. Martin, and Anguilla and the potsherds from Saba (Spring Bay 1 and 3, The Bottom, and Kelbey's Ridge 2).

Table 2.1. Associated Local, Associated Nonlocal, and Nonassociated Nonlocal Sherds from Kelbey's Ridge, Spring Bay, and The Bottom.

	Kelbey's Ridge		Spring Bay		The Bottom	
N	17		36		23	
total	**Ba (ppm)**	**Y/Zr**	**Ba (ppm)**	**Y/Zr**	**Ba (ppm)**	**Y/Zr**
Mean	403	0.153	392	0.159	569	0.160
2s	290	0.123	253	0.135	388	0.151
Median	477	0.130	449	0.132	591	0.132
Skewness	−0.787	2.046	−1.1	1.8	−1.26	1.24
Kurtosis	−1.141	3.624	−0.31	2.7	0.278	0.322
Local	**Ba (ppm)**	**Y/Zr**	**Ba (ppm)**	**Y/Zr**	**Ba (ppm)**	**Y/Zr**
Mean	498	0.126	472	0.121	621	0.131
2s	82	0.036	50	0.020	92	0.024
Median	499	0.123	474	0.119	619	0.130
Skewness	−0.623	0.148	0.053	−0.218	0.007	0.55
Kurtosis	0.014	−0.614	−0.412	−0.364	−1.3	0.38
N local (%)	11	(65)	19	(53)	13	(57)
N anl (%)	0	()	8	(22)	6	(26)
N nanl (%)	6	(35)	9	(25)	4	(17)

Figure 2.5 reports Y/Zr (Yttrium/Zirconium) and Ba (Barium) of the studied clays and potsherds. Y/Zr is a ratio of two trace elements that are insoluble in water under earth surface conditions, meaning their abundances are relatively unaffected by chemical weathering processes.

An element ratio is used to compensate for any sorting effects that might alter these elements' concentrations. Ba, together with Pb (lead), is the element that most strongly shows a multimodal distribution in concentrations. Both Ba and Pb are relatively soluble elements, so they are potentially mobile during chemical weathering. However, any weathering effects are apparently swamped by the naturally occurring variation between islands. Pb and Ba are also potentially sensitive to changes caused by firing of clay pots, so different production techniques may have played a role in at least part of the observed differences in abundance.

In a Y/Zr vs. Ba diagram, the clays from Saba and St. Eustatius define two distinct clusters. The four Saban clay samples plot in the lower right of the diagram. The two Statian clays plot in the upper left. Clays from Anguilla and St. Martin are scattered over much of the diagram. Sherds appear in two general clusters: one surrounding the Saban clays in the lower right, and one in the upper left half. In all likelihood, the sherds associated with the clay cluster in the lower right have been locally produced, while the sherds outside this cluster have different compositions and are probably of nonlocal origin.

The local population has been defined by determining the largest subset of samples in each site's data set that is normally distributed in both Ba and Y/Zr. This was done by iteratively excluding outlying samples from the set, based on 95 percent confidence, until the remaining population was symmetric and meso- or platykurtic (meaning its distribution has small tails). Sherds in this remaining group were termed "local." Excluded sherds were arbitrarily termed "associated nonlocal" (ANL) if they appeared to belong to the general cluster around the Saban clays, or "nonassociated nonlocal" (NANL) if they did not. The results are shown in Table 2.1. In general, nearly half of the total population has been excluded. However, in the case of Spring Bay and The Bottom, only a quarter or less of these nonlocals is actually nonassociated. The associated nonlocal sherds may or may not be local in origin. However, it is impossible to determine whether their composition is really different or if their exclusion from the "local" set is an artifact of the small numbers of samples in these analyses. The nonassociated nonlocals are very different from the local sherds and clays. It is suggested that these cannot have been produced from Saban clays and infer that they must have been imported from another island.

The very large spread, in both Ba and Y/Zr, of both the nonlocal sherds and clays from the neighboring islands of St. Martin and Anguilla, preclude the assignment of a definite source for these sherds at this moment. Clays from St. Eustatius,

St. Martin, or Anguilla could definitely well be sources for at least some of the non-local sherds.

Textural vs. Chemical Analysis. Three sherds were identified beforehand as possibly nonlocal based on textural analysis: 242, 261, and 262. All three were excluded from the local population by statistical analysis.

The composition of sherd 242 (The Bottom) is unlike that of any other sample in the data set, having extremely high Ba and low Y/Zr. The only clays found so far with extreme Ba contents are ANG-04 (Ba = 2903 ppm), from the hydrothermally altered basaltic basement of Anguilla (exposed near Sandy Ground) and STM-04 (Ba = 4698 ppm), from a volcanic ash deposit on St. Martin. The latter sample is from a quarry, so could be contaminated by anthropogenic chemicals.

Sherd 261 (Kelbey's Ridge 2) is chemically similar to many of the other NANL sherds. Sherd 262, however, is judged an associated nonlocal. So, while its chemical composition is only slightly different, its texture reveals a definite difference in origin. Whether the sherd was imported from elsewhere, or made from nonlocal raw materials, is not clear at this time. This example does show that both "conventional" and "innovative" techniques of ceramics analysis need to be used in tandem to allow reliable conclusions to be drawn.

Procurement, Provenance, and Distribution of Raw Materials

The mineral content of the samples reflects the difference in geographical position between the various sources on Saba. However, workability properties, fabric composition, and mineral contents may also differ among clays from the same source. The potters probably developed some experience in selecting their clays, and they must have been aware of the extant variations in quality, which had implications for the properties of the fabrics and also for their suitability to specific functions. One may also assume on the one hand that the potters knew how to improve at least some of their clays by "aging" (under strong humid conditions) and/or by adding temper materials. On the other hand, the nonstandardized way of working and the personal preference and choices of the potter likely also resulted in the variation of fabric type between various vessel categories.

Ethnoarchaeological research by Anneliese Vredenbregt among the Kari'na of the Lower Maroni River in Suriname may be illustrative in this context. The Kari'na use various types of clay, each with a different color and texture and taken from different locations. Generally, the clay used for making vessels is called *ori: no*. However, when referring to a specific clay, the *ori:no* is called after the locality where it is found. Clays can have specific purposes like slips to decorate vessels. At the source a small vessel is made to test the workability of the clay, which is then thrown into the river for the *ori:no akï:rï,* the spirit connected with the clay who resides at that place. The clay spirit is the manifestation of Okoÿumo, the water spirit, but it carries a different name for each sort of clay (Vredenbregt 2002:115; 2004).

Similarly Martijn van den Bel observed that the Palikur in French Guiana use a clay (*hibug*) obtained from an alluvial clay deposit rich in kaolin but in itself not very suitable (too dense and sticky) for the coiling technique (Van den Bel 1995). Therefore, the Palikur like the Kari'na add *kwep* ashes (from the bark of *Licania* sp.), as a temper material to the clay to make the substance suitable for coiling, with good results after drying and firing. After they burn the bark to form ash and charcoal they grind it in a wooden mortar. For large vessels they use a coarse grinding, while for smaller vessels a finer grinding is required (Vredenbregt 2002:115–116; 2004). Recent experiments with *kwep* evidenced that next to the fact that porosity of the fabric increases by adding burned bark, these ashes have the functional advantage of being highly absorptive (Jacobs and Van den Bel 1995:130; Van den Bel et al. 1995). The potters may have been aware of these advantages, but the preference for burned and pounded *kwep* used as a temper material among the Kari'na and Palikur has been defined by ancestral tradition. The knowledge of specific clay recipes was passed from mother to daughter, from generation to generation.

Local vs. Nonlocal Clays

The geological diversity of the islands of the Lesser Antilles results in a large varia- tion of clay sources. The volcanic islands are very rich in clays, whereas, in general, sources of usable clays are scarce on the limestone islands. This must have had di- rect repercussions for the gathering of raw materials for the production of pottery by the insular communities. We may assume that local clays, if available, were used for the manufacture of the majority of the pottery. However, the Saban case study showed that although clays are locally available, approximately one-third of the pottery has been manufactured of clays from other islands, mostly in the direct vi- cinity of Saba but in other cases from more distant locales.

Ethnoarchaeological research in the Guyana's shows that, sometimes, long dis- tances are traveled to gather clay even if clays are locally available in the direct vi- cinity of the settlement. In some cases it was clear that these sources were known from ancestral tradition and that a symbolic value was attached to them. Kari'na women, for example, collect their clays from Ura:ni, a place of a former village along the riverbank of the Maroni, which was located about 30 minutes upstream from the home village by motorboat (Vredenbregt 2002:115; 2004). Renzo Duin ob- served that Wayana potters from the Upper Maroni River travel nearly 20 km from their home village, requiring at least two hours by canoe upriver to gather clay.

Clay gathering among the Wayana is combined with a hunting and fishing trip of several days with the whole family (Duin 2000/2001:46).

Concluding Remarks

It is suggested here that the best way to determine provenance areas in the Lesser Antillean archipelago is to determine local sherd compositions for settlements from multiple islands and use these as a basis for comparison in combination with clay compositions that define the total chemical variability in locally available sources. The outcome of these analyses in combination with ethnoarchaeological information makes one aware of the sociocultural parameters and choices that may have been involved in the modes of procurement and selection of the clays and temper materials by the precolonial potters. As such, on Saba, while most of the pottery has been manufactured of local clays, there is also evidence that either distances have been traveled to purchase the raw materials, and/or that the exchange of raw materials was incorporated in a network in which also other materials, ideas, and people circulated (Hofman et al. 2007; Hoogland and Hofman in press).

In the coming years the refinement of these methods and the intensive collection of clays and pottery in the other islands of the archipelago should broaden our scope tremendously on the provenance, procurement strategies, and exchange networks of materials and goods among precolonial island communities.

Acknowledgments

We would like to acknowledge Arie Boomert, Gareth Davies, Alice Samson, and Luc Amkreutz for their useful comments and corrections of the original English text.

3

American Gold and European Brass

Metal Objects and Indigenous Values in the Cemetery of El Chorro de Maíta, Cuba

Jago Cooper, Marcos Martinón-Torres, and Roberto Valcárcel Rojas

Introduction

Gold was one of the most sought after resources for the Europeans arriving in the New World in the fifteenth and sixteenth centuries. Ethnohistoric sources have long formed the basis for discussions regarding the use, availability, and role of metals among the indigenous peoples of the Caribbean (Szaszdi Nagy 1984).

Early European interest in metals has left a second, less welcome, legacy, and that is the paucity of metal artifacts available for study today. There are only a handful of surviving examples of indigenous metalwork from the Caribbean dispersed among museums and private collections around the world (Oliver 2000) and the lack of archaeological sites where metal artifacts have been recovered has greatly restricted the opportunity for the use of new methods and techniques in the Caribbean (Oliver 2000; Vega 1979). However, research elsewhere in Latin America has shown how useful analytical instruments can be for determining the provenance of metals and investigating past technologies with important wider archaeological implications (Bray 1993; Fernández and Garita 2004; Gordus and Shimada 1995; Scott 1991; Sil et al. 2004).

For the present work, we have used some analytical techniques that are established in the field of archaeometallurgy, but which had not previously been systematically applied to the study of Cuban materials. Namely, we have employed optical microscopy, X-ray fluorescence and scanning electron microscopy, with micro-analysis to investigate an excavated metal assemblage from El Chorro de Maíta cemetery in eastern Cuba. The analytical data reveal particulars of the morphology, microstructure, and chemical composition of these artifacts, which, in turn, will furnish precious information regarding their manufacture and likely origins. This

Figure 3.1. Location of the site El Chorro de Maíta on Cuba.

information, when combined with ethnohistorical and archaeological data, provides an interesting insight into the supply, use, and value of different metals, to a level of detail that could not have been achieved without the application of scientific techniques. It is therefore hoped that this may serve as a stimulus for further applications of analytical methods to Caribbean material culture.

El Chorro de Maíta

El Chorro de Maíta is located 4 km from the north coast in the province of Holguín in eastern Cuba (Figure 3.1). A team of Cuban archaeologists directed by José Manuel Guarch between 1979 and 1987 (Guarch et al. 1987) surveyed and excavated the site. The cemetery, occupying an area of 2,000 m², is located in the center of an extensive settlement covering 22,000 m². Material remains from the site indicate long-term indigenous occupation, and this is supported by two initial radiocarbon dates taken from human bone in the cemetery. However, the validity of one of these dates, cal A.D. 1080 ± 70, is called into question by the findings presented in this chapter.

A comprehensive dating project to establish the chronology of the burials and the wider cemetery is under way and further samples are currently being dated at the Oxford Radiocarbon Accelerator Unit in the United Kingdom. It is hoped that these further radiocarbon dates from the cemetery will allow a refinement of the site's chronology.

Excavations in 1987 increased the number of skeletons found at El Chorro de Maíta to more than 120, and a study of physical characteristics, burial position, and cranial morphology has indicated the indigenous nature of the cemetery. Associated artifacts, or grave goods, were found in 25 of the burials clustered centrally in the cemetery. Metal objects form a large percentage of these grave goods. An osteological study of the human remains indicates that the metal objects were most commonly associated with female, adolescent, and child burials. A hypothesis was put forward that the differential distribution of the grave goods reflected the emergence of social inequality associated with inherited power (Valcárcel Rojas and Rodríguez Arce 2003, 2005). The catalyst for the development or material manifestation of this hierarchy was unclear.

Therefore, a comprehensive microanalysis of the metal objects from the cemetery was conducted to study their composition, manufacture, and origin in order to help interpret their relative value to the indigenous community that buried them.

Laboratory Methods

An initial study of a sample of the metal objects was carried out in the Centre of Nuclear Development and Technological Application, part of the Ministry of Science, Technology, and Environment in Havana, Cuba, by energy-dispersive X-ray fluorescence (ED-XRF) surface analyses. The corroded condition and small size of the metal specimens prevented a full quantitative analysis of the metal compositions; however, surface analysis indicated ternary gold/copper/silver alloys and zinc-rich copper alloys (Valcárcel Rojas 2002). Subsequently, a more detailed analytical study of the metal assemblage was carried out at the Wolfson Archaeological Science Laboratories, Institute of Archaeology UCL, London. These analyses employed ED-XRF, optical microscopy, and scanning electron microscopy with an attached energy-dispersive spectrometer (SEM-EDS).

ED-XRF analyses were performed with a Spectro X-Lab Pro 2000; the objects analyzed were smaller than the detector window (ø 25 mm), and were placed directly in the chamber without any preparation. These qualitative analyses of surface compositions allowed comparison with the ED-XRF results from Cuba, and also with the bulk compositions of mounted cross sections of specimens examined with the SEM-EDS.

Examination by optical microscopy involved the use of a standard Wild Heerbrugg stereoscopic microscope for complete objects, and a Leica DM LM for reflected light microscopy of metallographic cross sections. These were mounted in epoxy resin and polished to 1 μm grain size following established procedures (Scott 1991).

SEM-EDS was carried out using a Philips XL30 instrument with an INCA Oxford spectrometer package. Specimens were observed in secondary electron (SE) and backscattered electron (BSE) modes, and analyzed using the EDS system. Operating conditions for data collection were as follows: working distance of 10 mm; accelerating voltage of 20 kV; spot size of 4.7 to 5.3 (INCA conventional units) and process time 5, corresponding to a detector dead time of 25–40 percent; and acquisition time of 75 seconds. Based on previous analyses, the lower confidence limits for this instrument may be established at 0.3 wt percent, and values below this limit can be taken as indicative only. Bulk compositions given in this paper are averages of five measurements taken in areas of ~100 μm2, either on the surface of the artifacts analyzed noninvasively, or in the polished sections of those mounted for microstructural analysis. Further analytical details, images, and micrographs can be found in another publication (Martinón-Torres et al. 2007).

Analysis and Results

The metal objects from El Chorro de Maíta that were studied as part of this research can be divided into three categories: beads, laminar sheets, and tubes. An ornithomorphic pendant, a jingle bell, and a spherical bead were also found in the cemetery; however, they were not available for this study.

Beads

Two circular metal beads, measuring approximately 2 mm in diameter, were both found in association with an adolescent female skeleton in burial 57 in El Chorro de Maíta. Noninvasive SEM-EDS analysis of one of these beads showed it to be gold (93.4 wt percent) with smaller amounts of silver (5.2 wt percent) and copper (1.3 wt percent). These metal compositions are comparable to naturally occurring alluvial gold sources, some of which are known in the Holguín area near to El Chorro de Maíta (Ariosa 1977). Ethnohistorical sources attest to the exploitation of naturally occurring gold by indigenous peoples throughout Latin America (Bray 2003; Fernández and Garita 2004) and there is archaeological evidence for the exploitation of gold nuggets from alluvial sources in Puerto Rico (Chanlatte Baik 1977:47). The Amerindians in the Antilles called this metal *caona*. Therefore, it appears probable that these beads were made from individual gold nuggets collected from a local alluvial source. From microscopic observation it appears that the nuggets were shaped into a square elongated form using simple hammering and then bent into a circle before the two ends were heated and fused together to form a simple bead (Figure 3.2a). Thus, no high-temperature melting or smelting were involved.

Laminar Sheets

Four laminar sheets were found in burial 57 at El Chorro de Maíta; two are trapezoidal, one is triangular (CMP 1), and one is arrow shaped (CMP 2). All the sheets from El Chorro de Maíta are approximately 22 mm by 17 mm in size and have a small perforation (< 1 mm) located off center (Figure 3.2b).

Two of these sheets, CMP 1 and CMP 2, were analyzed by SEM-EDS and were found to be ternary alloys of copper, silver, and gold (CMP 1 Cu 47.9 percent, Ag 12.6 percent, Au 39.5 percent; CMP 2 Cu 55.1 percent, Ag 10.0 percent, Au 34.9 percent). Both samples show very similar compositions that reflect the alloy of one part of pure copper with one part of alluvial gold, the latter with an Ag:Au ratio of 0.3. Ternary alloys with these compositions have been found in indigenous con-

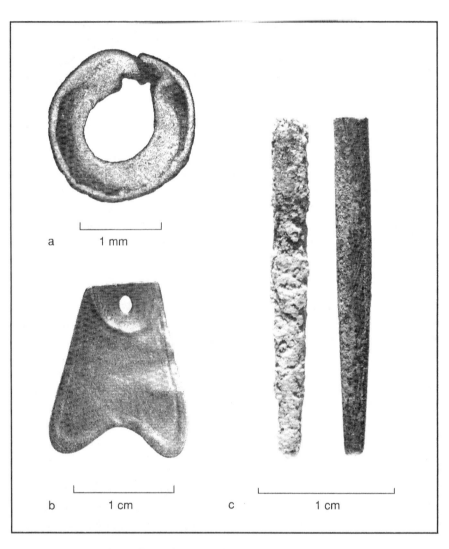

a

1 mm

b

1 cm

c

1 cm

Figure 3.2. a: image of one of the gold (*caona*) beads under the optical microscope; b: laminar ternary alloy (*guanín*) pendant; c: two of the brass (*turey*) tubes, one of them as found (left) and the other one after mechanically removing the corrosion layer.

texts elsewhere in the Caribbean and are commonly called *guanín* (Bray 1993, 1997; Oliver 2000; Siegel and Severin 1993; Szaszdi Nagy 1984; Whitehead 1990). Microscopic observations indicate that they were cut out of a thin sheet, the edges being subsequently polished to remove sharpness. Although some remnant casting porosity is visible on the surface of the objects, it is likely that the original metal sheet was subject to hammering after casting. The small < 1 mm perforation used for threading was not punched or drilled but cut, as suggested by repeated shallow cut marks in several directions. The sheets also exhibit some simple repoussé decoration, normally in the form of shallow grooves parallel to the edges (Figure 3.2b). These manufacturing details in conjunction with their excavated context make it likely that these sheets were used as pendants, perhaps forming part of a necklace in burial 57, where all four sheets and the ornithomorphic pendant were found. Macroscopic studies of the ornithomorphic pendant have made stylistic links with examples found in Colombia (Oliver 2000).

Ternary alloys with such high levels of copper are not known to occur naturally in the Caribbean, and there is no ethnohistorical or archaeological evidence for prehispanic ternary alloy production in the Caribbean. Therefore it appears likely that these ternary alloys found at El Chorro de Maíta were not produced locally but were imported from continental South America, where *guanín* objects are commonly found (Bray 1997; La Niece and Meeks 2000).

Tubes

Metal tubes, rolled from flat sheets < 0.4 mm thick, were found in association with 17 skeletons in the cemetery. In the majority of cases the tubes were found individually with different skeletons, however in burial 25, five tubes were found in association near the left knee of the skeleton. Complete tubes are approximately 30 mm in length and are tapered with a diameter ranging from 3 mm to 2 mm at each end (Figure 3.2c). ED-XRF surface analyses consistently showed these tubes to be made of brass. SEM-EDS data on cross sections of five specimens confirmed this. They were all found to be copper-based alloys containing high zinc contents (15.6–26.1 wt percent) with smaller amounts of lead ($\leq$ 1.7 percent), iron ($\leq$ 0.4 percent), nickel ($\leq$ 0.7 percent) with occasional traces of tin ($\leq$ 0.7 percent) and silver. The high zinc content of these brasses is particularly distinctive, as such high levels could only be produced using the process of crucible cementation, before zinc sublimation techniques were introduced in the eighteenth century. Previous analyses of brass artifacts from the German town of Nuremberg, a major European metal production center during the late fifteenth century, repeatedly showed brasses with a high zinc content in association with relatively high nickel (> 0.2 wt percent) and a virtual absence of arsenic (< 0.05 wt percent) (Mitchener *et al.* 1987). This metal composition is entirely consistent with the brass tubes found at El Chorro de Maíta. The zinc content of the tubes found in El

Chorro de Maíta is too high to be explained as a result of fortuitously smelting mixed copper and zinc ores. There is currently no evidence of brass production by cementation in the New World before the arrival of the Europeans. It therefore seems most likely that the brass used to make the metal tubes found at El Chorro de Maíta came from medieval foundries in central Europe.

The question then remains as to how this brass came to be in an indigenous cemetery in Cuba? Microscopic examination of the edges of the metal sheet shows vertical cut marks, suggesting that punching or striking with a sharp tool in one single cutting event was the method used to cut the sheet. This appears in contrast with the repetitive cut marks observed in the *guanín* pendants and described above. The metallography of these specimens shows recrystallized and twinned grains resulting from cold working followed by annealing, reflecting the manufacture of the sheets that have been beaten and bent into their tubular shape. Thus, both the chemical composition and the manufacturing traits set these objects apart from those manufactured in the Americas and discussed above. The analytical observations, coupled with the ethnohistorical sources suggest that, in all likelihood, these tubes were not crafted pendants but rather reused lace tags or aglets from European clothing. These aglets were common in Europe from the fifteenth century onward, and it is likely that the first Europeans to arrive in the Caribbean had aglets fastened to their doublets and hose. There are several mentions of copper-alloy aglets in the literature of the period, and they also appear in period paintings and domestic archaeological contexts in Europe (Egan and Pritchard 1991; Margeson 1993:22). Similar objects have also been excavated in early colonial settlements in Havana, Cuba, and North America, including Fort San Juan (Moore et al. 2004) and Jamestown (Kelso and Straube 2004:173–174). Thus, our analyses appear to confirm previous suggestions by Szaszdi Nagy (1984:133) that these aglets were used as a trade item by the Europeans arriving in the Caribbean at the end of the fifteenth and early sixteenth centuries. In order to interpret the role and significance of these different American and European metals within the indigenous context of El Chorro de Maíta, it is necessary to contextualize their role in Taíno society.

Metal Objects and Indigenous Values

A detailed review of the ethnohistorical and archaeological evidence for the role of gold within Taíno society is provided by Vega and Oliver (Oliver 2000; Vega 1979). Gold, or *caona*, was sourced locally and worked by the Taíno in Cuba, Hispaniola, and Borinquen. Interestingly, ethnohistorical accounts state that gold was the least valued of all the metals within Taíno society, possibly because it was the most easily sourced. The ternary alloy of gold, silver, and copper, or *guanín*, was held in much higher esteem. Indeed, the word *guanín* held much more significance than a simple description of the ternary metal alloy. The meaning of the word was implicitly bound up with a concept of the exotic, and it was used to describe other objects and concepts of value that shared similar aesthetic properties, such as rare feathers, stones, plants, and celestial bodies. *Guanín*, as both a metal and a concept, is most commonly associated with caciques in Taíno society, reflecting a link between social status and possession of these highly valued materials.

The Europeans, who valued gold as the most precious metal of the New World, exploited this differential value between *caona* and *guanín* metals in Taíno society. Bray (1997) discusses how the Europeans distorted the trade and exchange of metals by using exchange rates of 200 *caona* for 1 *guanín*. This provides one possible explanation for the relatively small amount of *caona* found at El Chorro de Maíta, even though it was the only metal that could be locally sourced.

Brass was only introduced to the Caribbean following the arrival of the Europeans, but it was soon integrated into the preexisting system of symbolic value. The aesthetic properties of the brass meant that it was associated with the sacred celestial, and according to Las Casas it was described as *turey*. "Anything made of latón [brass] was esteemed more than any other [metal]. . . . They called it *turey*, as a thing from the sky, because their name for sky was *turey* [or *tureyro, tureygua*]; they smelled it as if by doing so they could sense it came from heavens" (Oliver 2000:198). This link between brass and the sacred in Taíno society meant that it was a highly valued material.

Therefore, it is possible to conjecture that the first Europeans to arrive in the Caribbean found that a small, expendable clothing accessory became one of their most valuable items for trade with the indigenous population. This perhaps goes some way to explaining why European brass objects become the most common metal item to appear in an indigenous cemetery in eastern Cuba.

Conclusion

The cemetery of El Chorro de Maíta has produced the largest metal collection to be excavated from an indigenous context in the Caribbean. These metal objects are associated with a limited demographic subset of the burial population in the cemetery. This study has provided early indications of European artifacts being incorporated into the material culture of an indigenous community. Further discussion of the social and cultural significance of these grave goods and their reflection of a hierarchical society is detailed in further publications (Valcárcel Rojas and Rodríguez Arce 2003, 2005). This chapter has focused on an archaeometallurgical study of the objects themselves and concludes that three separate categories of metal object have been identified as having distinctively different origins and meanings. It is argued that the inverse ratio between the quantity of metal found and the distance from its likely source of origin is reflective of the value system that the metals held in the Taíno society that acquired them. The arrival of European brass and its occurrence at El Chorro de Maíta provides an insight into the early interactions between Europeans and indigenous peoples, highlighting the distinctly different value systems of the two cultures.

Further research is currently focused on providing a better chronological framework for the cemetery, contextualizing the site of El Chorro de Maíta in its wider archaeological setting, and making comparative archaeometallurgical studies with metal collections from other sites in Cuba and the wider region of the Caribbean.

4

Chert Sourcing in the Northern Lesser Antilles

The Use of Geochemical Techniques in Discriminating Chert Materials

Sebastiaan Knippenberg and Johannes J. P. Zijlstra

Introduction

One of the main topics in the present volume is the use of archaeometric techniques in determining the source of specific materials used by the Amerindian populations of the Caribbean realm. In the opening chapter of this volume, Hofman and colleagues mention that the introduction of these techniques in this area occurred relatively late as compared to other parts of the world, despite the fact that the Caribbean island archipelago lends itself well to archaeometric investigation of different materials, in particular rocks.

With regard to rocks, the Lesser Antilles form an excellent stage to perform this type of research. First, the islands in this region have different geological histories (Martin-Kaye 1969; Wadge 1994; see also Knippenberg 2006). This has resulted in a situation in which neighboring islands provide totally different settings with regard to rock material availability. Second, it can be stated that several islands are unique in this respect, such as St. Martin, Antigua, and La Désirade (Figure 4.1) (Bonneton and Vila 1983; Christman 1953; Martin-Kaye 1959; Montgomery et al. 1992; Multer et al. 1986; Weiss 1994). They are especially the islands, which host some very distinguishable and very unique rock materials, which crop out over a relatively small area and which have been used by the indigenous populations (Knippenberg 2006).

The discovery of significant amounts of siliceous, flaked stone artifacts at the Archaic and Early Ceramic Age sites of Norman Estate and Anse des Pères on St. Martin, initiated the research aimed at finding the source of these stone types, whereby petrographic and geochemical analytical techniques were used in sup-

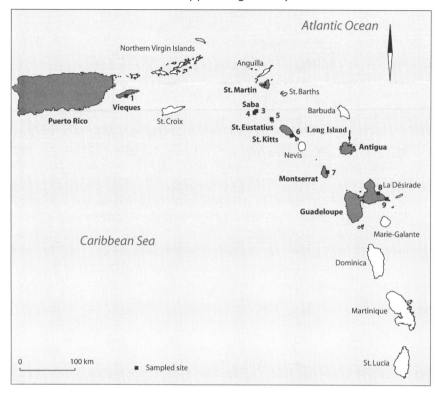

Figure 4.1. Map of the northern Lesser Antilles showing the islands with studied chert sources in bold font and sampled archaeological habitation sites indicated by rectangles. 1: Sorcé; 2: Anse des Pères; 3: Spring Bay 3; 4: Kelbey's Ridge 2; 5: Golden Rock; 6: Sugar Factory Pier; 7: Trants; 8: Morel; 9: Anse à la Gourde (see also Table 4.4.).

port of more traditional macroscopic analysis (Knippenberg 1995, 1999a, 1999b, 1999c).

Encouraged by the results of this preliminary study, the investigation was extended to include more sources on the islands of Antigua, St. Kitts, and Puerto Rico. In particular, attention was addressed to natural distribution of chert, which occurs as crypto- to microcrystalline, tabular, nodular, and diffuse precipitates of silica, in volcanic siliciclastic and biogenic calcareous sediments of the Lesser Antilles islands. This work has formed the basis on which the distribution of different chert rocks used as raw material for the manufacture of flake tools among the northern Lesser Antilles during the Ceramic Age was specified. The discussion of this distribution and the underlying exchange mechanisms responsible for it are beyond the scope of this chapter. They are extensively dealt with elsewhere (Knippenberg 2001, 2006).

The quality, appearance, and composition of chert changes with time and is a function of the early processes of genesis in the rock of formation, but also of later processes that occur during burial, erosion, exposure, weathering, and even after the manufacturing into artifacts. In order to improve the understanding of the variability of the different cherts, the investigation of the prearchaeological history of chert, and of the related petro-physical and geochemical properties needs to be addressed.

Therefore, in this study four aims were specified. The first objective was to map available chert sources and determine the relation between the quality, geological environment, and the geologic history. Second, the morphological and geochemical characterization of source materials had to be specified with the aim to identify objective criteria by which sources can be discriminated. In close relation to this source characterization, which focuses on the geochemistry of the chert, it was also attempted to find explanation(s) for why sources differ chemically. This provides a stronger empirical basis for source discrimination, and may yield guidelines for future research. Finally, a number of artifacts were analyzed and the sources were specified using multivariable statistical techniques.

Cherts in the Region

The Caribbean in general and the Lesser Antilles in particular host a wide variety of chert types, on a restricted number of islands though. In the northeastern Caribbean chert only occurs on Puerto Rico, St. Martin, St. Kitts, Antigua, La Désirade, and Martinique (Bérard 1999a, 1999b; Bérard and Vernet 1997; Bodu 1984; De Mille 1996; Knippenberg 1997, 1999a; Murphy 1999; Pantel 1988; Pike and Pantel 1974; Walker 1980a, 1980b). Macroscopically, the Lesser Antilles cherts can be distinguished on the basis of form and texture. They have been divided into three general groups based on color. These groups include (1) a multicolored chert, ranging in color from white, yellow, brown, gray, to almost black. This group represents most of the varieties used during the prehistory in the northern Lesser Antilles. It consists of nodular chert, which is often called flint when formed in limestone, of tabular chert, of irregularly silicified volcanic rock, and of silicified corals or wood; (2) a light to dark gray-green colored chert that is rare among flaked material in the northern Lesser Antilles. It predominantly can be found at Puerto Rican sites (Rodríguez Ramos 2001a), and its only known source locality is the tabular chert from the Mariquita Chert Formation in southwest Puerto Rico (Volckmann 1984a, 1984b); and (3) a red-colored chert, which is also rare among flaked material from northwestern Lesser Antilles sites, yet more common than green chert. To the contrary, on Martinique, red-colored (nodular) jasper is the most widely used material (Bérard 1999b; Bérard and Vernet 1997), and it is also found on St. Martin (Christman 1953). Furthermore, red-colored, tabular, radiolarian chert is found on La Désirade (Bodu 1984; Bouysse et al. 1983; De Waal 1999b; Montgomery et al. 1992), and in the eastern part of Puerto Rico (Rodríguez Ramos personal communication 2000).

Given the occurrence of a broad range of chert types in the northern Lesser Antilles, a choice was made about which material varieties were to be included in the characterization study and which were not. This choice was necessary to avoid having the series of source locations be too large, which would make success in petrographically or chemically distinguishing the different source types less probable. As the first group includes the large majority of available chert sources and prehistorically used materials in the northern Lesser Antilles, it will be the focus of this research. Sources can be found on Antigua, St. Kitts, and in the southwestern part of Puerto Rico.

On these three islands, chert is most common on Antigua and moreover still occurs in the rocks where it formed. On St. Kitts and Puerto Rico chert is less abundant and has only been found ex-situ. The rocks of Antigua can be subdivided into three types. In the southwest, one finds siliciclastic rocks of the early Tertiary Volcanic Suite (Figure 4.2) (Weiss 1994). They formed when the Atlantic plate subducted under the Caribbean plate and molten, relatively low density magma moved to the surface, depositing volcanic deposits above sea level. Subsequently, during the Eocene, the subsurface cooled and while the island slowly sank below sea level, the volcanic rocks were eroded and erosion products were deposited as near-coastal volcanic siliciclastic sediments of the Central Plain Group, which forms the central part of the island. During the Oligocene, most of the island was submerged again, and shallow-marine sediments were deposited, which received little volcanic siliciclastic sediment from land, and therefore consist mainly of very pure biogenic carbonates that presently form the northeast part of the island, and that belong to the Antigua Formation (Weiss 1994). As a consequence of Miocene tectonics, the island was uplifted again and tilted toward the northeast. During the Pliocene to Pleistocene Ice Ages, southwest-northeast-oriented river valleys were repeatedly eroded and filled with alluvial sediments derived from Volcanic Suite, Central Plain Group, and Antigua Formation, while the soluble carbonates of the Antigua Formation experienced also karstic dissolution and were covered by insoluble eluvial residue.

Also at St. Kitts, early Tertiary siliciclastic volcanic rocks crop out; however, limestone is absent, apart from a small patch of relatively young Pleistocene limestone (Figure 4.3). Puerto Rico exposes Mesozoic volcanic rock and limestone, which is covered again by early Tertiary volcanic rock covered by marine limestone (Figure 4.4).

From eight localities on Antigua, two on St. Kitts[1] and five on Puerto Rico, 15 in total, a source description was made and chert samples were collected for mac-

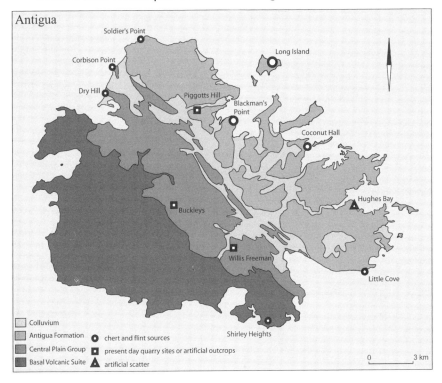

Figure 4.2. Geological map of Antigua showing the three main geological regions and the location of flint and chert sources, including the location of an artificial flint scatter at Hughes Bay, a limestone present-day quarry site at Piggotts Hill, and chert outcrops at Buckleys and Willis Freeman (geological map based on Multer et al. 1986:Figure 2.1).

roscopic, microscopic, and chemical analysis (Table 4.1). Basically, three types of context of occurrence were distinguished: (1) a primary, in which chert is still present in the host-rock; (2) a secondary, where chert occurs ex-situ, for instance as loose surface scatters along beaches and cliffs, in eluvial soil, or alluvial deposits; and (3) a tertiary context, where chert occurs as scattered flaked artifact material.

After macroscopic classification, during which color, type of cortex, texture, presence of inclusions, luster, and grain size were specified following a predefined set of attributes, at least four subsamples of each type of chert were processed into about 30 μm thin sections, and analyzed by means of a standard polarizing light microscope.

For all sources on Antigua, the relation with the rocks in which the chert was formed could be well established. Five of the sources belong to the Antigua Formation. At the three sources of Long Island, Little Cove, and Soldier's Point, chert oc-

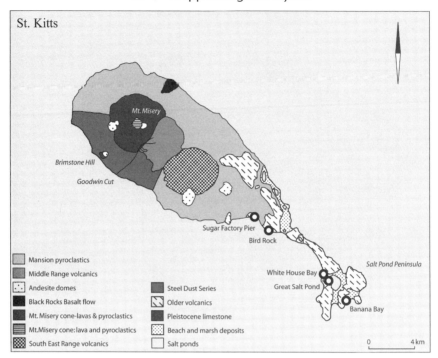

Figure 4.3. Geological map of St. Kitts, showing the location of flint scatters (geological map based on Baker 1968:Figure 1).

curs as flint in primary context and forms nodular layers in limestone. In addition, surface scatters of flint in secondary context as eroded from the limestone by the sea are common and in particular at Long Island, where the nodular flint layer occurs at sea level and where abundant scatters constitute a beach that protects this small island against wave erosion. The color of the flint is pale brown, brown, yellow brown, dark brown, dark gray, and with white patina. The flint is characterized by a rather "dirty" quartz matrix with fine, but varying, crystal size, in which fossils, calcite crystals, carbonate mud, opaque (organic) matter, and iron oxides are present.

The two other sources related to the Antigua Formation, Blackman's Point and Coconut Hall, exhibit flint that occurs only in a secondary context, with large boulders scattered over the surface. Besides the well-known Long Island site, these latter two localities, Blackman's Point and Coconut Hall, also show evidence of prehistoric exploitation in the form of scatters of flaked material.

The last three localities of chert on Antigua are associated with volcanic tuff deposits of the Central Plain Group and the Basal Volcanic Suite. At Corbison Point and Dry Hill, in close proximity to each other along the northwestern shore-

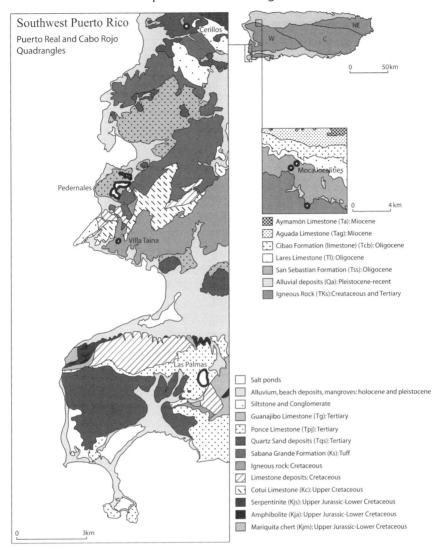

Figure 4.4. Geological map of the southwestern part of Puerto Rico showing the location of chert sources in white (geological map based on Volckmann 1984a, b).

line of Antigua, similar tabular chert occurs in primary context in clayey deposits and in a secondary context as subrecent marine erosion products along the beach. They are gray-brown colored, fossil rich, dirty, and often contain large amounts of carbonate, clay minerals, and opaque (organic) matter, resembling the flint of the Antigua Formation.

Finally, the last investigated chert source on Antigua is the Shirley Heights lo-

Table 4.1. Description of Chert and Flint Sources in the Northeastern Antilles, Included in This Study.

Island	Source locality	Geological setting	Type of (original) host-rock	Type of occurrence	Description
Antigua	Long Island (LI)	Antigua Formation	Limestone	primary, secondary, tertiary	Major flint occurrence on small island off Antigua's northern coast. Flint is scattered along the islet's northern shore and at surface scatters on large portions of the island.
	Little Cove (LC)	Antigua Formation	Limestone	primary, secondary	Limestone section and cobble beach along Antigua's eastern coast. Flint can be found on the cobble beach and in limestone sections.
	Soldier Point (SP)	Antigua Formation	Limestone	primary, secondary	Extended rock point along Antigua's northwestern coast. Flint can be found within limestone of this rock point as well as at both cobble beaches enclosing it.
	Blackman's Point (BP)	Antigua Formation	Limestone	secondary, tertiary	Exclusive secondary occurrence of flint at the Blackman's Point peninsula along Antigua's northern shore. Flint can be found scattered on the surface and along an eroded coastline.
	Coconut Hall (CH)	Antigua Formation	Limestone	secondary, tertiary	Exclusive secondary occurrence of inland scatters of flint at Coconut Hall along Antigua's northern coast.
	Shirley Heights (SH)	Basal Volcanic Suite	Tuff	primary, secondary	Chert boulders are exposed at the flanks of Shirley Heights in the southeastern part of Antigua, surrounded by secondary surface scatters.

	Site	Formation	Rock type	Source	Description
	Corbison Point (CP)	Central Plain group	Tuff	primary, secondary	Bedded chert layers exposed at a rock-point along Antigua's northwestern coast. Secondary chert is lying on the adjacent cobble beach.
	Dry Hill (DH)	Central Plain group	Tuff	primary, secondary	Bedded chert layers exposed at a rock-section along Antigua's northwestern coast, secondary chert is lying on the adjacent cobble beach.
St. Kitts	Great Salt Pond (GSP)	Unknown	Limestone	secondary	Secondary surface scatter of small cobbles situated along an artificial dam separating two salt lakes in the southwest peninsula of St. Kitts.
	Sugar Factory Pier (SFP)	Unknown	Limestone	secondary	Small cobbles scattered on a cobble beach predominantly consisting of igneous rock, along St. Kitts southern shore near the capital of Basse Terre.
Puerto Rico	Cerrillos (CE)	Guanajibo Formation	Limestone	secondary, tertiary	Significantly destroyed inland surface scatter near the village of Conde Avila within the southwestern part of Puerto Rico.
	Pedernales (PE)	Guanajibo Formation	Limestone	secondary	Extensive inland surface scatter of relatively large irregularly chert boulders in the immediate surroundings of the village of El Cerro in the southwestern part of Puerto Rico.
	Las Palmas (LP)	Ponce Formation Mariquita Chert	Limestone Chert	secondary, tertiary	Extensive inland surface scatter near the village of Las Palmas in the southwestern part of Puerto Rico. The surface scatter includes secondary green chert material from the Mariquita Chert Formation as well.

Continued on the next page

Table 4.1. *Continued*

Island	Source locality	Geological setting	Type of (original) host-rock	Type of occurrence	Description
	Villa Taina (VT)	Cotui Formation	Limestone	secondary	Small inland surface scatter of relatively large irregularly shaped chert boulders 2.5 km west to the village of Boqueron in the southwestern part of Puerto Rico.
	Moca (MO)	San Sebastián Formation	Conglomerrate	secondary, tertiary	Inland surface scatters of chert within the valley of the Culebrinans river in the western part of Puerto Rico.

* Note that primary stands for chert or flint material still present in its original host-rock, secondary for eroded material out of the host-rock, and tertiary for evidence of exploitation or working of the material at the locality in the form of scatters of flaked stone.

cality, where chert occurs in primary and secondary context along the slope of the Shirley Heights cliff. Outcrops of tuff occur with inclusions of irregularly shaped chert. The chert is white–pale brown colored, pure quartz with a relatively coarse crystalline matrix, and it typically lacks fossils or other carbonate matter. No chert in tertiary context as evidence of prehistoric exploitation was found at these three latter localities.

The occurrence of chert on St. Kitts and Puerto Rico is quite different. All sources on these islands are characterized by chert occurring in a secondary context. No clear relationship could be established with rocks in which the chert may have formed. Chert on St. Kitts is found on cobble beaches amid igneous rocks. It resembles flint of Antigua, but has a characteristic very fine crystalline quartz matrix and, on average, low amounts of fossils, calcite, and opaque (organic) matter.

On Puerto Rico, limestone in which flint might have formed is common; however, no relation between chert occurrence and limestone host-rock could be established. The chert consists of relatively clean, rather coarse crystalline quartz with common radial fibrous silica precipitates (chalcedony). Furthermore, it lacks calcite and opaque (organic) matter, but is occasionally impregnated by iron oxides, which cause a reddish-colored hue.

Chert Formation and Chert Chemistry

The properties of chert and its suitability for prehistoric manufacturing are a function of the type of rock in which it forms, of the processes during its precipitation from pore fluid (Bush and Sieveking 1986), and of the changes that occur after erosion, exposure, and subsequent weathering (Brownlow 1979; Lavin and Prothero 1992). They are reflected in macromicroscopic characteristics that allow a subjective classification by the trained eye, but also in trace element composition that allows a more objective classification without much prior knowledge.

Chert consists mainly (> 95 percent) of silicium dioxide, the matrix, which may occur in various crystal habits (polymorphs) as a function of age, each characterized by a specific molecular ordering or crystallinity and a related solubility. Most soluble is the poorly ordered silica in rapidly formed and fine-grained volcanic ash, but also in siliceous tests of microorganisms such as diatoms and radiolaria. In pore fluids of sediments containing large concentrations of this amorphous opaline silica, dissolved silicium dioxide concentrations may exceed 100 mg/liter. However, in time, better ordered silica polymorphs will form, such as cristoballite, trydimite, and finally quartz, which have decreasing solubility and silicium dioxide saturation concentrations, of 60, 30, and about 10 mg/liter, respectively.

In young host-rock, locally the silicium dioxide concentration in the vicinity of less soluble silica polymorphs is lower than the saturation concentration of the more soluble polymorphs distributed through the rock, the latter will dissolve, while the former grow at their expense. This autocatalytic recrystallization of silicium dioxide (Krauskopf 1956, 1959) is the driving force behind the ultimate genesis of dense tabular and nodular chert quartz concretions in sediments that were initially characterized by a more diffuse distribution of opaline silica.

It has been argued that early formation of relatively insoluble silica polymorphs is catalyzed by bacterial metabolism in sediments and that chert layers formed when sediment remained relatively long in such bacterial redox zones, in particular during periods of relatively low sedimentation rates (Zijlstra 1987). It is interesting to note that the Oligocene Antigua Formation and its flint are very similar to the Maastrichtian Chalk and its flint of northwest Europe (Zijlstra 1994, 1995). However, the flint of the Antigua Formation appears to occur in only a single meter-thick interval that can be traced throughout the island, and that seems to have been formed during a short period in the Oligocene, when deposition rates were relatively low, and depositional regime changed from transgressive to regressive in the middle of the Antigua Formation. From an archaeological point of view, this suggests that the distribution of flint and possibly associated workshop sites can be reconstructed from careful geologic mapping.

The chemistry of chert concretions is also defined by external factors and in particular the variation of pH in pore fluid as often caused by changes in carbon dioxide solubility. Thus, silicification is observed along faults, where rising hydrothermal fluids degas (jasper; Martinique and St. Martin), at the top of karstified limestone deposits (Puerto Rico), or in soluble aragonitic carbonate corals within siliceous sediments (top Central Plain Group, Antigua). The dissolution of chert, witnessed by a change from dark dense concretions, into lighter-colored and more porous concretions, moreover starting with development of a light-colored, more porous rind or patina, is caused by pore fluids that are undersaturated with respect to silica, such as may occur in soils with humic acids (Rottländer 1975a, 1975b, 1989).

Determination of trace element concentrations by means of destructive Inductively Coupled Plasma Emission Spectroscopy (ICPAES) has been proven to be an effective method to discriminate Lesser Antilles cherts (Knippenberg et al. 1995, 1999). Earlier studies elsewhere demonstrated the advantages of measuring trace-element composition in a few grams of dissolved rock. Measurement of readily quantifiable, objective, and independent variables like trace element concentrations provides a powerful tool besides more traditional subjective macroscopic and microscopic techniques for chert source discrimination (Cackler et al. 1999; Craddock et al. 1983; De Bruin et al. 1983; Glascock et al. 1998; Luedtke 1978, 1979, 1992; Shackley 1998; Sieveking et al. 1972; Thompson et al. 1986; see Church 1994 for an overview).

Trace element distribution in chert is a consequence of the inclusion of insoluble compounds during silicification and of their dissolution, diffusion, and reprecipitation in the pore space of the chert during later weathering (Bush and Sieveking 1986; Cowell 1981; Kars et al. 1990; Luedtke 1992). The following is proposed concerning distribution of trace metals in chert:

(1) Li and Cr, but also to a minor extent K, Al, and Na, can occur as impurities in the quartz crystal lattice itself, however generally in very low concentrations.

(2) Ca, Mg, and Sr may occur in fairly high concentrations, in particular if chert is formed in limestone and if less soluble and often coarse crystalline carbonate relics of the original host-rock have been incorporated and are still present.

(3) Al, K, Ti, and Cr, and to a lesser extent Fe, Ca, Mg, Sr, and Na may occur in relatively high concentrations if rather insoluble siliciclastic compounds have been included, such as clay, volcanic tuff, and detrital rock fragments.

(4) Al/K ratio is higher in chert with land derived siliciclastic inclusions as compared to chert with marine (authigenic) clay inclusions that have incorporated potassium from seawater.

(5) Fe, Mn, and S stem from sulfides, such as pyrite, that form authigenically in marine sediments, moreover as a consequence of bacterial metabolism.

(6) S is also associated with organic matter.

(7) Na is introduced by seawater and is concentrated in remaining interstitial water.

(8) Ca, Mg, and Sr concentrations may decrease as a consequence of weathering and the dissolution of carbonates, in particular at the margins of chert concretions.

(9) S and Fe concentrations decrease as a consequence of pyrite oxidation during weathering. Sulfate diffuses out off the concretion, while Fe^{2+} oxidizes and precipitates as rust colored Fe^{3+}, in particular toward the margin of the chert concretion.

Discussion of Trace Element Variability in Caribbean Cherts

More than 150 chert samples from the 15 different sources were analyzed using ICPAES. Thorough study of the chemical data from samples belonging to all these sources has come up with some clear results. First, variation in chert trace-element composition is much dependent on the type of host-rock in which it was formed and reflects the characteristics of the different geological formations. As a result, variation is seen between materials from different geological formations (Figure 4.5). Second, the trace element composition reflects a super imposed chemical weathering effect. Third, the trace element composition of chert derived from different localities in the same geological formation is comparable, but may vary in certain cases.

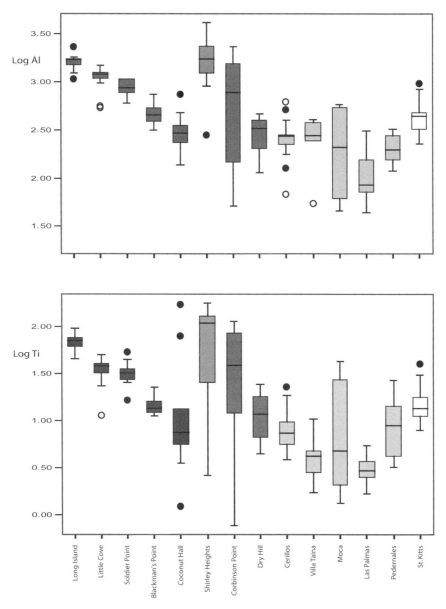

Figure 4.5. Box plot graphs showing the log-values of Al and Ti concentrations (mg/kg [ppm]) by source grouped according to geology. Solid circles are outliers; open circles are extremes.

Comparing chert from the Central Plain Group tuff and Antigua Formation limestone of the Antigua Island, allows distinction as based on Al/K ratios, reflecting mixed land derived/marine and mainly marine clay mineral assemblages, respectively (Table 4.2 and Figure 4.6). Chert that formed in tuff displays higher intrasource variability, reflecting formation in beds of low terrigenous input (low Al/K ratio), as well as in beds with high terrigenous input (high Al/K ratio). Comparing the Al/K ratio of the St. Kitts chert (flint) to the Antigua Formation chert (flint), suggests that also the former has a marine origin and was probably formed in limestone, although possibly of different type than the Antigua Formation, or else of the same type but affected by differences in later weathering, as follows from the differences between the trace element suites.

Weathering also has a significant impact on the trace-element composition. Prolonged exposure, by this we mean in geological rather than archaeological terms, to chemical processes in soils proved to be most severe, more than the effects of seawater. Comparing trace element composition of primary and secondary chert (flint) from the Antigua formation, suggests that Na, trapped as interstitial water, is lost in chert from secondary context (Table 4.3). The lower Ca and Mg concentration in chert from secondary context suggests dissolution of carbonates, increase of porosity and specific surface area, further promoting quartz dissolution and change to lighter color, during weathering. Porosity of the rock also induces iron and manganese oxidation. Depending on the water transport in the flint, Fe (and Mn) may be precipitated in bands in the outer parts of the rock. Slowly clay minerals and other terrestrial minerals, trapped in the quartz and calcite, are dissolved resulting in lower Al, K, and Ti concentrations. K and Ti decrease relatively more in concentration than Al, as they are more reactive. Decrease in Li and Cr indicate actual quartz dissolution. These elements are least affected by weathering suggesting relatively little quartz is dissolved. Depending on the Fe contents in the surrounding soil new Fe (and Mn) may be precipitated in the voids that are formed after solution. If Fe content is higher in the surrounding soil than in the flint this will result in an increase of Fe in the flint, as has been the case at the secondary Antigua Formation Blackman's Point source and some of the secondary Puerto Rican sources.

For some sources, intrasource variability may be low enough to assign samples to a single source, for others intrasource variability may be so high that trace element values of different sources overlap, and samples cannot be clearly assigned to a single source. This is particularly true for the secondary chert sources on Puerto Rico and St. Kitts.

Source Discrimination

The acquisition of quantifiable variables, the trace elements in chert, offers the possibility to employ multivariable statistical analysis, of which Discriminant

Table 4.2. Average Values, Standard Deviations (sd), and Relative Standard Deviations (RSD) of Trace Element Al/K Ratios in Caribbean Flints and Cherts by Source.

Sources	N	Al/K		
		mean	sd	RSD
Long Island	21	3.21	0.26	8.16
Little Cove	13	3.39	0.18	5.25
Soldier Point	10	3.08	0.42	13.68
Blackman's Point	12	4.60	1.52	32.97
Coconut Hall	11	3.26	1.03	31.62
Corbison Point	7	4.50	1.27	28.13
Dry Hill	13	4.50	1.58	35.14
Shirley Heights	9	4.66	3.87	83.00
Cerillo	13	5.26	3.04	57.77
Las Palmas	8	7.02	4.07	58.07
Pedernales	6	2.77	0.68	24.75
Villa Taina	11	1.85	0.86	46.49
Moca	8	2.36	1.31	55.41
St. Kitts	15	1.73	0.49	28.09

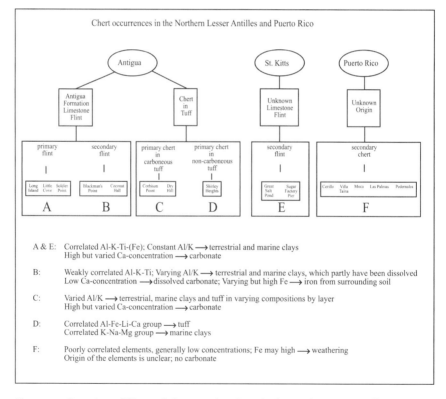

Figure 4.6. Overview of flint and chert geochemistry in the northeastern Antilles.

Table 4.3. Antigua Formation Flints. Average Values of Trace Element Concentrations (in mg/kg [ppm]) and Their Ratios in Flints from a Primary Context Compared to Flints from a Secondary Context by Source.

Source	Al	K	Na	Ti	Li	Cr	Fe	Ca	Al/K	Al/Na	K/Na	Al/Fe	Al/Li	Al/Ti	Al/Cr
Long Island															
primary	1484	481	1029	58.1	12.7	5.80	482	3303	3.06	1.45	0.47	3.23	115.4	25.52	254
secondary	1647	502	868	71.3	14.5	7.21	447	1007	3.29	1.94	0.60	4.65	114.6	23.15	234
Little Cove															
primary	1037	314	822	35.9	13.1	4.51	235	3121	3.32	1.33	0.40	5.98	81.4	30.35	231
secondary	1246	355	682	34.1	14.7	4.40	162	1640	3.50	1.88	0.54	11.52	88.5	37.15	337
Soldier Point															
primary	875	297	528	32.1	11.2	3.34	227	3570	3.06	1.72	0.59	3.97	79.8	28.29	268
secondary	878	283	680	34.6	11.4	3.62	241	1930	3.10	1.30	0.42	3.91	77.5	26.60	262

Analysis is considered most suitable (Craddock et al. 1983; De Bruin et al. 1983; Glascock et al. 1998; Luedtke 1979; Sieveking et al. 1972). Klecka (1980:7) defines Discriminant Analysis as "a statistical technique, which allows the researcher to study the differences between two or more groups of objects, with respect to several variables simultaneously." In relation to this study, the sources of chert material are the groups, and the different trace element concentration values represent the variables. This technique can be applied in two different ways: (1) Descriptive Discriminant Analysis that is used in interpreting group differences; and (2) Predictive Discriminant Analysis that is used for classification (assignment[2]) of cases to groups. The latter application has been widely used in provenance studies for stone materials.

In short, Discriminant Analysis (DA) determines which factors contribute most to group separation. It identifies functions, called canonical discriminant functions, that are linear combinations of the original variables. These functions maximally enhance group separation. The classification technique of DA calculates a centroid for each group, which is the mean value in multidimensional space based on values obtained from the canonical discriminant functions. It then compares the distance of the canonical value of an unknown case (an artifact for which one wants to identify the source) to the centroids of the different groups. This distance (D) is called the Mahalanobis distance. The artifact will be assigned to the group for which D^2 is smallest.

In this study, 12 trace elements were used for the discrimination of sources and for assigning artifacts to sources, as their concentrations appeared to be above the detection limit in most cases, and as their measurement provided relatively precise results. The elements are: Lithium (Li), Sodium (Na), Potassium (K), Magnesium (Mg), Calcium (Ca), Barium (Ba), Titanium (Ti), Vanadium (V), Chromium (Cr), Manganese (Mn), Iron (Fe), and Aluminum (Al).

In order to evaluate how well sources in this study are discriminated, only the source samples were entered in first instance, and tests were performed on the classification results, using the leave-one-out, or jack-knife method (Glascock et al. 1998). It appears that the success of individual assignment to the sources is moderately well. Using cross-validation classification in the SPSS statistical program produced a correct assignment rate of just above 73 percent. Different researchers working on northwestern European flints found similar or lower success rates (Craddock et al. 1983; De Bruin et al. 1983). This relatively low assignment rate as compared to, for example, obsidian studies (see Glascock et al. 1998) can be attributed to relatively large intrasource and relatively low intersource variation, as is in general the case for chert and flints.[3]

Considering this moderate correct assignment rate on a source specific level, the next step is to see how well the sources from the three islands can be discriminated. It appears that approaching this problem using two steps produces the best results. By first discriminating Puerto Rico from the two Lesser Antillean islands,

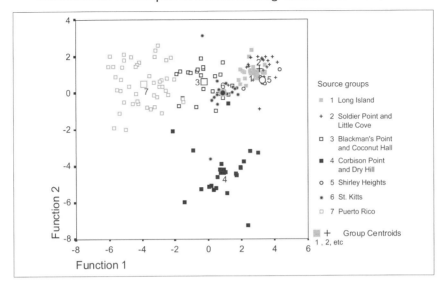

Figure 4.7. Scatter plot of the first two canonical discriminant functions by source groups.

an almost 100 percent correct assignment is obtained. The next step of discriminating Antigua from St. Kitts results in a 95.7 percent overall correct assignment. By grouping the sources following geology into related groups on Antigua, assignment is approved as well (Figure 4.7).

Source Determination of Artifacts

The usefulness of a more extensive characterization of chert with archaeometric techniques that comprise definition of source geology, macro-microscopic petrographic description, and trace element analysis, appears only when the methods are put to the test during assignment of artifacts to sources.

Artifacts from a number of Ceramic Age habitation sites were geochemically analyzed. These sites were taken from a larger sample of sites, which has been studied over the past years (Knippenberg 2006). The sampled sites are situated on a large number of islands and cover all four main phases of the Ceramic Age (Table 4.4). Single artifact sample specimens were taken from larger sets of artifacts that were grouped together on the basis of strong macroscopic similarity. Artifacts were analyzed following the same procedure as the source samples. They were assigned to sources by the step-wise approach, using SPSS. At first the samples are assigned to the different islands and then to the different sources. The main results are summarized as follows (see for more extensive discussion Knippenberg 2006).

All analyzed sites contain artifacts that are assigned to the Long Island source

Table 4.4. Source Assignment for Chert Artifacts Found at Different Habitation
Sites in the Northeastern Antilles.

Site	Island	Identified sources
Sorcè	Vieques	Long Island, Soldier Point, Coconut Hall, St. Kitts (?), unknown
Anse des Pères	St. Martin	Long Island, primary Antigua flint sources, St. Kitts (?), unknown
Spring Bay 3	Saba	Long Island
Kelbey's Ridge 2	Saba	Long Island
Golden Rock	St. Eustatius	Long Island, unknown
Sugar Factory Pier	St. Kitts	Long Island, Soldier Point, Coconut Hall
Trants	Montserrat	Long Island, Blackman's Point, Dry Hill, Shirley Heights (?), unknown
Morel	Guadeloupe	Long Island, unknown
Anse à la Gourde	Guadeloupe	Long Island, Coconut Hall

of the Antigua Formation on Antigua, and chert from this source has been most
widely used in the northeastern Lesser Antilles. Especially on the islands close to
Antigua, such as Montserrat, Guadeloupe, and St. Kitts, but also on islands farther away, Long Island flint makes up the majority of the flaked stone rock. Only at
Sorcé on Vieques is Long Island flint rare. Beyond the Saba-Guadeloupe region, the
abundance of Long Island flint significantly declines, suggesting down-the-line-
exchange (Knippenberg 2006).

The results of artifact trace element analysis furthermore suggest that chert
from other Antigua sources, such as Soldier Point, Blackman's Point, Coconut
Hall, and Corbison Point/Dry Hill were also used during prehistory, but they form
only a small fraction of the flaked stone found at habitation sites on Antigua and
adjacent islands.

Chert from St. Kitts has only been tentatively identified in the artifact collection, and interestingly, the majority of the artifacts of the Sugar Factory Pier site
on St. Kitts, initially believed to stem from the St. Kitts chert, are now assigned
to two Antigua sources, Soldier Point and Coconut Hall. This finding casts serious doubts on the natural origin of secondary flint scatters found on the island
of St. Kitts, which may well be imported during historic times, for instance as bal-
last stones.

None of the analyzed artifacts could be assigned to secondary context sources
in the southwestern part of Puerto Rico. These include a number of artifacts from
the Sorcé site on Vieques. Apparently these sources were of no significance to this

region. Closer look at the Sorcé samples revealed that most have an unknown origin, suggesting that there are sources in the region not known to us.

This highlights another outcome of this research: the existence of a number of unknown sources. A significant but generally minor portion of the analyzed samples produced chemical values that did not match the chemical characteristics of the different source sites. In particular for the Sorcé site on Vieques, where the majority of the chert artifacts could not be provenanced, this holds true. Most probable locations for these unknown chert sources are either the Central Plain Group on Antigua, where additional chert outcrops exist to the ones sampled, the western part of Puerto Rico, the Virgin Islands, and possibly St. Martin.

Conclusion and Final Remarks

In this chapter we have reviewed the methodology with which a number of potential chert sources in the northern Lesser Antilles and Puerto Rico were discriminated in order to be able to source prehistoric artifacts. Geochemical analysis using ICPAES in association with macroscopic and microscopic analysis not only provided a strong empirical basis for distinction but also offered a better understanding for source variability. From careful comparison of data between the sources, it is evident that intersource variation is primarily a result of host-rock variability and to a lesser degree dependent on variation in time and space. Weathering also has a significant effect on trace element composition. Generally, the final effect is disadvantageous for source discrimination, as intrasource variability increases. Under specific circumstances, however, as is shown by the Blackman's Point material, it can have a differentiating effect.

Correct artifact assignment to the level of source locations proves to be difficult in some cases due to significant overlap between sources from similar geological origins. Discriminating geologically related source groups, or distinguishing the three different islands, produces far better results. The analysis of a number of chert artifacts from different Ceramic Age sites in the northern Lesser Antilles showed that the Long Island flint source on Antigua was the major source for the manufacture of flake tools in this region throughout the entire Ceramic Age. These results show that the indigenous populations of the Lesser Antilles particularly chose this source for the manufacture of their flake tools and that other sources were of less importance. This knowledge has formed the basis of a more elaborate study on distribution and exchange of stone materials among the northern Lesser Antilles, which proved that not only Long Island flint but also other rock materials were widely distributed and exchanged among the different small islands.

This study has shown that the use of archaeometric techniques, though time consuming and expensive, provides a strong objective empirical basis for artifact provenance. When used systematically it will finally give us a detailed insight on chert source use through time and space. The outcome of the artifact analyses demonstrates that this type of research produces some very detailed data with regard to artifact provenance and makes this line of research in the northern Lesser Antilles a very exciting one, which definitely needs continuation.

Acknowledgments

The work discussed in this chapter was part of a broader research by the first author at the Faculty of Archaeology, Leiden University, the Netherlands. This research was financed by the Netherlands Organization for Scientific Research (NWO; research grant number 250-53-023). The authors visited the northeastern Antilles in 1998. Petrographic and geochemical analyses were performed at the Faculty of Earth Sciences, University of Utrecht.

In the course of this work many people were helpful to us. We would like to thank the following people at the faculty of Earth Sciences, University of Utrecht: Helen de Waard, who performed the ICPAES analyses and helped us out during the sample preparation procedure; Otto Stiekema and Jan Drenth, who prepared many of the thin sections; and Professor Bernard de Jong and Dr. Cees Woensdrecht, who were helpful in many ways.

We would like to acknowledge the following people for allowing us to analyze artifact samples from archaeological sites: Luis Chanlatte Baik and Yvonne Narganes Storde of the University of Puerto Rico, Río Piedras (Sorcé); Corinne Hofman and Menno Hoogland, Leiden University (Spring Bay 3 and Kelbey's Ridge 2); Aad Versteeg (Golden Rock); Jeffery Walker of the USDA Forest Service (Sugar Factory Pier); David Watters, Carnegie Museum of Natural History, Pittsburgh (Trants); and André Delpuech, Musée du Quai Branly, Paris (Morel and Anse à la Gourde).

Furthermore, special thanks go to Jeffrey B. Walker, Reniel Rodríguez Ramos (both Puerto Rico), and Reginald Murphy (Antigua) for helping us out during our field trip. Finally, we would like to acknowledge Annelou van Gijn and Corinne Hofman for their help during different parts of the research.

Notes

1. Out of five known localities on St. Kitts only two were sampled.

2. In this chapter we use the word "assign" for placing an unknown case (i.e., artifact) in a predefined group (a source), and the word "classify" for grouping a number of cases based on predefined criteria. Confusingly, in predictive Discriminant Analysis the term classify is often used for assigning unknown cases to known groups (e.g., Duarte Silva and Stam 1995).

3. This may well be explained by the different environments of genesis for both rock materials. In the case of obsidian, sources corresponding to remains of the same volcanic outburst event have very similar element concentration. While sources corresponding to remains of different events generally vary significantly in chemical characteristics, even if the remains stem from a single volcano. Furthermore, obsidian contains higher concentrations of trace and rare-earth elements as compared to chert, which increases the possibility of finding discriminating variables.

II
FUNCTIONAL STUDIES
OF ARTIFACTS

5

A New Material to View the Past

Dental Alginate Molds of Friable Artifacts

Charlene Dixon Hutcheson

Introduction

Palmettan Ostionoid pottery, or Palmetto ware dated to A.D. 850–1500 (see Hoffman 1967, 1970), in the Bahama Archipelago is primarily undecorated (Keegan 1997a:39; Rouse 1992:99), although very limited examples of punctate-incised and molded appliqué occur (Sears and Sullivan 1978). The primary decorations on Palmetto ware are negative basketry impressions, which occur to a varying degree (4 to 14 percent) in the reported assemblages. There is some debate concerning the purposefulness of the basketry impressions (cf. Berman and Hutcheson 2000; Hoffman 1970; Hutcheson 2001; Keegan 1997a; Rose 1987; Sears and Sullivan 1978). Regardless of the reason these negative impressions occur, they are invaluable in the reconstruction of the basketry and textile industries in the pre-Columbian Bahamas and elsewhere (Drooker 1992, 2001; Petersen et al. 1997), as actual fiber artifacts are extremely rare (Conrad et al. 2001). Thus, this class of material culture has been disproportionately underrepresented in archaeological models.

Negative basketry, cordage, fabric, and netting impressions on ceramics provide an avenue through which these technologies can be studied in the absence of the original fiber artifacts (Adovasio et al. 2001; Drooker 1992; Hutcheson 2001; Petersen et al. 1997), and offer the potential for understanding the cultural and political expressions associated with them (Berman and Hutcheson 2000; Drooker 1992:xiii–xiv; Petersen 1996:2).

Background

In 1995, under the auspices of the Lucayan Ecological Archaeology Project, directed by Mary Jane Berman and Perry L. Gnivecki, on San Salvador Island (Fig-

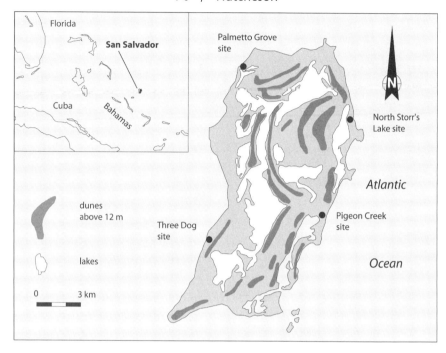

Figure 5.1. Map of San Salvador, Commonwealth of the Bahamas (original by Perry L. Gnivecki.

ure 5.1), the author began an ongoing study of negative basketry impressions on Palmetto ware. It became apparent that positive molds needed to be created from a large number of impressed pottery sherds (Pigeon Creek [SS1] no. 260; Palmetto Grove [SS2] no. 205) for later basketry analysis (Berman and Hutcheson 2000; Hutcheson 2001).

Many materials have been used over the years for creating positive molds and casts of impressed ceramics, none of which have been completely satisfactory, including clay (Holmes 1884; Sears and Sullivan 1978), latex (Rachlin 1955), Sculpey® (Drooker 1992, Reith 2004), Reprosil®, a dental compound (Stothert et al. 1991), and Plasticine® (see Drooker 2001 for details).

Dental alginate met our requirements for retention of design detail, easy release with minimal damage to friable unglazed ceramics, and ease of use in the field, even though there was some concern about long-term mold stability and shrinkage. As a result, dental plaster, or "dental stone," casts were also deemed necessary. Even though the casts exactly replicate the pottery sherds, measurements were taken from the artifacts whenever possible. A protocol was developed to enhance the stability of the alginate in the field providing adequate durability for long-term analysis of pattern and structure.

Methods and Materials

Dental alginate is readily available in many proprietary brands. Jeltrate® Plus Fast Set (Dentsply International, Milford, Delaware) was selected for this study. It is light and transports easily as a powder, has low dusting character, and requires no special apparatus. Table 5.1 outlines the protocol.

Any cool, clean, freshwater source is acceptable for mixing the alginate and dental stone. Saltwater adversely affects the alginate mix, preventing it from properly setting up. Casts can be made of any plaster material, but because of durability and fine detail retention, dental stone is preferred. Vel-Mix® dental stone (Kerr Lab, Orange, California) was used for this project.

Durability of the Molds

A shrinkage study was conducted to document the durability and stability of the alginate molds. Molds made in the field as well as fresh samples were used in the study. The first measurements were taken in August 1995 with the final measurements in December 2005. All of the molds were stored in individual zippered heavy plastic freezer bags in a covered cardboard file box in ambient temperatures of 68° to 75°F. At the time of the final measurements, all molds were firm to the touch, but many remained partially flexible and, with care, these were still usable for casting. New casts made from these partially dry molds do not provide accurate measurements. Pattern detailing was still clearly visible for study purposes even in the totally dry examples. All of the molds in bags that retained their integrity remained semiflexible.

The final range of shrinkage dimensions was 0.7–14 mm; 11 to 31 percent. Table 5.2 gives the shrinkage rates over time. Circular and elongated objects had the highest initial shrinkage rate, approximately 1 percent per week for the first three weeks, while irregular shapes had the highest dimensional stability during that time (Table 5.2). For the most part, this equalized by the end of the study, with rectangular forms ultimately shrinking the least, averaging 5 mm or 15 percent overall. After ten years, many of the molds stored in near optimal conditions remained in good condition. Mold durability is adversely affected by exposure to direct sunlight, heat, rough handling, compression, and exposure to air.

When evaluating the effects of the alginate compound on the study collection, no detectable surface residue or damage has been noted over the past ten years. However, at the time of molding, some crumbling was noted at the most friable edges. Additionally, water-based pigments painted on sherd surfaces are in potential jeopardy of removal by contact with the wet alginate (Drooker 2001). Slip decoration fired onto the ceramics will not be harmed. The 1999 Society for American Archaeology Working Group in Impressed Pottery concluded that since all of the compounds used for taking molds and casts of impressed ceramics may leave some form of residue, examples of each type should be set aside so that other analyses

Table 5.1. Mold and Cast Production from Dental Alginate and Dental Stone.

Molding Procedure	Equipment
• Clean artifact surface of excess loose dirt, do not scrub	• Flexible rubber bowl
	• Round-blade putty knife
• Make a foil form 1/4-in larger than artifact, secure with tape	• Aluminum foil
	• Cellophane tape
• Mix alginate with water in a 1:1 ratio in 30 ml increments	• Zippered freezer storage bags
	• Two 30 ml measures
• Pour mixture into form	
• Slowly roll the sherd into the mixture, this reduced chance of air bubbles	**Materials**
	Jeltrate® Plus Fast Set alginate
	Vel-Mix® dental stone
• Allow to set until firm, about 1 minute ± 30 seconds	
• Once the alginate is set, remove form and separate mold & sherd	**Alginate to Artifact surface area**
	30 ml = 1 measure
• Gently rinse off debris from mold	• 1 measure / 5 cm^2
• Store molds in a zippered freezer bag out of direct sunlight in a stable temperature of 70–75°F	• 2 measures / 8 cm^2
	• 7 measures / 15 cm^2
• Casts may be made immediately; for dimensional accuracy make within 24 hours	
	New molds from casts
	• New molds can be made from the casts at any time
Cast production	• To prevent the alginate mix from sticking, soak dry cast in water for 2 to 3 minutes
• Follow manufacturer's directions	
• Allow to dry completely before storing in paper or plastic bags	
• Use ballpoint pen or pencil to ID	

Table 5.2. Shrinkage of the Alginate Test Molds in Near Optimal Storage Conditions.

Time	1 wk	2 wk	3 wk	18 mo	24 mo	10 yrs
Average shrinkage percent	0–2 mm	0–2 mm	0–3 mm	7 mm	8.8 mm	18 mm

can be carried out. It was noted that some of the compounds commonly used left surface residues that hinder ^{14}C dating (Minar et al. 1999). This has not been determined for dental alginate (Drooker 2001), a seaweed derivative, but it seems advisable to follow this protocol regardless of the molding material being used.

Discussion

The methods described here were successfully utilized in the study of negative basketry impressions from several native Lucayan sites in the Commonwealth of the Bahamas (for details see Berman and Hutcheson 2000; Hutcheson 2001), most notably the Pigeon Creek (SS1) and Palmetto Grove (SS2) sites on San Salvador Island. Through the use of this technique, the basketry of the Lucayans has once again come to life. A classification system for the weave types has been created (Berman and Hutcheson 2000) and a basketry technology and style-grammar may now be studied and articulated.

The weaving classes identified are all forms of plaiting, which includes 1-over-1 (1/1) simple plaiting, often called "checkerboard weave," wicker—a form of simple plaiting, and 2-over-2 (2/2) twill plaiting (see Adovasio 1977 for basketry definitions). No examples of coiled or twined basketry have been found in the Bahamas to date (Berman and Hutcheson 2000; Hutcheson 2001). There is a predominance of 2/2 twill plaiting, which is the primary interval of interlacing in Lucayan basketry (Berman and Hutcheson 2000) and often produces the appearance of a herringbone pattern. This is especially true when a thick material is used causing an uneven surface; one having "topography." Additionally, a single instance of compact countertwined fabric with evidence of S-spin and S and Z twist rows from the Palmetto Grove site was noted (Hutcheson 2001:189). This is the only example of fabric thus far identified in the Bahamas.

Several very complex weave patterns have been deciphered, most of which utilize one primary shift sequence dubbed the "A pattern" due to its appearance in the pottery impressions (Figure 5.2). This ubiquitous shift mechanism is made up of a four row repeat sequence by one element that can be inverted or rotated to the left or right at set intervals within a design. The "A pattern" sequence consists of: (row one) 2 over/1 under/2 over, (row two) 2 over/3 under/2 over, (row three) 2 under/1 over/2 under, (row four) 2 under/3 over/2 under and has a 2 over/2 under primary interval of interlacing for the other element. Visual zigzags, chevrons, lozenges, as well as quartered and halved fields in the Lucayan weaves were identified. The term "visual" is used because the actual weaving is straight across, whereas the pattern appears as a zigzag or other design (Figure 5.2). This shift pattern often looks like one or more stacks of the capital letter "A." For example, a zigzag pattern will have evenly spaced upright and inverted "stacks."

Having the positive face of the weaving in the form of the mold is essential in

0   3 cm

Figure 5.2. Photo of a sherd and corresponding mold showing the difference in visibility of the weave pattern.

deciphering the more complex weaves, and when the weave is very tight, the impression is faint or otherwise obscured on the sherd. The optical confusion created by the negative impression on the pottery makes it extremely difficult to follow the interlacing. Note the difference in appearance between the sherd and the mold in Figure 5.2, where the mold actually looks like a basket surface. Casts offer a different visual perspective, and, due to their uniform coloration, they often reveal details that cannot be seen on the original artifact (Drooker 2001; Hutcheson 2001).

The Pigeon Creek site has produced the most complex use of the "A pattern" mechanism (Figure 5.3, no. 4), as well as a modification of the "A pattern" in the third and fourth rows, giving a staggered appearance creating a diagonal line (Figure 5.3, nos. 1a and 1b). Another pattern, very different from the "A pattern," has also been found where the warp and weft simultaneously alter intervals creating a borderlike pattern (Figure 5.3, no. 2) (Berman and Hutcheson 2000). Two versions of a quartered field have been found (Figure 5.3, nos. 3 and 5). One creates nesting lozenges while the other draws the eye inward. These designs speak of a weaving tradition that is complex and well developed, hinting that other such weaves are yet to be found.

Preliminary investigations by Lucinda McWeeney have suggested the identification of some of the fibers used in Lucayan basketry that includes several types of palm, most notably *Cocothrinax argentea* (silver thatch) and *Sabal palmetto* (palmetto), and monocotyledonous plants such as *Typha* sp. (a likely one being cattail) and *Poacea* sp. (one or more types of grass) (Hutcheson 2001; Hutcheson and

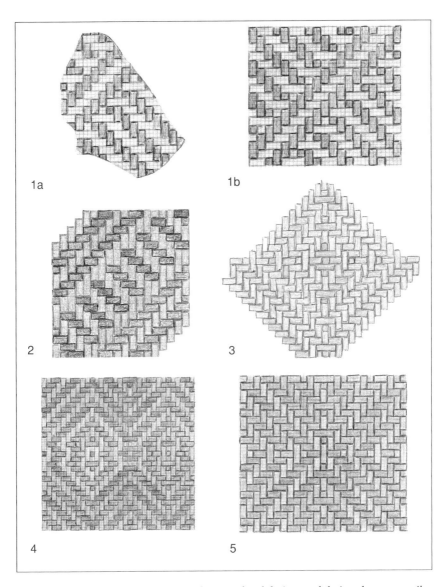

Figure 5.3. Weave pattern schematics and extrapolated designs and design elements. 1a: illustration of a sherd with basketry impression; 1b: pattern indicates a diagonal divide in the overall design; 2: pattern producing a border or division in the design field; 3: a quartered field creating multiple lozenges; 4: a multipart complex design; 5: a quartered field radiating out from the center (illustrations by C. D. Hutcheson, imaging by Bron Duncan, Totally Digital, Roanoke, VA. See details of 1a, 1b, 2, and 4 in Berman and Hutcheson 2000; details of 5 in Hutcheson 2001).

McWeeney 1999). Due to the often crisp, clear nature of many of the impressions, and the remarkable detail in the alginate molds, it is sometimes possible to make direct observations of plant morphology. A collection of materials, both plant and basketry, was amassed, with which to study these impressions. Some of the materials have been woven into mats, while others have been left relatively unprocessed; both are then impressed into clay after which molds are made. This aids in understanding what plant attributes can be expressed in the sherds and ultimately the molds.

Purposefulness vs. Production By-Product

Many of the basketry impressions are amazingly crisp, with the exception of very used worn pottery and the presence of heavy soot and other debris coating the artifacts. In many instances 5x magnification of the molds shows the vertical scraping of the cut edges of the basket elements in the clay. This, in conjunction with my experiments in pottery manufacture and impression (Berman and Hutcheson 1997), lends further support to my belief that these impressions are purposeful. This is not to say that the pots could not have initially been made on "mats" as Hoffman (1967, 1970) states, but rather that those imperfect markings were removed and crisp ones added at a specific time in the production sequence. Sears and Sullivan contend that the impressions are deliberate (1978:12–13). Modern support for this concept comes from Yde, who asked a Wai Wai woman in 1967 to make a clay cassava griddle. The clay was worked on a mat in the initial stages of the production sequence, but those markings were removed during the finishing process (Yde 1967:182). It is believed that the Lucayan potters used a similar production sequence.

Adovasio and associates (2001:65-67) discuss the fabric or basket impressions of the St. Johns assemblage, Tick Island site, ca. 500 B.C. to A.D. 100. They state: "These mats are doubtlessly the surfaces upon which the St. Johns vessels were placed in the still wet state and with some downward force as the indentations in the impressions are quite sharp" (Adovasio et al. 2001:67). While this statement does not indicate a belief of purposefulness, it does imply that the impressions were made in a single downward motion, as opposed to multiple multidirectional forces consistent with hand-built pottery production. If the Lucayan impressions are indeed intentional, then we must look for their cultural significance instead of continuing to assume they have no meaning because they were created by someone slapping some clay onto a piece of basketry (cf. Hoffman 1967, 1970).

Summary

The creation of dental alginate molds by the technique discussed here, while not one-step, is not difficult and works well in the field lab. The vast array of data available for study from these molds and casts opens many avenues of research into the perishable fiber industry of the Lucayans. This technique can be applied to other impressed, incised, and flaked materials where pattern details are being analyzed. Molds show excellent durability if stored with care after the field season. The information already obtained from the use of alginate molds in the Bahamas is vast and heralds new discoveries forthcoming.

Acknowledgments

I would like to thank Dr. William Frazier for his assistance with information on dental compounds. Thanks to Mary Jane Berman for getting me into this study and giving many hours of assistance and collaboration on weave terminology. Don and Kathy Gerace of the Gerace Research Center, and The Bahamas Department of Archives, must be thanked for making the ceramic assemblages available. Also, many thanks goes to Mike Anthony, Anne Sampson, and my husband, Bob, for editing assistance, and to Grace Turner for continuous support.

6
Saladoid Lapidary Technology
New Methods for Investigating Stone Bead Drilling Techniques

Christy de Mille, Tamara Varney, and Michael Turney

Introduction

Ancient lapidary traditions are frequent objects of interest and curiosity. The high degree of artistry and technical skill demonstrated by these industries worldwide is characteristic of both the Saladoid lapidary industry and the Saladoid occupation of the Caribbean (Watters 1997c). Stone beads, in particular, have played an important role in discussions of Saladoid socioeconomic systems and interaction. For example, the most frequently cited evidence for interisland movement is the common occurrence of exotic stone artifacts in Saladoid sites (Watters 1997c). In addition to the movement of raw materials, it has been demonstrated that both the local manufacture of items and import of finished goods occurs in Saladoid sites, and that both of these are differentially represented between islands (Crock and Bartone 1998; Murphy et al. 2000; Watters and Scaglion 1994). This has led to hypotheses of regional manufacturing centers and trade, with associated suggestions of craft specialization (Watters 1997c; Watters and Scaglion 1994). Such hypotheses have important implications for topics of interisland contact and trade, political and economic organization of production, and the Saladoid cultures. Many different lines of evidence are necessary for such broad-level questions; however, meaningful interpretation can only begin to be accomplished through specific and detailed understandings of the finer scaled participants in this production. One of the long-term goals of our research is to work toward a detailed understanding of bead manufacture on Antigua, which would provide a basis for later comparisons with other islands. While still exploratory, our present study is an initial step toward these larger goals.

This chapter continues research into the drilling technology of the Saladoid lapidary industries on the island of Antigua. The investigation focuses on the examination of manufacturing traces on the bore walls of stone beads in addition to other attributes such as bore hole shape and size. Focus is laid on drilling technology as it is one of the easier production steps to examine archaeologically; lapidary production typically does not produce large quantities of waste, and on finished beads most of the manufacturing traces have been obliterated by the final stages of bead production such as polishing. The examination of perforation methods could therefore allow one aspect of manufacture to be analyzed and compared between finished and partially manufactured beads. This is potentially important when comparing locally vs. off-island manufactured stone artifacts. Additionally, the drilling of the beads is usually considered the most difficult and technologically demanding of the steps in bead manufacture.

The specific methodology we employ in our bead drilling research is based on a series of studies into Near Eastern lapidary technology in which the bore holes of cylinder seals and beads were molded, cast, and then examined with a scanning electron microscope (SEM) (Gorelick and Gwinnett 1978; Gwinnett and Gorelick 1979, 1981). The underlying rationale behind their research was that different drilling techniques (types of drills, abrasive, motion) leave distinctive traces. Through a series of experiments and comparison with archaeological examples, Gwinnett and Gorelick demonstrated that at a broad level this did seem to hold true. The microscopic examination of manufacturing traces is essentially analogous to the better-established use-wear research, with production, rather than use, the object of the analysis.

Preliminary results from our trial application of molding bead bores for examination with an SEM were encouraging (De Mille and Varney 2003). Our primary objective was to establish the viability of producing replicas of bead bores, through molding and casting, that could then be analyzed for manufacturing traces. Through comparison with X-ray images taken of the beads, and SEM imaging of broken bead bores and the molds taken from them, we were satisfied enough with our ability to reproduce the bores in fine detail in molds. A second objective was to compare any features that could be seen on the Antiguan specimens with similar studies elsewhere to gain any preliminary insight into bead drilling techniques. One hypothesis gained from this comparison was that the beads examined were drilled with an abrasive (De Mille and Varney 2003).

The present study further explores and validates the methodology utilized to investigate drilling techniques. We continue to experiment with molding and casting techniques. In addition, the replicability of both molds and casts for recording manufacturing traces is further explored. Another goal is to enlarge our database of manufacturing traces from Antiguan archaeological examples. This study also initiates the experimental drilling portion of our research.

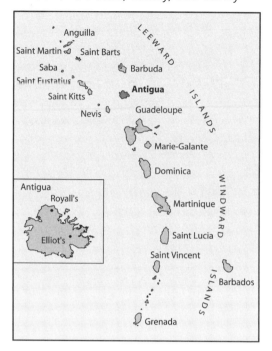

Figure 6.1. Location of the Royall's and Elliot's sites on Antigua.

Background

The small Lesser Antillean island of Antigua is unusually geologically diverse, which has resulted in the presence of archaeologically significant mineral and rock resources on the island (Murphy et al. 2000). The wealth of stone resources is demonstrated throughout the entire precolonial archaeological record of the island. However, the breadth of raw material use and types of artifacts produced are substantially greater during the Saladoid (A.D. 71 to 900) (Murphy 1999).

The two Saladoid sites of Royall's and Elliot's (Figure 6.1) have provided much of the information known about beads from this time period on Antigua. Most of the beads were recovered at these sites during surface reconnaissance and excavation by the Museum of Antigua and Barbuda and the University of Calgary field school (1997–2001). In addition, a number of beads were borrowed from a private collection on the island.

Mineral and rock identification was undertaken as an interdisciplinary effort with Reg Murphy and two geologists from the University of Calgary, Al Levinson and David Hozjan (Murphy et al. 2000). Two calcite artifacts, a partially drilled bead, and a drilled tablet, as well as an experimentally drilled calcite tablet, are discussed here.

Methods

As it is not possible to directly view manufacturing traces on the inside walls of the bore of intact beads, it is necessary to replicate the bores in order to examine them. Although our efforts at obtaining high quality replicas to date have been met with some challenges, we have been able to reproduce fine detail satisfactorily.

Initially, it was chosen to make molds of the bore with Resilpom Putty, a silicone-based putty, for its qualities of gentleness toward archaeological specimens, rapid curing time, and its ability to produce detailed replicas of an object. Previously (De Mille and Varney 2003), we noted some challenges in producing perfect molds with this putty. As such we consulted with a dental technologist whose expertise in reproducing fine detail for various types of dental prosthetics provided invaluable insights and new directions in seeking the optimal replication materials and techniques. This led to the use of a new molding material, Elite HD+ (manufactured by Zhermack), designed for creating high precision dental impressions. This light-bodied two-component silicon is available in a variety of colors, setting times, and consistencies. The "light bodied normal setting" form was utilized as it has a viscous yet fluid consistency and is prepackaged in a cartridge delivery device such that air bubbles are not introduced into the mold. It has the added advantage of being a medium blue color, which serves to enhance observing and imaging the relief on the mold.

In order to create a replica of the bead bores, the impression material was injected into the bore. When it was set (15–20 minutes), it was removed from the bore and placed into a "bowl" that was custom made to size using a fast-setting silicone putty. This container served to hold the mold securely in place as well as contain the liquid casting material in place until it set. This technique was adopted after some experimentation so that only half of the mold was cast at one time for intact beads, allowing us to create a cast that did not need to first be sawn in half in order to be viewed. The casting material was prepared using a mechanical mixer under vacuum that eliminated any air bubbles in the casts that were produced. Casts produce a more permanent and positive replica of the bead bores; however, our attempts at casting have not yet produced satisfactory results due to difficulties in capturing adequate images of the three-dimensional detail that exists on the casts. The best results were achieved using a museum grade casting material, Aqua-Resin, and we will next try coating the casts with a thin coating of carbon or metal before viewing under the microscopes to enhance imaging.

It was decided upon to use scanning electron microscopy due to its exceptional capability for observing fine topographical detail. Recent advances in SEM technology have allowed nonconductive materials to be imaged without being coated with a thin layer of metal (typically gold or platinum), thus both the artifacts themselves, when found broken with the bore exposed, as well as the casts could be examined. A second reason for employing this imaging technique is for the purposes of comparability with other work undertaken on manufacturing traces and drilling technology by Gwinnett and Gorelick (1979, 1981; Gorelick and Gwinnett 1978).

A scanning electron microscope/energy-dispersive spectrometer (SEM/EDXA) capable of imaging in environmental mode was utilized in the Lakehead University Instrumentation Laboratory (LUIL), and we were able to image our bead bores and molds without any modifications. The beads and bores and molds were scanned along their entire length, and at focal points of interesting features, and the images were saved as computer files. However, the SEM we now have access to at the LUIL could not produce images in the same low magnification (85x vs. 30x) as the SEM we utilized for our initial study (De Mille and Varney 2003). This meant that a greater detail (mostly of the mineral and rock itself) was visible, and that the smaller field of view required complete pictures of boreholes to be composites of a series of many images. The issue of direct comparability with our previous work and that of Gwinnett and Gorelick (1979, 1981; Gorelick and Gwinnett 1978) was raised. As such, we made use of a stereoscope fitted with a digital camera to visualize the bores and their replicas. Image Pro 5 software was then used to knit together a stack of serial images taken at different focal distances to produce an accurate 3D image. We are confident that the combination of the SEM and the 3D images taken through the stereoscope has allowed us a comprehensive view of the bead bores and their replicas.

Experimental Drilling

In this initial phase of our experimental program, one drilling trial, in which a 5 mm hole was drilled in a calcite tablet using a wooden drill bit and a quartz sand slurry as the cutting solution, was completed. We decided to begin our experiments with the relatively soft mineral, calcite, common in the Antiguan assemblages. The first experiment was chosen with wood as a drill bit, as no chert drill bits small enough to have been used on the beads have yet been recovered archaeologically. Further trials will include a variety of rock and mineral types, abrasives, and drill bits.

It took six hours to drill a hole 5 mm deep. The drilling mechanism was a rotary multitool (Einhell Model BSG30–40T) with speeds of approximately 10,000 rpm. A wooden toothpick, blunt end down, was inserted into the chuck of the tool. We purposely did not drill through the tablet, allowing us to examine the leading edge of the borehole. A small reservoir was built out of modeling clay to retain the slurry in the drill hole, particularly in the initial phase of drilling. Drilling was undertaken in half-hour stages. During these 30 minutes, the wooden drill would have to be replaced between 6 to 10 times due to attrition. If the drill bit were too long, it would snap immediately if too much pressure was applied to it. After about 30 minutes the sand particles from the drilling slurry became wedged into the bottom of the borehole and were difficult to remove. It was necessary to remove the compacted slurry, however, before further drilling progress could be made. To ease both molding and examination of the experimentally produced drilled materials, these pieces were cut in half, exposing the drill bore. This allowed examination of manufacturing traces on the actual bore surface as well as the mold.

Results

Figure 6.2 illustrates different images of the experimental piece (experimental calcite #1) and its mold taken with a stereomicroscope and SEM. The images taken with the stereomicroscope offer more realistic views of the item, due to the enhanced depth of field. They also offer excellent views of the general shape and macroscopic features of the borehole. In this case, the prominently conical shape of the borehole is very obvious. If the bottom of the actual borehole is examined (Figure 6.2a), it can be observed that the leading edge (arrow #1) is relatively flat. There are prominent furrows (arrow #2 and arrow #3) near the leading edge that give it a steplike appearance. The mold (Figure 6.2b), which offers a negative impression of the object, is particularly effective in illustrating the shape of the larger scale features such as a number of faint furrows (arrow #4), which are difficult to image on the actual experimental piece. These furrows are concentric features, but are less prominent than the ones closer to the leading edge, nor do they demonstrate the polish of the leading edge furrows visible on the SEM image, as described below.

SEM imaging is necessary in order to examine finer-scaled features. Two obvious features that can be observed on the composite SEM image (Figure 6.2c) are areas of localized and more generalized polish. The two prominent furrows giving the leading edge its steplike appearance (arrow #2 and arrow #3) are represented on the SEM images as linear polished bands extending around the borehole. Similar bands of polish are not in evidence in locations farther up on the borehole where the less prominent furrow features were observed on the mold (Figure 6.2b, arrow #4). There is also a prominent area of polish on one side of the borehole outlined by the oval in Figure 6.2c. Many of the other features and textures visible on the SEM image are that of the calcite itself, including a large fracture.

We were fortunate to have an archaeological example of a partially drilled calcite bead to compare with our experimental piece. Again, the mold imaged with the light microscope provides an excellent view of the overall shape of the bore

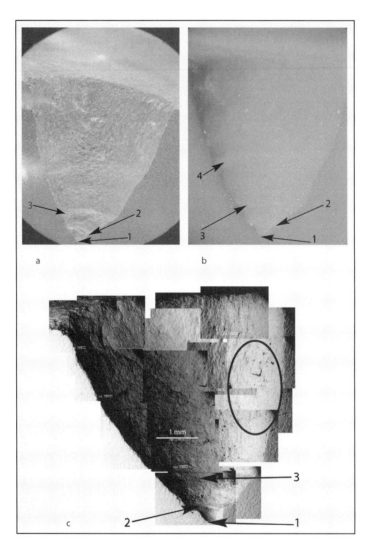

Figure 6.2. Three views of experimental calcite #1 and mold taken with stereomicroscope and SEM. Arrow #1 points out leading edge; arrows #2 and #3 point out furrows near leading edge; arrow #4 points out less defined furrows and oval defines area of polish. a: stereomicroscope, experimental calcite #1, actual; b: stereomicroscope, experimental calcite #1, mold 2; c: SEM, experimental calcite #1, actual.

Figure 6.3. Side view of mold of partially drilled calcite bead, stereomicroscope.

(Figure 6.3). Drilling did not proceed very far on this bead; its shallow nature is apparent from the side view of the borehole mold (Figure 6.3). Despite its limited perforation, preliminary comparisons of general shape between this bead and our experimentally drilled example are possible. One similarity between both items is the appearance of the leading edge. Like that of the experimental piece, the leading edge in the calcite bead is flat and has a stepped appearance down to the bottom of the borehole. One observed dissimilarity is that the bore walls above the immediate leading edge of the partially drilled calcite bead are more parallel than the prominently conical walls of the experimental piece.

Figure 6.4 shows two composite SEM images of the partially drilled bead borehole. The top image is one of the actual artifact (Figure 6.4a), while the bottom image is of the mold (Figure 6.4b). If the two are compared, it is clear that the detail replicated on the mold is considerable and accurate. The mold is particularly useful for allowing the very bottom of the bore to be viewed, as it is difficult to focus in on the very bottom of the actual artifact. The immediate leading edge, as observed with the mold, is quite pitted. Farther up on one side of the wall there is a large patch of polish. With the top down view, the concentric abrasion features defining the borehole are very apparent.

The final artifact described here is a partially broken calcite tablet with two boreholes paralleling each other; likely representing misaligned bores (Figure 6.5).

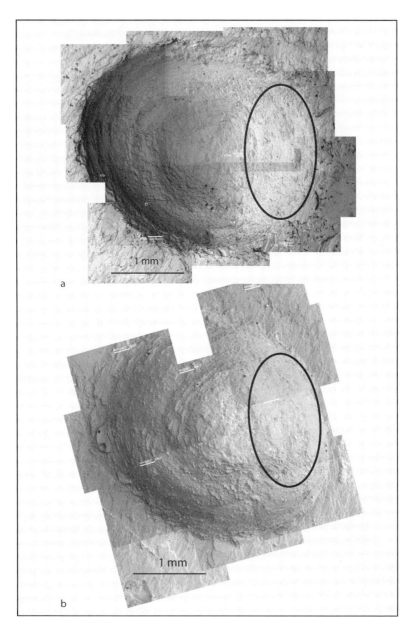

a

1 mm

b

1 mm

Figure 6.4. SEM images of partially drilled calcite bead and mold taken from the bead. Oval outlines area of polish. a: SEM, actual bead; b: SEM, mold.

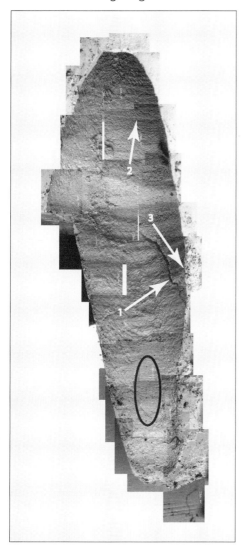

Figure 6.5. SEM image of partially drilled calcite tablet. Oval defines polished area, arrow #1 points to fracture, arrow #2 to abrasion rings, and arrow #3 to deeper furrows.

A portion of the end of one of the boreholes has been broken off, allowing direct imaging of part of the bore wall. Only this limited portion is available for discussion, as we have not yet produced a satisfactory mold from this artifact. If the SEM composite is examined (Figure 6.5), a number of characteristics that appear to be common with calcite are in evidence, including the general texture and the presence of a fracture (arrow #1). In terms of manufacturing evidence we see numerous concentric abrasion rings (arrow #2), some of which are quite prominent and furrowlike (arrow #3), in addition to smoother more polished areas (outlined by the oval). Although it is difficult to tell from this view, the borehole is parallel.

Discussion

We offer tentative interpretations of our findings based on comparisons with those of Gwinnett and Gorelick (1979, 1981; Gorelick and Gwinnett 1978). Their investigations remain the most extensive utilizing these general methods. In general their findings seem to suggest that the nature of the drill, objective piece type, and abrasive (if utilized) can all contribute to the appearance of the manufacturing traces on the inside of bead boreholes.

The manufacturing traces resulting from our first experimental trial with a wooden drill mimic those described by Gwinnett and Gorelick (1979). A particular characteristic of a wooden drill is a stepped or terraced appearance at the leading edge of the borehole, hypothesized to be a result of changes in the wooden drill bit due to attrition (Gwinnett and Gorelick 1979). The leading edge of the experimental piece conforms to the expected stepped appearance. The partially drilled calcite bead also has this characteristic leading edge, strongly suggesting the use of a wooden drill or material similar in its drilling properties.

The use of softer drills such as wood requires the use of an abrasive as a cutting agent. On the basis of their experimental work, Gorelick and Gwinnett (1978) cite the presence of concentric abrasion rings and the occasional more prominent furrow as characteristics of the use of abrasives. In the archaeological and experimental examples thought and known to be drilled with wooden drills, Gwinnett and Gorelick (1979) describe a common pattern of irregular (spacing and size) concentric abrasion rings characterizing the borehole, with smoother polished patches also in evidence. They hypothesize that localized polishing is the result of the breakdown of the abrasive into finer particles that then act in a polishing rather than cutting fashion. Similarly, it is possible that deeper furrows that appear to cut into the bore walls may result from the compaction of the abrasive in the bottom of the borehole, resulting in a more outward rather than downward cutting action.

Concentric abrasion rings are present on all the experimental and archaeological objects described above. However, they are definitely more prominent on the archaeological items, reflecting differences in abrasive use. The experimental piece presented an interesting feature, as the more prominent furrows near the leading edge were found to be more highly polished than the immediate area surrounding them. A similar highly localized polishing effect was not observed on the archaeological examples.

A prominent difference we observed between the experimental piece and the archaeological beads from Antigua is the prominently conical borehole of the experimental piece. Many of the Antiguan examples are remarkably parallel-sided with slight flaring near the end, indicating bidirectional drilling (De Mille and Varney 2003). Evidently, our drilling procedure allowed continued cutting of the upper sidewalls, an occurrence that did not appear to occur as frequently in the archaeological examples.

Conclusion

To conclude, we remain convinced of the viability and utility of this technique as a method for investigating bead manufacturing, specifically drilling, techniques. However, we are continuing to refine our methods. In terms of understanding the manufacturing techniques utilized by the Antiguan Saladoid craftspeople, the use of an abrasive with a softer drill, such as wood, is strongly suggested for the softer calcite examples. The use of abrasive, as demonstrated by concentric abrasion rings, is more strongly evidenced in the archaeological examples, rather than the experimental piece, where we know for sure that an abrasive was utilized. Further experimentation with abrasive use and different stone types should be profitable.

Acknowledgments

We would like to extend our gratitude to Paul O'Neill of Balmoral Dental Designs for providing expertise and aid in the replication of the bead bores, and Al McKenzie of the Lakehead University Instrumentation Laboratory for assistance at the SEM.

7

Lithic Technology

A Way to More Complex Diversity in Caribbean Archaeology

Benoît Bérard

Introduction

Caribbean archaeology has been essentially built on the analysis of only one type of remains: ceramics. This focus has been a good choice in the pioneering days of Caribbean archaeology, and this for a number of different reasons. First, pottery often constitutes the major part of the remains we find during excavation of archaeological sites in the Caribbean. Second, the making of pottery in Caribbean prehistory is not only the production of artifacts but also—perhaps more significantly, due to the important technical and symbolic value of pottery—the production of meaning. Thus, the "interrogation" of this one, but major, witness has been a success that has enabled the founders of Caribbean archaeology to build the chrono-cultural framework we still use today.

Yet for the last twenty years we have had to deal with new, more complex questions, and it is not possible to find answers with only one witness to interrogate. We have to develop a multiwitness approach. In this way Caribbean archaeology will start to become a more complex science, adapted to answering more complex questions. Lithic technology is one of the steps on the road to methodological complexity—even if stone tool production is essentially utilitarian with a low social investment. Still, like all technical production lithic technology is also a cultural production, and therefore it can give us some essential answers.

The aim of this chapter is to present ways in which lithic technology studies can be useful for Caribbean archaeology. Thus I will first present the theoretical framework supporting this type of study. Then I will present, as an idealized research program, the different questions lithic technology studies can help to answer. As an example of what is possible to do, I will specifically focus on one of

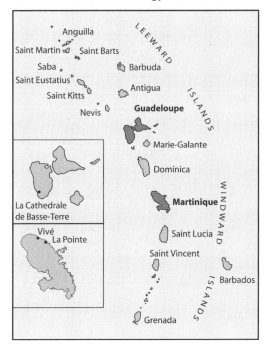

Figure 7.1. Location of the archaeological sites on
Guadeloupe and Martinique.

the major questions today: the distinction between early Cedrosan Saladoid and
Huecan Saladoid.[1] To do this I will present the results of a comparative analysis of
the early Cedrosan Saladoid *débitages* from Martinique and a Huecan collection
from the site of La Cathédrale de Basse-Terre in Guadeloupe (Figure 7.1).

Lithic Technology

Technological studies are supported by the conception of technical action as a fully
cultural one. Following the pioneering works of Marcel Mauss (1947), who has extended the field of technical actions into body techniques, technological studies in
social sciences have been first developed by ethnologists. But very quickly archaeologists have invested this new field of research, perfectly adapted to the nature of
their findings: the material expression of culture (Leroi-Gourhan 1943, 1964). This
new approach was also, in the 1960s, an answer to the traditional way of characterizing cultures that had been inspired by natural sciences and was based on the
identification of different guide fossils. Therefore, for a long time technological
studies have remained associated with a paleoethnological (synchronic) approach

to prehistoric cultures. It has just been two decades that technological studies have started to be used in comparative diachronic approaches. Comparisons are based on the characterization of a set of *chaînes opératoires* that, in an associative system, constitute a technical system specific for each culture.

The *chaîne opératoire* concept gives to these studies a dynamic vision, putting each technical act into an associative sequence.[2] It is this sequence that gives a technical and social meaning to these acts. In order to study the lithic technology researchers have to analyze all the steps from the procurement of raw materials to the abandoning of the used tools (Balfet 1991; Inizan et al. 1995). The *débitage* remains are especially well adapted to this type of study. The knapping of siliceous stones follows the physical laws of the conchoidal fracture. This specific breaking mode leaves different stigmata on the stone. The stigmata on the upper face of a flake, if correctly analyzed, indicate the direction and the sequence of preceding removals, and on the lower face they show the nature of the type of percussion that has produced its own removal. In this way it is possible to read on each piece of a collection a more or less lengthy sequence of gestures by the flint knapper. The association of these different sequences in a coherent framework allows the reconstruction of the *chaîne opératoire*.

Studies of lithic technology are generally constructed in parallel with an experimentation program. The experimentation is essential in developing an intimate understanding of the techniques and the methods associated with lithic technology. It is indispensable for the analysis of the percussion techniques, which cannot be correctly identified without a comparative approach with experimental collections.

Indeed, by means of studies of lithic technology European archaeologists are building a fine characterization of Paleolithic cultures, allowing them to identify technical traditions as well as regional groups, and enabling a discussion of the level of social relations that have existed between different groups, for example, between Chatelperronian (Neanderthal) and Aurignacian (*sapiens*) groups (Pelegrin 1995). As I have to deal with this type of questions in Caribbean archaeology, lithic technology can help.

Lithic Technology in the Caribbean: A Research Plan

Although some researchers in the Caribbean started early to study stone tools, the first real technological studies have only been conducted during the 1980s. The best example of this first effort in the 1980s may be the work of J. Walker on the *débitage* remains from the Sugar Factory Pier site on St. Kitts (Walker 1980a, 1980b, 1983). It constitutes a very complete research program in lithic technology, including experimentation and wear-trace analysis. More or less contemporaneous studies are the works of A. Gus Pantel on Lithic Age cultures (Pantel 1988).

These first studies were followed in the last seventeen years by a new generation of researchers who essentially concentrated their efforts on the studies of the first agro-ceramist groups (Bartone and Crock 1991; Bérard and Giraud 2002; Bérard and Vidal 2002; Crock and Bartone 1998; Rodríguez Ramos 2001a, 2001b). The first comparative diachronic or synchronic studies were published during this same period (Bérard 2001; Rodríguez Ramos 2001b, 2005a). Thus we now have a first set of findings on Amerindian lithic technology. It concerns essentially the first agroceramist groups and more specifically the early Cedrosan Saladoid ones. Still, there are large gaps in our knowledge and lithic technology can help us solve different problems or see them from a new point of view.

First of all, studies of lithic technology make a major contribution to the understanding of Preceramic cultures and groups. In this field we have to improve our analysis concerning identification of the continental origins of the cultures of the Caribbean Lithic Age. Through their ability to identify enduring technical traditions, studies of lithic technology are able to give us a definitive answer. To be able to deal seriously with I. Rouse's migratory hypothesis, which postulates the arrival of Ortoiroid groups from Trinidad (Rouse 1992), we also have to look at the mechanisms of transition between the Lithic and the Archaic Age, and maybe more than that, at the diffusion of Archaic groups in the northern part of the Lesser Antilles.

For the transition between the Archaic and the Ceramic Age, the first work conducted by Rodríguez Ramos (2005a) shows all the interest this type of study has for identifying the importance of intergroup relations (Archaic and Ceramic) and of the acculturation phenomena in the progression of the agro-ceramist way of life in, especially the northern Antilles. This type of study has been really successful in the last ten years in western Europe, advancing the understanding of the mechanism of neolithization of the Mesolithic groups.

For the Ceramic Age a precise diachronic analysis of knapping technologies will allow us to identify enduring traditions and cultural rupture. It will give us a new perspective for the analysis of cultural change during this period. More than that, studies of lithic technology can contribute actively to the identification of regional groups, an approach that has started in the last few years, essentially supported by the analysis of ceramic remains.

Following this *pro domo* pleading, and as a first small step toward a future research program, the results of a comparative analysis of early Cedrosan Saladoid and Huecan Saladoid knapping technologies is presented.

Early Cedrosan Saladoid vs. Huecan Saladoid Knapping Technologies

No other study of this type has been undertaken previously except one by R. Rodríguez Ramos (2001a, 2001b). Based on the analysis of the collections from Puerto Rico and Vieques, it has been concluded that real differences have existed between

Cedrosan and Huecan Saladoid production technologies. The specificity of the Huecan Saladoid *débitage* lies in the use of a technology called "Levallois-like" by Rodríguez Ramos. It consisted in the centripetal removal of flakes in the core, prior to the removal of flakes with a predetermined shape. He associated the discoidal cores presented in those collections with this specific method of reduction. The first step of the *chaîne opératoire* consists of the splitting of nodules by means of bipolar percussion, followed by the production of smaller flakes by bipolar percussion.

Early Cedrosan Saladoid Knapping Technology

The early Cedrosan Saladoid lithic *débitage* has been well described since the first publications of J. Walker (Bartone and Crock 1991; Bérard 2004; Bérard and Giraud 2002; Bérard and Vidal 2002; Crock and Bartone 1998; Rodríguez Ramos 2001a, 2001b; Walker 1980a, 1980b, 1983). The focus of the present chapter will be the study of two early Cedrosan Saladoid sites, Vivé and La Pointe on Martinique. The results of the technological analysis of the lithic collections coming from Martinique, St. Kitts, Montserrat, and Vieques has shown them to be comparable, so the example from Martinique can be considered representative of the early Cedrosan Saladoid knapping technology in general.

Two types of raw materials have mainly been used by the Cedrosan Saladoid knappers in Martinique: a set of hydrothermal amorphous silicifications (jasper in majority) and a set of igneous stones more phaneric (basalt and andesite). Those two types of stones have been knapped in two different ways. The raw materials supplied were of poor quality. Those materials have been introduced untreated in the residential sites, sites that will not be discussed further in this chapter.

The goals of the reduction sequence are the production of flakes (average length: 30 mm) with sharp cutting edges useable as multipurpose knives (Figure 7.2f) and, second, the production of small straight flakes (average length: 15 mm) classified as "manioc grater teeth" (Figure 7.2b).

Both types of raw materials can be used to realize the first goal. There is no specific organization of the *débitage* (see problem above) during that phase. During this process, the reorientations of the *débitage* are frequent and, in fact, there is not, in general, a preferential striking platform. The first flake of the pebbles can be realized with the bipolar technique (Crabtree 1972), but direct percussion with a stone hammer is mainly used in this phase of production. There is no specific intention on the part of the knappers to predetermine the flakes' morphology. The only exceptions to that general scheme are some nodules that are knapped by the bipolar technique along a preferential axis. Those cores have a morphology commonly described as a *pièce esquillée* (Figure 7.2e).

The *débitage* of the small flakes is realized only on the hydrothermal amorphous silicifications. The knappers make that production on small pebbles or on

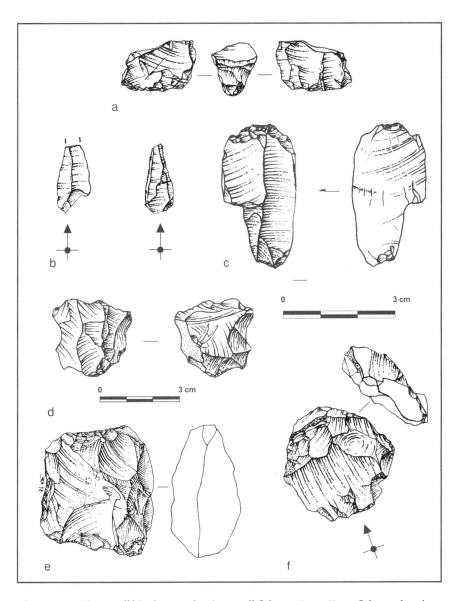

Figure 7.2. a: Vivé, small bipolar core; b: Vivé, small flakes; c: Basse-Terre, flake produced by bipolar technique; d: Basse-Terre, discoid core; e: La Pointe, *pièce esquillée*–type core; f: Vivé, "large" flake with secondary work.

thick flakes produced during the first phase. This work is realized by the bipolar technique using a preferential striking platform (Figure 7.2a). The knappers try to obtain small straight flakes. That second phase of the *débitage*, which is recurrent and well organized, is realized more carefully. The very small size of some cores implies the use of some specific prehensile systems.

Different elements can be highlighted in that short presentation. The method of reduction is relatively simple. The reduction process is very short, and, in general, only a few products are obtained (especially during the first phase). However, the method used is really efficient and quick: a minimum of time and of percussion instances is necessary to obtain a small set of flakes. Even though the early Cedrosan Saladoid reduction strategies are simple and poorly organized, they are not entirely opportunistic. This is proven by the clear articulation existing between the two goals described above. Rather than opportunism, the *débitage* reveals that the knappers have a large freedom of action, freedom linked with a low level of social and cultural investment. The most characteristic element is the knapping of the small flakes by the bipolar technique. I will try to see now if that cultural investment is sufficient to support our comparative study.

Huecan Saladoid Knapping Technology

The presentation here of the Huecan Saladoid reduction technique is based on the analysis of a collection coming from the site of La Cathédrale de Basse-Terre in Guadeloupe. The site was excavated in 2002 under the direction of Bonnissent and Romon.[3] It is composed of an Early Ceramic Age occupation partially disturbed by a colonial cemetery. The *débitage* remains presented here come from the test pits 1 (a 2 x 2 m test pit) and 7 (a 3 x 5 m test pit). Two occupational levels, none clearly individualized, constitute the Amerindian occupation of that site. Following the analysis of the ceramic remains (Bonnissent in Bonnissent and Romon 2004), the lower level is associated to the Huecan Saladoid subseries and the upper one is considered as a mix or a transitional level associating elements linked to the Huecan and the Cedrosan subseries. At this stage, I have not been able to identify a pertinent technical variation in the lithic collection associated with that chronological or spatial division, therefore I will make a global presentation of the *débitage* remains coming from the two test pits and the two levels. Two hundred and forty eight pieces of *débitage* constitute that collection.

The raw materials used are mainly Long Island (Antigua) flint (64 percent). This type of flint is characterized by the presence of a white chalky cortex and a clear brown to dark gray color. Long Island is the major source of siliceous raw materials for the northern part of the Lesser Antilles (see Knippenberg this volume). Igneous stones (andesite and basalt, 10 percent), red jasper (7 percent), and a set of amorphous silicifications (sedimentary or hydrothermal) compose the rest of the sample. Igneous stones can be found around 10 km away from the site to the north. Red jasper can be found on the leeward coast of Basse-Terre island and on Les Saintes islands. The pieces of the collection show a low degree of corticality.[4] With the exception of the igneous stones introduced in the site untreated, all the other types of raw materials have been brought to the site at least partially prepared (there are no fully cortical flakes associated with those raw materials).

The goals of the reduction sequence are difficult to identify. Only two pieces have clear evidence of secondary work. But six other pieces show macrowear traces. All those pieces can be regarded as flakes; their average length is 28 mm. They have no specific morphology but they are in general thinner than the rest of the collection. Thus we can suppose that one of the objectives of the reduction sequence is the production of thin, amorphous flakes that were not morphologically predetermined. However, the presence of small scar negatives on the cores seems to indicate a second objective of the reduction sequence: that of small flakes. Some of those last removals are in average only 13 mm long. Thus, there are two goals of the reduction sequence: the production of "large" thin flakes and the production of small flakes. However, small flakes were not produced on the igneous stones.

Two types of percussion techniques have been identified in the collection, direct freehand percussion with a stone hammer and bipolar techniques.[5] The percussion techniques have been used for different purposes or at different stages of the chaîne opératoire.

The "large" thin flakes have been obtained by two methods. First, some cores have been knapped with direct freehand percussion following a simple discoid method. This method, first identified for the middle Paleolithic cultures, is defined by bifacial conception of the core volume associated with a centripetal recurrent production of flakes. This is one of the simplest recurrent knapping methods. The identification of that method is easy by the observation of the cores (Figure 7.2d) and can be supported by the presence of éclats débordants. The second method uses the bipolar technique (Figure 7.2c). Those débitage are conducted according to a main axis and the cores have at the reduction sequence end a pièce esquillée morphology. This type of production is realized on small blocks or on thick flakes produced during the manufacture of the "large" thin flakes by the discoid method.

The small flakes have been produced on thick flakes or on exhausted discoid cores. Those flakes and cores were first split by means of bipolar percussion. Subsequently, the production of the small flakes is realized by means of the bipolar technique to use the thickness of the half thick flakes (or the half discoid cores) as flaking surface.

Comparison

Now it is possible to realize point by point a comparison between the early Cedrosan Saladoid and the Huecan Saladoid débitage technologies (Figures 7.3, 7.4).

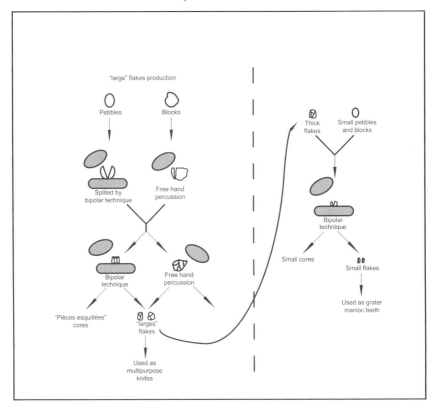

Figure 7.3. Early Cedrosan Saladoid *chaîne opératoire* of *débitage.*

Concerning the raw materials used, no serious comparison can be made be-tween collections from different islands. In regard to the way those raw mate-rials were introduced in the sites, some differences have been identified. In the early Cedrosan Saladoid sites, the stones have been introduced untreated. On the site of La Cathédrale de Basse-Terre, the majority of the stones have been intro-duced at least partially preprocessed. That point is in contradiction with the obser-vations of R. Rodríguez Ramos about the sites in Puerto Rico and Vieques. In fact, the mode of introduction of the raw materials may not have a cultural significance.

The major difference existing between the reduction methods is the presence in the collection from La Cathédrale de Basse-Terre of the discoid method of re-duction. That method has never been identified in early Cedrosan Saladoid sites. The other elements of the *chaînes opératoires* are quite similar. There is no real dif-ference between the results of that study and those of R. Rodríguez Ramos. The only difference is a terminological one. The use of the term "Levallois" implies an important level of predetermination of the final products.[6] That predetermina-

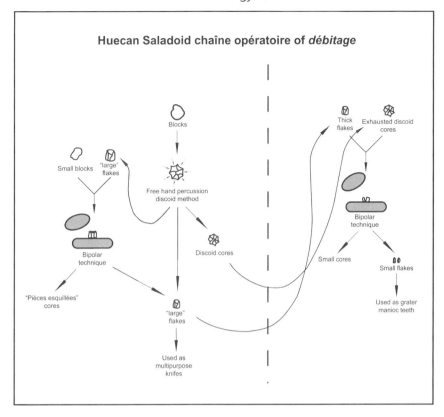

Figure 7.4. Huecan Saladoid *chaîne opératoire* of *débitage*.

tion seems to be absent in the *débitage* of La Cathédrale de Basse-Terre, which is why I prefer to associate this *débitage* with the discoid method than with the Levalloisian one.

Conclusion

Different elements can be emphasized from the short analysis above. First, the distinction between early Cedrosan Saladoid and the Huecan Saladoid, initially based on the analysis of the ceramic remains and subsequently extended to other elements (Oliver 1999) can also be identified in the lithic reduction methods as far as the actual southernmost extension of the Huecan culture: Guadeloupe. This assertion gives a greater importance to the distinction between the Cedrosan and the Huecan Saladoid. However, some of the differences identified seem to vary according to the geographical context. This is the situation for the mode of introduction of the raw material. As so often with the evaluation of the degree of relation that existed between the Cedrosan and the Huecan groups, we will need more studies to deal properly with the internal geographical and chronological variations of those two sets.

The results of this study are more or less concomitant with those of the ceramic remains analysis. Cedrosan and Huecan subseries seem to be clearly two distinct cultural assemblages, but linked at different levels. We cannot expect that this situation of concomitant evidence will be systematic in the future. With the entrance of Caribbean archaeology in a time characterized by multiple sources of evidence, we will have to learn to deal with contradictory data. The story we will have to write will be more complex but may be nearer to reality.

Notes

1. In this chapter I have chosen to use the term "Huecan Saladoid." This choice is not depending on a personal, theoretical position in the important, ongoing debate on the qualification of this cultural assemblage. The choice has simply been made because it was easier to make a choice than to use a more careful but a longer definition.

2. Chaîne opératoire: "enchaînement de faits techniques dont les opérations sont articulées comme des maillons au long d'un processus tendant à un certain résultat, de telle manière que l'observateur doit pouvoir rapporter un acte technique même isolé à la série dans laquelle il prend sens, techniquement et socialement" (Balfet in Balfet 1991). English: Chaîne opératoire, or operational sequence: a sequence of technical facts of which the operations are articulated as a link to a process leading to a certain result, of such manner that the observer must be able to associate a technical act, even isolated, to the series in which it makes sense, technically and socially.

3. Institut National de Recherches Archéologiques Préventives, Guadeloupe

4. The corticality degree is the part of cortical surfaces present on a flake.

5. For the identification criteria of the two techniques, see Bérard 2001, 2004; Bertouille 1989; and Mourre 1996.

6. Levalloisian method is also associated with a specific preparation of the striking platform before the removal of the objective pieces.

8

Tool Use and Technological Choices

An Integral Approach toward Functional Analysis of Caribbean Tool Assemblages

Annelou L. van Gijn, Yvonne Lammers-Keijsers, and Iris Briels

Introduction and Theoretical Background

Archaeological research relies on the material remains of past peoples. Although this may seem obvious, it is remarkable that especially material objects have not always received maximum attention and, during much of the last century, were mainly used as chronological markers. In the last decade interest has shifted toward material culture studies, both in archaeology and in cultural anthropology. We have realized that tools are not only indispensable in subsistence and craft activities, but are also intimately connected with the social and ideational aspects of society. They are not only reflective of the social and cultural identity of their makers, but they also, through their role in daily life, structure and reinforce existing social relationships and play an important role in mediating social changes (DeMarrais et al. 2004; Dobres 2000; Graves-Brown 2000; Meyers 2001; Miller 2005; Schiffer 2001). In the same vein, even apparently insignificant objects made of stone, coral, and shell were not only essential for subsistence and craft activities but may also have structured society by the routine of their daily use. The meaning of objects may also have changed during the course of their use-life. A tool could have been used, resharpened, modified into another object, or placed as a burial gift in a grave. Each tool has therefore its biography: it was made in a specific way particular to the social and cultural traditions of its producers; it was used, maybe modified again, and finally it was rejected or deposited.

In order to achieve a better understanding of the social biography of prehistoric implements, we must first understand their function. Use-wear and residue analysis offer a possibility to identify the actual use of stone tools. Experimental studies have shown that using tools made of flint, hard stone, bone, and antler result in characteristic traces, each linked to specific activities, that can be examined microscopically (Hamon 2004; Keeley 1980; Nieuwenhuis 2002; Van Gijn 1990, 2005). Additionally, identifiable residue may be left behind (Fullagar 1998; Fullagar and Furby 1997; Nieuwenhuis 2002, this volume). This is equally as relevant for distinct tool types, like arrowheads, as for unmodified shell and stone tools. The results of the use-wear analysis of stone, shell, and coral implements thus provide a clue to the past function of these implements. However, just as a kitchen chair and a royal throne are both used to sit on (thus presumably displaying the same traces of wear), their social and ideational function is entirely different. Similarly, a lithic tool like a strike-a-light, can have a direct functional application (to make fire) but may also have an ideational connotation if found in burial context (Van Gijn et al. 2006). It is therefore always very important to examine the results of use-wear and residue analysis in the archaeological context from which they derive. Tables of results are not enough.

Not only is it important to examine the archaeological context in which objects were found, we also must understand the technological and functional relationships between tools made of different raw materials. In other words, we must attempt to reconstruct toolkits used for different tasks (Van Gijn in press). Traditionally, functional analyses have focused on stone tools (mostly flint) and have neglected tools made of bone, antler, shell, or coral. Methodological research in use-wear analysis over the past decade has made clear that use-wear analysis also works for these "other" materials (see Kelly and Van Gijn this volume; Lammers-Keijsers 2007; Maigrot 1997; Van Gijn 2005, in press). The functions of the toolkits in a technological system form a basis to trace the choices past people made in the selection of raw materials, in the production techniques used, and in the selection of tools. Such choices are reflective of the social and cultural identity of the users because of the cultural embedding of technology (Appadurai 1986; Lemonnier 1993a, 1993b). By examining these technological choices in a wider archaeological context, it may be possible to understand the meaning of objects for past people and the role they play in structuring society.

Obviously, this approach requires extensive functional studies of a range of different sites, something that has not yet been done on Caribbean find assemblages. Elsewhere, comparative data are available, indicating some remarkable differences in the choice of tools between sites from different periods or different regions (Van Gijn 1998, 2005, in press). In this chapter some initial results of high-power functional analyses and residue studies will be presented, outlining the possibilities of an integral approach toward tool use. This will be done by means of three case studies: Plum Piece on Saba and Anse à la Gourde and Morel on Guadeloupe. Clearly, more research is necessary before a social biography of different tools can be made and the cultural significance of simple, domestic tools can be investigated. In the meantime we can obtain, al least at site level, some insights into the organization of the technological system, especially about those aspects thereof that are usually not preserved.

Methodology

Use-wear analysis as a method to study the function of prehistoric tools was first introduced by the Russian S. A. Semenov. Although several researchers had been interested in the function of prehistoric artifacts before, Semenov was the first to include experimentation, ethnographic observation, and microscopy in his research. He not only studied flint tools but also examined hard stone, bone, and antler tools (Semenov 1964). His book on use-wear analysis was first published in Russia in 1934, but it was not until 1964 that an English translation appeared. This book, titled *Prehistoric Technology*, inspired several researchers in England and the United States to study the function of all those artifacts, which until then had only been used as chronological markers. Obviously, this new approach toward studying the function of tools fitted in well with the ideas of the New Archaeologists at that time who wanted to know about the people behind the artifacts.

In the United States, Tringham and Odell were the first to do systematic research of tools, stressing one aspect of Semenov's research, that of the macroscopic wear traces (Tringham et al. 1974). This included edge removals (often referred to as use retouch) and edge rounding, whereas the general presence or absence of polish could often be determined as well. This approach makes use of a stereomicroscope, using magnifications of 10x to 100x, occasionally 160x. In England another American, Keeley, emphasized another aspect of Semenov's method. Keeley concentrated on polish and striations that can only be observed under high magnification (100–560x), making use of reflected light microscopes (Keeley 1980). The method of Tringham and Odell is commonly referred to as the Low Power approach, that of Keeley as the High Power approach. In the 1970s several articles appeared that stressed the relative benefits of each approach. Basically, the issue is between those emphasizing relative speed and ease of analysis (the advocates of the Low Power approach) and those more concerned with obtaining detailed functional information by means of the more tedious High Power method (Juel Jensen 1988).

The debate has pretty much abated and most researchers nowadays stress that the two approaches should be used in a supplementary way. The choice of method should be determined by the degree of preservation of the assemblages studied and by the archaeological questions asked. Low Power microscopy is ideal to detect residues, to find the location of polish and edge rounding, in short to obtain a general idea about the function of an implement. High Power analysis is crucial to arrive at a more detailed statement about the nature of the contact material and often also about the motion executed. However, most European researchers still predominantly use High Power microscopy, whereas Low Power studies are preferred in the Americas. Because in the Caribbean area too, High Power analyses have so far been rare, this chapter demonstrates the relative benefits of such an analysis for well-preserved and well-documented find assemblages. Residue studies form an essential aspect of this approach but will be dealt with elsewhere in this volume (Nieuwenhuis this volume).

The Laboratory for Artifact Studies in Leiden, the Netherlands, where the functional studies presented in this book have been conducted, has a range of microscopes and other facilities, including stereomicroscopes, incident light microscopes (fitted with polarizing filters and differential interference contrast [DIC]), and a transmitted light microscope. One incident light microscope has a free arm, allowing the examination of large objects like celts and ground stone tools. Equipment to extract and process residue samples is present (see also Nieuwenhuis this volume) and reference collections for residue, phytoliths, and (to a lesser extent) starch analysis are present.

There is also a large experimental reference collection of used implements, including almost 300 experiments specifically geared toward the Caribbean environment. These experiments include tools made of Antigua flint, shell (bivalves and *Strombus gigas* for the celts), coral (*Porites porites*, *Acropora cervicornis* and *Acropora palmata*), and stone. The experiments are essential for use-wear and residue analysis. Functional inferences are based on a comparison of experimental and archaeological wear traces and residue. The more alike the two sets of observations are, the higher the probability that the activity responsible for these traces is the same.

Case Studies

Plum Piece

Plum Piece is located on Saba and dates to the Archaic Age (Figure 8.1). It is situated away from the coast ca. 400 m above sea level, in a forested environment (Hofman and Hoogland 2003; Hofman et al. 2006). The midden deposits found contained flint (Briels 2004), shell celts, various ground stone tools such as hammer-stones and querns (Nieuwenhuis this volume), and coral. Most of the flint has been brought in from Antigua (Knippenberg personal communication). Faunal remains include fragments of the mountain crab and the soldier crab, both occurring at higher elevations, as well as a large amount of bird bones of the Audubon's Shearwater. This bird only resides on the island between February and July, providing a very good seasonal indicator (Hofman and Hoogland 2003; Hofman et al. 2006; Van den Bos 2006).

Preliminary functional and residue studies of flint and hard stone tools have been carried out so far (Briels 2004; Nieuwenhuis this volume). A small sample of

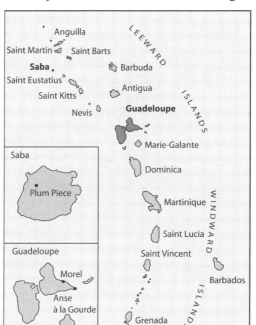

Figure 8.1. Location of the sites of Plum Piece, Saba, and Morel and Anse à la Gourde on Guadeloupe.

the shell celts has been analyzed, showing them to have been used for heavy wood-working (Figure 8.2a, b). With respect to Plum Piece the shell celts are assumed to have been involved in canoe making, an activity that is likely to have taken place in the tropical forest surrounding the site (Hofman and Hoogland 2003). Woodwork-ing traces were also found on three flint implements (Briels 2004), but the small size of these flakes makes it unlikely that they were put to use in canoe making; they were probably used for finely shaping wooden objects.

Besides wood, other plant material must have been important for subsistence and craft activities as well. This can be inferred from the use-wear analysis of a small selection of the extensive flint assemblage (Briels 2004). Of those tools dis-playing wear traces, the majority concerned siliceous plants (Figure 8.2c). The edge on which these traces were found was invariably obtuse. The polish found is very bright, with a smooth texture and an undulating and domed topography (Figure 8.2c, d). Striations were not pronounced. Where present the striations and the di-rectionality in the polish distribution indicated a perpendicular motion such as scraping or planing. Two varieties of plant polish could be distinguished: one with and one without tiny "pin pricks." This variation probably relates to two different

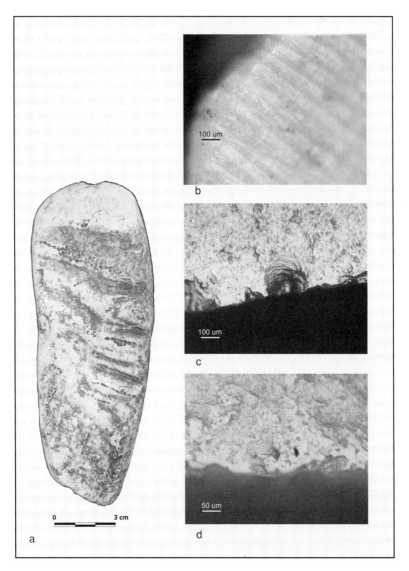

Figure 8.2. Toolkit for wood and plant working from Plum Piece, Saba. a: shell celt; b: wear traces from woodworking seen on this celt (original magnification: 100x); c, d: plant polishes on flint tools, original magnification 100x (c) and 200x (d).

species of plants, but it is not yet clear which plants were responsible. More experimentation is needed to clarify this issue. Whether the two varieties of plant working polishes, both predominantly oriented perpendicularly, are related to subsistence tasks such as peeling tubers, or to craft activities like scraping plants for producing fibers for rope making or basketry, is also unclear. It is argued here that the perpendicularly oriented polishes on the flint implements more likely were involved in making objects of plants. From ethnographic sources we know that, as the need arose, many objects in the tropical forest are made of the ample plant material present in the forest, to be rejected after use. Scraping shoots or stalks for weaving or plaiting is therefore a very plausible explanation of the transversely oriented plant working traces. The querns with plant working traces found at Plum Piece are mote likely to be connected to food processing, like crushing palm fruit. However, the querns too may have been used for processing fibers from palm (Nieuwenhuis this volume).

Considering the relative rarity of good quality flint and the effort that must have been expended in its acquisition, it is puzzling that most of the flint implements selected did not display any traces of wear. Flint is not locally available and one would expect it to be heavily used. Although some activities, like cutting meat, leave few traces on flint, the lack of extensive use-wear is yet another argument for seasonal occupation of Plum Piece. The attraction of the location lies indeed in the plant resources surrounding the site. The use-wear analysis of different categories of tools further corroborates this supposition, showing the important role of the plant and woodworking toolkit.

Anse à la Gourde

Anse à la Gourde is situated on the east part of Grande-Terre, the limestone island of Guadeloupe (Figure 8.1). The site is located on a narrow piece of land that ends at the Pointe des Chateaux. On the basis of the ceramic assemblage generalizing four phases are distinguished belonging to the Saladoid (A.D. 400–A.D. 850) and Troumassoid series (A.D. 850–A.D. 1400) (Hofman et al. 1999, 2001). The site was excavated on a large scale and yielded an enormous amount of artifacts: ceramics, shell, stone, flint, coral, and bone were encountered. Flint was mainly brought from Antigua, stone pebbles and rocks had to be imported from La Désirade or Basse-Terre. Shell was therefore considered a valuable substitute, serving as a raw material for tools and ornaments. Anse à la Gourde has revealed a rich variety of shell beads, adornments, and three-dimensional objects, as well as a range of tools such as celts (axes, adzes, and wedges), bivalve-scrapers, and knives, fishhooks, gauges, and spoons (Lammers-Keijsers 1999, 2007). Only a limited range of shell species was employed, all of which can be obtained rather easily around the reefs. Two hundred bivalves, of which some were clearly gathered after the death of the animal, indicate that these shells did not form an important part of the diet. More likely they were foremost considered as a raw material for tools.

Celts made of *Strombus* sp. were probably produced on the site. We find both the production waste and the toolkit involved in their production. The hammer stones were used to break off and roughly shape the lip of the shell (Fig. 8.3a). The blanks were then brought into shape by grinding and polishing, using stone and coral grinding tools with the addition of sand and water. One big slab of coral of *Acropora palmata* displayed use-wear traces from polishing shell in a longitudinal direction, thus serving as a "grinding stone" (Figure 8.3b, c). The "angle abraded artifacts" of coral may have served to resharpen the edges of the celts during use. Experiments have shown them to be very effective for this task. Another task at Gourde seems to have been the manufacture of shell beads from *Chama sarda,* as waste products from all stages of production are present (Figure 8.4a). The first stage of production is breaking up the shell into fragments, probably with a hammer stone. The flattening was probably done on coral, whereas the perforation was made with a flint drill (Figure 8.4b). Experiments have shown small drills to be effective for this task (Figure 8.4c). A few flint flakes display traces of cutting and drilling shell (Figure 8.4d). These traces were also found on experimental pieces used to make bell-shaped tinklers.

Wood- and plant working was done with a variety of tools: shell celts for the rougher tasks, flint flakes and bivalves like *Codakia* for activities requiring less tool mass like cutting and scraping, and coral scrapers for polishing and rasping the wood (Figure 8.5). The use-wear traces demonstrate that the celts were used intensively. Many (30 percent) display traces of woodworking, both burned and fresh (Figure 8.5a). They were hafted as axes as well as adzes. Battering on the opposite side of the edge implicates that celts were also used as wedges. The flint flakes were used both in a cutting and a scraping/transverse motion, predominantly on plant, occasionally on wood (Figure 8.5c, d). Bivalves were mainly used in a scraping or transverse motion on silicious plants (Figure 8.5b). One species (*Tellina radiata*) was used exclusively in a longitudinal cutting motion, most probably on plant. The hard stone tools had a role in plant processing activities as well, but because only the Low Power approach was used on this material, the information on contact materials is limited.

Several abraded potsherds display traces of wear that are attributed to scraping the inside of pottery vessels (Van Gijn and Hofman in press; see also Lopez Varela et al. 2002 for an example from Maya context). Several bivalves, notably *Codakia,* were used for the same purpose (Figure 8.6a). Coral played a role in pottery production as well, as some of the "angle abraded artifacts" were used for scraping clay (Kelly 2003; Kelly and Van Gijn this volume).

The composition of the toolkits used for other activities is less clear. The majority of the celts studied (70 percent) display a mixture of use-wear polishes. It is

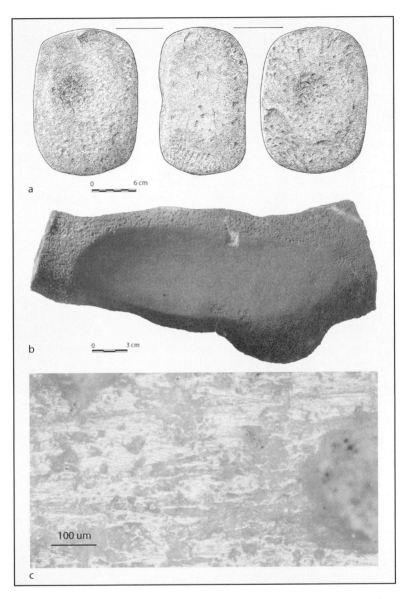

a

0   6 cm

b

0   3 cm

100 um

c

Figure 8.3. Toolkit for the production of shell axes from Anse à la Gourde, Guade-loupe. a: hammer stone; b: grinding slab made of *Acropora palmata;* c: use-wear polish observed on the coral grinding slab of b (original magnification 100x).

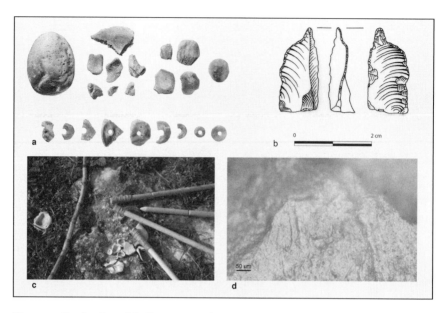

Figure 8.4. Production of shell ornaments from Anse à la Gourde, Guadeloupe. a: production sequence of shell beads from *Chama sarda* displaying the (waste) products at the various stages; b: flint drill from Anse à la Gourde with traces from perforating shell; c: experiment with perforating shell beads with hafted flint drills; d: use-wear polish from shell seen on archaeological flint drill of Figure 8.3b (original magnification 200x).

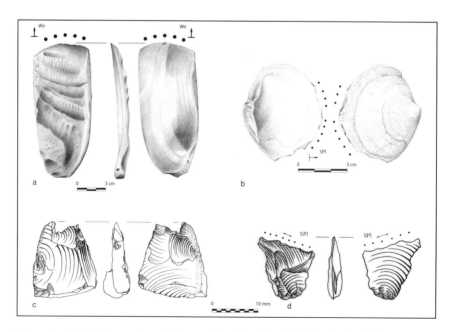

Figure 8.5. Toolkit for wood and plant working from Anse à la Gourde, Guadeloupe. a: shell celt with traces from chopping wood; b: *Codakia* bivalve used to scrape silicious plant material; c: flint tool used on wood; d: flint tool used on silicious plants.

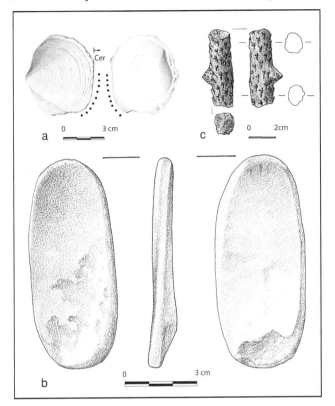

Figure 8.6. Toolkit for pottery production from Morel and Anse à la Gourde, Guadeloupe. a: *Codakia* shell used to scrape clay; b: abraded sherd used to scrape leather-hard clay; c: piece of coral (*Acropora cervicornis*) with clay residue.

suggested to interpret this as a result of multiple usages, comparable to the modern use of a machete. The presence of shark and manatee bones in the excavation demonstrates that the former inhabitants were in need of sturdy tools to slaughter these animals. It is unlikely that this task was carried out with the aid of a shell bivalve or flint flake (Lammers-Keijsers 2007).

Morel

The site of Morel is situated on the northern shore of Grande-Terre, Guadeloupe (Figure 8.1). Excavations at Morel by a team of Leiden University and the Directions Régionales des Affaires Culturelles (DRAC), Guadeloupe, focused on the two earliest occupation phases of the site. The oldest one is dated between 320 B.C. and A.D. 300 (Huecan/Cedrosan Saladoid, Morel I) followed by a second phase dating from A.D. 300 to A.D. 850 (Cedrosan Saladoid, Morel II) (Hofman et al. 1999). Because the larger part of the site has disappeared in the sea, it has to be considered that the artifacts studied form only a sample of the actual assemblage. Artifacts found washed upon the shore in the previous decades demonstrate that the variety in shell ornaments and tools must have been comparable to the range at Anse à la Gourde. It is remarkable that only five coral tools have been found, considerably less than at Anse à la Gourde.

The use-wear analysis was hampered by the bad state of conservation of much of the shell assemblage. The evidence obtained, however, indicates the same range of tools and toolkit composition as at Anse à la Gourde. Plant and wood were worked with flint flakes and shell bivalves. The majority of the hard stone tools can also be connected to the processing of plants and wood. Shell celts were hafted as axes and adzes. Five of them (10 percent) broke during use. Shell ornaments were made by means of flint. Some flint artifacts displayed traces from contact with bone. This may relate to slaughtering prey animals.

Two additional sets of tools will be discussed for Morel: the pottery manufacturing tools and fishing implements. The range of ceramic artifacts at Morel was much larger than at Anse à la Gourde (Van Gijn and Hofman in press). They formed part of the toolkit for pottery manufacture (Figure 8.6b). This also applies to one piece of coral (*Acropora cervicornis*) that displays a reddish brown residue, interpreted as clay (Figure 8.6c). Whether shell bivalves formed part of this toolkit as well, like at Anse à la Gourde, could not be ascertained due to the bad conservation of the shells.

We frequently assume that fishing played an important part in coastal communities, but the actual fishing implements are often not found. Morel has produced one small fishhook, made of *Cittarium pica* (Figure 8.7a). Other implements related to fishing are a series of small round pebbles. These stones display a band of black residue, interpreted as resin, in which, incidentally, imprints of fibers can be distinguished. These stones may have been braided into the edges of a fishing net (Figure 8.7b).

Conclusion

The three case studies presented above show how use-wear and residue analysis can shed light on tasks that, due to poor preservation circumstances, otherwise leave few archaeological traces. Examples are woodworking and plant processing activities such as fiber or rope making, netting, and so forth. Although at Morel and Anse à la Gourde it seems that shell, especially the bivalves, and coral tools seem to be just as multifunctional as flint implements, this may be a specific choice that has to be investigated for each new site. By looking at only one category of material culture, like flint tools, it is easy to miss some activities that were habitually carried out on sites. Use-wear and residue analysis of as many categories of objects as possible is therefore a vital method to extract more information regarding subsistence tasks, duration of occupancy of the site, and craft activities carried out.

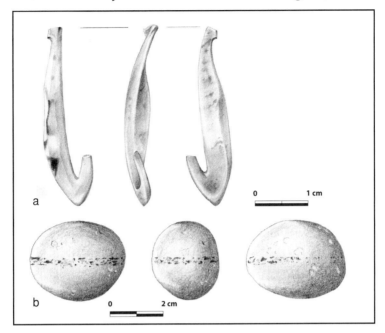

Figure 8.7. Toolkit for fishing from Morel, Guadeloupe. a: fishhook made of shell; b: stone pebble with black residue interpreted as a net sinker.

Another advantage of such an integral approach toward functional analysis, incorporating different categories of material culture for the presence of use-wear traces and residue, is that we may be able to reconstruct toolkits. This directly relates to the technological choices made by the people in the past. At Plum Piece we found that flint implements and shell celts formed part of the woodworking tool kit. This seems to be the case in Anse à la Gourde and Morel as well, supplemented by the incidental use of shell bivalves. It is also clear that shell celts were made with a toolkit composed of hard stone implements for shaping the rough out, coral grinding slabs for finishing the blanks, and coral scrapers for rejuvenating the edges. Flint objects served to roughly shape the blank of shell ornaments and objects and for making perforations. The blanks were subsequently finished on coral or hard stone grinding slabs. Shell bivalves, coral tools, and rejected pottery sherds constituted the toolkit for ceramic production. The toolkit for plant processing also consists of implements made of different materials: shell bivalves and flint tools for cutting and scraping, hard stone tools for milling and grinding plant material. For now it is not entirely clear whether the ubiquitous plant working traces found on a variety of tools are reflective of subsistence or of craft activities. Future experiments will hopefully clarify this issue, whereas residue analysis of the starch and phytoliths may provide clues as well (see Nieuwenhuis this volume).

By examining the production and use of different implements in relation to one another, it is thus possible to obtain insight into the choices people made with respect to the raw material selected for tool manufacture, the production technique, the way of use, and ultimately the loss, rejection, or deposition of the different objects. In this manner we can at least partially reconstruct the technological system. Research elsewhere indicates that the choice of raw material, production technique and use, as well as the composition of toolkits, may vary both diachronically and between different areas (Van Gijn 2005, in press). Such choices not only reflect the relationships established with other groups by means of the raw material exchange (see also Knippenberg this volume), but also the cultural preferences of the groups themselves. Obviously, in most archaeological cases the greater part of the material world will have disappeared. However, use-wear and residue analysis may shed light on aspects of the technological systems that are no longer directly visible in the shape of tangible objects.

Eventually it will be possible to do comparative studies of tool use between islands and through time, adding a further dimension to questions about cultural identity. Not many Caribbean find assemblages have yet been studied for the presence of use-wear and residue. The find assemblages are, however, so rich and varied that they certainly merit a detailed functional analysis, not only by means of the stereomicroscope but also by more detailed High Power and residue examination. With respect to the Caribbean situation there is the added advantage of an ethnographic and ethnohistoric knowledge base (Boomert 2000), providing ample information about tools and processes that can be replicated experimentally. It would be a shame not to tap this rich contextual information and maybe extend the inferential possibilities of microwear analysis. In the meantime the integral approach toward tool use applied to three Caribbean sites has shown that the Amerindians had a very flexible technology in which tools made of different raw materials were to some extent interchangeable. The producers and users of the tools were, however, always aware of the physical properties of the various materials they made their implements of and how these properties would affect the task at hand.

9

Understanding the Function of Coral Tools from Anse à la Gourde

An Experimental Approach

Harold J. Kelly and Annelou L. van Gijn

Introduction

Coral objects are found throughout the Caribbean in archaeological excavations. A magnificent example is the mask from Anse à la Gourde (Hofman et al. 2001). Other examples are the *zemis* made of *Acropora palmata* and *Porites* sp. found at Golden Rock on St. Eustatius and several Saban sites (Hoogland 1996; Steenvoorden 1992). However, coral fragments also were collected as raw material for the manufacture of tools. Sometimes these pieces of coral were not further modified; sometimes they were shaped into standardized artifacts. These tools have been recognized for some time and reported by various researchers (e.g., Rostain 1997; Steenvoorden 1992). Coral tools that were reported included grinders, metates, and rasps, functions that were basically inferred from morphological characteristics of the artifacts and by means of analogy to tools whose function was known. So far, however, use-wear studies of these tools by means of microscopic analysis are lacking.

In order to better understand the role of the coral tools in the technological system of the native peoples of the Caribbean islands, it was decided to examine a selection of tools for traces of wear (Kelly 2003). The tools derived from the site of Anse à la Gourde, a Saladoid-Troumassoid (A.D. 400–1400) site on Grande-Terre, Guadeloupe (Hofman et al. 1999; Hofman et al. 2001) (Figure 9.1). Tools of shell, flint, and hard stone from this site had already been microscopically studied, the results of which could be integrated with the study of the coral tools (Van Gijn et al. this volume).

No experiments with the use of coral tools were yet available in the Laboratory for Artifact Analysis of Leiden University. A first objective of the present research

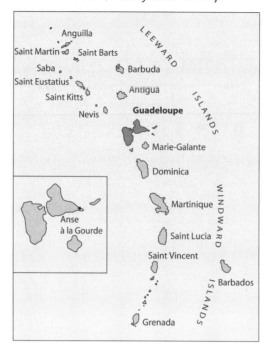

Figure 9.1. Location of the site Anse à la Gourde on
Guadeloupe.

was therefore to establish an experimental reference collection and to determine
whether interpretable wear traces developed on the coral tools. The approach was
subsequently applied to a selection of the coral tools from Anse à la Gourde. The
second objective was to understand the role of coral in the technological system of
the Amerindian inhabitants of Anse à la Gourde.

Methodology and Sampling

Use-wear traces on flint tools include use retouch, edge rounding, polish, and striations. Use retouch and rounding can be observed by stereomicroscope (Low Power
microscopy), polish and striations by incident light microscope (High Power microscopy) (Van Gijn 1990; Van Gijn et al. this volume). Initially, it was thought
that it would only be possible to look at macroscopic use-wear traces like abrasion and breakages. It was assumed that use-wear polish and striations would not
be visible, considering the coarseness of the coral. However, as it was not possible to distinguish the traces from the various contact materials by stereomicroscope, it was decided to attempt to use the incident light microscope, with magni-

fications of 100–560x. As it turned out from the experiments, the corallite ridges within the honeycomb structure of the coral behaved very much like other fine-grained surfaces such as flint or shell, displaying clearly developed polishes with topographical features similar to the ones observed on flint tools (Van Gijn 1990). The topography and relative smoothness of the polish can be assessed within the spatial confines of these ridges. The only difficulty is that, in order to evaluate the extent, distribution type, and limit of the polished zones, one has to "jump" as it were from one ridge to the next to obtain an idea of the extent of the wear. Polish does not develop on the coarse-grained interstices between the corallite ridges. Contrary to our expectations, therefore, the macroscopic wear such as edge removals and rounding was sometimes difficult to distinguish. It was decided to concentrate on High Power analysis, using the stereomicroscope only to obtain an overall view of the macroscopic wear and to detect residue.

The polish was described the same way as on flint tools, making use of the same attributes such as polish brightness, topography, directionality, and so forth. Problematic was the limit of the polish, in other words, whether it gradually fades out or whether the polish stops abruptly. This is because of the fragmented polish distribution: only on the corallite ridges. A few extra attributes were added to account for the specific physical properties of coral, the most important one being the degree of beveling visible on the ridges (a hard contact material will "bevel" the top of the corallite ridge, whereas a soft material will round the ridge).

The use-wear analysis was performed using a Nikon Optiphot incident light microscope with magnifications in the range of 10–560x (equipped with differential interference contrast [DIC] and polarizing filter) and a Wild stereoscopic microscope (10–160x). Photographs were taken with a Nikon DXM1200 digital camera. Some of the tools were cleaned in distilled water in an ultrasonic cleaning tank in order to remove adhering dirt, but the majority of the tools were just wiped clean with alcohol to remove finger grease. Chemical cleaning was not done in order not to damage the artifacts.

A large number of coral artifacts were found in Anse à la Gourde, not all of which could be subjected to a time-consuming microscopic analysis. It was therefore decided to focus on one type of tool: the tools with abraded angles made on *Porites* sp. The 52 *Porites* sp. artifacts selected displayed varied shapes and types of abraded angles (Figure 9.2). A categorization into different groups was made according to morphological similarities between the artifacts in terms of tool shape, degree of angle, occurrence of one or multiple abraded angles, and one- or two-sided abraded angles. The objective was to assess whether this morphological variation reflected differences in function. In addition, a few abraded implements of *Acropora cervicornis* were included in the sample (see Van Gijn et al. this volume, Figure 8.6c).

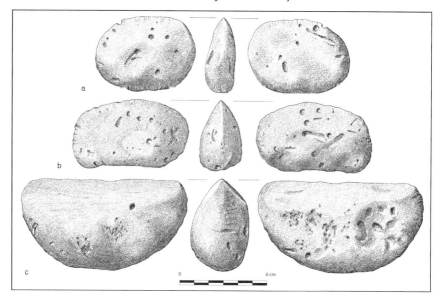

Figure 9.2. Angled abraded *Porites* sp. artifacts.

The Experiments

At Anse à la Gourde three types of coral predominated in the assemblages: *Porites* sp., *Acropora palmata,* and *Acropora cervicornis.* They each have different properties, making them appropriate for different kinds of tools. The *Acropora palmata* has thick flat branches that form excellent blanks for grinders and metates. It is also very hard and resistant. *Acropora cervicornis* grows in branches that have a rough surface, comparable to *Acropora palmata.* Fragments of these branches are very suitable as rasps to polish wood, shell, and bone, as well as for scaling fish (Steenvoorden 1992). *Porites* sp. is softer than the previously described species and can therefore more easily be modified into tools and objects than *Acropora palmata.* We concentrated on *Porites* sp. and *Acropora cervicornis* because they were the species the most common coral tools at Anse à la Gourde were made of: that is, scrapers (or angle abraded tools) and rods, respectively.

Coral has abrasive properties that most stones, shell, and wood lack. Because of the corallite ridges, surrounded by softer interstices, it resharpens itself during use, a bit like vesicular basalt. However, it does not provide a very sharp cutting edge. For cutting purposes flint, and to a lesser extent shell or hard wood, is a very wanted raw material.

The *Porites* sp. artifacts from Anse à la Gourde showed a wide range of shapes along with clear usage patterns such as abraded angles, polish traces, residues, striations, and hammer traces. Our assumption was that they were probably used for a wide variety of tasks. The experimental program therefore focused on a broad range of activities in order to obtain a wide variety of use-wear traces for the reference collection.

The experimental tools were made on coral gathered far from the site to exclude the possibility of using probable archaeological coral pieces. Since the *Porites* sp. artifacts from Anse à la Gourde appeared to have been used both unmodified and modified, the experiments were divided into two sets. The first set consisted of experiments based on the natural shape of the coral; the second consisted of experiments with modified *Porites* sp. (angled abrasions). These angled abrasions were made either one or two sided, depending on the aim of the experiment. Both sets of tools were used on the same type of contact materials. Additionally, the modified *Porites* tools were also used in experiments for which an unmodified piece would not be suitable, that is, cutting and incising calabashes and de-barking of branches, tasks for which a ground cutting edge is needed.

Contact materials included various types of (tropical) hardwood, shell, seeds, stone, ochre, clay, various plant species like calabashes, charcoal, and bone. The motions included cutting/sawing, scraping, sanding, rasping, polishing, incising, crushing, and pounding. Each tool was used an average of 30 minutes. If no traces were visible after the first 30 minutes of use, the tools were used another 30 minutes and observed again. The maximum time the tools were used was 1.5 hours.

A total of 37 experiments were carried out on the *Porites* sp. coral (Figure 9.3). The experiments not only served as a means to build up a reference but, more importantly, also provided insight into the way in which coral handles and behaves on different types of materials.

Microwear Analysis of the Experimental Tools

Contact with hard materials as shell, coral, and stone all caused a flattening of the corallite ridges (referred to as beveling) and a similar polish distribution (Figure 9.4b). Other attributes of wear, however, such as polish brightness and amount of striations, varied between the three materials. Contact with shell caused a bright polish, whereas rubbing coral with coral resulted in a dull, rather rough polish. Moreover, the corallite ridges of the tools used on shell developed deep gorges with a rounded bottom. Both materials produced a polish distribution that could be characterized as "streaks" (Figure 9.4b). So even though the wear traces from contact with these three hard materials overlapped to some extent, other characteristics were associated with specific contact materials. However, it may not always be possible to differentiate between these contact materials in archaeological context.

Another inorganic contact material, clay, resulted in quite different traces. The

Figure 9.3. Experiments with coral tools. a: pounding seeds; b: rasping hard wood.

wear traces obtained from experiments on clay were characterized by the development of rounded (rather than a beveled) corallite ridges in combination with a bright polish with flat topography, a lot of randomly oriented striations can be discerned in the polished zones.

Contact with materials such as wood, plant material, and bone showed some overlapping similarities in terms of resulting use-wear traces. However, each of these materials also provided specific features of wear. Working bone resulted in a dull to bright polish and a cratered and pitted polish topography (Figure 9.4c). A variable number of randomly oriented striations are also visible. The wear traces that resulted from the experiments with wood were characterized by the occurrence of rounded to very rounded corallite ridges (Figure 9.4a). Furthermore, a bright to very bright, smooth polish with a domed topography developed, with

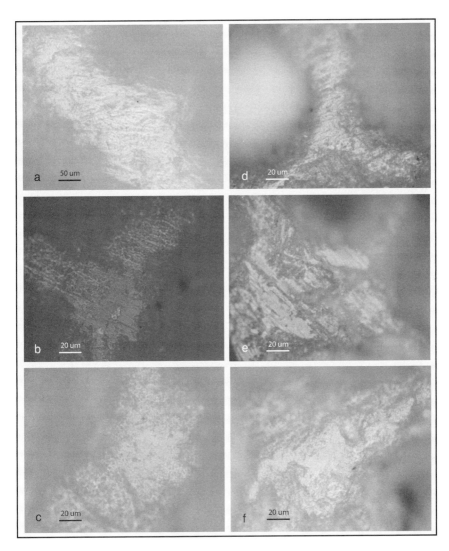

Figure 9.4. Matching experimental and archaeological use-wear traces. a: polishing tropical hardwood for 45 minutes (original magnification 200x); b: sanding *Strombus gigas* shell lip 30 minutes; c: polishing the shoulder blade of turtle for 90 minutes; d: scraper of *Porites* sp. with polish interpreted as having been used on wood; e: scraper of *Porites* sp. with traces from working shell; f: scraper with traces resembling experimental bone working traces (original magnification of Figures 9.4b–f 500x).

a clear directionality, as well as a limited number of striations. Experiments with plant materials resulted in a rather variable corallite ridge shape, ranging from rounded to slightly flattened. The polish was bright to very bright and striations were generally absent. Topographical features in the polish included the presence of small craters.

To conclude, use-wear traces that resulted from experiments carried out on hard materials such as shell, stone, and coral were clearly different from the wear traces that resulted from experiments on softer material types such as wood, plant, bone, and clay. Characteristics specifically related to the hard materials are a flat to very flat or beveled corallite ridge, streaked polish distribution, a rough texture, and the occurrence of a lot of striations. The softer contact materials resulted in more rounded corallite ridges and a smooth, bright polish with a clear directionality. Striations do occur but in lesser quantities.

The Archaeological Tools from Anse à la Gourde: Matching Traces

The *Porites* sp. angle-abraded artifacts were classified into nine different groups. This classification was based on the basis of general shape, the shape of the edge (straight, concave, or convex), and the occurrence of single- or double-angle abrasion on the artifact.

In order to test the hypothesis that the angle-abraded tools made of *Porites* sp. were indeed used for a variety of activities, 52 artifacts were selected. Each typological group was treated separately to examine its functional homogeneity. Traces on the archaeological tools were compared to the experimental ones in order to infer the probable contact material and the movement applied (e.g., longitudinal or transverse).

Unfortunately, 18 archaeological implements displayed postdepositional surface modifications that made a functional analysis impossible. It is not entirely clear how these secondary modifications developed. More research into the taphonomic conditions under which use-wear traces on coral tools are affected is first needed. On three other tools the traces could not be matched to experimental equivalents and were classified as unknown. It may actually involve multiple usages, causing the superimposition of different types of traces making identification impossible. The traces on one tool were insufficiently developed to allow a functional inference. In all other cases it turned out to be possible to match the traces on the archaeological tools with those seen on the experimental reference samples (Figure 9.4d–f). Eleven tools displayed polish attributes closely resembling those on experimental woodworking implements (Figure 9.4d). Seven artifacts were most likely involved in scraping clay. Five tools were interpreted as shell-working implements (Figure 9.4e), six as bone-working implements (Figure 9.4f), and three as plant-working implements.

It turned out that there is little relation between tool form and function. Characteristics such as similarity between tool and edge shape, amount of abraded angles, and degrees of abraded angles of tools are not specifically related to one contact material or motion. This may relate to our own classification system, based on etic criteria that probably did not correspond to the emic approach of tools of the inhabitants.

Conclusion

The experimental use of coral tools and subsequent analysis of the resulting wear traces indicates that use-wear analysis of coral artifacts can be carried out successfully. Coral has a totally different contact surface—corallite ridges in a honeycomb structure on which the traces develop—as compared to materials such as flint that display a flat smooth surface. Nonetheless, wear traces that resulted from use of coral on a specific type of material were clearly visible and comparable to traces that occur on materials such as flint. The High Power approach proved to be more efficient compared to the Low Power approach during the analysis of the experimental tools and artifacts. Low Power analysis did prove to be very useful as a means to get acquainted with the surface of the coral (e.g., characteristics and distribution of the corallite ridges), possible wear traces, and residues. However, it was through High Power analysis of the experimental tools that the potential of microwear analysis on coral became clear. Not only was it possible to obtain insight into the general hardness of the contact materials (e.g., soft, medium, or hard), but it was also frequently possible to reach a more detailed inference regarding the contact material (e.g., clay, bone, and shell). The experimental program was not only important to build up a reference collection, it also gave insight in the manner in which the coral handled and the types of probable tasks for which it was suitable. Furthermore, the experiments also provided an insight about the tool life (i.e., length of use vs. degree).

Taphonomic processes such as dissolution or abrasion of the corallite ridges complicate the analysis and interpretations of the artifacts. Even so, postdepositional surface modifications can frequently be distinguished from wear traces. On the one hand, postdepositional traces usually are located across the entire tool, whereas the use-wear traces are limited to the functional edge. On the other hand, traces seen outside the abraded angle should not immediately be categorized as postdepositional traces. They could also be handling traces (recognized on some of the experiments).

The present research constitutes a methodological innovation in that it demonstrated the possibilities of use-wear analysis on coral tools. It also provides a more in-depth view of the manner in which the Amerindians interacted with their surroundings in the sense of resource exploitation. Last, the use-wear study gave coral a place in the technological system of the native peoples of the Caribbean islands. It turns out that they used coral tools for various activities. They carefully selected their tools for specific purposes and obviously had a thorough knowledge of the physical properties of the various raw materials from which their tools were made. Coral tools therefore played a vital role in carrying out various activities and formed an integral part of the technological system. Their rough surfaces, ideal for rasping, scraping, or polishing, make them very suitable for such tasks as the grinding or sharpening of shell tools or objects of very hard wood types. It makes clear that the inhabitants of Anse à la Gourde had a flexible technological system in which tools made of different materials were to some extent interchangeable.

10

The Significance of Wear and Residue Studies

An Example from Plum Piece, Saba

Channah J. Nieuwenhuis

Introduction

Many archaeologists agree that statements on the function of stone tools cannot be made without the study of microscopic wear traces. Although the morphology of stone tools is still the first criterion to separate "tools" from "waste," the presence and type of use-wear on the surface of stone artifacts is a better indication of use than morphology (Nieuwenhuis 2002). Complementary to these wear traces, the study of residues can refine insights into specific tool uses and environmental conditions and improves the effectiveness, accuracy, and applicability of wear-trace analysis. This chapter demonstrates this complementary approach, illustrating this by means of an archaeological example.

Hard stone tools like querns, grinding stones, mortars, and pestles have long been interpreted on the basis of their typo-morphology and macroscopically visible wear on one or more surfaces. Hollowed areas and smoothened surfaces indicate which area was most intensively used. Macroremains found in association with these artifacts may give some clues to processed material. In this chapter it will be argued that microscopic analysis can extend the limit of inference. A selection of hard stone implements from an Archaic Age site on Saba, one of the Lesser Antilles, serves as a case study.

Residues

Microscopic remains of worked material, adhering to the stone surface, can survive thousands of years if buried under favorable conditions. These residues are microscopic elements of either processed plants, animal, or (bio-)mineral prod-

ucts, like starch grains, phytoliths, resins, ochre, hairs, feathers, or collagen. For the
present study focus was laid on phytoliths and starch grains.

Phytoliths are silica bodies that form in plants. Soluble silica from the groundwater is absorbed by the roots and carried up into the plant. This silica precipitates in and around the cellular walls and copies the morphology of the cell or cell
groups. When the plant decays, phytoliths can be preserved in the soil over long
periods of time. They are subject to mechanical breakage, erosion, and deterio-
ration in high pH soils, but survive in heavily leached and oxidized tropical soils
(e.g., Piperno 1988). Phytoliths are not species-specific, like pollen, but their morphology and size can inform us on plant families and genera, on plant parts, and
possible domestication. Phytolith analysis can be used as a supplement to pollen
and macrofossil analysis.

Starch grains can inform us on processed roots, tubers, seeds, or starchy plants
like palm, especially because some of these plants do not leave pollen or phytoliths. As a general rule, starch grains from roots and tubers have eccentric hila
(which means that their hilum, which often appears as a dark spot under the microscope, is off-center). Seeds, in contrast, usually produce starch grains with centric hila (Scott Cummings 2006).

Case Study: Plum Piece

Archaic Age occupation of the Antilles is mainly known from coastal sites. Plum
Piece, in the northwestern part of Saba, one of the northern Lesser Antilles, is an
inland site with evidence of Archaic Age occupation in a tropical forest setting,
400 m above sea level (Hofman and Hoogland 2003; Hofman et al. 2006) (Figure 10.1). The site, which has been excavated from 2001 onward, consisted of dense
midden deposits and dates from approximately 3300 B.P. The variety of exploited
food resources seems to be rather restricted, as the deposits mainly consist of terrestrial faunal remains (land crab and bird), while fish and shellfish (marine resources) are nearly absent (Van den Bos 2006). Therefore, it is suggested that single
groups recurrently occupied the site seasonally, alternating with sites in the coastal
area. The inland site may have been used for specific activities, like woodworking for the building of dugout canoes (Hofman and Hoogland 2003; Hofman et
al. 2006).

The tools found on the site include shell adzes, large quantities of flaked-flint
tools, and hard stones for hammering, pounding, battering, and grinding, all made
of volcanic rock. These rocks were carried up the mountain from the seashore.
There are also coral artifacts and fragments of red ochre.

The sizeable number of hard stone tools suggests that plants were processed
at the site, either for consumption or for the extraction of fibers for the manu-

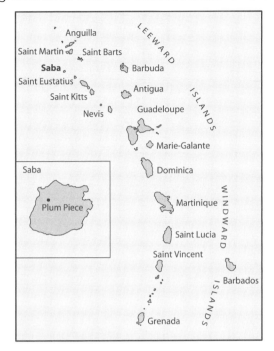

Figure 10.1. Location of the site of Plum Piece on Saba.

facture of baskets, mats, or fish weirs. Grass seeds may have been processed (Hofman and Hoogland 2003; Hofman et al. 2006). Certain plant species may have already been cultivated in "house-gardens" by Archaic Age people (Davis 2000:96; Newsom 1993; Newsom and Pearsall 2003; Newsom and Wing 2004).

In pre-Columbian times the area was probably covered with rainforest. The modern vegetation consists of secondary rainforest with some species reflecting the remnants of the original forest. One of the characteristic trees now growing in the area of the site is the palm *Prestoea montana,* or Mountain Cabbage (Lugo et al. 1998; Rojer 1997). The slopes below Plum Piece are said to be suitable habitats for grasses and fruit trees such as papaya (*Carica papaya*), soursop (*Annona muricata*) and sweetsop (*Annona reticulata*), arrowroot (*Maranta arundinacea*), and tuna cactus (*Opuntia* spp.) (Hofman and Hoogland 2003; Hofman et al. 2006).

Sample Selection and Treatment

Four artifacts were first selected for a pilot study in order to determine their condition and suitability for this type of analysis. Three of these artifacts were excavated; one was from surface recollection. When the pilot study proved successful, seven additional artifacts were chosen for analysis.

The implements are all made of volcanic rock and vary in size from 9 x 11 x 4 cm to 36 x 29 x 23 cm. The sample includes three complete querns, or grinding bases (metates, PP17, PP329, PP18), four grinding stones (PP1, PP3, PP5, PP7), two pounding stones, or *manos* (PP10, PP12), one large unmodified flake (PP14), and one tool labeled as "hammer stone" due to its shape, which resembles a modern hammer (PP30). The querns and grinding stones have at least one smooth, in some cases hollowed, surface. Most artifacts were covered either with sediment or a chalky scale, or both.

All stones have been slightly rinsed before storage. Before choosing further cleaning procedures, all artifacts were first analyzed with a stereoscopic microscope (Wild M3Z) with two obliquely reflected light sources, magnifying between 10x and 160x, and a Nikon Optiphot metallographic microscope (100x and 200x) to detect microscopic wear traces and to localize spots with possible residue.

As this study aimed at recovering *any* residue present on the artifacts, it was tested whether microremains could be recovered and distinguished without the usual chemical treatment. Chemical treatment for the preparation of phytoliths will mostly destroy starch. Besides, it is extremely time consuming. In many cases the analysis of residues can be done with untreated samples. This depends on the structure of the sediment (clayish or loose) and its chemical composition. Therefore, it was decided to make a first attempt running a very simple extraction procedure, which had given positive results in former studies (Nieuwenhuis and Van Gijn 2006).

To remove sediment, the artifacts were first cleaned in distilled water in an ultrasonic tank for at least two hours. This liquid was preserved and sampled. Then the upper and lower sides of each artifact were separately soaked in distilled water for one hour. This water was also sampled.

To reduce the amount of liquid, samples were centrifuged for five minutes at 3,000 rpm and the supernatant was decanted. For a third sample the entire artifact was soaked in distilled water during one hour. Again the liquid was centrifuged at 3,000 rpm during five minutes, then decanted and extracted.

Extractions were mounted on slides with DPX mountant and analyzed with a Nikon Optiphot transmitted light microscope (magnifications of 150x, 300x, and 560x) with a cross-polar illuminator to analyze starch grains. After analyzing the obtained samples it was decided to sample five of the artifacts again after another cleaning in water (in two cases with a 10 percent HCl solution in water). A small area was then brushed with a rotating electronic toothbrush and ultrapure water in order to remove possible residues still present.

A soil sample from the direct vicinity of the midden was analyzed for reference (see below). No other soil samples were available.

Results
Wear

Specific wear traces like striations or polish were detected on seven tools: the two pounding stones, the large flake, one of the complete querns (PP18), two of the grinding stones (PP1 and PP3), and the hammer stone. If interpretable, the polish was either caused by contact with plant (PP18, PP3), wood (the large flake), or hard and medium-hard material (pounding stones). Striations and direction of the polish on the querns and grinding stones were mostly linear, indicating a longitudinal motion (Figure 10.2a). One of the artifacts with pounding traces from use on hard or medium-hard material may have been hafted; it has spots of a reddish resin or mastic and fragments of fibers. On the other pounding stone possible residue of ochre was found next to the wear traces (Figure 10.2b).

Residues

Analysis of residues revealed that starch grains, phytoliths, raphides (needlelike calcium oxalate crystals), hafting material, and possibly ochre were preserved on some of the tools.

The most remarkable phytoliths found on the stones were round and elongated spherical phytoliths, which will be further referred to as spheres. These spheres have rounded nodular projections evenly distributed over the entire surface. Some have more pointed projections. They appear in all sizes, between 1 and 10 μm. These spheres are from palm, possibly Mountain Cabbage, *Prestoea montana*. Experimentally ground fruit from this palm yielded the same type of phytoliths (Figure 10.3a, b). They were found on all implements except one of the pounding stones (PP10) and the large flake with wood polish.

Processing of palm is also evidenced by the presence of starch grains found on two artifacts (PP3 and the hammer stone) and raphides on a large quern (PP18), which match the microremains obtained from processing fresh fruit of *Prestoea montana* (Figure 10.4a, b). The starch grains from palm are very round with an average diameter of 4 μm (at 50x) and have centric hila. As some kind of processing is needed to release starch from plants, the presence of starch grains from palm on two artifacts supports the supposition that palm was indeed processed.

Starch grains found on three other tools seem to be different: not round but elongated with eccentric hila. This second type of starch grains may be from a rhizome like arrowroot (*Maranta arundinacea*) or yam (*Dioscorea* spp.) but could also be from grass seeds (Fullagar et al. in press; Figure 10.5).

The soil sample analyzed for reference contained the same type of spherical phytoliths as the ones found on the artifacts. It also contained a modest number of grass phytoliths. Neither starch grains nor raphides were found in these samples. It is possible that the presence of spheres on most of the artifacts is simply a re-

Figure 10.2. a: plant polish with linear striations; b: polish from contact with hard material and residue, possibly ochre.

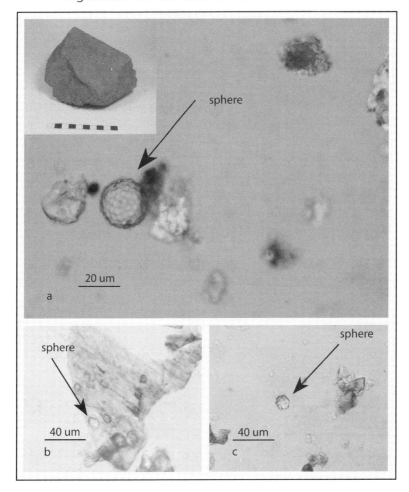

Figure 10.3. a: sphere found on quern fragment; b, c: spheres obtained from crushing fruit from *Prestoea montana*.

flection of the naturally present microremains and does not imply at all that parts of this palm were processed at the site. However, if palm were processed, it is to be expected that palm phytoliths are also present in the soil directly surrounding the site, and even at a farther distance. After all, the palm used was growing in the area, which may have been one of the reasons why the site was chosen for specific activities.

Grass processing was hypothesized as one of the possible activities executed with the hard stones (Hofman and Hoogland 2003). Therefore, it was expected that grass phytoliths would be amply present on the tools. This was not the case.

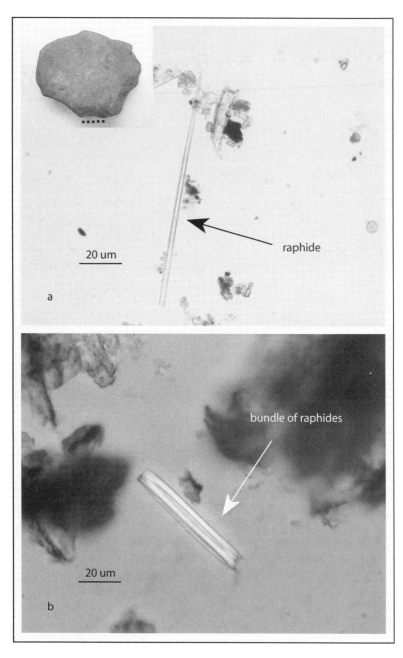

Figure 10.4. a: raphide found on quern; b: bundle of raphides obtained from crushing fruit from *Prestoea montana*.

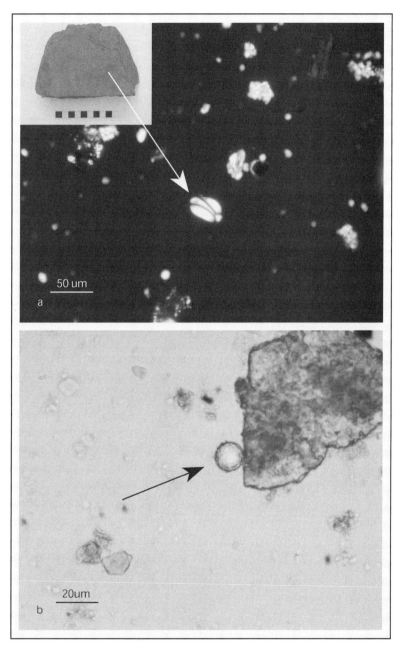

Figure 10.5. a: starch grain with eccentric hilum found on quern fragment, possibly grass or yam; b: worn sphere found on quern.

They were found on seven implements (the hammer stone, PP17, PP18, PPS29, PP1, PP3, and PP5), but compared to the number of spheres the number of grass phytoliths found on the implements is remarkably low. Samples of two grinding stones were counted (PP3 and PP5). These contained spheres and grass phytoliths. One-third of the slide was counted. One contained 35 spheres and one grass phytolith (PP5), the other one contained 120 spheres and 10 grass phytoliths (PP3). Grass phytoliths were found in the soil sample, suggesting that grass was growing in the area, but apparently it was not processed on a large scale with the hard stone tools. It may have been done incidentally, some of the querns and grinding stones may well have been used for a variety of activities.

One pounding stone (PP10) contained possible hafting material, which has not yet been identified. Mastic bully (*Mastichodendron foetidissimum*) did grow in the area. The sticky fruit juices are white; the sapwood is thick and yellow. The residue found is reddish or orange, but this can be colored by elements from the sediment.

The function of the artifact labeled as "hammer stone" is unclear. On one side the hammerhead has a reddish residue, possibly ochre. Fragments of ochre were found at the site. This artifact was one of the two that contained round starch grains, which may be from palm. The tool has primary impact traces on the whole upper side and pecking traces on one of the edges of the hammerhead. The entire surface is polished but the "handle" of the hammer seems more polished, possibly due to handling.

Conclusions

Wear and Residue

In two cases wear-trace analysis would lead to specific inferences: plant traces on an oval quern (PP18) and a grinding stone (PP3) and wood on a flat large flake with a relatively sharp edge. Contact with hard or medium-hard material was detected on two pounding stones, one of which may have been hafted. On two artifacts microwear did indicate use, but this could not be further specified. This observation strengthens the importance of residue analysis.

Phytoliths were found on nine artifacts. These were mostly spheres of various sizes with nodular projections, some pointed. They were all from palm, probably *Prestoea montana*. The experimentally processed palm fruit yielded spheres, raphides, and starch grains. Unfortunately, there were no other parts of this palm available for experiments. Palm leaves are known to contain spheres in abundance (Piperno 1988). Starch can be found in other parts as well, like the trunk or the leaf stems. Raphides can be found in roots, stems, leaves, flowers, fruits, and embryos of some palms (Zona 2004). Various parts of this palm can be used, either for consumption or for other purposes. Fibers for roofing or for manufacturing a variety of products may have been produced from the palm leaves. The wood from this palm is now used for constructing floors. The fruit may have been consumed, as it forms a good source for proteins, oil, and carbohydrates. There are no ethnographic accounts of present-day consumption by humans. Now birds eat it. Palm hearts from the Mountain Cabbage are edible and may have been consumed in the past (Lugo et al. 1998:426).

In a few cases the spheres from the tools seem to have smoothened surfaces. This may be insignificant, they may simply have a different origin, but this was not traceable. However, this might also be due to processing. Experiments and the analysis of larger samples should answer this important question.

Starch was detected on five implements. There seem to be two types of starch. The smaller round starch grains may well be from *Prestoea montana*. The elongated starch grains could be from grass seeds (Fullagar et al. in press), but there are other candidates, like yam.

The presence of a few starch grains that could originate from grass seeds and a very low amount of grass phytoliths on the tools is not enough to confirm the hypothesis that wild grasses were processed at the site. If grasses were processed, larger numbers of either grass starch or of grass phytoliths should have been found on the tools. Grasses were present in the area, according to the soil samples, though not in high numbers. The low percentage of grass phytoliths and high incidence of nongrass phytoliths, like the spheres, reflects a shaded forest vegetation. It is argued that little or no wild grasses were processed with the hard stone tools at this site.

Wear analysis of flaked flint tools revealed that the largest number of tools with wear traces were used to process siliceous plant (Briels 2004; Van Gijn et al. this volume). It is not clear whether these were grasses or, possibly, palm leaves. In view of the results of the present study the latter is suggested. Again, experiments are needed to further confirm this hypothesis.

Methodology

Finally, wear-trace and residue analysis are complementary methods, which should be integrated. Both types of analysis require different approaches, which may seem incompatible. On the one hand, if tools are not clean, wear traces are not detectable. On the other hand, if tools are cleaned, residues may disappear. To complicate this, the clean extraction of each type of residue often needs a different chemical treatment.

Scholars involved in wear-trace and residue studies are well aware of this (e.g., Field and Fullagar 1998). The order of analytical steps to be followed is, to a certain extent, inevitable: residues should be extracted first, after which cleaning for wear-trace analysis can follow. On relatively clean tools, a stereoscopic microscope can detect the location of residue and even of possible wear traces. However, residues may not come off after a first sampling procedure. It may also be uncertain whether the observed residue is sediment deposition or use related. Often a second, third, or even fourth extraction may be needed, as was the case with the Plum Piece samples. If tools are very dirty, this could imply that wear cannot be analyzed until the implements are released for cleaning procedures needed for wear analysis. As soon as this is done, one will probably destroy any residue still present on the artifact.

In the present study, cleaning and analyzing was done step by step. At each step the least invasive and destructive approach was chosen to further analyze and sample the tools. On some of the tools wear traces were analyzed after the second and/or third extraction procedure, or tools were only partially cleaned for wear-trace analysis in order to preserve possible residue (e.g., ochre on a pounding tool). No chemicals were used to prepare the residue samples, although the visibility of the mounted samples would certainly improve with chemical treatment. However, the samples were considered clear enough for inferences. If the structure of the adhering material allows it and if one does not wish to rule out specific residue categories, chemicals should be avoided.

It is considered a great advantage in this type of study to carry out all steps of analysis at one single laboratory, thus being able to carefully control the extraction and cleaning procedures, and at the same time preserving the use-wear traces. By doing so it is possible to take full advantage of the inferential possibilities of both residue and use-wear analysis, two methods to infer the function of prehistoric artifacts that are clearly complementary.

Acknowledgments

I want to thank Eric Mulder from the Laboratory for Artifact Studies for his assistance in preparing the samples and in determining cleaning procedures. I also thank Annelou van Gijn and Annemiek Verbaas for their assistance in detecting and interpreting wear traces.

11

Starch Residues on Lithic Artifacts from Two Contrasting Contexts in Northwestern Puerto Rico

Los Muertos Cave and Vega de Nelo Vargas Farmstead

Jaime R. Pagán Jiménez and José R. Oliver

Introduction

This chapter discusses the preliminary results derived from the analysis of 15 starch residue samples obtained from seven ground stone tools recovered from Los Muertos Cave (SR-1) and Vega de Nelo Vargas (Utu-27) sites, both located in the karst mountain region of northwestern Puerto Rico (Figure 11.1). This study provides new data that contribute to a better understanding of the nature of the agrarian economy of ancient Puerto Rico, one of the main objectives set forth in the Utuado-Caguana Archaeological Project, codirected by Oliver and Rivera Fontán (see Oliver 1998, 2005; Oliver et al. 1999).

The time frame pertinent to this study is bracketed between A.D. 680 and A.D. 1450, covering Periods IIIa–b (early to late Ostiones) and IVa (Capá), if one follows the regional chronology devised by Rouse (1992). Period IIIb (ca. A.D. 900–1200/1300) is a momentous time, as it was when inequality and social complexity seem to have emerged in tandem with "monumental" architecture in the form of sites with multiple plaza and ball court precincts (Curet 2005:22–26, 90–91; Curet and Oliver 1998; Siegel 1999). By Period IVa (ca. A.D. 1250/1300–1500) complex polities, with varying degrees of centralization and hierarchical (and perhaps also heterarchical) organization, dominated the political scenario of ancient Puerto Rico, although not all polities in the island were necessarily subject to a paramount chief, and may have maintained a certain degree of decentralization and political autonomy (see Oliver 2003).

Earle and Johnson (2000:257–258) and Earle (1991:1–15), among others, have argued that the political economy of chiefdoms and states were financed by exercising political control over staple crops (staple finance) and/or over material wealth

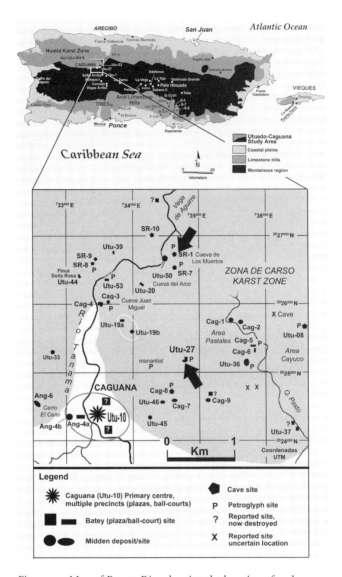

Figure 11.1. Map of Puerto Rico showing the location of archaeological sites; the Utuado-Caguana study area, showing the distribution of various types of archaeological sites. Arrows indicate the location of Cueva de Los Muertos (SR-1) and Vega de Nelo Vargas (Utu-27).

of various kinds (wealth finance). Earle (1997:70–75) remarked that staple crops seem to play a larger role than wealth in financing chiefdoms than in states. For the historic Taíno, Moscoso (1986:414–432) compiled data from the early Spanish colonial documents that suggest that paramount caciques (chiefs) exhibited direct control over vast *conucos,* or plantations, cultivated principally with *yuca,* or manioc (*Manihot esculenta*), and *ajes,* or sweet potatoes (*Ipomoea batatas*), with other crops playing less important roles.

Questions about the emergence of elites (caciques) and the nature of their political economy, however, are difficult to address given that the remains of crops from pre-Columbian archaeological contexts are few and far between despite all the recent advances (De France and Newsom 2005; Newsom and Wing 2004).

The significance of most of the identified plant (and animal) species are still largely discussed at a coarse level of resolution (subseries and series) with the consequence that understanding what is going on at the levels of household and local community and discrete social groups remains vague. It is in this context that the foregoing starch residue analysis is an initial effort toward gaining new insights on the ancient agrarian economies of the Caribbean.

The preliminary data emerging from this study suggest that the phyto-cultural dynamics of northwestern Puerto Rico do not neatly conform to the widely accepted, conventional views on the nature of the pre-Columbian agricultural economies of the Caribbean. The evidence points to different agricultural production scenarios that coexisted in the intra- and interisland contexts.

Site and Tool Contexts

Los Muertos Cave (SR-1)

The karst zone in the Utuado-Caguana region exhibits an abundance of caves, some of which were selected for human utilization. One such cave is Los Muertos Cave (SR-1), located some 2.8 km due north of the Vega de Nelo Vargas site and 1.5 km north of the civic-ceremonial site of Caguana (Figure 11.1). The cave consists of a relatively large and well lit main chamber (A), with its mouth opening to the northeast, and a dark, long gallery into the back of the cave extending some 25 m before it reaches a dead end. The main chamber contains a dozen or so petroglyphs and a single human burial. The long back gallery yielded a human skeleton laid to rest on its surface, while two secondary burial bundles were found in a niche sealed with a limestone slab along this gallery.

This cave has an unusually high frequency of exogenous igneous rocks (metavolcanic); many were subjected to postmanufacture firing. The closest source of igneous rocks is Pasto Creek located to the southeast (Figure 11.1). The metavolcanic materials included a variety of modified tools, nuclei, *débitage,* and unmodified rocks, suggesting that their manufacture was in situ. Given the high number of plant-processing stone implements, the question arises as to what kinds of plants were being processed and why these were processed in what appears to be, at first glance, a ritual-religious burial site. Seemingly, there is something about the location and the use into which the resulting tools would be put that made it necessary to manufacture them in this cave and not back at home or at a workshop nearer the Pasto Creek.

The three tools analyzed for starch came from a 2 x 1 m test excavation adjacent to a human burial pit (see Figure 11.2). Artifact 2 (FS-905) came from Stratum II, characterized by loose dark soil and ashes mixed with abundant land snails and a few animal bones. The few ceramics recovered are all Ostiones style. Artifact 3 (FS-916), came from Stratum IIIa, whereas Artifact 1 (FS-998) came from Stratum IIIb. Stratum III is a dense and compact midden, with abundant ashes, charcoal, land snails, and *buruquena* crab claws (*Epilobocera sinuatifrons*), and registered the highest frequency of ceramics (also Ostiones style) and metavolcanic implements. The three implements are from granodiorite rocks (Utuado Pluton). Stratum IV is similar to Stratum IIIb but for two key differences. First, the still abundant *buruquena* claws are mostly from juvenile or immature specimens; second, pottery is absent.

A preliminary assessment of the lithic assemblage by Reniel Rodríguez Ramos suggests that the reduction protocol and formal end products for metavolcanic rocks from Stratum IV do not show major or obvious differences with that of the upper strata. Nevertheless, at this stage it cannot be determined with certainty whether Stratum IV represents an Archaic or a Ceramic Age component. Two dates were obtained: sample GrN-30060, from Stratum IIIa, dates to cal A.D. 1020–1190 (2σ), and GrN-30059 from Stratum IIIb dates to cal A.D. 680–950 (both at 2σ using OxCal v. 3.10). These dates agree with those from nearby habitation site Utu-44 and Juan Miguel burial cave site (Oliver and Narganes Storde 2005; Rivera Fontán and Oliver 2005).

Vega de Nelo Vargas (Utu-27)

The Vega de Nelo Vargas site is located less than 2 km due northeast of the major civil-ceremonial center of Caguana (Figure 11.1). The site is typical of other dispersed settlements (farmsteads) in the karst area of Utuado-Caguana (Rivera Fontán and Oliver 2005:235; Oliver et al. 1999). Located on a "saddle" between the karst hills (hereafter *mogotes*) it overlooks a small circular valley. The site has a *batey,* or plaza, demarcated with limestone slabs decorated with petroglyphs and a single midden deposit spilling down slope from the edge of the saddle (Oliver and Rivera Fontán 2004). Several test pits and long trenches were conducted on the midden area and the plaza in 2001. The midden was rich in both artifacts and subsistence remains, reaching a maximum depth of 90 cm below surface. The plaza area was scraped with a backhoe (machine scraped) in 2002, over which two long trenches

Figure 11.2. Lithic tools from Los Muertos Cave and Vega de Nelo Vargas: top left: artifact 1, FS-998, granodiorite mortar/edge grinder; top middle: artifact 2, FS-905, fragmented granodiorite mortar implement; top right: artifact 3, FS-916, a spherical granodiorite mano or pounding/grinding stone; middle left (two views): artifact 4, FS-996, dorsal and lateral views of a mortar-mano edge grinding implement made of granodiorite rock; middle right: artifact 5, FS-XXX, limestone mortar with a central concavity; bottom left: artifact 6, FS-946, a spherical granodiorite mano; bottom right (two views): artifact 7, FS-881, a coarse mano with edge battering made of a brittle species of granodiorite, showing the lateral and anverse facets.

(N-S, E-W) were excavated. The plaza area had a significantly lower frequency of cultural materials. Two assays from Stratum II calibrated to A.D. 1300–1430 (GrN-26413) and to A.D. 1290–1400 (GrN-26412; both 2a). Stratum III assays calibrated to A.D. 1290–1400 (GrN-30051) and A.D. 1280–1400 (GrN-30050; both 2σ).

Artifacts 4 (FS-996), 5 (FS-XX), and 6 (FS-946) (see Figure 11.2), came from the machine-scraped exposed surface of the *batey* area, corresponding to Stratum I of the North-South Trench profile (Table 11.1). Artifact 7 (FS-881), came from Test Unit 3, Stratum III (Table 11.1). Artifacts 4 and 5 are made of a compact grano-diorite stone, whereas Artifact 7 is made of a meteorized granodiorite with large hornblende crystals (Oliver and Rivera Fontán 2004:10). Artifact 5 is the only lime-stone implement to be analyzed in this study.

To summarize, Artifacts 1, 2, and 3 at Los Muertos Cave came from a midden deposit associated with Ostiones-style ceramics (ca. A.D. 850 and 1250/1300). These implements are made of imported igneous materials probably brought from Pasto Creek into a cave site that seemingly had a religious function, but which does not exclude other kinds of (secular?) activities.

Artifacts 4 to 7 came from a late Capá period (cal A.D. 1280–1430) habitation site, Vega de Nelo Vargas, where farmstead-level domestic activities combined with the civic-ceremonial activities carried out in the plaza. The site probably was oc-cupied by a single household whose members may have been of some standing (elite?), as several prestige/wealth items were found (Rivera Fontán and Oliver 2005). However, the site is nowhere near Caguana's (Utu-10) "monumentality" and its impressive iconographic display (Oliver 1998, 2005).

Materials and Methodology of Starch Residue Analysis

Table 11.1 describes the possible functional attributes of the seven lithic imple-ments selected for analysis. All the selected lithic implements were bagged in the field and subsequently transported to the project's laboratory in San Juan. None of these lithics were washed at any point in time. At a later date, Pagán Jiménez ex-tracted the sediment samples from each artifact.

The sediment samples were extracted from one or more pinpoint locations for each tool (Table 11.1). The reason for multiple point sampling was to insure that these were recovered from different facets or aspects of the same tool that had evi-dent use-wear patterns and which could have had different plant-processing func-tions. In other instances, samples were extracted from the periphery of the (evi-dent) use-wear areas, thus allowing a comparison of the results obtained from different sections or facets of the same tool, with or without evident use-wear signs. Of the 15 samples analyzed, 11 (= or >0.006 g each) were processed for the separation of starch grains with cesium chloride (CsCl), as discussed in the sec-tion below. The remaining six samples were mounted directly on the slides with a

Table 11.1. Summary of Artifacts Selected for Analysis by Provenance, Type, and Location/Number of Point Samples.

Artifact Number (Cat. #)	Site and Provenance	Artifact type and raw material	Use-wear sections and number samples points in parenthesis
Artifact 1 (FS-998)	Cueva de Los Muertos (SR-1) Strat. IIIb-Lev. 4. 128–165 cm BD	Mortar and possible edge-ground tool: granodiorite	Concavity (1), faceted section (1), lateral facet (1) and use-wear periphery (1)
Artifact 2 (FS-905)	Cueva de Los Muertos (SR-1) Strat. II-Lev. 2	Mortar fragment: granodiorite	Concavity (1) and use-wear periphery (1)
Artifact 3 (FS-916)	Cueva de Los Muertos (SR-1) Strat. IIIa-Lev. 3 125– cmBD	Spherical mano (pestle): granodiorite	Pecked surface (1) and use-wear periphery (1)
Artifact 4 (FS-996)	Vega de Nelo Vargas (Utu-27) Block E (mss)*	Mortar and possible edge ground tool: granodiorite	Concavity one (1), concavity two (1), faceted surface (1) and use-wear periphery (1)
Artifact 5 (FS-XXX)	Vega de Nelo Vargas (Utu-27) Block E (mss)*	Mortar: limestone	Concavity (1)
Artifact 6 (FS-946)	Vega de Nelo Vargas (Utu-27) Block C: N940.72–W852.15 (mss)*	coarse spheroidal mano, granodiorite	Faceted surface(1)
Artifact 7 (FS-881)	Vega de Nelo Vargas (Utu-27) Test Unit N951–W857.5 Stratum 3	Mortar: meteorized grandiorite (large hornblende crystals)	Faceted surface (1)

*(mss) = machine-scraped surface; that is, on top of Stratum I as recorded in the North-South Trench

solution of water and liquid glycerol, since the volume and weight (< 0.006 g) of the sample was insufficient to process with CsCl.

The work surface of the implement was thoroughly cleaned with a new, moist rag. To handle the artifacts, talc-free latex gloves were used at all times. A sterile paper was placed on the working surface and, over the paper, the portion of the artifact to be sampled. Next, sediment residues (dry method) were extracted using a sterilized dental pick (see also Pearsall et al. 2004; Perry 2004). Before each new point sample was taken, the workspace was cleaned again, and materials were replaced. Finally, the extracted sediment was placed on sterile white paper, which was then placed inside a sterile plastic zip-lock bag with the appropriate label.

For 11 of the samples, the following protocol was applied, modified from Atchison and Fullagar (1998), Barton et al. (1998) and Pearsall et al. (2004). Each sample was placed in a sterile plastic centrifuge tube, and then a solution of CsCl with a specific gravity of 1.79 g/cm-3 was added. The objective was to separate the starch grains through flotation and to isolate them from other particles, as the starches are known to have an average specific gravity of 1.5 g/cm-3 (Banks and Greenwood 1975). A centrifuge running at 2,500 rpm and lasting for 12 minutes during the first phase effected the separation. The supernatant, where the starch grains would be contained, was decanted and poured into a new sterile centrifuge plastic tube. The next step was to add distilled water to the sample and agitate the mix for ten seconds. This process reduced the specific gravity of the mixture through the dilution of salt crystals with the objective of eliminating, with repeated washes, their presence. This last step was repeated two more times, but adding less water in each successive step, and running each sample through the centrifuge at 3,200 rpm for 15 minutes. A droplet taken from remaining residue was then placed on a sterile slide. Half a drop of liquid glycerol was added and stirred with a stick or needle in order to increase the viscosity of the medium and enhance the birefringence of the starch grains.

The Taxonomic Ascription of the Recovered Starch Grains

The study of starch grains in archaeology provides a useful means to address questions about plant utilization. It is not meant to be a substitute for other macro- and microbotanical (phytolith, pollen) analytical techniques but rather to complement them. As other studies have shown, starch residues can preserve for a long time in the imperfect, irregular (i.e., pores, fissures, cracks) surfaces of lithic tools related to the processing of plant organs (e.g., Haslam 2004; Loy et al. 1992; Pagán Jiménez 2002a, 2002b, 2005a, 2005b; Pearsall et al. 2004; Piperno and Holst 1998). If starch grains can be extracted from a tool and correlated to the starch of a known plant then a direct link can be established between the implement and the starch-rich plant or plants that it processed.

At present we have assembled a comparative reference collection of starch grains obtained from modern economic plants. It includes 40 specimens that have been formally described, along with 20 others informally described, together representing 30 genera and 51 species that encompass wild, domesticated, and cultivated species from the Antilles, continental tropical America, and some from the Old World (Pagán Jiménez 2004, 2005b [Appendix B]). The detailed bidimensional description of the morphological traits of the modern starch, through comparison, allows us to identify the taxon of the archaeological starch—so long as these grains exhibit the necessary and sufficient diagnostic traits. The latter are previously established from the descriptive analysis of the modern samples in the reference collection. If these conditions are not met by the archaeological starch gains, then the taxonomic identification is deemed less secure. In such cases we use the categories "cf." (in reference to the closest tentative classification) and "unidentified." A reliable or secure identification will not be established if archaeological starch grains exhibit traits that are not documented in our reference collection or in the published literature (Pearsall et al. 2004; Perry 2002a, 2002b, 2004; Piperno and Holst 1998; Piperno et al. 2000; Ugent et al. 1986).

The identification of archaeological starch grains was effected through an IROSCOPE PT-3LIT (with polarizer) employing a 10x eyepiece and a 40x objective. The principal diagnostic (but not exclusive) element to discern starch gains from other residues is the presence of the extinction or Maltese cross observable under polarized light. The slides with the archaeological samples were comprehensively examined and their X, Y coordinate positions noted to facilitate location and perspective in later inspections. After the analysis, the slides were sealed with varnish and stored in standard cardboard slide holders.

Results

The results of the identification of the plants and organs through starch signatures obtained from the archaeological tools (Tables 11.2–3) show the existence of a dynamic "phyto-cultural" scenario in the Utuado-Caguana region. This is the first time that several of these plants have been identified for late pre-Columbian contexts in Puerto Rico.

Los Muertos Cave (SR-1) is a nonresidential site, whose most overt functions relate to religious activities having to do with burial and postburial rituals and/or ceremonies related to the numinous petroglyphs (Oliver 2005; Oliver and Narganes Storde 2005). The preliminary archaeobotanical data (Table 11.2, Figure 11.3) indicate that the three sampled tools were utilized to process *Zamia; guáyiga,* or *marunguey (Zamia amblyphyllidia)*; maize, or *maíz (Zea mays)*; sweet potatoes, or *batata; boniato (Ipomoea batatas)*; yams, or *ñame (Dioscorea* sp., possibly domesticated); *lerén (Calathea allouia)*; *yautía (Xanthosoma* sp., possibly two spe-

Table 11.2. Total Distribution of the Identified Taxa from Lithic Implements at Cueva de Los Muertos (SR-1).

Artifact/ Taxa	Artifact 1 Concavity	Artifact 1 Faceted section	Artifact 1 Lateral facet	Artifact 2 Concavity	Artifact 3 pecked surface	Peripheral sediment Artifact 1	Peripheral sediment Artifact 2	Peripheral sediment Artifact 3	Total grains	Ubiquity [1] (%)
Zamia amblyphyllidia	19	1				4	1	1	26	62.5%
cf. *Zamia* sp.		1					1		2	25%
Zamia sp.	1					2			3	25%
Calathea allouia	4			1	2				7	37.5%
cf. *Calathea allouia*		1			1				2	25%
Zea mays	1			2	2	2	5	1	12	62.5%
cf. *Zea mays*	1		1	1		2	1		6	62.5%
cf. *Xanthosoma undipes*	1	8			2	ca. 480 cluster in cellulosic tissue			ca. 491	50%
Xanthosoma sagittifolium	1				2				3	25%
Ipomoea batatas						2		2	4	25%
cf. *Ipomoea batatas*			1			1			2	25%
cf. *Ipomoea* sp.						1			1	12.5%
Manihot esculenta				1	3				4	25%
cf. *Manihot esculenta*		4						1	5	25%
Dioscorea sp. (poss. domestic)			1						1	12.5%
cf. *Acrocomia media*		1			1				2	25%
cf. *Bixa orellana*					1				1	12.5%

										Ubiquity[1]
Fabaceae					2	6	1	1	10	50%
Phaseolus vulgaris						1			1	12.5%
Maranta arundinacea						1		2	3	25%
Not identified	1	5	0	0	1	1	0	0	8	—
Total grains	28	21	3	5	17	ca. 502	10	8	ca. 594	—
Species richness[2]	4	1	1	3	5	5	2	5	—	—

[1] The ubiquity in Table 11.2 refers to the occurrence of a reliably identified taxa between the analyzed samples (there may more than one simple per analyzed tool); tentative identifications are excluded from consideration.
[2] To determine species richness per sample only the secure identifications are considered; tentative or insecure simples are excluded.

Table 11.3. Total Distribution of the Identified Taxa from Lithic Implements at Vega de Nelo Vargas (Utu-27).

Taxa/Artifact	Artifact 4 Concavity 1	Artifact 4 Concavity 2	Artifact 4 Faceted surface	Artifact 5 Concavity	Artifact 6 Faceted surface	Artifact 7 Faceted surface	Artifact 4 Peripheral sediment	Total grains	Ubiquity[1] (%)
Zea mays			4		1		2	7	42.86%
cf. *Zea mays*					1	1		2	28.57%
Fabaceae			1		1	4		6	42.86%
Zamia amblyphyl.	1		1					2	28.57%
Zamia sp.				11				11	14.29%
cf. *Zamia* sp.						3		3	14.29%
cf. *Xanthosoma undipes*				ca. 331				ca. 331	14.29%
Xanthosoma sagittif.	2		1		1			4	28.57%
cf. *Manihot esculenta*			1					1	14.29%
cf. *Ipomoea batatas*				1				1	14.29%
Dioscorea sp. (wild)			1					1	14.29%
cf. *Canavalia* sp.			Fragments (MN = 4 starches)					1	14.29%
Canna cf. *indica*							1	4	14.29%
Not identified	1	—	0	0	0	0	1	2	—
Total grains	4	0	8	ca. 345	7	8	4	ca. 376	—
Species richness[2]	2	0	4	2	3	1	1	—	—

[1] The ubiquity in Table 11.3 refers to the occurrence of a reliably identified taxa between the analyzed samples (there may more than one simple per analyzed tool); tentative identifications are excluded from consideration.

[2] To determine species richness per sample only the secure identifications are considered; tentative or insecure samples are excluded.

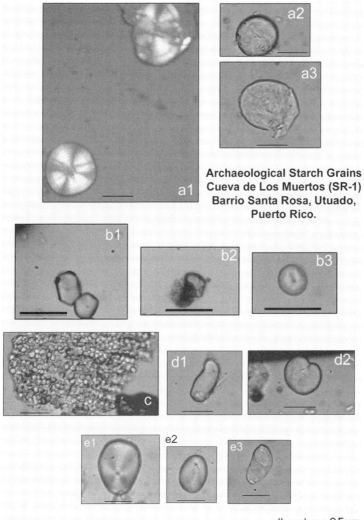

Archaeological Starch Grains
Cueva de Los Muertos (SR-1)
Barrio Santa Rosa, Utuado,
Puerto Rico.

all scales= 25µm

Figure 11.3. Archaeological starch grains from Cueva de Los Muertos site. a: *Zamia amblyphyllidia*. Starch grains show symmetric lamellae and extinction crosses. Image a1 is taken in a bright field and cross-polarized light. Images a2 and a3 were taken with a white nonpolarized light. b: *Zea mays*. Starch grains of maize with a central hilum visible in images b1 and b2, and possibly evincing two different maize sources (soft and hard endosperms). All images were taken with a white nonpolarized light. c: cf. *Xanthosoma undipes*. Starch grains show as a cluster in a cellulosic tissue. Image was taken with a white nonpolarized light. d: *Disocorea* sp. Starch grains from a possibly domesticated yam shown in image d1, and *Phaseolus vulgaris* in image d2. Both show concentric lamellae. Both images were taken with a white nonpolarized light. e: *Maranta arundinacea*. Starch gains show concentric lamellae and eccentric open hilum (images e1, e2). All images were taken with a white nonpolarized light.

cies); corozo palm seeds (*Acrocomia media*); beans, or *frijol* (*Phaseolus vulgaris*); arrowroot, or *yuquilla* (*Maranta arundinacea*); manioc; and the seeds of *annatto*, or *achiote, bija* (*Bixa orellana*) for red pigment. This suite of economic plants (and their derivates) would seem to have two possible areas of significance: one as a nutritional/dietary resource and the other as a ritual/religious resource.

The temptation is to assume that at Los Muertos Cave the principal objective of visitors was to conduct activities of a religious nature. Certainly, at several points in time religious rituals had to be the main focus of activity, when the individuals were laid to rest (funerary rites). It is reasonable to hypothesize that plants were processed for consumption (foods) or other uses (*achiote* colorant) during funerary feasts and/or in subsequent commemorative celebrations. But it can be argued that these plants were processed also for other more mundane or "secular" activities instead of, or in addition to, religious ceremonies. One should consider that the starches in these implements do not provide any clues as to how they might have been prepared into different kinds of meals or point to the ways in which they might have been displayed, served, distributed, or employed. Whether religious or not, and unlike other burial cave sites (Oliver and Narganes Storde 2005), Los Muertos has an unusually high number of metavolcanic tools manufactured and used in situ to process edible plants. Although only three tools have been analyzed for starch content, there are many more implements of similar morphologies and use-wear characteristics that point to plant processing (and tool manufacture) as a significant activity, and also point to the cost of transporting (heavy) stones uphill from the Pasto Creek. The frequency of metavolcanic implements and detritus from their manufacturing process would be expected from a habitation site such as at the contemporaneous site of Finca de Doña Rosa (Utu-44).

By contrast, the Vega de Nelo Vargas site (Table 11.3, Fig. 11.4), firmly dated between cal A.D. 1280–1430, is primarily a farmstead settlement that also had a domestic *batey*, where periodic religious rituals, civic ceremonies, and feasts (including trade and exchange) took place. Both religious and secular activities, in the context of a domestic (residential) environment, have to be considered in regarding the use of the suite of economic plants identified (Table 11.3, Figure 11.4): *Zamia*, maize, beans, *yautía*, sweet potatoes, wild yams, and the *gruya* or *achira* (*Canna indica*, a root crop), the latter showing up only in Artifact 7 recovered from the midden. The plants processed by the four implements reflect everyday food preparation activities as much as the confection of particular meals for religious ceremonies or civic (public) events conducted in the farmstead.

The tool and starch sample, of course, is too small to execute a balanced comparison between the two sites (Tables 11.2 and 11.3) or to make any solid inferences between the sites. Nevertheless, on the basis of the analysis of the ubiquity of the taxa of the studied tools, it is possible to sketch two distinct scenarios. Since the local landscape, implements, and native population can be invested with meanings

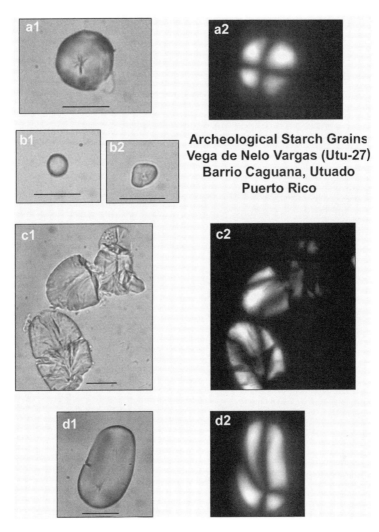

Archeological Starch Grains
Vega de Nelo Vargas (Utu-27)
Barrio Caguana, Utuado
Puerto Rico

Figure 11.4. Archaeological starch grains from Vega de Nelo Vargas site. a: *Zamia amblyphyllidia*. Starch grains show asymmetric lamellae and diagnostic central stellate fissure. Image a1 is taken with a white nonpolarized light. Image a2 is the same as a1, but taken in a dark field and cross-polarized light. b: *Zea mays*. Starch grain from possibly two different maize sources (soft and hard endosperm); the grain in image b2 has a central open hilum. Both images (b1, b2) were taken with a bright nonpolarized light. c: *Canna* cf. *indica*. Damaged and fragmented gruya starch grains. Both images are the same, but c1 is taken with a white nonpolarized light while c2 is taken in a dark field with cross-polarized light. d: *Dioscorea* sp. (wild). The starch grain shows eccentric linear fissures. Both images are the same, but d1 is taken with a white nonpolarized light while d2 is rotated and taken in a dark field with cross-polarized light (cf. Pagán Jiménez et al. 2005:Figure 3c).

through social interactions to which they were integrated (Gosden and Marshall 1999), it is viable to think that the identified plants, and the resulting end products, would have different meanings as a result of the varying social environments in which they were utilized, as would appear to be the case of the two sites here considered. The lithic implements do not present use histories that would indicate a particular, specialized plant-specific processing function. Rather, the artifacts' wear patterns and starch residues displayed multiple functions: they were used to macerate tubers, roots, corns, and tuberous trunks and, as well, used to grind mature green seeds. The identified plants can provide opportunities to discuss the production processes they represent, to offer insights about the subsistence system that furnished the raw plant products at each site, and to inform about the intra- and interregional and diachronic plant-human interactions.

Discussion

For reasons of space we will concentrate the discussion on the relative importance of some of the identified plants, which contrast with the accepted general perception that dominates the current understanding of subsistence strategies deployed by the natives of the Greater Antilles.

Even though several early Spanish chroniclers (e.g., Las Casas 1909) commented on the existence of several distinct agricultural systems, and on their floral components, there is no certainty about how these systems operated in different areas, much less in prehispanic time periods. Despite its limitations, this study suggests a tantalizingly different scenario than that contemplated by many Caribbean scholars. For example, the high ubiquity of *Zamia* starch in both sites alludes to a much more prominent economic role for this plant in nurturing societies, including those with more complex forms of sociopolitical organization (i.e., *cacicazgos;* Curet 2003).

The range of tuberous and seed plants obtained from the tools analyzed here are indicative of a broad spectrum of potentially high-yield food plants, countering the Spanish colonial insistence that the Taíno staples were manioc and *ajes* (varieties of sweet potato). The varied floral assemblage deduced from lithic implements points to the underlying complexity of both the productive and nutritional systems in operation in Puerto Rico.

On the basis of the identified plants, we suggest a continuity in some of the culinary practices that extends from the Archaic period until the end of the fifteenth century (Newsom and Wing 2004; Pagán Jiménez et al. 2005). The presence of starch grains of *zamia*, maize, beans, sweet potato, yam, *gruya* (*achira*), *yautía*, manioc, and *corozo* (a palm seed) in the Ostiones and Capá (A.D. 700–1450) contexts are most revealing. Other plants, like arrowroot and *lerén* (a root crop), have been identified by Pagán Jiménez (2005b) for the Huecoid tradition (ca. 200 B.C.

onward) of Puerto Rico and Vieques (see Figure 11.1), which refutes Sturtevant's (1969) argument that the introduction of arrowroot (*Maranta arundinacea*) occurred during the European contact period (Rodríguez Suárez and Pagán Jiménez this volume).

Using other techniques besides starch residue (De France and Newsom 2005; Newsom and Wing 2004), several other plants, such as *annatto*, or *achiote*, have been documented for sites of exclusively "Taíno" (A.D. 1250–1500) affiliation. The use of maize, which until very recently was deemed of little agro-economic or nutritional consequence, seems now to have played a more prominent dietary role. Newsom and Deagan (1994) and Deagan (2004) have suggested the social and ritual importance of maize as an elite-controlled plant at the protohistoric Taíno site of En Bas Saline, Haiti. But maize, while controlled by elites is, nonetheless, still regarded as a minor component in the overall diet at En Bas Saline.

Starch grain evidence indicative of maize cultivation now appears to have had an early presence and ubiquity in Puerto Rico, as attested at the Archaic sites of Maruca on Puerto Rico and Puerto Ferro on Vieques Island. While its presence alone is insufficient to propose maize as a staple diet, the consistency with which its starch grains has been detected in stone implements in Puerto Rico from the Archaic onward, and in clay griddles from Cuba (Macambo II and Laguna de Limones), calls for caution (Pagán Jiménez 2005b; Rodríguez Suárez and Pagán Jiménez this volume). The presence of maize starch in a burial cave (SR-1), in a dispersed farmstead (Utu-27), in the villages of Macambo II and Laguna de Limones, and the large nucleated En Bas Saline village of chief (presumably) Guacanagarí, also suggest a wider range of social contexts in which maize was processed and consumed.

Manioc, still regarded to be *the* staple "supercrop" that underpinned the development of complex societies (*cacicazgos*) in the Caribbean, seems to have a lower than expected visibility in this study. That does not mean that manioc was insignificant or marginal, particularly since the lithic implements that were most likely involved in processing, such as the triangular flakes inserted on wood boards (i.e., *güayos*), are absent from the tool sample analyzed.

From the "optimal foraging" theoretical perspective among other things invoked to evaluate the changing conditions of sociocultural development as different food resources enter a diet (Keegan 1986; Oliver 2001; Piperno and Pearsall 1998), the starch evidence from the Utuado-Caguana sites and others in Puerto Rico (Pagán Jiménez 2005b) raises the question of why some of the indigenous groups in the Caribbean did not develop "sophisticated" social structures much earlier, given that a good proportion of the economic plants were available well before the process of emerging complex societies began around A.D. 900.

Given the available information, it seems plausible to think that the changes that resulted in the social and organizational complexity of the Taíno populations would have more to do with the "optimization" of the "operative chain" of the systems of production and redistribution (with their implications in the different sociocultural spheres), than with the specific plants that are considered high yield, such as manioc or maize. In this regard, and considering the aggregate value that *Zamia* spp. had—as a carbohydrate and also a protein source (Las Casas 1909)—it is notable the high esteem that the meals prepared from this tuberous had. Las Casas (1909) described that since *Zamia* contains lethal toxins (analogous to bitter manioc) insect larvae were added and encouraged by the natives to nest and develop in the grated pulp mass (dough) and thus fulfill their role in eradicating these toxins (Veloz Maggiolo 1980:89, 1992, 1996:101–114). The presence of larvae in the rich carbohydrate dough may have positively favored the intensification of this endogenous plant over that of other plants with high protein value, like maize, legumes. Although an educated guess, because the effects and technological means of neutralizing the toxicity of the endogenous *Zamia* must have been well understood by Archaic times (as evidenced at Puerto Ferro, Vieques, and El Porvenir sites) this knowledge may well also have readily predisposed Archaic societies to adopt and incorporate the exogenous and likewise toxic manioc plant.

The Reliability and Confidence of Starch Grain Analysis

The presence of archaeological starch grains in the lithic implements studied has led to skepticism on the level of confidence placed on this method; namely, that: (a) the starch morphology cannot be a secure source to ascribe a taxon (taxonomic viability); (b) the recovered starch grains are not representative of all the plants processed by the tools (preservation); and (c) the starch present in the tools may be incidental or intrusive and adhered to the tool during or after they processed plant (pedology, soil contamination). For quite some time, experts in microbotany have determined that the starch coming from different sources exhibits sufficient morphological and bidimensional traits that allow their taxonomic differentiation (e.g., Banks and Greenwood 1975; Bello and Paredes 1999; Buléon et al. 1998; Cortella and Pochettino 1994; Reichert 1913). We have assembled a comparative reference botanical that is sufficiently detailed (using 12 metric and morphological variables) to allow us to establish the diagnostic traits of the different groups of starches (e.g., Pagán Jiménez 2005b).

Researchers like Haslam (2004) have demonstrated that the molecular variation in starch has a direct relationship to the differential preservation of one over another starch grain. Therefore, we think it is possible that the analyzed starch grains represent a limited range of the full spectrum of processed plants. Nevertheless, the starch grains that have been recovered were found in the tools precisely because while processing plants, starch grains were embedded in the tools.

In contrast to other microbotanical remains, starch does not participate in the natural processes of dispersion, similar to pollen "rain" or the integration of phytoliths into the sediments. In the case of pollen, "rain" is a natural mechanism of plants to insure species diversity during reproduction, while for phytoliths it is the result of the mineral acquisition and remodeling on the part of the plant and its eventual disposal into the soil due to the decomposition of the organism. Starch, however, is produced within the plants from the polymerization of glucose residues during photosynthesis. Hence, these are subcellular bodies (grains) that remain in the interior of the plant. During their natural growth process, the plant uses the starches to fulfill determined processes of development. In this process the starch undergoes, through oxidation, a transformation into carbon dioxide and water. In their natural state plants do not deposit starch in the soil, or become airborne, or disperse through other mechanisms. Starch grains could only reach the soil if they are intentionally liberated from the plant's organs by exogenous mechanisms, such as human or animal interventions, or as a consequence of natural "accidents" (e.g., a plant squashed by rock-fall). Even when such events occurred, Therin's (1998) study demonstrated how insignificant the dispersal of starch is in different types of sediment regimes and under different mechanical (force) conditions. Ultimately, some starch specialists (e.g., Fullagar et al. 1998; Pearsall et al. 2004; Perry 2004) argue that the presence of these residues (outside the tools) is due to various reasons: the contamination of the sediments on the part of the tools themselves and the contamination of the soils as a result of the intentional processing of plant sources over or on a particular surface of a terrain.

Final Remarks

An examination of Tables 11.3 and 11.4 shows the relative importance that *Zamia*, maize, legumes, and *yautía* processing had, along with the presence of a fairly broad range of edible cultivars. The data minimally account for which kinds of plants were indeed gathered or cultivated during two consequent periods of human occupation and processed in two different kinds of sites. That *Zamia*, maize, and beans turn out to be so preponderant at both sites may well be a function of our limited tool sample (size, type). The differences in plants between the two sites cannot be taken as representative of the full range of plant-human interactions and plant processing activities at either. This study is an initial effort in testing whether starch grains were present and identifiable from processing tools. Our initial results provide an avenue for further fruitful research to complement other archaeobotanical methods. Starch residue analysis remains the one method that allows a direct plant-use (via implements) correlation. The next phase would be to assemble a larger and statistically meaningful tool sample that encompasses a fuller range of artifacts and from a wider variety of contexts amenable for interpreting the social behaviors involved in plant preparation.

Table 11.4. Comparative Summary of Total Starch Grains and Ubiquity per Taxa.

Taxa/Site	LOS MUERTOS CAVE ca. A.D. 680–1190		VEGA DE NELO VARGAS cal. A.D. 1280–1430	
	Total number of grains (ubiquity within 8 point samples)	Ubiquity %	Total number of grains (ubiquity within 7 point samples)	Ubiquity %
Zea mays	12	62.5	7	42.86
cf. Zea mays	6	62.5	2	28.57
Phaseolus vulgaris	1	12.5		
Fabaceae	10	50.0	6	42.86
cf. Canavalia sp.			1	14.29
Zamia amblyphyllidia	26	62.5	2	28.57
cf. Zamia sp.	2	25.0	3	14.29
Zamia sp.	3	25.0	11	14.29
cf. Xanthosoma undipes	~491	50.0	~331	14.29
Xanthosoma sagittifolium	3	25.0	4	28.57
Ipomoea batatas	4	25.0		
cf. Ipomoea batatas	2	25.0	1	14.29
cf. Ipomoea sp.	1	12.5		
Manihot esculenta	4	25.0		
cf. Manihot esculenta	5	25.0	1	14.29
Calathea allouia	7	37.5		
cf. Calathea allouia	2	25.0		
Canna cf. indica			4 (MN fragments)	14.29

Dioscorea sp. (pos. domest.)	1	12.5	
Dioscorea sp. (wild)	1		14.29
Maranta arundinacea	3	25.0	
cf. *Acrocomia media*	2	25.0	
Non-edible/industrial			
cf. *Bixa orellana*	1	12.5	
Not identified	8		2
Total grains	~594		≈376
Species richness per site	11		8

Acknowledgments

The authors acknowledge Juan Rivera, Reniel Rodríguez, Miguel Vázquez, and students from the Institute of Archaeology and the University of Puerto Rico for their work on the two sites. For use of their facilities, we are grateful to the Laboratory of Paleoethnobotany-Paleoenvironment and Photomicroscopy at IIA-UNAM, Mexico. The Institute of Puerto Rican Culture is to be commended for their support. This study was funded by the British Academy, División General de Estudios de Posgrado (UNAM) and the Consejo Para la Protección del Patrimonio Arqueológico de Puerto Rico. We dedicate this chapter to the memory of Irving Rouse, who stimulated younger generations to improve, deepen, and go beyond what he began building through more than six decades of dedication and hard work.

12

The *Burén* in Precolonial Cuban Archaeology

New Information Regarding the Use of Plants and Ceramic Griddles during the Late Ceramic Age of Eastern Cuba Gathered through Starch Analysis

Roberto Rodríguez Suárez and Jaime R. Pagán Jiménez

Introduction

Our understanding of the way of life of the precolonial populations of Cuba and their interrelations with the environment has changed due to new approaches that, in our opinion, mark an important advancement in our knowledge of the foods consumed. One of these approaches is the analysis of direct evidence, such as fats, carbohydrates, and proteins from food remains, that was preserved on the artifacts related to the preparation of these foods. In addition, the analysis of starch grains through means of new analytical techniques, which we are just beginning to explore, forms a new source of information (see also Rodríguez Suárez and Pagán Jiménez 2006).

This preliminary work has applied an archaeobotanical study of starch grains in griddle (or *burén*) fragments to two late agro-ceramic communities in the eastern region of Cuba: the sites of Macambo II and Laguna de Limones, both in the province of Guantánamo (Figure 12.1). We intend to illustrate an initial approach of this kind of study utilizing an example of ceramic analysis of artifacts related to the production of foodstuffs; these artifacts appear in great quantities in Cuban agro-ceramic sites and other Antillean islands. The archaeological starches recovered from these artifacts give us the first direct evidence of Cuban use and potential consumption of products generated by plants, which have economic importance in both sites. At the same time, we are providing additional information that refutes the generalized conception that the *burén* was an artifact used solely for the production of cassava bread.

We have yet to find evidence in archaeological literature dealing with this kind of study of archaeological ceramics. However, our interest in exploring the pos-

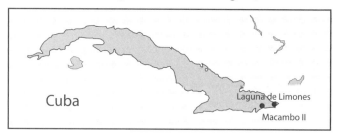

Figure 12.1. Island of Cuba, location of the Macambo II and Laguna de Limones sites.

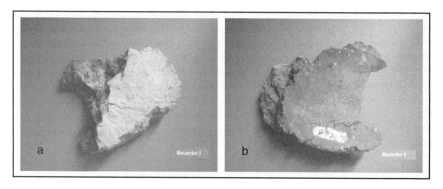

Figure 12.2. *Burén* fragment, Macambo II site. a: work surface with visible whitish crust; b: the opposite side of the same fragment.

sibility of the existence of starch grains in griddles started by noticing a whitish crust preserved on the work surface of the Macambo II fragment (Figure 12.2), followed by the evidence that it had not been exposed to heat. In the case of Laguna de Limones, the analyzed fragments did present traces of heat, and we consider the possibility that there still are starches preserved in some of their less affected areas.

We were a bit skeptical, considering that the *burén* had been a traditional artifact presumably used to cook the cassava bread (*torta de casabe, pan de yuca,* or *mandioca* [*Manihot esculenta* Crantz]). It is commonly assumed that starches are not preserved after heating. However, the obtained results point to another direction as will be shown in the next sections of this chapter. A previous investigation (Rodríguez Suárez et al. 2001; see also Rodríguez Suárez 2004), employing gas chromatography, was able to determine the presence of animal and plant fatty acids, such as Palmaceae and fish. At that time, this led to the conclusion that the *burén* was a multipurpose artifact in which not only the cassava bread was prepared but also foods coming from other sources. It seemed that the multifunctionality of the *burén* was not seen or documented clearly during the contact period (ca. A.D. 1492–1550).

These previous studies planted the seed of doubt regarding the contribution of varied vegetable foods to the diet, especially if the *burén* had been utilized solely for the preparation of cassava. Since it is known that well-defined artifacts existed for grating and mashing manioc and other plants and tubers, it could be clearly conceived that this artifact could contain starch grains from other vegetable sources. Following these new doubts, we designed this study with the intention of starting to elucidate these and other problems of Cuban and Antillean archaeology.

The Macambo II Site

The site is located in San Antonio del Sur, Guantánamo province, in the southeastern region of Cuba (Figure 12.1). It was discovered in 1987 and excavated by personnel from the Centro de Antropología del Ministerio de Ciencia Tecnología y Medio Ambiente. The excavations confirmed that the precolonial inhabitants who settled there can be affiliated with a highly evolved late agro-ceramic cultural level (e.g., ca. A.D. 1200–1600).

The Site of Laguna de Limones

This agro-ceramic site is located in the second terrace that forms the coastal plain of Maisí, some 600 m south of the embankment that allows access to the town of Maisí, also in the Guantánamo province (Figure 12.1). At approximately 1 km north of the site the canyon of the Maya River opens up, which remains dry for the greater part of the year. The location received its name from a small lagoon some 100 m from the archaeological site. Excavations in the lagoon itself took place under the direction of the archaeologist Ernesto Tabío in 1964. A radiocarbon date from this settlement showed a calibrated age of A.D. 1050–1613 [2σ] (A.D. 1150–1490 with 98 percent probability) (Guarch 1978).

Materials and Methods

The samples used in this study (~0.008 g each) come from dust obtained by dry scraping of the work area of the fragments. The instrument used in this procedure was a sterile scalpel blade. The protocol followed for the extraction of the starch grains was that proposed by Pagán Jiménez (2005; see also Pagán Jiménez and Oliver this volume). In order to compare morphologies and metrics of the found starches and propose identifications we made use of previously published work of other authors (Pearsall et al. 2004; Perry 2002a, 2002b, 2004; Piperno and Holst 1998; Piperno et al. 2000; Ugent et al. 1986) and our own work (Pagán Jiménez 2003, 2004, 2005).

Results and Discussion

The results obtained from both sites are summarized in Table 12.1, where the identifications are registered by taxa for each of the analyzed fragments. The use of plants such as maize (*Zea mays*), beans (Fabaceae, *Phaseolus vulgaris*), sweet potato (*Impomoea batatas*), maranta (*Maranta arundinacea*), *yautía* or *malanga* (*Xanthosoma* sp.), and wild plants like *Zamia* (*Zamia pumila*), including the uncertain identifications from this last case, illustrate the development of flexible adaptive strategies by the inhabitants of the studied sites in what refers to the incorporation, production, and use of plants, both endogenous and exogenous. Some of the plants that the identified grains came from were described by Antillean chroniclers. It must be stressed, though, that grains of manioc were not found on the slides we analyzed under the microscope, which implies that the rigid form-function correlation of an artifact (e.g., *burén* preparation of manioc dough) is called into question by our preliminary results. We can add to this Linda Perry's data (2002a and 2004) from the Pozo Azul Norte-1 site, located in the middle valley of the Orinoco in Venezuela, where she found that the stone teeth related to the *guayos* to grate manioc did not show this plant to be represented in the identified taxa by means of starch analysis. Through these means she was able to find in these small artifacts other plants like maize, *ñame* (*Dioscorea* sp.), maranta, *guapo* (*Myrosoma* sp.), and ginger (Zingiberaceae), all of which suggest, from a different area and cultural context, that artifacts traditionally related to the preparation of bread from cassava or manioc were not exclusively utilized in the preparation of those products.

In the case of the *batata*, or sweet potato, identified in the *burén* fragments in both sites (Figure 12.3a.1, a.2) some chroniclers wrote on the preparation of a "*pan de aje*" (bread of *aje*), as it is called by the aborigines and the first chroniclers, that could be eaten raw, roasted, or boiled (Las Casas 1909). The information now collected permits us to generate some inference with regard to the manner of preparation of the tuberous root of this plant; meaning, the use of shell or stone artifacts for the grating of the skin, like was done with manioc, and the posterior grating or pounding of the pulp. For if the *burén* is an artifact of traditional use in the production of cassava bread it can be assumed that a similar manner of preparation would produce this said "*pan de aje*." In accordance with Rodríguez Ramos (2005), the sweet potato could have been converted into a paste to mix with other products to give these a sweeter taste or just as well to turn it into bread, a reasoning that derives from an experimental analysis conducted with edge-ground cobbles.

Table 12.1. Plant Identification by Starch Grains Recovered from Five Burén Fragments, Macambo II and Laguna de Limones, Guantánamo, Cuba

Site and artifacts	*Zamia pumila*	cf. *Zamia pumila*	*Phaseolus vulgaris*	cf. *Phaseolus vulgaris*	Fabaceae	*Zea mays*	cf. *Zea mays*	Poaceae	*Ipomoea batatas*	cf. *Ipomoea batatas*	*Maranta arundinacea*	cf. *Xanthosoma* sp.	No ident.	Total grains
Burén 1 Macambo II	2				2	2						2		8
Burén 1 Lag. Limones		1	1	1				1	2		1		1	8
Burén 2 Lag. Limones		3	297			1	1		2		1			305
Burén 3 Lag. Limones		4	2			4				2			1	13
Burén 4 Lag. Limones			9				4		4				2	19
Total	2	8	309	1	2	7	5	1	8	2	2	2	4	353
Ubiquity (%)	20%	60%	80%	20%	20%	60%	40%	20%	60%	20%	40%	20%	60%	—

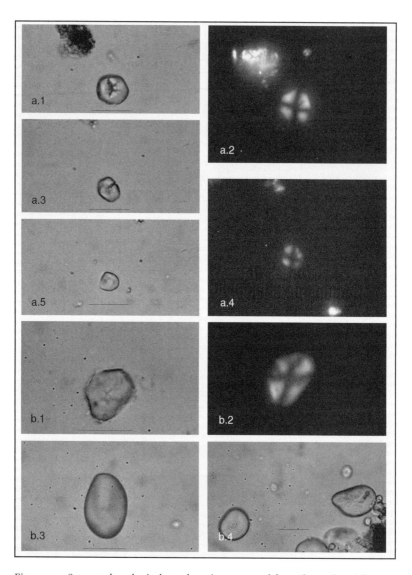

Figure 12.3. Some archaeological starch grains recovered from the analyzed fragments. Micro-photographs taken with a Iroscope PT-3LIT (400x) microscope with polarizing lens. Bar scale = 25μm. a: Macambo II, *burén* 1: a.1, a.2: *Ipomoea batatas;* a.3, a.4: *Zea mays;* a.5: *Xanthosoma* sp. b: Laguna de Limones, *burenes* 1 (b.1, b.2) and 2 (b.3, b.4): b.1, b.2: *Zamia pumila;* b.3: *Maranta arundinacea;* b.4: *Phaseolus vulgaris.*

It is worth noting that in a study by Pagán Jiménez and Oliver on Taíno sites in Puerto Rico (this volume), starches of sweet potato were identified on various lithic artifacts for grinding/pounding, for example, in the lateral protrusion of one of them and in the central concavity of the other. These data give ground to the previous affirmations regarding the pounding of this plant's tuber to release its starches. However, it does disregard that the sites here studied have used other techniques like scraping, seeing as how we have not yet conducted studies on lithic artifacts related to this process.

The presence of maize starch grains on some of the *burén* fragments (Figure 12.3a.3, a.4) contrasts with what chroniclers and some archaeologists (e.g., Newsom and Deagan 1994; Rouse 1992) have said about the consumption of fresh, boiled, roasted, or creamed maize. In effect, these cases do not require any shell or stone artifacts for their preparation or previously mentioned treatment. Yet the presence of maize on some of the analyzed *burén* fragments reinforces the idea that there was some other type of treatment of the grains for which artifacts for grinding, pounding, or grating were used. This would account for a possible culinary practice related to maize not clearly documented for the Greater Antilles by the chroniclers.[1] Keeping this point of view in mind, there have been other documentations of grains of maize starch in the same Puerto Rican Taíno archaeological sites, found on six of the seven analyzed grinding and pounding artifacts. This point confirms, even if from a different late agro-ceramic context, previous processing of maize by means of grinding and pounding with the goal of freeing their starches in order to generate some type of dough. In Venezuela, Perry (2002a, 2004) also found starch grains of maize on the microflakes related with the *guayos* associated with the grating of tubers (e.g., manioc), an aspect that points to possible grating of the maize husk while it was, perhaps, still tender.

In the light of what we have proposed and based on the above results, we think that in future investigations the following must be considered: that the processing of maize in whatever state (e.g., mostly tender, softened, or in some kind of "flour" variety [of soft endosperm]) could have been carried out with artifacts like edge-ground cobbles, *guayos*, grinding stones, mortars, and stone pestles. The fact that traces of dry seed pounding, like those of dry maize, are absent could well indicate that a variety of soft endosperm seeds or still tender and/or soft seeds was pounded after prolonged water immersion. Rodríguez Ramos (2005b) has conducted an experiment to prove that a paste made from hard maize, but previously immersed in water and pounded, can be made in an efficient manner with edge-ground cobbles over a flat stone-grinding base, the edge-ground cobbles being a relatively common artifact in aceramic and agro-ceramic Antillean sites. This information, together with what we have shown, offers new possibilities on the production and consumption of other products (nutritional and/or ritual powders?) derived from maize not considered by the investigators of the region.

In the case of tentative identifications of *yautía,* or malanga, in the Macambo II fragment (Figure 12.3), we would propose the same food treatment we explained before, since, as has been pointed out (Pagán Jiménez 2005b), starches can be released from plants and their respective organs through deliberate action like pounding, grating, or grinding in the preparation process. As the starches of *yautía* and other documented plants were found on the surface of the *burenes,* it is very probable that the tubers were previously converted into dough for the preparation of some kind of bread or paste. If it would have been preferred to consume boiled tubers and seeds, then the pounding, grinding, or grating of the tubers would not have been required. If the plant tubers would have been pounded later and worked over the *burén* (after boiling them) their starches would not display the characteristic extinction cross that was observed on the samples. This particularity, and the shape of the starches, is lost when they are submitted to temperatures up to 40 to 60°C. Considering the making of bread, it is reasonable to think that the flour would have been mixed with some substances that could have acted like a gluten and given flavor, while the paste could have been pounded and mixed for food preparation, but perhaps they were covered with leaves or some other type of covering to be cooked by means of boiled water or over an open flame.

De Las Casas (1909) tells us that bread rolls were produced after pounding and fermenting dough made from the tuberous trunk of the *zamia.* The presence of this plant in the analyzed *burenes* of Laguna de Limones (Figure 12.3b4) is not surprising, given that diverse species of that plant were clearly being used on other islands of the Antilles much earlier (Pagán Jiménez 2005b; Pagán Jiménez et al. 2005; Veloz Maggiolo 1992). The interesting thing is that this plant's starches were now documented on some *burenes.* For the first time, this provides direct evidence for the possible preparation of dough that coincides with some descriptions referred to in the literature (see Veloz Maggiolo 1992). The *Zamia pumila,* as a wild plant, is concentrated right in the southern zone of the Guantánamo region in evergreen forest and xeromorphic subspinous brush over serpentine (González 2003); even more to the northeast, in the province of Holguín, it is found in two other locations. *Z. amblyphyllidia* is also very abundant in the eastern extreme of Cuba, which would mean that generally all of the precolonial population in this area must have had a well-established tradition of using these plants. Even today, this plant's use is prolific in eastern Cuba.

The presence of *maranta* starches in Laguna de Limones (Figure 12.3b.4) and other precolonial Antillean sites (see Pagán Jiménez 2005b; Pagán Jiménez and Oliver this volume) shows that it is a plant that was underestimated by some investigators of the region (e.g., Sturtevant 1969) because it was considered a late introduction from South America during the colonial period. Sturtevant (1969), recognizing the nutritional and medical properties that the Antillean indigenous peoples attributed to the flour extracted from the rhizomes of this plant, deduced, mainly for linguistic reasons, that the documented traditions surrounding this Antillean plant were a recent acquisition (during the early colonial period), encouraged by the same process of European colonization in the region.

With regard to legumes, the presence of bean starches in some of the *burén* fragments (Figure 12.3b.4) would suggest that these types of seeds could have been previously pounded or ground in a similar manner as that described for other plants, that is to say, made into some type of flour or dough. Just as in the Puerto Rican Taíno sites mentioned before, Fabaceae and bean starches have been documented in six of the seven analyzed lithic artifacts, which again supports the idea of pounding and/or grinding the beans before making the dough that would later be worked and cooked on the *burén* fragments studied here. We believe that grinding and/or pounding were the only options available to free the flour from the beans because these seeds are individual, which would make it almost impossible to grate or rub them over a *guayo*. In nutritional terms, the possible joint usage of various foods cannot be discarded since it is known that the nutritional value of maize increases, for example, when consumed with beans in a synergetic process that permits one to supplement the deficiencies of the other.

As one can see, this analysis confirms previous conclusions obtained by one of the authors (Rodríguez Suárez et al. 2001) in chromatographic studies, in which the *burén* is shown to be a multipurpose artifact. That is, this large ceramic plate could have been used as a medium to create an array of nutritional recipes.

As we have pointed out before, in the specific case of the analyzed Macambo II *burén* fragment, it was established that it has not been affected by heat exposure for cooking purposing. Besides it was made with an impure clay with very thick particles of additives. Thus, its production was crude and fragile. These conditions suggest that it was probably used by the aborigines of the site more as a support for the preparation of the nutritional dough than for its cooking. In the same way, the fact that we found starch grains from different plants in the same fragment suggests that they were either mixed to prepare some kind of special dough, or this support was used in multiple occasions to process one of these plants. In the case of Laguna de Limones, the study of various *burén* fragments offered better possibilities to analyze the variety of botanical remains. However, those analyzed fragments did show evidence of being subjected to heat for food production. Therefore, it seems worthy to consider the factors that in our opinion influenced the preservation of the recovered and analyzed vegetable residues at both sites.

On the Preservation of the Grains of Starch on the Studied *Burén* Fragments

In one of the cases that concerned us, which, as we have noted is the one in which the *burén* fragment has not been heated (from Macambo II), it would not be difficult to explain the starch grain preservation in light of the fact that the most evident degrading factor was not present. At the same time, the fact that the analyzed sample comes from the whitish crust stuck to the work surface would suggest an intense use of the artifact. This would guarantee preservation that in addition could have been aided by glutinous substances from other sources, for example fats. It is possible that the group of elements involved in the preparation of the determined foodstuffs (e.g., vegetable oil, animal, resins, minerals) when mixed with the starch in a medium missing intentional exposure to an open flame, could have provoked an isolating, consolidating environment that would permit the starches to "survive" inclement in situ exposure, that is, on the surface on which the previously mentioned product was processed.

The *burén* fragments from Laguna de Limones show evidence of having been exposed to heat with well-preserved morphological grains that show the extinction crosses at different states of birefringence. We believe that there are various factors that explain this phenomenon. We will present a number of factors that will be considered in future studies.

Clay is a bad heat conductor, and even when it heats up this occurs very slowly, in a gradient. The *burenes* are fairly thick, and even if some are relatively thin and of fine temper, the following possibilities must be considered. If the starches are exposed to heat in a dry environment (e.g., in the already prepared dough and in a soft state over a hot surface), the present water component in the molecular structure would respond slowly to the temperature gradient in the *burenes;* that is, the grain would dehydrate little by little and the loss of water could have helped it to preserve its structure and morphology, behaving like a body buried in the desert that mummifies by dehydration. This same principle could even apply if the *burén* had reached high temperatures, because the dough that was placed on the cooking surface would have been cold or at room temperature. It could be expected that the dough warms up slowly. Dehydration of the starches that were not in direct contact with the artifact's cooking surface would have occurred in the same way. Under these circumstances, the starches would not be in a liquid environment that would allow them to gelatinize, and since they are not strictly organic material they could not carbonize by contact with hot surfaces. This would explain why hydrating the starch grains during the process of sample flotation or by analyzing the sample directly would return them to their original state, unless they were broken by some other cause (like we have seen in some cases, particularly in the sample obtained from the Laguna de Limones fragments).

Another possibility is that the Amerindians perhaps did not wash his or her hands during the handling of the starch-rich foods when processing them in the *burén* and could have been carrying grains on himself or herself; we do not consider that they ever washed the *burén* between one preparation and the other. Starches have been found on both sides of one *burén* fragment, and as we know, this piece does not heat up uniformly, in which instance the grains could have been well preserved in the less heated areas.

Another explanation could be that the clay was sufficiently porous to trap some unaffected grains. If we consider what we have previously said concerning temperature gradients, all of the starches may not have been exposed to the same level of heat, and thus some may have been preserved better than others.

One last possibility for the preservation of starches on the *burén* fragments is that the artifacts were used in their last stage (i.e., after their use as a cooking utensil) or before their disuse and abandonment (i.e., after their usefulness as cooking tools) to process fresh material (e.g., pounded material or "flour" derived from starchy plants) on work surfaces (the *burén* like a table work surface).

Unfortunately, at this time we cannot present or suggest a more detailed and precise picture on the subject discussed in this chapter due to the study's preliminary character. We hope to elaborate on each aspect we have dealt with here as well as on other subjects (e.g., social organization and systems of production) that are related to the data we have gathered.

Notes

1. The French chronicler Guillaume Coppier ([year 1645] translated by Cárdenas 1981:151) said that the Carib Indians of the Lesser Antilles have maize "that they forcefully crush on concave rocks or stones, a kind of mortar; once beaten they shape it like sausage and wrap it in *balliris* leaves and then they boil it in hot water and it serves as bread which (thank God) nourishes very well (italics in original text)." Although this information was recovered 145 years after the start of the conquest and the colonization of the Greater Antilles, it should not be ignored that this practice could have been shared by the Taíno of the Lesser Antilles centuries before European intervention in the islands.

III

NEW TRENDS IN PALEOETHNOBOTANICAL AND PALEO-OSTEOLOGICAL RESEARCH

13

Caribbean Paleoethnobotany

Present Status and New Horizons (Understanding the Evolution of an Indigenous Ethnobotany)

Lee A. Newsom

Cibolles des Yndes (Onions of the Indies). "These are the onions, sweet and very large, more so than those of France, being white inside and red outside. The Indians eat them as we eat apples—they have some all the time. They grow them from seed in their gardens and harvest them three times a year."
—*Histoire Naturelle des Indies* (The Drake Manuscript,
middle sixteenth century [Pierpont Morgan Library 1996])

Introduction

Humanistic botanical knowledge and practices in the Caribbean culminated an ancient and richly textured ethnobotanical tradition, a complex-adaptive process that was the multidimensional product of centuries of human-plant interactions and that also involved a fusion of earlier botanical traditions transferred from different source regions. At the time of European contact, Caribbean indigenous people exploited a variety of plant taxa for diverse purposes. Many of these were managed in specifically prepared agricultural grounds or in multifunctional home gardens, venues that separately and together incorporated unique combinations of native and exotic cultigens, quasi-domesticates, and other taxa esteemed for their edible fruit or for other products.[1]

The consumers and gardeners themselves are of central interest, of course, as the people who depended to one degree or another on plant resources for their existence—both managed and wild—and who developed the specialized knowledge and skill to locate, exploit, and maintain particular plant resources for the purposes to which they were put. We can reasonably assume that the native ethnobotany was an integral part of Caribbean Indian cultural and ecological dynamics, and I would argue that we can be fully cognizant of neither one without a thorough understanding of the roles and significance of plant resources in the daily lives, ritual activities, and broader social sphere (e.g., issues of sustainable resources, economy, trade, and related interactions among groups) of the various indigenous peoples of the region.

Archaeobotany is the key to decipher the historical development and specific details of Caribbean Indian ethnobotany. It is the means to discover the deep history of the myriad interactions between particular groups of Caribbean islanders and their local floras, providing an idea of the developmental pathways and processes behind plant-use traditions, as well as some of the elements inherent in human-landscape dynamics at any number of scales. Paleoethnobotany potentially also can reveal key information concerning the significance of plant resources vis-à-vis human social developments in the region, and at minimum can provide some confirmation and ground-truthing of the human-plant dynamic revealed in early historic documents.

The theme of this volume is about explicating new directions in Caribbean archaeology and the study of material culture. I begin my chapter with some musings about Caribbean paleoethnobotany stemming first from ethnohistoric documents and then gleaning from the archaeobotanical record, emphasizing garden or otherwise nonfuelwood economic taxa. I proceed with some ideas for new directions.

A Native Ethnobotany

First Base: Insights from the Ethnohistoric Record

Ethnohistoric sources indicate that Caribbean Indians grew crops in specially prepared fields in which tropical root crops, particularly manioc, were the centerpiece (Table 13.1). We can specify that agricultural tools included at least a planting stick, known in the Taíno language as a *coa,* and additional native terms distinguishing the agricultural plots *conucos,* as well as weedy plants, *carabucos* (presumably volunteer ruderals in and around the anthropogenic settings of village and field), and forest, *ar(c)abuco* (Granberry and Vescelius 2004:Table 12), provide a little more sense of the depth and breadth of indigenous ethnobotanical knowledge. Furthermore, aside from the basic descriptions of agricultural plots and the crops produced, there are indications that separate varieties (e.g., different landraces of maize and peppers) and seasonally scheduled harvests of some taxa occurred, and crop intensification measures were undertaken in at least limited areas of the Greater Antilles (Tables 13.1 and 13.2).

Groves of fruit trees (Table 13.1) were evidently cultivated by Caribbean Indians, and otherwise useful plants for food and other purposes were tended in home gardens in which were grown a variety of species, many undoubtedly deeply ingrained in the fabric of daily life. Tobacco and the tree legume known as *cojóbana,* the source of a narcotic snuff (Table 13.2), functioned as special purpose plants among the Taíno of the Greater Antilles, at least (Nieves-Rivera et al. 1995). Evidently also among such restricted-use plants was the mysterious herb *gioia* that I have proposed may be a species of evening primrose.[2]

Plants such as these—tobacco, *cojóbana, gioia,* and perhaps others deemed to

Table 13.1. Selected Excerpts and Comments Based on Ethnohistoric Documents Regarding the Cultivation Practices and Garden Venues of Caribbean Indians.

General impression of cultivated landscape, first Columbus voyage

- "All of this island and that of Tortuga is **all cultivated**" (December 16, 1492 [Dunn and Kelley 1989:233]) (emphasis added).

Field preparation

- "The Indians **first cut down the cane and trees where they wish to plant** it [maize] . . . **After the trees and cane have been felled and the field grubbed, the land is burned over and the ashes are left as dressing for the soil,** and this is much better than if the land were fertilized" (Oviedo [1526] 1959:13–14) (emphasis added).

- After initial plot preparation to clear woody growth, as indicated in the quote, Indian cultivators built individual growing platforms consisting of small circular earthen mounds, termed *montones* by Spanish observers, of about 1 ft high and 3–4 ft in diameter. A variety of crops were grown in these *conuco* plots, including manioc, sweet potato, other root crops, and maize (Las Casas [1527–1565] 1971:110; Sauer 1966:51–54).

Intensification practices

- In some locations native agriculture involved more labor-intensive construction and management practices, including building terraces on mountain slopes in Puerto Rico (Oliver et al. 1999; Ortíz Aguilú et al. 1991) and extensive networks of irrigation ditches in the low terrain of arid southwestern Hispaniola (Krieger 1930:488).

- For example, "Morales noted that in Xaragua and about the lakes it rained rarely and irrigation was practiced: 'in all these parts there are ancient ditches by which the water is led to irrigate fields with no less art than do the inhabitants of Cartagena and Murica'" (Peter Martyr, Decade III, Book 9, quoted in Sauer 1966:53).

Vegetative propagation of manioc, first Columbus voyage

- "These lands are very fertile; the Indians have them full of *ñames* [or "naimes," i.e., yucca or manioc] which are like carrots and have the taste of chestnuts" (November 4, 1492 [Dunn and Kelley 1989:133]).

- "**They have sown** yams, **which are some little twigs that they plant**, and at the foot of the twigs some roots like carrots grow, which serve as bread; and they scrape and knead and make bread of them. **And later they plant the same twig elsewhere** and it again produces four or five of those roots which are very tasty, having the same flavor as chestnuts" (December 16, 1492 [Dunn and Kelley 1989:233]) (emphasis added).

Agricultural cycle

- The planting cycle had seasonal aspects (Kimber 1988:85, 91), however staple root crops, particularly manioc, could be propagated and harvested practically year round. Individual manioc plants were tended up to three years until harvest, when the plant was removed completely, then new stem cuttings made and reinserted into the *conucos* (Oviedo y Valdes [1535] 1851, 271–72, chapter 7, paragraph 2 [quoted in Kimber 1988:91]).

Continued on the next page

Table 13.1. *Continued*

- Oviedo observed that two types of maize were grown in the Greater Antilles (and see Table 13.2 notes), one that matured in three months and the other after about four: "Este maíz desde a pocos días nace, porque en cuatro meses se coge, y alguno hay más temprano, que viene desde a tres" (Oviedo y Valdes 1996:93). [translation, courtesy R. Rodriguez Ramos: "This corn from to few days it is born, because in four months it catches/matures, and some is earlier, that comes from (ripens) at three."]

Home or "dooryard" gardens

- **"They planted small trees** of *manzanillas* for purgative use **adjacent to their houses,** as something they esteemed greatly" (Las Casas in Sauer 1966:57) (emphasis added).

- "wee traveyled two or three miles further, passing through **many goodly Gardens,** wherein was abundance of Cassada [stet.], Potatoes, Tobacco, Cotton-wool-trees, and Guiava trees . . . (John Nicholl, 1606–1607 voyage of the *Olive Branch* [Hulme and Whitehead 1992:72]) (emphasis added).

- "The Indians of this island had a bad vice among others, which is taking a smoke they called tobacco, to leave the senses. This herb was most precious by the Indians, and it was **planted in their orchards and farm lands**" (Oviedo 1556, quoted in Nieves-Rivera et al. 1995) (emphasis added).

have special magical properties (e.g., the Yanomamö of the Orinoco region in Venezuela use certain plants and botanical concoctions for charms and "casting spells" [Chagnon 1997:69]; similarly, consider that the black and red body paints used by Caribbean Indians [Table 13.2] was deemed to effect more than simple decoration)—were central to indigenous ritual and curative practices. It is reasonable to assume that such plants or even varieties that were restricted in use may have been grown in separate areas of the home gardens or "special beds" (Sauer 1966:57).

Who in Taíno society were the gardeners? Who precisely undertook field preparation and who was responsible for the daily care, cultivation, and harvest of plant resources, both domestic and wild? Unfortunately, Caribbean ethnohistoric sources are silent or vague on the roles of adult men and women or different ages and social classes (see Keegan 1997b) in terms of the agricultural cycle, much less ethnobotanical practices as a whole. Among many Amazonian groups (e.g., see Chagnon 1997:69–71) men prepare the fields, and women are the planters and shepherds of crops and garden produce. A similar division of labor may have existed in the Caribbean such as Keegan suggests (2007:61), but the evidence remains to be discovered. Perhaps also such special purpose plants as mentioned above were exclusively maintained by individuals such as the *behiques*—the specialists under whose purview was the sacred knowledge of their use and practice, whether male or female—representing both an additional venue of plant care and control, and

Table 13.2. Plant Taxa Indicated in Early Historic Records of European Chroniclers.[1]

Plant Taxa	Latin Name	Vernaculars[2]	Details[3]
Root crops:			
manioc	*Manihot escultenta*	*yuca* or cassava (*cazabi*)	(1) (6)
sweet potato	*Ipomoea batatas*	*hage, batata, aje* (or "*age*")	
tanier	*Xanthosoma* sp. (*X. sagittifoluim*)	*yautía*, tannia	
arrowroot	*Maranta arundinacea*	*araru*	
sweet corn-root	*Calathea* sp. (*C. allouia*)	*ileren*, topitambour	
yam	*Dioscorea trifida*	*yampee*, kush-kush	
edible canna	*Canna* sp.	maraca, toliman	
zamia	*Zamia* sp.	*guayiga*, coontie	
rhubarb-like plant	unknown	unknown	(2)
Maize	*Zea mays*	*mahiz, máhici*	(3)
Legumes:			
beans	*Phaseolus* spp., probably *P. vulgaris* and *P. lunatus*	common bean, lima bean	(4)
peanut	*Arachas hypogaea*	*cacahuete, maní*	
Peppers	*Capsicum* spp.	*axi, hatty*, red pepper, pimiento	(5)
Pineapple	*Ananas comosus*	*yayagua*	(6)
Narcotics:			
tobacco	*Nicotiana* sp.	*tabaco* and *cohoba* (tobacco powder)	(6) (7)
anadenanthera	*Anadenanthera peregrina*	*cojóbana*	(8)
unknown herb	possibly *Oenothera* sp.	*gioia*	(8)
Utilitarian:			
cotton	*Gossypium* sp.	*carobei*, cotton	(9)
annatto	*Bixa orellana*	*bija, achiote*, annatto	(10)
genipop	*Genipa americana*	*xagua, jagua*, genip	

[1]Key sources: Dunn and Kelley 1989; Hulme and Whitehead 1991; Kimber 1988; Layfield [1598] 1995; Nieves-Rivera et al. 1995; Oviedo [1526] 1959; Pané [1505] 2001; Sauer 1966.
[2]Taíno vernaculars (in italics) are primarily from Granberry and Vescelius 2004; see also Sauer 1966.
[3]Relevant details from ethnohistoric documents:
(1) **Manioc, "*yuca*,"** also known as cassava (particularly the bread product) see Table 13.1.
(2) **Unknown root crop**: ". . . Vicente Anes, its [the *Niña*] captain, affirmed that he had seen rhubarb . . . and that he had recognized the stalks and roots. They say that rhubarb puts out small stalks above the ground and some fruits that look almost like dry, green mulberries; and the stem,

Continued on the next page

Table 13.2. *Continued*

which is close to the root, is yellow and handsome as the best possible color for painting, and under the ground it forms a root like a big pear" (December 30, 1492 [Dunn and Kelley 1989:297]).

(3) **Maize**: "when the ears are tender they are eaten almost like milk" (Oviedo [1526] 1959:14–15; and see Ortega and Guerrero 1981; Sauer 1966; Sturtevant 1961). And "it is a grain of very high yield, of the size of the lupine, of the roundness of the chick-pea, and yields a meal ground to a very fine powder; it is ground as is wheat and yields a bread of very good taste; many chew the seeds when in need of nourishment" (Coma quoted in Sauer 1966:55). The following excerpt from Layfield ([1598] 1995) suggests bread was produced from two races of maize present in the islands: "Además del casabe [cassava, yuca] cuentan con el maíz, del caul se hace un pan muy fino, que usan mucho. Hay dos clases de maíz, el más pequeño no se diferencia mucho del arroz; en proporción, tamaúo y gusto: éste nunca le ví en plantíos o crudo, pero lo he visto en la fuente, y al principio lo tome por arroz, exceptuando que yo me creí que estaba un poco inflado. Los que lo comían que sabía a arroz. La otra clase la he visto en plantíos y es la misma o se parece mucho al grano que nosotros llamamos trigo; crece con un tallo nudoso como una caña con grandes hojas esparcidas; crece hasta la altura de braza y media por lo menos, y en la misma punta brota la mazorca" (my clarifications added in brackets).

(4) **Beans**: "and they have varieties of bean very different from ours . . ." (November 4, 1492 [Dunn and Kelley 1989:133]).

(5) **Peppers**: "There is also much chili, which is their pepper, of a kind more valuable than [black] pepper, and none of the people eat without it, for they find it very healthful" (January 15, 1493 [Dunn and Kelly 1989:341]). According to De Las Casas (in Sauer 1966:57), the Taíno Indians regularly used three types of pepper. Two of these were evidently domesticated--one with long red, finger-shaped fruit (e.g., *Capsicum annuum*) and the other with a smaller round, cherrylike and more pungent fruit (perhaps [?] *C. chinensis* [see Pickersgill 1984]), and the third was considered wild, with a small fruit. It seems likely that all three were potentially grown or casually tended in and around home gardens or in more formal plots.

(6) **Pineapple and other taxa cultivated in the Lesser Antilles**: "and fetching from their houses great store of Tobacco, as also a kind of bread which they fed on, called Cassavi, very white and savourie, made of the rootes of Cassavi [cassava, manioc]" (Hakluyt's Principal Navigations, 1585–86 [Hulme and Whitehead 1991:53]) (and see Table 13.1 on home gardens).

(7) **Tobacco use in the Greater Antilles**: "The Indians of this island had a bad vice among others, which is taking a smoke they called tobacco, to leave the senses. This herb was most precious by the Indians, and it was planted in their orchards and farm lands for what I said; they insinuate if you take the weed and to smoke it was not only a sane stuff, but very sacred" (Oviedo 1556, quoted in Nieves-Rivera et al. 1995). Columbus diary: "The two Christians found along the way many people going back and forth between their villages, men and women with a firebrand of weeds in their hands to take in the fragrant smoke to which they are accustomed" (November 6, 1492 [Dunn and Kelly 1989:139]).

(8) **Cojoba (narcotic snuff)**: "the cohoba is a certain snuff, which they use sometimes to purge themselves and for other uses . . . they take it with a cane about the size of an arm and a half; then putting one side in the nose and the other in the snuff, they inhaled it and this makes them purge greatly" (Pané 1498, quoted in Nieves-Rivera et al. 1995). The snuff was made from pulverized and powdered seeds of the tree *cojóbana* (*Anadenanthera peregrina*) combined with crushed shell or lime. This mixture was inhaled directly into the nostrils through tubes made of pottery or wood as part of the important *cojoba* ritual (Alegría 1997; Nieves-Rivera et al. 1995). *Cojóbana* seeds contain an adrenergic agent known as bufotenine, a powerful hallucinogenic drug that strongly affects the cardiovascular and nervous systems (Dobkin de Rios 1984:120). Ritual practices also involved vomiting induced mechanically (Alegría 1997; Kaye 2001; Olazagasti 1997), with the shaman entering into a trance state, including for the treatment of disease or general ill state of being. Evidently such healing rituals often began with the use of the herb called *gioia* (Rouse 1992:14).

(9) **Cotton in the Greater Antilles**: "and much cotton, which they do not plant; and there grow in the mountains very large trees of it; and I believe they have cotton to pick in all seasons because I saw open pods, and others opening, and flowers, all on one tree" (November 4, 1492 [Dunn and Kelley

1989:133–135). (This reference may pertain to wild or feral cotton, or to specimens in misinterpreted tropical home gardens, which are often very junglelike and "untamed" in appearance, or alternatively to the native "silk cotton tree" or *ceiba* [*Ceiba pentandra,* Bombacaceae] that produces a similar seed fiber.) On Guadeloupe (Lesser Antilles) during Columbus's second voyage in 1494 (report of Dr. Chanca [Hulme and Whitehead 1992:33]): "They had much cotton, spun and ready for spinning, and many cotton cloths, so well made that they lose nothing by comparison with those of our own country."

(10) **Red colorant**: "their skinne coloured with some painting of a reddish tawney" (Hulme and Whitehead 1991:53).

another dimension as to who indeed were gardeners in the society, over and above everyday and more-or-less mundane gardens, gardening, and gardeners. Can paleoethnobotany be employed to illuminate these kinds of details, that is, the personal or humanistic side of the indigenous ethnobotany? Perhaps so, particularly if examined in conjunction with studies of symbolism and ideology, agricultural implements recovered with human burials, and so on. But this avenue of research has yet to be realized in the Caribbean. What else can we learn? Specifically, how can Caribbean paleoethobotany help us to resolve things beyond these basic understandings and suppositions concerning the indigenous human-plant dynamic?

Second Base: The Caribbean Paleoethnobotanical Record

Caribbean paleoethnobotany has reached a stage of maturity in recent years. A number of sites have been studied from throughout the region using a variety of approaches, and they represent nearly the entire span of human occupation in the archipelago. Recent syntheses of archaeobotanical data from the Caribbean are available (e.g., Newsom and Wing 2004; Pagán Jiménez 2005b) and do not need to be reiterated here. Rather, I highlight some of what we have learned with an emphasis on early human settlement and subsistence adaptations in the region and from a paleoethnobotanical perspective to reflect on the current breadth and depth of our data and the unique strengths of this avenue of research.

One thing readily apparent from a cursory comparison (Figure 13.1) between the list of plants mentioned in ethnohistoric documents and current inventories of archaeobotanical identifications derived from both micro- and macrobotanical data sets is that more types of plants and representing a wider range of uses have now been identified via archaeobotany, relative to the number and variety described in the chronicles. This makes quite clear that great strides have been made in recent years toward detailing the paleoethnobotany of the region.

Gardeners from Day One. Caribbeanists have for some time surmised that the first human occupants of the region—focusing on the period between about 4000–100 B.C. (Keegan 1994)—were mobile or perhaps partly sedentary hunter-gatherer-fisher people (Dacal Moure and Rivero de la Calle 1996; Keegan 1994; Rodríguez

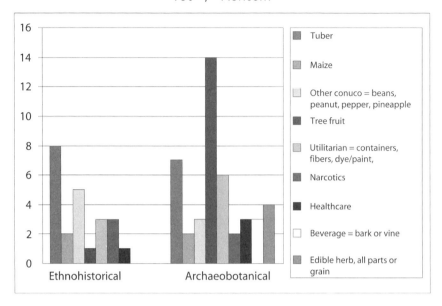

Figure 13.1. Comparison of major classes of economic plant taxa from the ethnohistorical vs. archaeobotanical records.

López 1997; Rouse 1992), and a few of us have suggested that at least some among these original groups were part-time or "low-level" cultivators (to use Smith's [2001] term), based on a number of lines of reasoning (Davis 1988; Newsom 1993; Newsom and Wing 2004; Oliver 2004; Pagán Jiménez 2002b, 2005b; Rodríguez Ramos in press). In fact, archaeobotanical data (Table 13.3) are providing mounting evidence that the earliest islanders were indeed familiar with plant cultivation, having introduced and propagated fruit trees from outside the area, for example, yellow sapote (*Pouteria campechiana*, Sapotaceae); sapodilla, or *níspero* (*Manilkara zapota*, Sapotaceae); and perhaps also avocado (*Persea americana*, Lauraceae), which come from Central America (Newsom and Wing 2004). Maize (*Zea mays* ssp. *maize*) and several edible tubers, particularly manioc (*Manihot esculenta*, Euphorbiaceae)—all based on Pagán Jiménez's (2005b) starch grain analyses—represent additional plant introductions and may well derive from South American sources.

Sooner or later, with increasing intensity of South American colonization or via continued trade networks with that region, other taxa such as papaya (*Carica papaya*, Caricaceae), peppers (*Capsicum* sp., Solanaceae), peanut (*Arachas hypogaea*, Fabaceae), and pineapple (*Ananas comosus*, Bromeliaceae) appeared in the Caribbean. The expanding suite of imported trees and herbs included others with spiritual and symbolic significance, for example, *jagua* (*Genipa americana*, Rubiaceae), *achiote* (*Bixa orellana*, Bixaceae), and *cojóbana* (which was mentioned above).

Native economic plant resources including a number of fruit-bearing and beverage-making trees, as well as the cycad *zamia*—this latter apparently as early as the Archaic Age based on Pagán's evidence—were eventually incorporated into the original garden systems and so became a part of this unique fusion of economic plants and gardening traditions. Root crops seem to have remained the mainstay of subsistence spanning the so-called Ceramic Age and into the contact era (Keegan 1996a, 2000; Olsen 1974). I have argued (Newsom 2006) that maize, even though now understood to have been introduced relatively early, seems to have retained a rather restricted pattern of use in the Caribbean, perhaps ultimately and primarily associated with high-status and/or communal (feasting) contexts, never having achieved the status of a staple crop in the islands. The culmination of all this was a uniquely Caribbean approach to plant production that includes interesting island and subregional variation, particularly when examined in combination with use of faunal resources (Newsom and Wing 2004).

In general, we now have the benefit of a more complete understanding of the types and diversity of plant resources that separately and together, at various times and in various places, comprised the ancient ethnobotany of Caribbean Indians. We have a much more solid basis on which to begin to model the evolution of plant use in the region, and to provide important context and clarification of the ethnobotanical details provided in ethnohistoric documents. We are to the point that we are beginning to be able to infer the relative importance and respective roles of plant resources in ancient subsistence economies and among social segments (e.g., see Deagan 2004), and we can specify that plant cultivation was part of the cultural milieu of Caribbean Indians from the outset of colonization and settlement. Plant use and husbandry in the ancient Caribbean was complex and multifaceted, mirroring the implications from ethnohistoric record, with individual taxa gathered from the wild, others maintained in prepared fields, or tended in home gardens, and perhaps others grown in specialized garden settings, for example, the specialty plants, as suggested above. The apparent pattern of increasing presence and diversity of plant taxa over time (Table 13.3) may attest to the evolution, diversification, and intensification of plant production practices and reliance, topics that we are now better poised to examine.

Third Base and Home Stretch

The next challenge, as we continue to build on the archaeobotanical database, is to provide a clearer spatial and temporal framework of understanding, on a regional, subregional, and island-by-island basis. We should work to address some of the unique historical circumstances underlying the development of local cuisines,

Table 13.3. Key Plant Resources Identified from Caribbean Archaeological Deposits.[1]

	Taxon	Vernacular	Ethnobotany
Trees & Shrubs	Anacardiaceae, *Spondius* sp.[4]	mombín, hog-plum	edible fruit
	Annonaceae, *Annona* sp.[4]	soursop, guanábana	edible fruit
	Bignoniaceae, *Cresentia* sp. cf. *C. cujete*	calabash tree, higüera	container fruit and health care
	Bixaceae, *Bixa orellana*[4]	annatto, achiote	red colorant (fruit)
	Caricaceae, *Carica papaya*[4]	papaya, lechosa	edible fruit
	Euphorbiaceae, *Manihot esculenta*[4]	manioc, yuca	edible root
	Fabaceae, cf. *Anadenanthera*[5]	cojóbana, cojoba, cojobilla	narcotic seeds
	Fabaceae, *Hymenaea courbaril*	stinking toe, locust	edible pulp
	Fabaceae, cf. *Inga* sp.	guaba	edible fruit
	Fabaceae, *Piscida* sp., cf. *P. carthagenensis*	fish poison	fish poison
	Lauraceae, *Persea americana*[4]	wild avocado	edible fruit
	Malpighiaceae, *Malphigia* sp.	West Indian cherry	edible fruit
	Malvaceae, cf. *Gossypium* sp.[5]	cotton	seed fiber
	Myrtaceae, *Psidium guajava*	guava, guayaba	edible fruit
	Palmae, *Acrocomia media*	corozo, spiny palm	edible fruit, fiber
	Rhamnaceae, cf. *Colubrina* sp.	snake-bark, maví	beverage (bark)
	Rubiaceae, cf. *Genipa americana*[4]	jagua	black dye (fruit)
	Rutaceae, *Zanthoxylum* sp.	wild lime	health care
	Sapotaceae, *Chrysophyllum* anatomical group	star apple or caimito, and close relatives	edible fruit
	Sapotaceae, *Manilkara* sp. and/or *Sideroxylon* sp.	bulletwood, níspero, and/or mastic bully	edible fruit
	Sapotaceae, *Manilkara* sp. cf. *M. zapota*[4]	níspero, sapodilla	edible fruit
	Sapotaceae, *Pouteria campechiana*[4]	yellow sapote	edible fruit
	Sapotaceae, *Pouteria* sp.[5]	bully-tree, jácana, almendrón	edible fruit
	Sapindaceae, cf. *Meliccocus bijugatus*[4]	genip, quenepa	edible fruit
	Sterculiaceae, *Guazuma ulmifolia*	guácima	beverage (seeds)
	Sterculiaceae, *Sterculia* sp. cf. *S. apetala*[4]	Panama tree	edible fruit
Herbs	Acanthaceae, *Siphonoglossa*[3]	cossie balsam	health care
	Aizoaceae, *Trianthema* sp.	trianthema, verdolaga	all parts edible
	Araceae, cf. *Xanthosoma* sp.[4]	yautía	edible root
	Cannaceae, *Canna* sp.[5]	canna	edible root

Archaic Age				Early Ceramic Age				Later Ceramic Age			
GA	LA	BTC	SC	GA	LA	BTC	SC	GA	LA	BTC	SC
									x	x	
					[x]			x	x		
								x	x		x
								x			
								x			
x	[x]				[x]			x	[x]		[x]
								x			
									x		
				x				x			
					x			x	x	x	
x											
x				[x]				x			
								x			
					[x]			x			
x				x	x			x	x		
								x			
								x			
	x				x			x	x	x	
					x			x	x	x	
x	x				x			x		x	
x											
x											
								x			
								x			
								x			
				x				x			
	x										
x				x	x			x			
x								x			
								x			

Continued on the next page

Table 13.3. *Continued*

	Taxon	Vernacular	Ethnobotany
Herbs	Cycadaceae, *Zamia* sp.	zamia, guayiga	edible stem (cycad)
	Fabaceae, *Arachis hypogaea*[4]	peanut	edible ground nut
	Fabaceae, *Phaseolus* sp.[4]	common bean, frijol	edible seed
	Marantaceae, *Calathea* sp.[5]	ileren, lerenes, galatea	edible root
	Marantaceae, *Maranta* sp. (*M. arundinacea*)[4]	arrowroot	edible root
	Onagraceae, *Oenothera* sp.[5]	evening primrose	all parts, medicinal
	Poaceae/Paniceae, cf. *Setaria* spp. and relatives[3]	panicoid grasses, e.g. foxtail millets	edible grain
	Poaceae, *Zea mays*[4]	maize	edible grain, sugary vegetative organs
	Solanaceae, *Capsicum* sp. cf. *C. annuum*[4,5]	chili pepper, pimiento, ají	edible fruit
Vines	Convovulaceae, *Ipomoea* sp., cf. *I. batatas*[4]	sweet potato, batata	edible root
	Cucurbitaceae[5]	gourd/squash family	edible fruit, container
	Passifloraceae, *Passiflora* sp.	Passion flower, parcha	edible fruit

[1]Source data: Berman and Pearsall 2000; Pagán Jiménez 2003, 2005a, 2005b; Pagán Jiménez et al. 2005; Newsom and Pearsall 2003; Newsom and Wing 2004; Pearsall 1985, 1989, 2002a.
[2]Subregions: GA = Greater Antilles and Virgin Islands; LA = Lesser Antilles; BTC = Bahamas, Turks and Caicos; SC = Southern Caribbean Islands.

cultivation practices, cultivators (i.e., the questions posed above about roles), and consumers, as well as the possibility of independently domesticated taxa, which would represent a truly unique Caribbean development. I next offer something of a road map for Caribbean paleoethnobotany, some potential future directions to pursue via this line of inquiry focusing on three basic thematic issues.

I. Clarifying Environmental Dynamics. What can we do to discern more the landscapes and cultural biogeography of prehistoric human settlement in the Caribbean? Scarry and Reitz (2005) recently reflected on our shying away from considering climate change as a causal factor in cultural behavior, largely because of negative impressions generated by unsupported or poorly supported claims in past years. But they urge it is time to return to environmental issues as a potentially "important ingredient in culture change" and which can clarify significant aspects of the human-landscape dynamic (Scarry and Reitz 2005:118). Certainly we cannot preclude environment as a causal factor unless and until we understand it, including the nature of stochastic variations such as in rainfall and the potential

Table 13.3. *Continued*

Archaic Age				Early Ceramic Age				Later Ceramic Age			
GA	LA	BTC	SC	GA	LA	BTC	SC	GA	LA	BTC	SC
x								x			
								x			
[x]				x				[x]			
								x			
								x			
								x			
x					x			x			
x								x			
								x			
x								x			
								x			
								x			

[3] Member of the cosmopolitan weed flora. [4]Taxon is believed to have been introduced or dispersed from outside the region. [5]Taxon may be introduced, naturalized, or native (uncertain).

effects of periodic natural disturbances. At the very least, even simple baseline information about environmental context is necessary to appreciate the circumstances with which past inhabitants of the region coped on a daily basis, not to mention how they may have responded to specific environmental issues and disasters (see Alley 2000; Diamond 2005) and changed their environments.

A number of circum-Caribbean paleoecological records are now available in increasingly higher resolution. For example, a significant cyclical and multiscalar drought history has been documented for Central America (Curtis et al. 1996; Curtis et al. 2001; Hodell et al. 1995; Hodell et al. 2001; Hodell et al. 2005; Peterson and Haug 2005; and see Black et al. 1999; Haug et al. 2001, 2003), and this has been compared with micropaleontological and geochemical records from the Caribbean itself (Curtis and Hodell 1993; Higuera-Gundy 1991; Kjellmark 1996; Nyberg et al. 2001; Street-Perrott et al. 1993). A recent study by Beets and colleagues (2006) of oxygen and carbon isotopic variation in the shells of land snails recovered from Anse à la Gourde, Guadeloupe, is a superb example. The study produced a chronological record of annual and seasonal moisture fluctuation and proceeded to link the climate variability with separate episodes of human occupation on the island.

This type of multidisciplinary research will undoubtedly continue to be pursued in the islands. But given that wood charcoal is the most abundant and ubiquitous class of terrestrial archaeobotanical remains preserved and routinely recovered from Caribbean sites, a complementary avenue of research involves tracking species frequencies and presence (forest succession and species turnover) and the use of tree ring evidence.

Temporal and spatial changes in species assemblages reflected in wood charcoal can shed light on ecosystem (forest) dynamics and health, as well as human impact on forest environments (Redman 1999), over and above simple notions of wood preferences and taxon availability. Tree-ring data are a proven proxy of rainfall patterns and other environmental cycles and perturbations, including in the seasonally dry tropics as encompasses much of the Caribbean. Methodological refinements (Baillie 1995; Schweingruber 1988) enable work with samples comprised of multiple short-ring series, such as is the situation with charcoal assemblages. Thus, the carbonized remnants of fuelwood we typically recover can potentially serve not only as longitudinal records tracking natural succession, human extraction of forest resources, including perhaps human-induced changes in forest composition and structure, but also as a record of the local and regional paleoecology and climate variation (Schweingruber 1988, 1996).

Some ultimate goals for Caribbean research combining multiple proxy environmental data sets—including dendroecology, micro- and macrobotanical remains—might include to examine more broadly across the region the Caribbean hydrological cycle and drought record, as Beets and colleagues (2006) have done for Guadeloupe. A number of areas in the Caribbean are quite arid; with or without fertile soils we can reasonably infer that extended droughts would have significantly impacted the success and productivity of plant production, if not at times rendering horticulture a complete failure.[3]

We should attempt to gain a better appreciation too of the past presence and impacts of other Caribbean-specific environmental perturbations, for example, volcanism, earthquakes, tsunamis, hurricanes, and storm surges (e.g., Ricklefs and Bermingham 2001; Schoener et al. 2001; Ten Brink et al. 2006; Tomblin 1981), that potentially impacted food webs, the food supply and overall well being of prehistoric human communities. Clarifying this underlying complexity of the human-environment relationship would also facilitate studies of risk avoidance, including responses to natural environmental variation and the constraints on cultural investments in an agricultural way of life. All of this bears also on the sustainability of biotic resources in the region (see, for example, McKee 2003), and in general the carrying capacity of anthropogenic environments (Abel 1998). Already we can point to some tree taxa, for example, lignum vitae (*Guaiacum* sp., Zygophyllaceae), which seem to have been preferred or commonly targeted for fuelwood early in the record that we see less of or that disappear entirely from later records. Does this change represent the cultural values and preferences of different human groups, changes in human activities involving wood use, or does it signal the local extirpation of particular taxa necessitating a switch to other species? Can pulses of carbon particulate matter in sediment cores (e.g., Burney and Burney 1994) be used to clarify such changes, assuming we can discern forest clearing from the residues of natural fire events? In combination these lines of evidence may help to establish the scale of past human influence in the Caribbean landscape. Perhaps we can distinguish, if we are very creative, between the carbon and other residues of single-event or short-term clearing for horticulture, even some crop residues, vs. the effects of repeatedly impacted areas, including continuous fuelwood extraction. And since such human influence on local forests, and one way or the other fragmentation of natural habitats, represents a complex and multiscalar process, necessarily extending to faunal communities, soils, and adjacent watersheds (successional changes induced by and under the influence of human extraction pressure), understanding the entire human-ecosystem dynamic is essential to our interpretation of the history of human-landscape interactions (and certainly paleoethnobotany and paleobotany are important parts of this equation).

II. Making the Most of Excavations. What can be done to gain greater insights into the prehistoric ethnobotany of the Caribbean? How can we overcome some potential pitfalls, particularly the loss of archaeobotanical data, (i.e., we get what we look for . . . or we certainly will not find what we do not look for . . . or we can [and have] caused data to be lost)? We need to rethink, or at least consider in greater depth, sampling and recovery issues, in other words, about planning and implementing sufficient data collection in Caribbean archaeology. This has been said before, but is worth reiteration.

We all recognize the inherent complexity of archaeological sites, including details of their internal organization and how this may reflect and prove to be the key to understanding the underlying social dynamics of ancient settlements. Household archaeology has become a topic of interest in our region, and necessarily involves as one aspect of ancient households and communities, trying to discern specific details of foodways and the internal circulation and distribution of food items and other commodities (Sheets 2006). This includes among other things trying to discover the patterns and venues of production, distribution, and consumption; food storage, management, and control of surpluses; and so forth. Accordingly, this scale of analysis necessitates a very detailed and comprehensive sampling effort, for one thing, to recover evidence related to all the links and separate aspects of subsistence and economy, if not simply to adequately assess species richness and diversity (Lepofsky and Lertzman 2005), thus diet breadth, and so on.

In other areas, intensive sampling (coupled fine-scale recovery methods) across house floors and other activity surfaces has enabled researchers to identify differences in the types, distributions, and relative quantities of plant food items among structures, that is, households, and to discern between food preparation, storage, and consumption areas and activities. Hastorf's (1988) work with ancient Peruvian settlements is a good example. Deagan's (2004) recent interpretation of ritual (feasting, burial) and residence (elite, nonelite) contexts at En Bas Saline, Haiti, emphasizing the nonrandom distribution of cultivated and wild plant taxa illustrates the benefits of insights made possible due to having carried out very specific sampling and recovery of plant remains. Some other sites in the region have been sampled fairly intensively for plant macroremains—Maisabel, Luján I, Golden Rock, Anse à la Gourde, to name a few—and the samples have been analyzed or are in various stages of analysis. In general we need to apply this more broadly to achieve greater resolution of the archaeobotanical record in the Caribbean, including point sampling across house floors and activity surfaces (Pearsall 2000:73), in conjunction with the feature and stratum sampling that is already done, and be attentive to matching the size (volume) of samples with the size of the contexts sampled (i.e., larger features should as a general rule be sampled in greater volume; we standardize according to volume later in the laboratory for intersample comparisons). The benefits of factoring in and planning for both micro- and macrobotanical analyses, as complementary data sets, should be self-evident by now.

Can we locate those home gardens and crop venues inferred or hypothesized through the archaeobotany and the ethnohistoric documents? Consider that Amerindian groups in the Upper Orinoco, Venezuela, grow two partially domesticated species of *Solanum* (the potato and nightshade genus), including individual varieties of each, but those of one species are cultivated in swidden plots and those of the other in home gardens; the distinction as to venue is based on economic use and domestication status, the latter as recognized and defined by the native cultivators (Volpato et al. 2004). Can we discern equivalent distinctions and patterns of cultivation and use in the ancient Caribbean, perhaps even the *behique*'s nexus of activity, including any specially groomed habitats or gardens for the plants central to his or her practice? Can we finally associate specific assemblages of food items and other economic plants with individual dwellings, particular households, or separate social segments? These are all achievable goals, but they will never be realized unless we make a directed effort to do so. We can only achieve such an exacting level of resolution of the archaeobotanical record by instituting a broad and appropriately tuned sampling effort combined with suitable recovery procedures (fine sieving, flotation, direct collection, depending on the material and the depositional environment).

Somewhat similarly, wet-site archaeology has great potential to illuminate Caribbean paleoethnobotany and any number of broader issues due to the more complete preservation of organics entombed in anaerobic deposits (see Van de Noort and O'Sullivan 2006). Wet sites are well documented around the region, particularly in coastal Belize and in Florida,[4] and wetlands and submerged deposits abound in the Caribbean (sloughs, ponds, cenotes, marshes, mangrove swamps, and estuaries). At least one Caribbean wet site is under investigation, Los Buchiollones, Cuba (Pendergast et al. 2002), and waterlogged strata below the water table were encountered at En Bas Saline, Haiti, and the Bastion de San Justo del Muelle (San Juan Federal Building, Puerto Rico) (Newsom 1993, 1996). All have yielded well-preserved uncarbonized wood and seeds, and many other unique items. Similar sites surely exist around the region. Although not a simple undertaking, when and where possible, we should seek to avail ourselves of the opportunities inherent in wet sites. This is not for the sake of simply locating unusual objects, but to recover a more complete and potentially more revealing record of the past, and in the context of our planned research agendas and theoretical concerns (e.g., sea-level change, human migrations, coastal settlement, trade and maritime resources, among others).

III. Gleaning More of the Archaeobotanical Record (Clarifying Details . . . but Be Careful What You Look For!). Sassaman (2003) recently highlighted the opportunities available to directly date ceramics and other cooking vessels using carbon or soot encased in smudged surfaces. But the same call to arms can apply to analysis of any surface-adhering and internally bound organic residues (e.g., lipids) that may be extracted and used not only for dating, but also to identify original foodstuffs, parallel to blood residue analysis. In the Caribbean we should be alert to analyze and identify any of several types of chemical residues that may be retained on tool and ceramic surfaces or bound in ceramic fabric to clarify function, if not specifically plant presence and use. Griddle sherds occasionally harbor burned or baked-on food (?) residues that can be analyzed using gas chromatography mass spectrometry (GC/MS) or other chemical means. Likewise, compounds bound in the vessel walls of clay pots may help identify the contents of soupy, so-called pepper pots, and various ritual paraphernalia, such as pipes or snuff inhalers (Kaye 2001), may preserve traces and residues from their use, helping to confirm what was actually smoked or inhaled, and whether used singly or combined, for example, mixing *cajoba* and tobacco as a highly potent snuff (Stevens-Arroyo 2006). This type of analysis is now underway with my laboratory group on a bone inhaler from Tibes.

An important first step in this type of analysis is the development of chemical standards, such as analyzing modern tobacco leaves and *Anandenanthera* sp. seeds for their precise organic chemical signatures to then compare with archaeological residues (along with careful consideration of diagenetic factors). The analytical standards are critical, just as sufficient and adequate comparative collections and other supporting data (published identification keys, floras, anatomical and morphological treatments, etc.) are required to conduct mainstream analyses of plant remains of any type.

With this in mind, recent efforts with starch and other microremains data sets have made it possible to specify an early presence for manioc, if not virtually all of the root crops listed in ethnohistoric documents, as well as maize. This is an exciting new development in Caribbean paleoethnobotany. However, it is essential that those working with starch and phytoliths, and this is true also of seed and pollen analysis, continue to build on the background database, the comparative universe. Direct morphological matching—that is, assigning identifications of taxa primarily on the basis of perceptible morphological characteristics—presents a number of challenges and potential pitfalls that are not unique to archaeobotany.[5]

Interpretation is typically by comparison with living species; however, it is neither an easy nor simple matter to distinguish between homologous and homoplastic (having the same form but unrelated taxonomically) forms, that is, to discern whether shared characteristics represent true relatedness (i.e., a correct identification) or are superficially similar (i.e., similar form, but an incorrect assignment).[6]

When the comparative universe is small and limited, the full range of intraspecific and interspecific variability is unknown, not to mention variation associated with ontogeny and growth conditions (particularly considering the inherent genetic plasticity of many taxa under a range of selection pressures, that is, some polyploid taxa have multiple independent origins, culminating in ecologically distinct races and species; see, for example, Levin 2001), which in fact represent another set of problems and potential pitfalls to correct assignments. In reality, the potential to mis-assign an archaeological taxon is quite large, particularly given that we are dealing with degraded (decay), altered (cooking/heating/shredding, carbonization, mineralization), typically fragmentary plant organs and tissues or simply the mineral inclusions originally contained within tissues (e.g., starch, crystals, cystoliths, opal phytoliths). Archaeological remains of all types inherently present considerable and serious potential to faithfully but incorrectly assign taxa, to match them based on comparison with the observed structure of modern representatives that appear to be the same when in fact they may not be. This is a problem that is heightened when there are few ancient specimens (e.g., see Smith 2006), few comparative specimens, and/or few replicate specimens to account for genetic, ecological, and functional variation within each candidate taxon. In other words, things can look quite similar and appear to be a really great match, unless and until a broader range of inherent variation, of within—and between—species diversity, is encountered, at which time it may be realized that a particular morphology is less diagnostic, less specific to a given taxon than once appeared, and perhaps that assignments have overreached. So accurate and comprehensive comparison is critical and must proceed with considerable caution and recognition of all taxonomic "realities." We must continue to build on comparative databases, and routinely sample background soils for indications of the natural seed/pollen/starch rain.[7]

Finally, the archaeobotanical record is more than just a reflection of the plant resources used by people of the past. It IS, quite literally, *those plants*. Caribbean species extinctions resulting from natural catastrophes and human pressures have occurred on a massive scale (Brooks and M. L. Smith 2001). As a reservoir of ancient taxa, the archaeobotanical record bears directly on past and present biodiversity issues. Although long dead in the life history sense, and generally existing only as fragments of or a particle from the original plant, archaeobotanical remains nevertheless exist to the present in their various states of preservation. In a very real sense the archaeobotanical record is a repository of ancient taxa and their genetic material, including in some cases the last traces of heirloom cultivars, of the ancestral forms of plants present today, and of others now extinct (consider here again the pitfalls of direct comparison with extant forms).

We know from the ethnohistoric accounts (Tables 13.1 and 13.2) and archaeological kernel morphologies that at least two races of maize were present in the Caribbean by the time of European contact, one of which may be related to the modern race Early Caribbean (Newsom 2006; Newsom and Deagan 1994), but can DNA be used to clarify that assignment, to discern more? We have suggestions of several tropical root crops from the ethnohistoric documents, carbonized tubers, and plant microremains, but suppose DNA or some chemical residue analysis revealed that other taxa, varieties, or landraces were present? This would be important to the overall understanding of subsistence patterns and the evolution of crop systems in the region. And whereas ancient DNA analysis might be difficult or impossible with carbonized remains, the chemical signatures still may be attainable. Furthermore, certainly there are numerous caves and wetlands in the Caribbean— thus very arid or perpetually waterlogged environments—in which uncarbonized material may be recovered and become available for study. Archaeobotany can inform on the past record of biodiversity, as well as clarify the history of cultivars, cultivation, and cultivators. It is essential to continue to work to clarify whether some of the taxa documented archaeologically in fact represent plants introduced by humans (vs. natural dispersal, wild pepper and wild avocado being two possibilities), and whether they indeed represent domesticates, semidomesticates, or wild taxa, including whether some cultivars were developed in situ from native or introduced sources. This has important cultural implications and is central to understanding the indigenous ethnobotanical heritage. DNA analysis can be one source of information in this regard, including comparisons of modern taxa in the region, to detect genetic distances between wild and domesticated forms.

Discussion and Conclusions

Caribbean archaeobotanical data have potential significance and application well beyond simply generating lists of plants—their presence and time depth—to explore the complex history of plant use, the development of cultivation practices and self-organizing dynamics of agriculture systems, and the role of plant resources in human social evolution. By the time Europeans arrived in the region, Caribbean Indians managed plant resources variously in venues ranging from casual gardens to formally prepared agricultural plots. The ethnohistoric documents, as well as what we now understand directly from paleoethnobotanical research in the region, have provided some key insights, including the levels of commitment required to produce and maintain different economic species. We now have a reasonable understanding of when reliance on cultivated species began, and so have an indication of when Caribbean islanders began to exert some measure of control over their food supply (from the outset!). Caribbean paleoethnobotany is getting to the point where we can begin to consider the complexity and multiple dimensions of the indigenous ethnobotany. I have attempted in this chapter to offer some ideas for the road ahead by proposing or highlighting some new initiatives as well as describing ways to strengthen current research avenues in coming years, all as means to further illuminate the ancient ethnobotany.

We still have much yet to learn about the degrees of reliance on crops and other plant resources, such as their importance relative to faunal resources, exactly how intensively (and where specifically and generally) were crops grown, whether any represented manipulatable (by elites) surpluses, what were the circumstances behind the importation of exotic species, and so on. These are questions among others that remain to be explored through a culturally informed archaeobiological approach.

In my opinion, exotic tree taxa—being several, early, and widespread—collectively comprise the best evidence for the presence of home gardens in Caribbean antiquity because they suggest quite overtly that propagules were intentionally transferred and successfully reproduced in the region. The plant microremains would seem to do likewise for swidden-type horticulture, but in both cases we still lack a good understanding of the underlying factors and motivations behind these introductions. The presence also of certain herbaceous plants such as evening primrose and passionflower suggests that at least late ceramic age home gardens were diverse and multistrata, incorporating herbs, vines, shrubs, and trees (Table 13.3). They were also multifunctional, and gardens of all types were almost certainly important foci of individual households and communities, including in ways in which we have yet to discover.

Home gardens, it should be pointed out, are perfect venues for experimentation with plants (Niñez 1984). Some of the species, such as cotton (Tables 13.2 and 13.3) may be the products of local West Indian domestication where the idea of controlled breeding of a plant was applied to endemic species. The current data are insufficient to explore this possibility; nevertheless, as alluded to above, two-way DNA analysis of particular ancient taxa and their modern relatives may shed important light on this issue. Currently we lack solid evidence to demonstrate that particular plants were domesticated locally in the islands, although the presence of two races of maize at En Bas Saline may provide some suggestion of this, and it may be that we will eventually find that *zamia* was manipulated by Caribbean Indians. An early broad Ceramic-Age range and later postcontact disappearance of evening primrose may reflect domesticated status, given the taxon's apparent inability to survive in the absence of human intervention after the human population crash and cultural decline in the wake of European contact (Newsom and Wing 2004). The Native American role and influence on Caribbean biodiversity, including as plant breeders (e.g., Zaldivar et al. 2004 on Amerindian manioc breeding and perpetuation of high levels of genetic diversity), possible domesticators (e.g., Volpato et al. 2004), and the stewards and curators of unique germplasm (i.e., maintaining and perpetuating ancient cultivars, e.g., see Brush 2004; Minnis and Elisens 2000), is a particularly exciting new area that we should endeavor to pursue.

Acknowledgments

My thanks to Corinne Hofman and Annelou van Gijn for including me in the original SAA symposium (Puerto Rico, 2006) on which this volume is based. I thank Bill Keegan for his generosity and helpful comments offered as the discussant in the symposium, particularly his unwavering encouragement to push the envelope.

Notes

1. For example, edible leaves, stems, roots, and other structures; for use as vegetables, condiments, beverages, medicines, narcotic substances, fish poisons, insecticides, colorants, fibers, containers, tools, and more.

2. The plant may equate with the archaeological evening primrose (the genus *Oenothera* sp., Onagraceae [Table 13.3]), which is mildly narcotic (see Newsom and Wing 2004).

3. Certainly such situations would have impacted Caribbean Indians in different ways, depending on social organization, settlement patterns, degree of reliance on cultivation, and so on, and in general how risk was managed. Consider the questions surrounding the settlement history of Puerto Rico and the apparent abandonment of sites

in the south-central region around ca. A.D. 1200. A transdisciplinary paleoecological and environmental approach would help to resolve at the very least the environmental context of this particular issue.

4. My experience with Florida wet sites has been that they typically reveal much more quantitatively and qualitatively of the archaeobotanical record due to the characteristically more complete preservation of plant remains. Particular examples include bowel contents (last meals), plant-fiber clothing, wooden implements, and other items associated with human burials (Newsom 2002), and highly perishable seed types, for example, squash seeds that demonstrate a longitudinal record of plant domestication (Newsom 1987). Dry terrestrial deposits at a Calusa site yielded a few fragments of gourd/squash seed, whereas the adjacent, contemporaneous and older wet deposits yielded numerous complete or nearly complete specimens that could be identified to finer resolution. Moreover, the dry component produced only fragments of carbonized wood, whereas the waterlogged deposits had both the charcoal as well as hundreds of specimens of uncarbonized wood *débitage,* the debris of woodworking operations carried out in a specific activity area (something for which there otherwise was no direct evidence at the site) (Newsom and Scarry in press; Newsom et al. in press).

5. Being shared with paleontology and paleobotany, which similarly take incomplete evidence and work forensically to recover as much salient information as possible to reconstruct past taxonomic and biological relationships.

6. In recent years there has been a lot of discussion in paleontology about multiple-effect factors and in general the difficulties and inconsistencies of identifying taxa according to morphological characteristics, lacking genetic or other supporting data.

7. Also, whereas wood anatomy, and seed/fruit and pollen morphological studies all have the benefit of being able to draw upon long previous years of research by wood anatomists, botanists, and palynologists—thus an expansive information base of published floras, keys, and replicate studies—there is no equivalent body of previous research for starch grain and phytolith analysis. Researchers working with starch and phytoliths have to work very hard to build original baseline data for direct comparison (e.g., see Pagán Jiménez 2005b). Moreover, unlike seeds and pollen, the morphologies and anatomies of which are intimately tied to the reproductive biology and dispersal mechanisms of the plant taxa (and in many cases also to their associated and coevolved faunal dispersers), starch and phytoliths form from internally deposited substances that culminate in durable structures bound within plant tissues and are not subject to quite the same evolutionary selective pressures, thus fewer of the mechanisms that result in taxonomically distinct morphologies. This adds another layer of difficulty and caution where these two data sets are concerned.

14

New Evidence of Two Different Migratory Waves in the Circum-Caribbean Area during the Pre-Columbian Period from the Analysis of Dental Morphological Traits

Alfredo Coppa, Andrea Cucina, Menno L. P. Hoogland, Michaela Lucci, Fernando Luna Calderón, Raphaël G. A. M. Panhuysen, Glenis Tavarez María, Roberto Valcárcel Rojas, and Rita Vargiu

Introduction

The circum-Caribbean area is formed by the southeastern part of the Mesoamerican continent, the northern part of South America, the archipelagos of the Bahamas, Florida, and the Greater and the Lesser Antilles (Figure 14.1). The ocean and the Caribbean Sea represented a way of communication, rather than a barrier, that allowed population movements and the interaction among the various groups (Watters 1997c; Watters and Rouse 1989).

The early human migrations into the Caribbean, documented so far only by the archaeological evidence, started around the fourth millennium B.C. (Rouse 1992; Rouse and Allaire 1978) and are thought to have originated from the Mesoamerican realm along the coasts of Belize (Veloz Maggiolo 1980; Veloz Maggiolo and Ortega 1976; Wilson et al. 1998).

The first migratory waves from South America led the aceramic Ortoiroids into the area around the second millennium B.C. (Veloz Maggiolo and Ortega 1976). Later, the Saladoids (the name comes from the site of Saladero in Venezuela; Siegel 1989) migrating from the Orinoco Valley introduced pottery and agriculture around 500 B.C.. This population rapidly expanded northward through the Lesser Antilles and Puerto Rico up to Hispaniola. The process lasted about

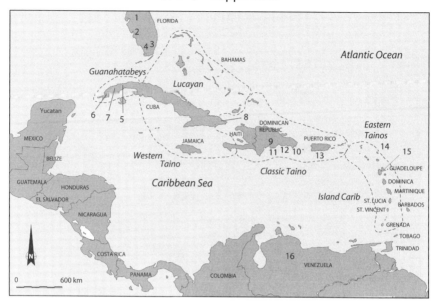

Figure 14.1. Geographical distribution of the samples (each number represents a sample; see Table 14.1).

four centuries, too short a time to establish permanent settlements in every is-land (Keegan 1992). The rapid movement was caused by the islands' small size and limited availability of terrestrial resources, which bound the human groups to seek for marine resources and concentrate along the coasts (D. Harris 1965; Keegan 1992). Rouse (1986) suggested that the Saladoids' expansion was halted in the eastern part of Hispaniola by the long-settled hunter-gatherer populations (Casimiroids).

The Ostionoids, a Saladoid subseries, would eventually evolve into the well-known Taíno culture (Veloz Maggiolo 1993), which started again the expansion process around A.D. 600. They moved along the southern and northern coasts of Hispaniola, reaching Jamaica and eastern Cuba. Here Rouse (1986) identified yet another barrier along the mountain chains in east Cuba, represented by what he considered the original hunter-gatherer settlers.

The Taíno, who originated from the South American continent (Lalueza-Fox et al. 2001), expanded into the Bahamas, the Greater Antilles, and the northernmost Lesser Antilles (Figure 14.1). Rouse (1992) divides them into Western Taíno, living in Jamaica, Cuba and the Bahamas; Eastern Taíno for those inhabiting the Lee-ward Islands and the Virgin Islands; and then the Classic Taíno for those in Puerto Rico and Hispaniola.

In the western part of Cuba, Lovén (1935) identified the remains of the aceramic culture that had been originally described by Harrington (1921) and Cosculluela (1946). Lovén hypothesized that the aceramic archaeological deposits in Cuba belong to the Guanahatabey, who settled the island as a consequence of a migration that took place before the arrival of the Taíno, probably from Florida, and who had been marginalized by the expansion of the Taíno from Hispaniola (Lovén 1935). However, he concluded that there was no proof that primitive groups were still living in the westernmost part of Cuba at the time of the conquest (Keegan 1992).

The initial frame depicted after the archaeological investigations was based, among the others, also on the ethnohistoric sources. Keegan (1992) calls into question this old-fashioned view of the Ciboney hunter-gatherers in Cuba being marginalized by the expansion of the Taíno and surviving there until the European conquest. His detailed review put emphasis on the bias introduced by the ethnohistoric sources and its misuse in the archaeological realm, in particular with regard to the Ciboney, who he underscores should be more properly called Guanahatabey. Indeed, Keegan (1992:8) highlights the fact that the Guanahatabey were the creation of the Spaniards and/or the Taíno, so that we should "dispense with the Guanahatabey until more conclusive archaeological evidence for their existence is uncovered, and we must explain the aceramic remains found throughout the Antilles solely on the basis of material evidence." According to Keegan (1992), at present we lack sufficient evidence to support the idea that this population still inhabited western Cuba at the time of the European conquest.

Previous anthropological studies highlighted that the human archaeological samples that had been originally identified as belonging to the so-called Ciboney (or Guanahatabey) showed a dental morphological pattern that was remarkably different from the one described for all the Taíno (Coppa et al. 1992; Coppa et al. 1995; Coppa et al. 2003; Cucina et al. 2003). Such difference motivated the present investigation on the morphological variation of dental traits of skeletal populations from different times and regions in the Caribbean and circum-Caribbean area, which updates the previous ones and aims to expand the understanding of the biological relationships between the human groups pertaining to different chronological or cultural horizons that peopled the Caribbean area before the European conquest.

We assume that, through the analysis of dental morphological traits in this cultural and diachronic sequence, it is possible to infer on the genetic component that the human groups inherited from the genetic pool of their direct ancestors or from gene flow from surrounding areas. We consider that the morphological differences, when analyzed by multivariate techniques, do possibly result in topologies that can be assessed for their coherence with patterns of continuity and discontinuity or for their random, chaotic distribution that limits its interpretation.

Specifically, our study aims to:

1. Assess the biological differences among the populations that occupied the same area during different periods of time;
2. Compare the biological information with the evidence from the material culture in order to understand whether the archaeological differences were to the product of "biologically" distant populations or of cultural transformations of populations that shared the same "biological" substrate;
3. Explore the diffusion model to infer whether the hunter-gatherers were "pushed into marginal locations by the expansion of the agriculturalists or assimilated into the expanding culture;
4. Expand the knowledge on the pattern of peopling of the Lesser Antilles;
5. Infer the possible role played by continental populations from Venezuela and Florida.

Dental Morphology

Recent studies have shown that morphological dental traits may circumvent supposed limitations of metric traits and provide useful information of microevolutionary processes (Scott and Turner 1997). The importance of dental morphological traits in anthropological studies was first perceived by Hrdlicka (1920) and Dahlberg (1945, 1949) who reported significant differences in frequency among the major geographic populations. Turner and collaborators (1991) developed a standardized method to score dental morphological traits (Arizona State University Dental Anthropology System), on the basis of Dahlberg's method (1956). It proved to be potentially highly discriminating in micro- and macroregional analyses of biological relationships (Scott and Turner 1997). Their potentiality rests upon the large number of traits available, the slow evolutionary rates that permit long-term diachronic studies (Turner 1969), the reduced influence of environment on dental morphology with the only exception of attrition (Dahlberg 1971; Larsen and Kelley 1991), and their strong hereditary components (E. Harris 1977; Larsen and Kelley 1991; Nichol 1989; G. Scott 1973; Townsend and Martin 1992; Townsend et al. 1988; Townsend et al. 1992; Townsend et al. 1994; Turner 1967). Estimations on heritability suggest that the genetic influence on dental traits can be as high as 60 percent (Berry 1978; Harris and Bailit 1980). Several papers have successfully used morphological dental traits to address questions concerning the emergence of modern humans (Irish 1998a; Scott and Turner 1997; Stringer et al. 1997) and the peopling of Africa, Americas, Asia and Europe (Coppa et al. 1997; Coppa et al.

1998; Coppa et al. 2000; Coppa et al. 2004; Cucina et al. 2003; Irish 1993, 1997, 1998b, 2000; Scott and Turner 1997).

Materials

The populations' samples analyzed in this study come from six geographical areas (Table 14.1). Because of the difference in sample size, dental collections that were sufficiently large were analyzed as single units. In turn, small samples that were geographically, chronologically, and culturally similar were pooled together to form larger groups. A total of 15,497 teeth and 1,932 individuals were retrieved from 16 dental collections.

As far as chronology is concerned (Table 14.1), the Florida samples are from four independent and chronologically different sites. Tick Island and Republic Groove are the most ancient ones, referred to a period spanning between 4500 B.C. and 3000 B.C., Fort Center is dated between A.D. 200 and 600, and Highland Beach around the A.D. 1200. Among the sites from the Dominican Republic, Cueva Roja is the most ancient, and it is dated between 2500 B.C. and 2000 B.C.. The samples of El Soco and Andres were pooled into the larger Ostionoid group and encompass a time range between A.D. 800 and 900. Juan Dolio and La Caleta belong to the Chicoid period, which dates between A.D. 1000 and 1500. The Cuban necropolises that were thought to pertain to the Ciboney culture date between A.D. 500 and 1500 and are geographically located in the westernmost part of the island. Two of them, Cueva del Perico and Cueva el Infierno, are sufficiently large to be analyzed independently. Even though we acknowledge Keegan's critics on the misuse of the term "Ciboney," this large group from Cuba will be labeled here as Ciboney from Cuba for no other reason than simple matter of simplicity. On the contrary, only one Taíno sample was retrieved from Cuba, El Chorro de Maíta, dated between A.D. 1000 and 1500, and located on the easternmost part of the island. All the collections from Puerto Rico pertain to the Saladoid period (150 B.C.–A.D. 0). The sample from the U.S. Virgin Islands pertains to the Saladoid and Chican periods. From the Lesser Antilles, so far we collected data only from the Troumassoid sample of Anse à la Gourde in Guadeloupe, which spans a period between A.D. 1000 and 1400. The samples from Venezuela are chronologically dated between A.D. 200 and 800.

Methods

In the present study, the permanent dentitions have been scored for 31 morphological traits (14 maxillary and 17 mandibular) according to the Arizona State University Dental Anthropology System (ASUDAS) with the help of rank-scale ref-

Table 14.1. List of the Samples and Their Chronology, Grouped by Cultural Pertinence, Total Number of Individuals and Teeth Analyzed.

N. of Site	Site	Initial	N. Teeth	N. Individuals	Culture/Chronology
	FLORIDA				
1	Tick Island	TIC	646	93	3500–3100 B.C.
2	Republic Groves	RGR	307	57	2000 B.C.
3	Higland Beach	HIG	1644	189	600–1200 B.C.
4	Fort Center	FRC	2403	430	450 B.C.–A.D. 1700
	CUBA				
5	Cueva el Infierno	CEI	956	96	Guanahatabeys/ A.D. 500–1400
6	Cueva del Perico 1	CUD	233	61	Guanahatabeys/ A.D. 500–1400
7	Ciboney Cuba	CIB	398	74	Guanahatabeys/ A.D. 500–1400
	Baracoa Maisi		*11*	*3*	
	Boca del Purial		*9*	*2*	
	Cueva Calero		*16*	*2*	
	Cueva Fria Maisi		*14*	*4*	
	Caivarien		*9*	*1*	
	Canimar		*11*	*1*	
	Cuba Ciboney		*79*		
	Guayabo Blanco		*117*	*24*	
	Las Mueles		*3*	*1*	
	La Santa		*15*	*8*	
	Maria 2		*75*	*14*	
	Maisi		*10*	*2*	
	Punta del Este		*9*	*2*	
	Pio 1		*13*	*1*	
	Saza del Medio		*2*	*1*	
	Seboinco		*5*	*1*	
8	El Chorro de la Maíta	ECD	1250	119	Taíno/A.D. 1000–1500
	DOMINICAN REPUBLIC				
9	Cueva Roja	CVR	435	86	Preceramic 2500– 2000 B.C.
10	Ostionoids	OST	1645	168	Ostionoids/ A.D. 800–1000
	Andres		*397*	*48*	
	El Soco		*1248*	*120*	
11	La Caleta	LCL	1719	263	Chicoids/ A.D. 1000–1200
12	Juan Dolio	JDL	1692	114	Chicoids/ A.D. 200–1400

N. of Site	Site	Initial	N. Teeth	N. Individuals	Culture/Chronology
	PUERTO RICO				
13	Saladoids	SAL	415	39	Saladoids/250 B.C.–A.D. 0
	Barrio Canas Ponce		*17*	*1*	
	Barrio Coto		*233*	*25*	
	Barrio Monserrate		*165*	*13*	
	U.S. VIRGIN ISLAND				
14	Saladoids-Chican	VIR	477	34	Saladoids-Chican/A.D. 650–1500
	Salt River		*36*	*2*	
	Tutu Site		*441*	*32*	
	GUADALOUPE				
15	Anse a la Gourde	ANS	529	34	Troumassoid/A.D. 450–1400
	VENEZUELA				
16	Venezuela	VEN	748	75	A.D. 200–800
	La Cabrera		*433*	*32*	
	La Marta		*315*	*43*	

erence plaques (Scott and Turner 1997; Turner et al. 1991). They have been chosen among those present in all the samples at the same times with a number of observations not inferior to at least ten. Each trait was elaborated by considering only the tooth (left or right) in which its expression was higher. This procedure presumes that the greater value represents its highest genotypic expression (Turner et al. 1991; Scott and Turner 1997). Individual traits scored along the rank-scales of expression were then dichotomized into presence/absence. The frequency of traits, number of observations and the dichotomic breaking points, recorded according to Turner and colleagues (1991), are listed in Tables 14.2a (maxilla) and 14.2b (mandible). Previous studies indicate that very few significant differences occur between sexes (Coppa et al. 1998; Hanihara 1992; G. Scott 1973; Turner et al. 1991). However, many workers have found differences in the expression of Carabelli's trait (Scott et al. 1983; Townsend and Brown 1981), and in the distal accessory ridge of the upper and lower canine (G. Scott 1977; Scott et al. 1983). The absence of sexual dimorphism in dental morphology is supported by this study. Fisher's Exact Test (Guo and Thompson 1992) was applied to the set of traits between sexes for

Table 14.2a. Frequencies of Traits Used and Dichotomic Breaking Points for the Maxillary Dentition.

	Dichotomy		TIC	RGR	HIG	FRC	CIB
I2 Shoveling	3–7/0–7	%	70,6	100,0	66,7	84,1	57,1
		N	17	5	48	69	7
I1 Double Shoveling	2–6/0–6	%	52,9	77,8	88,2	93,2	60,0
		N	17	9	51	59	5
I2 Double Shoveling	2–6/0–6	%	50,0	100,0	55,8	68,2	50,0
		N	14	5	43	66	6
I2 Interr. Groove	1/0–1	%	61,5	60,0	48,9	51,6	60,0
		N	13	5	45	64	5
C Mesial Ridge	2–5/0–5	%	0,0	0,0	0,0	1,1	0,0
		N	14	6	47	89	8
M1 Metacone	4–5/0–5	%	94,1	100,0	89,3	94,7	100,0
		N	51	19	84	170	25
M2 Metacone	3.5–5/0–5	%	100,0	100,0	100,0	100,0	94,1
		N	48	17	74	119	17
M3 Metacone	3–5/0–5	%	91,7	100,0	100,0	88,0	80,0
		N	36	11	44	50	5
M1 Hypocone	4–5/0–5	%	95,1	86,7	96,0	86,4	88,5
		N	41	15	75	169	26
M1 Cusp 5	1–5/0–5	%	7,1	25,0	30,3	27,2	42,9
		N	14	8	33	103	14
M1 Carabelli's Cusp	2–7/0–7	%	80,0	85,7	59,2	69,2	63,2
		N	15	7	49	143	19
M1 Enamel Extension	2–3/0–3	%	20,0	20,0	50,9	51,1	25,0
		N	30	15	55	131	20
M2 Enamel Extension	2–3/0–3	%	54,2	42,9	74,5	76,3	64,3
		N	24	14	51	93	14
M1 Root Number	3/1–3	%	92,9	77,8	93,3	92,6	80,0
		N	14	9	45	81	10

the adults for which the sex diagnosis was possible. No statistically significant differences (at the 0.05 probability level) between sexes were found. For this reason, frequency data are based on combined observations.

In order to evaluate the phenetic affinities between groups, multivariate analyses were applied on traits' percent values (Principal Component Analysis and Maximum Likelihood Method) (Felsenstein 1973), and on measures of distance (Mean Measure of Divergence and Multidimensional Scaling). By using the method of Maximum Likelihood we obtained a tree whose robustness was tested with by the bootstrap technique (Felsenstein 1985). Bootstrap values are reported only when higher than 50 out of 100 replicates, since these data are morphologic and not ge-

Table 14.2a. *Continued*

CEI	CUD	ECD	CVR	OST	JDL	LCL	SAL	VIR	ANS	VEN
36,7	40,0	50,0	33,3	75,6	57,6	73,2	62,5	53,3	72,7	71,4
30	5	46	12	41	33	41	8	15	22	14
57,1	63,6	19,4	83,3	20,7	29,7	42,3	14,3	40,0	45,0	70,0
28	11	36	6	29	37	26	7	10	20	20
39,3	100,0	38,6	50,0	24,1	38,9	12,9	33,3	28,6	27,3	61,5
28	5	44	12	29	36	31	9	14	22	13
45,0	50,0	23,3	44,4	13,3	33,3	20,0	28,6	57,1	33,3	20,0
20	4	43	9	30	33	25	7	14	21	10
0,0	0,0	9,4	0,0	5,7	3,6	0,0	0,0	0,0	0,0	10,0
34	8	32	10	53	56	53	5	14	14	20
100,0	100,0	100,0	100,0	100,0	98,6	98,8	100,0	100,0	78,9	100,0
82	15	58	21	75	73	81	21	27	19	37
98,6	100,0	98,1	94,1	93,1	98,5	100,0	100,0	100,0	100,0	97,1
74	9	54	34	58	66	63	14	18	17	35
87,9	75,0	100,0	78,3	96,6	96,0	93,3	90,9	100,0	81,8	100,0
58	4	23	23	29	25	30	11	7	11	19
81,9	73,3	83,6	82,4	89,6	92,0	91,4	100,0	95,8	100,0	91,9
83	15	55	17	77	75	81	17	24	17	37
54,5	50,0	11,8	31,2	10,2	8,8	12,5	16,7	28,6	13,3	16,7
66	8	51	16	59	68	56	6	14	15	24
79,2	90,0	56,0	81,2	56,7	61,8	72,6	37,5	60,0	56,2	76,5
72	10	50	16	67	68	73	8	15	16	34
25,5	37,5	9,8	13,3	28,4	25,7	45,3	10,5	22,7	22,2	50,0
51	8	51	15	67	70	75	19	22	18	34
77,6	71,4	51,0	55,6	62,5	55,0	67,3	71,4	43,8	62,5	80,0
49	7	49	27	56	60	55	14	16	16	30
100,0	80,0	87,0	100,0	90,1	92,2	94,0	100,0	88,9	93,8	77,3
13	5	23	20	71	64	50	9	18	16	22

netic (Piazza personal communication). The Multidimensional Scaling was calculated starting from the Mean Measure of Divergence matrix (C. Smith 1977), applying the Freeman and Tukey angular transformation (Freeman and Tukey 1950; Green and Suchey 1976; Sjøvold 1973) to correct for small sample sizes.

Results

Frequencies of the 31 traits for all samples are shown in Table 14.2a (maxilla) and 14.2b (mandible).

Table 14.2b. Frequencies of Traits Used and Dichotomic Breaking Points for the Mandibular Dentition.

	Dichotomy		TIC	RGR	HIG	FRC	CIB
I2 Shoveling	2–3/0–3	%	56,2	80,0	28,3	67,7	31,2
		N.	16	10	53	62	16
C Dist. Acc. Ridge	1–5/0–5	%	21,4	50,0	15,2	49,2	44,4
		N.	14	6	46	65	9
P4 Cusps Number	2–9/0–9	%	58,3	25,0	8,5	22,2	0,0
		N.	12	8	47	72	7
M1 Anterior Fovea	2–4/04	%	20,0	83,3	61,1	68,3	60,0
		N.	5	6	18	41	5
M1 Groove Pattern	Y/Y,X,+	%	92,3	100,0	80,9	86,2	84,6
		N.	13	13	47	109	13
M1 Cusps Number	6/4–6	%	12,5	46,2	40,5	28,6	54,5
		N.	16	13	37	98	11
M2 Cusps Number	4/4–6	%	55,0	42,9	45,2	51,2	53,8
		N.	20	7	42	80	13
M1 Middle Trigonid Crest	1/0–1	%	37,5	44,4	15,0	35,1	0,0
		N.	8	9	40	77	9
M2 Middle Trigonid Crest	1/0–1	%	9,1	16,7	0,0	7,8	12,5
		N.	11	6	32	64	8
M1 Protostylid	2–7/0–7	%	41,7	15,4	36,6	33,0	46,7
		N.	12	13	41	100	15
M3 Protostylid	2–7/0–7	%	77,8	50,0	84,4	87,8	92,3
		N.	18	8	32	41	13
M1 Cusp 5	3–5/0–5	%	100,0	92,3	100,0	97,0	90,9
		N.	16	13	39	101	11
M2 Cusp 6	2–5/0–5	%	5,9	0,0	2,5	14,7	18,2
		N.	17	6	40	75	11
M1 Cusp 7	1–4/0–4	%	5,9	0,0	0,0	6,1	0,0
		N.	17	12	42	115	14
M1 Root Number	3/1–3	%	0,0	0,0	0,0	0,0	0,0
		N.	13	12	45	59	14
M2 Root Number	1/1–3	%	46,7	27,3	51,5	40,6	50,0
		N.	15	11	33	64	10
M3 Root Number	1/1–3	%	63,6	14,3	55,0	61,3	0,0
		N.	11	14	20	31	5

Table 14.2b. *Continued*

CEI	CUD	ECD	CVR	OST	JDL	LCL	SAL	VIR	ANS	VEN
50,0	30,8	59,6	14,3	70,5	31,1	41,3	42,9	40,0	73,9	52,4
50	13	52	14	44	45	46	21	20	23	21
25,8	57,1	35,3	55,0	55,6	48,6	54,5	10,0	71,4	31,2	42,3
62	7	51	20	36	37	55	10	7	16	26
14,5	0,0	43,1	33,3	32,8	47,4	31,2	30,8	64,3	31,8	27,3
62	6	51	9	61	76	93	13	14	22	33
77,3	88,9	47,1	78,6	67,6	52,3	62,2	100,0	77,8	50,0	40,0
44	9	34	14	37	65	74	4	9	6	10
87,5	100,0	69,8	77,8	83,6	67,5	67,0	71,4	46,7	76,9	71,0
72	12	43	18	55	77	91	7	15	13	31
54,4	64,3	14,0	35,7	15,7	24,4	35,7	50,0	21,4	11,1	37,9
68	14	43	14	51	82	84	8	14	9	29
33,3	63,6	60,0	17,6	54,2	70,1	54,8	36,4	66,7	45,5	34,5
42	11	45	17	48	77	84	11	15	11	29
11,8	11,1	47,4	6,2	34,1	17,1	21,9	33,3	25,0	14,3	51,6
51	9	38	16	44	70	73	6	12	7	31
12,9	0,0	28,2	0,0	0,0	0,0	4,9	14,3	0,0	30,0	16,0
31	8	39	16	43	75	82	7	12	10	25
69,1	66,7	31,7	78,9	26,3	16,7	48,9	16,7	62,5	22,2	48,5
68	12	41	19	57	78	92	6	16	9	33
98,3	100,0	75,0	86,7	40,7	39,6	71,1	100,0	83,3	100,0	92,9
58	8	16	15	27	53	45	10	6	8	14
94,6	100,0	97,6	94,1	96,2	95,1	100,0	100,0	100,0	100,0	100,0
74	13	42	17	52	81	85	8	13	9	31
20,0	20,0	4,7	23,5	9,1	4,0	10,8	0,0	8,3	30,0	13,6
35	10	43	17	44	75	74	9	12	10	22
2,6	0,0	15,9	5,6	21,0	11,5	27,6	27,3	20,0	7,7	11,9
76	14	44	18	62	87	98	11	15	13	42
10,0	11,1	3,6	5,3	11,7	7,5	6,8	0,0	10,5	13,3	0,0
10	9	28	19	60	67	74	14	19	15	34
37,5	50,0	23,1	17,4	22,6	26,7	15,0	37,5	20,0	50,0	59,1
16	8	26	23	53	60	60	8	20	14	22
36,8	42,9	30,8	11,8	33,3	19,0	26,3	55,6	25,0	20,0	58,3
19	7	13	17	24	42	38	9	8	10	12

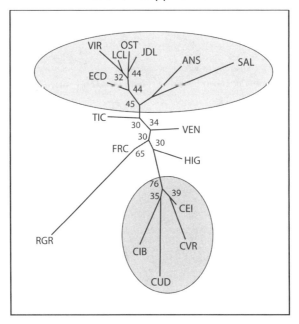

Figure 14.2. Maximum Likelihood tree.

Maximum Likelihood Method (ML)

The ML data elaboration highlights the presence of two main groups (Figure 14.2). In the upper part of the tree, we can observe all the Taíno. This cluster is tied to two branches sporting the Saladoid and Troumassoid samples, though both nodes are represented less than 50 percent of the time in the bootstrap. In the lower part of the tree, the Ciboney from Cuba and Cueva Roja cluster together with a node that appears in 76 percent of the iterations.

The Florida samples are distributed in between the two main groups without forming a clearly defined group by themselves. A significant bootstrap node (65 percent) connects Fort Center and Republic Grooves from Florida. Interestingly, the Venezuela group is in between the Florida ones.

Principal Component Analysis (PCA)

Figure 14.3 shows the PCA scatter plot, with the first two components explaining the 40.33 percent of all the variance (Table 14.3). The scatter plot clearly shows two distinct clusters. The first one, on the left part of the plot, gathers together the Taíno groups along with the Saladoid and Troumassoid samples. The second cluster, on the right side, links up all the Ciboney groups, both the recent ones

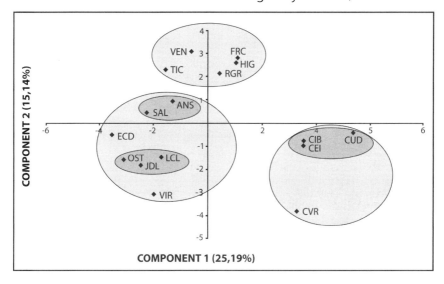

Figure 14.3. Scatter plot of the Principal Component Analysis showing the distribution according to the first and second components.

from Cuba and the more ancient one of Cueva Roja in the Dominican Republic. A third grouping gathers together the Florida samples along with the ones from Venezuela.

Within the first two major clusters, we can spot some tendency to form internal grouping. More specifically, in the Taíno cluster the samples from the Dominican Republic seem to separate from the Saladoid and Troumassoid samples. As far as the Ciboney are concerned, the three recent groups from Cuba set aside from Cueva Roja, marking the chronological gap between them.

Factor loadings are listed in Table 14.3. In the upper dentition, only M1 cusp 5 shows positive values above 0.7. Along the first component, this trait discriminates the Ciboney (Cuban samples 40–50 percent, Cueva Roja 31.2 percent) while the Taíno present lower frequencies (10–15 percent). The Saladoid and Troumassoid samples fall within the same range of variability as the Taíno, while the groups from the Virgin Islands are set at the 28.6 percent. The samples from Florida do not match any specific group, due to their variability between 8.1 percent and 30.3 percent.

Also in the mandibular dentition one trait (M1 cusps number) discriminates the samples with a positive value higher than 0.7. As for the maxilla, its frequency is higher in the sample of Cuban Ciboney (55–65 percent), and decreases in all the other island groups including the preceramic sample from Cueva Roja (14.0–35.7 percent). The Floridians again present a large variability (12.5–42.9 percent). Sig-

Table 14.3. Factor Loading for the Principal Component Analysis.

Trait	Contribution of the Components			
	Component 1		Component 2	
I^2 Shoveling	−0,4125		0,6190	
I^1 Double Shoveling	0,6716		0,4074	
I^2 Double Shoveling	0,5911		0,4690	
I^2 Interr. Groove	0,5371		0,1458	
C' Mesial Ridge	−0,4513		0,1181	
M^1 Metacone	0,1054		−0,3913	
M^2 Metacone	−0,1147		0,4338	
M^3 Metacone	−0,6993		0,2298	
M^1 Hypocone	−0,6429		0,2164	
M^1 Cusp 5	**0,8945**	*	−0,1279	
M^1 Carabelli's Cusp	0,6107		0,0933	
M^1 Enamel Extension	0,2191		0,4570	
M^2 Enamel Extension	0,3624		0,3878	
M^1 Root Number	−0,1473		−0,3175	
I_2 Shoveling	−0,4167		0,4741	
C, Dist. Acc. Ridge	0,0926		−0,5194	
P_4 Cusps Number	**−0,7455**	*	−0,2633	
M_1 Anterior Fovea	0,3651		−0,3287	
M_1 Groove Pattern	0,5653		0,4521	
M_1 Cusps Number	**0,7559**	*	0,0473	
M_2 Cusps Number	−0,3196		−0,1007	
M_1 Middle Trigonid Crest	−0,6049		0,4849	
M_2 Middle Trigonid Crest	−0,2401		0,3652	
M_1 Protostylid	0,6234		−0,4248	
M^3 Protostylid	0,4929		0,1800	
M_1 Cusp 5	−0,3424		0,2618	
M_2 Cusp 6	0,5339		−0,2151	
M_1 Cusp 7	**−0,7299**	*	−0,3441	
M_1 Root Number	−0,0096		−0,5808	
M_2 Root Number	0,3650		**0,7151**	*
M^3 Root Number	−0,1227		0,6367	
Percent of variance explained by the components	25,19		15,14	
Total percent of variance explained by the first two components		40,33		

Values in bold report correlation coefficients higher than 0.7.

nificant negative, discriminating values characterize the second premolar's cusp number and cusp 7 in the first molar. The Ciboney from Cuba show low values, as low as 0.0 percent in Cueva del Perico and the pooled Ciboney. In turn, frequencies are higher in the Taíno, the Saladoid, the Troumassoid samples, and those from Venezuela. The frequency of both traits ranges between 30 and 50 percent and peaks up to 64.3 percent in the U.S. Virgin Islands. Large variability can be found in the expression of the premolar's trait in the groups from Florida (8.5–58.3 percent), and reduced expression in the cusp 7.

The mandibular M2 root number is the only trait that discriminates the second component. Its frequencies are in the 40 to 50 percent range for the Cuban Ciboney, while the Taíno vary between 15 and 25 percent, with Cueva Roja (17.4 percent) falling within the latter. Frequencies between 40 and 60 percent characterize the Saladoid, Troumassoid, and Venezuelan samples, while the Floridians range between 30 and 50 percent.

Mean Measure of Divergence (MMD)

The MMD matrix is shown in Table 14.4. The major distances (> 0.13) always separate the Taíno from both the Floridians and all the Ciboney. At intragroup level, the Taíno from Cuba and the Dominican Republic present low but significant values, and nonsignificant values in the comparison with the samples from the U.S. Virgin Islands. It must be underscored, anyway, that the latter shows low, nonsignificant values also with Tick Island, Cueva Roja, and the pooled Ciboney. All the Ciboney groups show low, nonsignificant distances among them, regardless of geography and chronology. The Floridians bestow significant MMD values, with the exception of the two Archaic Age samples. The Saladoids do not diverge much from the groups of the U.S. Virgin Islands, Troumassoids, and Venezuela, and neither from the Ciboney's Cueva el Infierno. The Troumassoid sample reveals low values with Venezuela, Saladoids, and the U.S. Virgin Islands, but also with Tick Island and the pooled Ciboney. Last, Venezuela, shows nonsignificant distances with some of the Florida and Ciboney groups, along with it is those geographically close to them.

Multidimensional Scaling (MDS)

The MDS applied to the MMD matrix (Table 14.4) produces fairly similar results to those generated by the PCA analysis (Figure 14.2) and the ML tree (Figure 14.3). The scatter plot of the first and second dimensions (Figure 14.4) indicates that the Cuban groups cluster with Cueva Roja in the upper left quadrant. A second group on the right is formed by the Taíno. A third group, composed of the Saladoid and Troumassoid sample, is placed in between the Taíno. The other groups from Florida gather on the lower left part of the plot. Venezuela gets closer to the other groups from Florida as in the previous analysis.

Table 14.4. Mean Measure of Divergence Matrix.

		TIC	RGR	HIG	FRC	CIB	CEI
Tich-Island-Forida USA	TIC	0	0,0383	0,0193	0,0172	0,0352	0,0201
Republic Groves-Florida USA	RGR	0,0747	0	0,0298	0,0279	0,0458	0,0307
Highland Beach-Florida USA	HIG	**0,0532**	**0,1214**	0	0,0084	0,0267	0,0114
Fort Center-Florida USA	FRC	**0,0463**	**0,0570**	**0,0422**	0	0,0248	0,0096
Ciboney-Cuba	CIB	**0,0746**	0,0587	**0,0569**	**0,0836**	0	0,0275
Cueva el Infernio-Cuba	CEI	**0,1165**	**0,1616**	**0,0890**	**0,1119**	–0,0171	0
Cueva del Perico-Cuba	CUD	**0,1173**	0,0421	**0,0723**	**0,0692**	–0,0673	0,0002
Chorro de Maíta-Cuba	ECD	**0,0423**	**0,1239**	**0,1873**	**0,1816**	**0,1751**	**0,1893**
Cueva Roja-Dominican Republic	CVR	**0,1249**	**0,1104**	**0,1128**	**0,1167**	–0,0157	0,0203
Ostionoids-Dominican Republic	OST	**0,0728**	**0,1071**	**0,1761**	**0,1378**	**0,1475**	**0,1961**
Juan Dolio-Dominican Republic	JDL	**0,0535**	**0,1468**	**0,1291**	**0,1541**	**0,1079**	**0,1889**
La Caleta-Dominican Republic	LCL	**0,0658**	**0,1476**	**0,1123**	**0,1125**	**0,0902**	**0,1175**
Saladoids-Puerto Rico	SAL	**0,0730**	**0,1212**	**0,0917**	**0,1005**	**0,0674**	0,0389
Virgin Islands-USA	VIR	0,0215	**0,1195**	**0,1079**	**0,1092**	0,0734	**0,1223**
Anse à la Gourde-Guadeloupe	ANS	0,0076	**0,0854**	**0,0998**	**0,0583**	0,0202	**0,0718**
Venezuela	VEN	0,0024	0,0674	**0,0568**	0,0334	0,0448	**0,0808**

* MMD values are listed in the lower left triangle (bold numbers mark significant distances); the upper right triangle reports the standard deviations.

Discussion and Conclusions

It is worthwhile to underscore that all different statistical methods (ML, PCA, MMD, and MDS) produced consistent outcomes. The results of the analysis on the biological affinity among the samples that inhabited the circum-Caribbean area can be summarized into seven main points:

1. The phenetically different groups are also culturally different and vice versa. This result suggests that no substantial admixture between groups of different cultures occurred.
2. Results from the previous analyses, which differentiate between Taíno and

Table 14.4. *Continued*

CUD	ECD	CVR	OST	JDL	LCL	SAL	VIR	ANS	VEN
0,0392	0,0199	0,0277	0,0189	0,0178	0,0179	0,0360	0,0301	0,0306	0,0241
0,0503	0,0306	0,0385	0,0297	0,0287	0,0288	0,0463	0,0409	0,0408	0,0350
0,0310	0,0115	0,0191	0,0102	0,0091	0,0092	0,0274	0,0221	0,0222	0,0155
0,0292	0,0096	0,0173	0,0083	0,0072	0,0074	0,0252	0,0202	0,0202	0,0137
0,0471	0,0275	0,0354	0,0266	0,0256	0,0257	0,0432	0,0379	0,0376	0,0319
0,0321	0,0126	0,0200	0,0112	0,0103	0,0105	0,0279	0,0224	0,0226	0,0164
0	0,0321	0,0395	0,0310	0,0301	0,0302	0,0472	0,0423	0,0419	0,0362
0,2360	0	0,0200	0,0113	0,0102	0,0103	0,0281	0,0232	0,0231	0,0166
0,0231	**0,1902**	0	0,0191	0,0181	0,0182	0,0357	0,0304	0,0303	0,0243
0,2118	0,0610	**0,1482**	0	0,0091	0,0092	0,0270	0,0220	0,0219	0,0155
0,1935	0,0578	**0,1358**	0,0285	0	0,0083	0,0259	0,0208	0,0207	0,0144
0,1464	0,0798	**0,0836**	0,0278	0,0342	0	0,026	0,0209	0,0208	0,0146
0,1158	0,0740	**0,0894**	**0,0683**	**0,0886**	0,0436	0	0,0384	0,0388	0,0322
0,1063	0,0235	**0,0356**	0,0345	0,0103	−0,0077	0,0671	0	0,0337	0,0270
0,1451	0,0602	**0,0656**	0,0557	**0,0944**	0,0494	−0,0114	0,0557	0	0,0269
0,0534	**0,0992**	**0,1097**	**0,1012**	**0,1273**	**0,0680**	0,0369	**0,0918**	0,0356	0

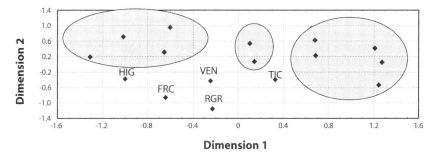

Figure 14.4. Multidimensional Scaling (Stress: 0.153).

Ciboney, are substantially confirmed by the fact that the Taíno group from Cuba differs from its coeval Ciboney samples from the most western side of the same island, which suggests that they belong to different migratory flows.

3. Cueva Roja, a more archaic Dominican but non-Taíno sample, shows strong affinities with the more recent Cuban Ciboney. This strong association indeed indicates that the Ciboney, confined to the far western side of Cuba, might have been the last representatives of a culture that was more widely spread in the Greater Antilles at the times before the expansion of the Taíno culture during the Late Ceramic period. The more the Taíno migrated through the Greater Antilles, the more the Ciboney were slowly confined to the western part of the most western island in the Caribbean Sea, in a cul-de-sac fashion.

4. The U.S. Virgin Islands (Saladoid-Chican), Guadeloupe (Troumassoid), and to some extent also Puerto Rico (Saladoid) samples show a good level of affinity with the Taíno, which suggests that all these samples belong to the same migratory wave. The present data on dental morphological traits do not seem to separate the sample from the northern part of the Lesser Antilles.

5. Florida and Venezuela do not show a regular association with any group. The unexpected result of the collections from Venezuela, in contrast with the archaeological data, might be due to admixture and/or drift processes, which could have changed the biological structure after the first settlement of the Caribbean islands. This might have masked the original affinity between the continental and the islands populations. The Florida samples do not show any clear affinity with the island groups. This is consistent with the notion that the populations from the northern continental areas might not have played a role in the peopling of the Caribbean Islands, as the archaeological models state, and is in contrast with the hypothesis by Lovén (1935) of an involvement of populations from Florida in the earliest migrations. Therefore, in this case the biological data are consistent with the cultural information sustaining the absence of genetic exchanges between the populations from Florida and those from the Caribbean islands.

6. On the base of the present data set, very little can be inferred on the so-called Island Carib and on their relationships with the other Caribbean populations.

7. The present results and interpretation do not solve (and do not intend to) the issue of labeling "Ciboney" the aceramic groups; nonetheless, they open a window on the chronological and geographic biological diversity in the Caribbean until the European conquest.

In conclusion, the morphological dental traits were able to detect two major migrations in the Caribbean area before the conquest. A more ancient one introduced groups of hunter-gatherers and a more recent one the agriculturalists.

The present anthropological data do not seem to support the hypothesis that different migrations brought the agriculturalists into the area, since the ancient Saladoids from Puerto Rico do not substantially differentiate from the more recent Ostionoids, Chicoids, and Troumassoids respectively from the Greater and the Lesser Antilles.

We can only infer that the second migration likely headed to the northwest from the southeast, while not much can be said on the first migration. Unfortunately, the lack of archaic dental samples from Belize and the Yucatán peninsula hampers the possibility to test the Mesoamerican hypothesis of an early migration from this part of the continent.

Also, the dental evidence clearly reveals a difference between those groups that Lovén (1935) labeled "Guanahatabey" and the Taíno. This is in disagreement with the DNA evidence, which indicates no substantial difference between the Taíno and the Ciboney (Lalueza-Fox et al. 2003). On the contrary, the similarity between the Guanatahabey and the pre-Taíno samples from the Dominican Republic (Cueva Roja) is suggestive of the bond that the groups who settled the western part of Cuba in the centuries immediately before the conquest had with the early hunter-gatherers. Obviously, this kind of data and the fact that they are all precontact samples does not help assess whether these Guanahatabey groups survived until the conquest (Keegan 1992).

The samples from both Florida and Venezuela are apparently not related to the Caribbean groups. Nonetheless, while the Floridians consist of distinctive, well-represented samples from different chronological periods, those from Venezuela are reduced in size and of little significance, which implies caution in drawing conclusions. It is necessary to expand our anthropological knowledge on the samples from Venezuela, as well as of the more ancient ones from Central America from one side, and of the samples from the Lesser Antilles from the other side in order to be able to fully understand the dynamics, directionality, and modality of the migratory waves from the areas.

Acknowledgments

The present research has been granted by MIUR COFIN and the Italian Ministry of External Affairs.

15

Tracing Human Mobility with $^{87}Sr/^{86}Sr$ at Anse à la Gourde, Guadeloupe

Mathijs A. Booden, Raphaël G. A. M. Panhuysen, Menno L. P. Hoogland, Hylke N. de Jong, Gareth R. Davies, and Corinne L. Hofman

Introduction

The presence of nonlocal pottery, lithic material, shell, and bone at Anse à la Gourde suggests the existence of interaction networks in the Lesser Antilles in which raw materials and exotic items circulated (Hofman et al. 2001; Hoogland and Hofman in press; Knippenberg 2006).

In this study we assess the applicability of strontium isotope ratios in teeth to distinguish nonlocal burials from local burials in order to determine the extent of residential mobility of the buried population at the site. Strontium isotope ratios are increasingly successfully used to make a distinction between local and nonlocal burials recovered from archaeological sites (e.g., Bentley et al. 2004; Price et al. 2002; Wright 2005). Generally, this technique is applied in areas with variable strontium ratios.

The site of Anse à la Gourde is located in the Lesser Antilles in the eastern part of the island of Guadeloupe (Figure 15.1). The Lesser Antilles island arc, to which Guadeloupe belongs, is theoretically a suitable area for this type of provenance research since large variations in geochemistry occur along the arc (e.g., Macdonald et al. 2000; Van Soest 2000). From Marie-Galante and Guadeloupe northward the Lesser Antilles separate into an outer arc (Limestone Caribbees) and an inner arc (Volcanic Caribbees). As a consequence the soil on different islands is characterized by different geochemical and isotopic compositions. It is expected that this variation will be reflected in the composition of the remains (bone and enamel) of the humans who collected a significant proportion of their food from these soils.

Focus will be laid on the analysis of dental enamel samples. Tooth enamel is not altered biologically after it is formed during childhood. The densely packed crystal

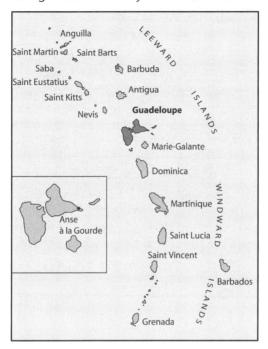

Figure 15.1. Map of the Antilles and the position of
Anse à la Gourde on Guadeloupe.

structure of apatite in tooth enamel protects the biogenic strontium isotope signature from outside diagenetic influences, such as microbial attack and dissolution
by groundwater (Budd et al. 2000). Hence, enamel preserves the isotope signature
of an individual's diet during childhood. Bone is constantly remodeled during life
and will tend to equilibrate with the dietary strontium consumed in vivo. Moreover, the more porous crystal structure of bone makes it more vulnerable to postmortem diagenetic alteration (Budd et al. 2000).

In order to distinguish locals from nonlocals, the local strontium signature
was determined and the distribution of strontium isotope ratios in the population were analyzed. The local strontium signature was determined by means of the
analysis of enamel of rice rats and soil samples from the burial pits. In addition, a
simple statistical procedure as used by Wright was applied to analyze the distribution of human enamel isotope ratios. Wright (2005) suggests that the local population in a data set is best defined as the largest possible subset of samples that is
normally distributed, that is, is symmetrical around the mean and contains 95 percent of cases within two standard deviations of the mean. We attempted to determine this subset by iteratively excluding outliers from the data set, defined based

on a 95 percent confidence interval, until no further statistical outliers are identified and the skewness of the subset is approximately 0.

Geology

The island of Guadeloupe consists of two sister islands: the volcanic Basse-Terre to the west and the limestone-dominated island of Grand-Terre to the east. Anse à la Gourde is located on the extreme eastern end of the latter, Pointe Chateaux (Figure 15.1). Maury and colleagues (1990) provide an overview of the geology of Guadeloupe and La Désirade. The surface of Grand-Terre consists entirely of Pliocene and Quaternary limestone (Andreieff and Cottez 1976). A reef platform was uplifted during the Pleistocene, starting in the southwest, and later followed by the northern and eastern parts. Basse-Terre has been the locus of active volcanism for at least 4 million years. Volcanic activity has shifted over time in a southerly direction and is currently concentrated in the Soufrière volcano.

Anse à la Gourde is located directly on the shoreline of the northern coast of Pointe Chateaux. It is exposed to continuous northeastern trade winds and strong surf, causing abundant sea spray that will add marine strontium to the local soils. The Late Ceramic occupation phase of the site (A.D. 1000–1350) coincides with a wetter phase in climate and a higher frequency of storm events (Beets et al. 2006).

No direct data are available on the isotope composition of the local bedrock. However, the coral limestone cap of Grand-Terre is known to be of Pliocene to Quaternary age (Andreieff and Cottez 1976). This means the $^{87}Sr/^{86}Sr$ of the carbonate bedrock cannot be lower than ~0.7090 as this is the lowest ratio known for seawater during these periods (Hess et al. 1986). In effect, the carbonate bedrock will probably have an oceanic $^{87}Sr/^{86}Sr$.

Archaeological Context

The site of Anse à la Gourde was occupied between cal A.D. 450 to 1350 based on radiocarbon dates and the occurrence of ceramics of the late Cedrosan Saladoid, Mamoran, and/or Troumassan Troumassoid and Suazan Troumassoid subseries. Between cal A.D. 1000 and 1250 Anse à la Gourde was the most densely occupied. The settlement of that time consists of a habitation area surrounded by a refuse midden. A total of 2,400 features have been encountered there belonging to houses and other domestic structures, hearths, refuse pits, and 83 burials containing the human remains of 93 individuals (Hofman et al. 2001). Burials mainly occur in clusters within the habitation area, each comprising 3 to 10 burials. The location of these clusters coincides with that part of the habitation area where the majority of the postholes are situated. The close association of the burials with postholes provides an indication that the burials were situated in the houses (Hofman et al. 2001). The buried population is composed predominantly of adult individuals with 11 infants (12 percent of the population) under the age of 12. The discrepancy between the number of children and adults cannot be attributed to the state of conservation of the skeletons because child bones have been conserved on the site in the different types of soil and context. It is suggested that children belong to another category of social persons and received a different mortuary treatment than the adults. At this point, sex determination revealed 36 female and 32 male individuals.

Sources of Strontium

Strontium taken up in the human body is derived, through the consumption of food and water, from the surrounding environment. After ingestion, strontium is incorporated into the human body as a substitute for calcium. Three major reservoirs of strontium are present at Anse à la Gourde: the local soil, the carbonate bedrock, and the Atlantic Ocean.

Oceanic water has globally uniform [87]Sr:[86]Sr ratio of 0.709175 (EN-1 standard for seawater (Howarth and McArthur 1997). Strontium from oceanic water can enter the human body through the consumption of seafood, such as fish or mollusks, and through sea salt adhering to the seafood. In addition, oceanic strontium is introduced into the environment by rainwater (e.g., Kennedy et al. 1998).

Strontium from the soil or the carbonate bedrock enters the body in vivo in two ways: through the consumption of groundwater and through the consumption of plants (and products and animals derived from them) growing on the local soil. Strontium from both water and food reflects the isotopic signature of the soil and/or the underlying carbonate rock of Grand-Terre. Because the site is situated in close vicinity to the sea it is most likely that food and water at Anse à la Gourde are enriched with oceanic strontium.

Material

The sampled material consists of human dental elements ($n = 50$), rice rat (*Oryzomys* sp.) dental elements ($n = 4$), and soil samples from the site of Anse à la Gourde ($n = 4$). One tooth is collected per individual, preferably a premolar to ensure a comparable age of formation for each sample. A total of 46 permanent teeth were sampled, comprising 4 central incisors, 1 lateral incisor, 17 first premolars, and 24 second premolars. The 4 deciduous teeth included in the study consist of 1 incisor, 1 canine, and 2 molars. The selected teeth represent a biological age between birth and 7 years. A low degree of dental wear and a good state of preservation of the enamel were prerequisites for the selection of teeth. The state of preservation was determined macroscopically. The enamel crowns of the teeth used in this study were free from visible cracks, lustrous, and either white or covered by only a thin and easily removed outer layer of dull, yellowed enamel, with white enamel underneath. Four enamel samples from rice rats were included in the study to determine the local isotope signature. Rice rat enamel was sampled from mandibles of four rice rats, collected from midden deposits at Anse à la Gourde that were contemporary with the human burials. Soil samples of at least 500 g have been collected from the fill of the graves.

Methods

Enamel Samples

Teeth were washed in water to remove dust and residual soil. Tooth enamel was sampled using a steel ball-shaped microdrill. The outer layer of enamel and any adhering dirt was first removed using the drill until only white enamel was visible. The drill was then cleaned in 1N HCl and Milli-Q water and used to drill a hole of ca. 1 mm in diameter and up to ca. 1 mm depth. The teeth were usually sampled on the buccal or lingual side of the enamel crown, but occasionally on the occlusal surface if it was smooth. Approximately 1 mg of enamel was gathered per tooth. The enamel powder was collected in glass sample containers that had been precleaned with 6N HCl and Milli-Q water. Rice rat teeth were halved, fixed in resin, and drilled with a diamond-tipped drill. Again ca. 1 mg of enamel was collected.

Soil Samples

The soil samples were oven dried, crushed in a jaw crusher, and homogenized. An aliquot (ca. 10 percent wt) of each was taken and powdered in an agate planetary ball mill. Five g of this powder is used to produce a tablet for X-ray fluorescence (XRF) measurement, which determines, among others, the elemental abundance of strontium. Based on these data, approximately 2 g of powdered sample was separated to be used for Sr-Nd-Pb isotope analysis. In a clean room this aliquot was transferred to an acid-cleaned Teflon beaker and precisely weighed. The sample was then treated with 6 ml 40 percent distilled HF and 1 ml concentrated distilled HNo_3 for two days for destruction of silicate bonds, after which it was dried down. The sample was then dissolved in ~25 ml 6N HCl to produce a stock solution from which an aliquot is separated containing approximately 200 ng strontium, calculated based on XRF data. This aliquot was dried, and 2–3 drops of concentrated HNo_3 were then added and dried, twice.

Strontium Separation

Strontium separation was performed in a clean room under class 100 air. The enamel was suspended in Milli-Q water, transferred to an acid-cleaned Teflon beaker, dried down, and dissolved in 1N HCl, then dried down again. The sample was then dissolved in 2 to 3 drops of concentrated HN03 and dried down. This step was repeated. The residue was dissolved in 0.5 ml 3N HN03, and this solution was centrifuged for 4 minutes at 12,000 rpm to remove any possible nonsoluble constituents (none were visible in any of the samples). The upper 90 percent of the solution was then transferred to a Strontium Spec resin chromatography column for strontium extraction, according to standard procedures (Heumann and Davies 2002). Strontium isotope ratios were determined on the FinniganMat 262 RPQ Plus thermal ionization mass spectrometer at the Free University Amsterdam. Statistical analysis of the collected data was done using SPSS 12.0.

Measurement Accuracy

Blanks

Laboratory blanks yielded 80 to 500 pg of strontium. The higher value is typical for the samples measured at the end of 2005 and is due to the use of a batch of Strontium Spec of substandard quality. The blank strontium is derived from the Strontium Spec resin used in column extraction and to a lesser extent from laboratory chemicals. It has an $^{87}Sr/^{86}Sr$ of ~0.7075. On a 200 ng sample this amounts to 0.25 percent of the total strontium present. The presence of this contaminating strontium decreases the accuracy of our measurements on typical ($^{87}Sr/^{86}Sr$ = 0.7091) samples by 0.001 percent (one unit in the fifth decimal place). This error is approximately equal to the analytical error and is therefore negligible compared to the natural variation in $^{87}Sr/^{86}Sr$, so no blank correction has been applied.

Standards

NBS 987 is used to assess measurement accuracy. Standard analyses over 2003 yielded mean $^{87}Sr/^{86}Sr$ of 0.710245 ± 8 ($n = 7$), whereas analyses over 2005 yielded mean $^{87}Sr/^{86}Sr$ of 0.710241 ± 4 ($n = 8$). The means are equal within error to the long-term mean of 0.710243 ± 9 ($n > 200$) so no correction has been applied to samples measured during different analytical periods.

Results

The mean strontium isotope ratios for the samples are presented in Table 15.1, and the individual results for the human and rice rat enamel samples are listed in Table 15.2. The mean $^{87}Sr/^{86}Sr$ of human enamel is 0.708989 and is lower than the mean found for the soil and rice rats. The mean values found for the human enamel samples are similar for all types of dentition. There is, for example, no significant difference between strontium isotope ratios in permanent incisors and premolars (ANOVA, $f = 0.132$, $n = 49$, $p = 0.88$).

Two well-preserved teeth have been sampled in multiple spots to determine

Table 15.1. Mean Value for Strontium Ratios of the Four Sample Categories.

	Number of samples	mean $^{87}Sr/^{86}Sr$	SD
Rice rats	4	0.709173	0.000038
Soil	4	0.709156	0.000030
All individuals	50	0.708989	0.000359
Local individuals	36	0.709137	0.000051

the variation in strontium isotope ratios in a single enamel crown. The spread in strontium ratios within the multiple sampled teeth is considerably smaller (nearly two orders of magnitude in the case of these extreme samples) than the spread in isotopic ratios between the local and nonlocal samples, and approximately half that of the standard deviation of the local group. We conclude that isotopic composition does not vary significantly within well-preserved single teeth.

Statistical Analysis

The subset of possible local individuals was distinguished from the nonlocal individuals by iteratively excluding outliers from the data set, until no further outliers are identified. Outliers were defined as values outside the 95 percent confidence interval. For the whole series the enamel strontium isotope ratios show a distribution (Figure 15.2) that is skewed to higher ratios (-2.63) and is leptokurtic (7.77). Two successive iterations and the exclusion of 14 outliers were sufficient to reduce the data set to an approximately normal distribution ($n = 36$, skewness -0.51 with a standard error of skewness of 0.39, kurtosis -0.18, mean and median coincide) (Figure 15.3). The local population is defined as having a mean $^{87}Sr{:}^{86}Sr$ ratio of 0.70914 and standard deviation of 0.00005 (five times higher than the analytical reproducibility). Samples with a strontium ratio between 0.70903 and 0.70924 are defined as local.

Discussion

$^{87}Sr/^{86}Sr$ Provenance

In the enamel samples a relatively homogenous group, with normally distributed strontium isotope ratios, was recognized. The mean strontium ratio of this homogenous group was in agreement with the local strontium signature determined from soil and rice rat enamel samples. Thus the homogenous group was considered to represent the local population. The samples of 14 individuals have been categorized as nonlocal because of strontium ratios outside the range of a normal distribution. These 14 individuals represent the minimum number of nonlocal individuals in the sample. As is visible in the distribution of strontium ratios in

Table 15.2. Strontium Ratios of Human Teeth ($n = 50$), Rice Rat Molars ($n = 4$), and Soil Samples ($n = 4$).

Feature	Label	^{87}Sr:^{86}Sr	2 SD
F0050	Local human	0.709171	0.000008
F0089	Local human	0.709161	0.000007
F0108	Local human	0.709172	0.000015
F0139	Local human	0.709034	0.000009
F0159	Local human	0.709146	0.000009
F0171	Nonlocal human	0.708636	0.000020
F0196	Local human	0.709038	0.000009
F0202	Local human	0.709127	0.000012
F0206	Local human	0.709127	0.000009
F0207	Local human	0.709116	0.000013
F0212	Local human	0.709083	0.000010
F0241	Local human	0.709058	0.000008
F0253	Local human	0.709162	0.000015
F0288	Nonlocal human	0.708646	0.000008
F0292	Nonlocal human	0.708755	0.000010
F0304	Local human	0.709122	0.000040
F0307	Local human	0.709165	0.000008
F0311	Nonlocal human	0.708849	0.000014
F0332	Nonlocal human	0.708278	0.000009
F0342	Local human	0.709031	0.000007
F0349C	Nonlocal human	0.708590	0.000009
F0350	Local human	0.709182	0.000010
F0377	Local human	0.709071	0.000027
F0378	Nonlocal human	0.707490	0.000009
F0430	Nonlocal human	0.708794	0.000009
F0447	Local human	0.709090	0.000011
F0450	Nonlocal human	0.708690	0.000009
F0451	Local human	0.709113	0.000008
F0452	Local human	0.709182	0.000006
F0454	Local human	0.709164	0.000009
F0706	Local human	0.709168	0.000018
F0726	Local human	0.709228	0.000013
F0953	Local human	0.709162	0.000012
F1203	Local human	0.709131	0.000012
F1226	Local human	0.709068	0.000009
F1413	Local human	0.709193	0.000018
F1496	Local human	0.709158	0.000007
F1651	Local human	0.709168	0.000006
F1944	Nonlocal human	0.709287	0.000010
F1945	Local human	0.709166	0.000007
F1947	Local human	0.709237	0.000013
F1948	Nonlocal human	0.708895	0.000009
F2005	Nonlocal human	0.708475	0.000012
F2107	Local human	0.709149	0.000008

Continued on the next page

Table 15.2. *Continued*

Feature	Label	^{87}Sr:^{86}Sr	2 SD
F2211	Nonlocal human	0.709412	0.000014
F2212	Local human	0.709100	0.000008
F2214	Local human	0.709156	0.000012
F2215	Nonlocal human	0.707747	0.000007
F2216	Local human	0.709165	0.000006
F2217	Local human	0.709168	0.000005
k617	Rat	0.709205	0.000011
k619	Rat	0.709207	0.000007
k623	Rat	0.709132	0.000009
k628	Rat	0.709149	0.000013
F1651	Soil	0.709192	0.000012
F430	Soil	0.709119	0.000017
F196	Soil	0.709150	0.000027
F454	Soil	0.709163	0.000014

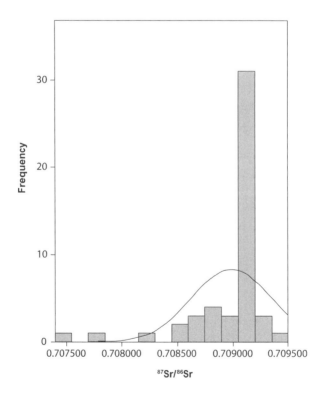

Figure 15.2. Distribution of all strontium ratios in all human enamel samples ($n = 50$).

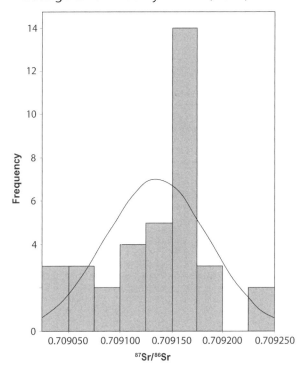

Figure 15.3. Distribution of strontium ratios of those human enamel samples that fall within the range of a normal distribution ($n = 36$).

Figure 15.4 there are individuals with strontium ratios at the extremes of the distribution that may also be of nonlocal origin.

How Local Were the "Locals"?

It is most probable that the majority of individuals with a local strontium ratio had been living on or near the site of Anse à la Gourde in their youth. We cannot be certain whether this is the case for all individuals categorized as locals. The local group has a mean ^{87}Sr/^{86}Sr (0.70914) similar to that of present-day seawater (Howarth and McArthur 1997). Also, the local soil samples and the enamel from rice rat dentition have mean ratios similar to the seawater value. This supports the view that all food and water sources of this coastal settlement had strontium isotope ratios close to the seawater value. However, similar geochemical and dietary conditions are likely to have existed in other coastal settlements on the limestone bedrock of Grand-Terre. Therefore, populations with a comparable subsistence living on limestone islands may have had equal strontium isotope ratios.

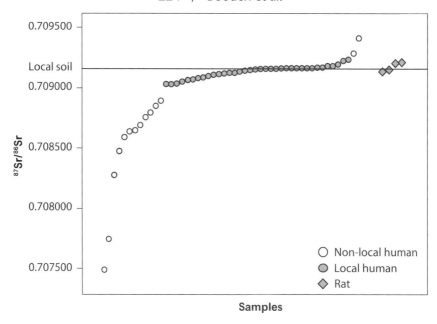

Figure 15.4. Sr isotopic ratios for human enamel and rice rat enamel samples. Samples are sorted in order of increasing $^{87}Sr/^{86}Sr$ within each group. The horizontal bar represents the mean strontium ratio found for the local soil.

Provenance of Nonlocals?

Nonlocal individuals were raised in another geochemical environment. Where exactly they came from cannot be determined at present since sufficient geochemical and bioarchaeological data from the region are missing. The majority of individuals with a nonlocal strontium isotope signature have lower values. Because the local rock values for the volcanic islands are known to be significantly lower (MacDonald et al. 2000) it seems plausible that these individuals had spent their childhood in the volcanic part of Guadeloupe (Basse-Terre) or other volcanic islands. Individuals growing up on these islands are expected to have $^{87}Sr/^{86}Sr$ values between the local rock value and seawater values.

Further Study

The strontium isotope values from Anse à la Gourde indicate that it is possible to acquire information on residential mobility in a population from the Late Ceramic period. However, more data are needed concerning the diet of the population to assess the contribution of various sources of strontium to the biogenic strontium ratio of the enamel. In order to determine the provenance of the non-local individuals, three approaches are necessary. More strontium isotope data of soils and large burial assemblages from archaeological sites on islands in the region should become available. Furthermore the isotope composition of an element that is not present in significant concentrations in seawater should be studied (e.g., neodymium or lead). Complete Sr-Nd-Pb analyses of the Gourde samples will be undertaken to assess if combined isotope data can better constrain an individual's provenance area.

Conclusions

[87]Sr/[86]Sr has been determined for 50 well-preserved enamel samples from human skeletal remains from the site of Anse à la Gourde. Iterative exclusion of outliers based on a 95 percent confidence interval has allowed the definition of a normally distributed subset of teeth, inferred to represent the range in [87]Sr/[86]Sr of the local population. This local group has mean [87]Sr/[86]Sr of 0.70914 and standard deviation 0.00005. Fourteen teeth (28 percent) were identified as outliers. The outlying teeth are thought to represent individuals who migrated to Anse à la Gourde after the completion of enamel formation. At present a definite provenance area cannot be assigned to nonlocal individuals. Regarding the local burials, a provenance from sites situated in a similar geochemical environment in the region cannot be ruled out. Local soil and enamel [87]Sr:[86]Sr ratios largely correspond with that of seawater-derived strontium, which may have dominated in the diet and the environment. The data suggest that in coastal environments the marine environment may create a common coastal signature instead of a specific local signature.

16
Epilogue
The Correct Answer Requires the Right Question
(and the Technology to Back It Up)

William F. Keegan

Let me start with an anecdote. When I first started working in Caribbean archaeology in 1978, I happened to be associated with several biologists who were studying Queen Conch (*Strombus gigas*). I was in the Caicos Islands and at the time they were still shipping millions of dried conch per year to Haiti (until the conch population crashed a few years later). It already had been pointed out that "Indian opened" or punched conch had a small round hole in the spire, which contrasted markedly with the linear cut made by modern fisherman. At one of the first meetings of Caribbean archaeologists that I attended I asked if anyone knew how the native peoples had removed the animal from the shell using this small round hole. There were a number of incorrect answers, but the bottom line was that no one had really thought about it. No one asked the question.

The same attitude prevailed with regard to the production of conch tools. Only shell artifacts with a ground work-edge were then considered tools. Thank god for Ramón Dacal Moure (1978) and Doug Armstrong (1979) who first raised the question of whether recurrent and unmodified shell forms were "scrap" or tools. At the time it was assumed that the rough form of these tools could be achieved by smashing the shell on a rock. I can assure you that this is not an easy procedure, and that it does not yield useable tools. A few years later, at my next meeting, I demonstrated how these expedient forms had to have been purposely manufactured (Keegan 1981, 1984). To my chagrin, in the process of making a tool I slit my wrist on the sharp edge of a *Strombus* lip, and *Strombus* tool replication quickly was christened "Arawak suicide." I still have the scar to prove it!

Preamble

There seems to be a general impression that Caribbean archaeologists have lagged behind their colleagues in the application of methods and theories. This is especially apparent when new investigators enter the region and fail to acknowledge the vast amount of work that has preceded them (e.g., Fitzpatrick 2004). For them, everything is a "new" perspective. Nothing could be further from the truth. The chapters in this volume demonstrate that Caribbean research is still on the cutting edge; it has always been so and we should expect no less. In their *History of American Archaeology*, Willey and Sabloff (1974) identified Irving Rouse as the foundation, the base of the tree, for modern archaeology for his contributions to the classificatory-historical period. In addition, Rouse's (1939) model, although Ben never liked the word model, of the cultural and behavioral patterning of artifacts is as relevant today as it was 70 years ago. Elizabeth Wing was a pioneer in the field of environmental archaeology (Wing and Reitz 1982), and many of her early studies involved faunal remains from the West Indies. Lee Newsom (1993) and Deborah Pearsall (2000), using Caribbean data, are pioneers in the field of archaeobotany. David Watters (1982) was one of the early practitioners of the subfield now called island archaeology. Marxist approaches were used to interpret developments in the Caribbean long before these became popular in the United States and Europe (Curet et al. 2005; Veloz Maggiolo et al. 1981). Kathleen Deagan (2004) and Lourdes Domínguez (2005) were instrumental in the development of historical archaeology, and became so based on research in the Caribbean. In Deagan's study of En Bas Saline, Haiti, she was one of the first to use electromagnetic conductivity as a remote sensing device (Williams 1986); Mary Collins used ground penetrating radar at the Coralie site on Grand Turk in the days when the readout was generated by carbon scoring (Hardman et al. 1998); and a Caribbeanist wrote the section on remote sensing for the *Encyclopedia of Cultural Anthropology* (Keegan 1996b). Schoeninger and associates (1993) made the first study of stable carbon isotopes for coastal human populations, which included samples from the Bahamas; the very first study of nitrogen isotopes in an aquatic setting came from samples collected in the Caribbean (Keegan and DeNiro 1988); and Anne Stokes (1998) made one of the earliest studies of whole diet using stable isotopes extracted from bone apatite. In the late 1970s, Shaun Sullivan (1981) did a metallurgical analysis of a brass nose ornament from MC-6 on Middle Caicos; further, he and Castellanos (1981) were among the first to investigate archaeoastronomy in the Americas. Judith Fandrich (1991) did a trace element study of stone axes from Grenada; samples from the Bahamas were used in Jim Burton's initial study of barium and strontium ratios; and human bones from the Caribbean were used in an early effort to extract DNA from ancient bone as part of a study to identify the remains of an Irish martyr (his skull was found in one place and his body in another). The first application of optimal foraging theory to a horticultural society was made using Caribbean data (Keegan 1985, 1986), and 20 years later we finally have an edited book on the subject (Kennett and Winterhalder 2006). Luis Fortuna (1978) was an early practitioner of pollen analysis; Sylvia Scudder (2001) is a founding practitioner of soils analysis and investigated evidence for changes in eustatic sea level in the Turks and Caicos; David Hodell and colleagues used a variety of methods to reconstruct past environments in the Caribbean (Higuera-Gundy et al. 1999; Hodell et al. 1991); David Steadman, although starting in the Pacific, is among the first to investigate human-induced animal extinctions on islands (Steadman and Stokes 2002); and Betsy Carlson's (1999) investigation of faunal remains at the Coralie site, especially marine species, has led biologists to reconsider the near-shore impacts of pre-European populations in the Americas (Jackson et al. 2001). One of the earliest CRM projects was conducted at El Bronce, Puerto Rico (Robinson et al. 1985); it is a case study for how scientific objectives can be met in a contract archaeology framework. Corinne Hofman and Menno Hoogland (1999) have implemented one of the most comprehensive research strategies executed in any archaeological context (as evidenced in this volume). Peter Roe (1980) was the first to address the conclusions of "ceramic sociology" (Deetz 1968; Hill 1970; Longacre 1970), and although his study was based on the Shipibo-Conibo of South America, his contributions to the study of Caribbean iconography are well known (Roe 1995). We can go back even further in time. Gaylord Bourne (1906) called Ramón Pané's 1494 account of Macorix religion the first ethnological study in the Americas, and the concept of chiefdoms is based on the *cacicazgos* of Hispaniola (Oberg 1955; Redmond and Spencer 1994). There are many other examples.

My point is that the Caribbean has never been lacking in technological or theoretical innovation. The problem has been that there were not enough people asking the right questions. Far too often the description of pottery styles has been the main objective, and far too often U.S., Hispanic, French, and Dutch scholars have not read the works of their colleagues; the dissemination of information is complicated by the publication of results in at least five different languages. A further problem is the dissection of the West Indies into discrete archipelagos. In this regard, several people have told me that the Bahamas, where I did my earliest work, is not Caribbean archaeology! Fortunately, times are changing, and it has taken the Leiden group to chart the way forward. I am somewhat embarrassed to admit this, but Hofman, Hoogland, Boomert, van Gijn, Louwe Kooijmans, their students, and colleagues (I should mention André Delpuech) have developed the most sustained and integrated program of technological innovation and application in the West Indies to date. I have tried to recognize the efforts of those who preceded them, but the ancestors whose shoulders they proudly ride upon often were working in isolation. In contrast, the Leiden group is a team, and it has been my privilege to work with them. The chapters in this volume reflect their efforts.

The chapters also reflect a profound change in how Caribbean archaeology is structured. Until recently, the major paradigms focused on classification. The two main approaches were Rouse's time-space systematics (1992), and, among Hispanic archaeologists, the Marxist emphasis on *modo de vida* (Ensor 2000; Veloz Maggiolo et al. 1981). Both tend to homogenize the prehispanic Caribbean, and ignore the diversity that is present—often just below the surface (Keegan and Rodríguez Ramos 2005). I do not mean to disregard the work of French (notably Jacques Petitjean Roget and his sons, Henry and Hughes); Dutch, such as Josselin de Jong; Cuban (José Guarch Delmonte, Ramón Dacal Moure, Manuel Rivero de la Calle); Dominican (Marcio Veloz Maggiolo, Elpidio Ortega, Fernando Luna Calderón); Puerto Rican (Ricardo Alegría, Luis Chanlatte Baik); or even U.S. archaeologists such as Ripley and Adelaide Bullen; was never considered mainstream by most North American archaeologists.

Case Studies

The pottery and clay studies of Hofman and colleagues are exemplary. In the past, when clays were even collected, the tendency has been to look solely at their chemical and physical properties. By examining the workability of various clays, they promise to provide a better understanding of clay sources and the manufacture of pottery vessels.

The characterization of gold and brass objects from the remarkable El Chorro de Maíta site in Cuba is certain to bring the production, distribution, and sources of these materials into sharper relief. The tendency has been to look at these objects through the eyes of the Spanish chroniclers. More complete information about the objects themselves will improve our interpretation of the roles they played in native West Indian culture.

Initial studies of lithics tended to focus on the classification of stone tools, especially for Archaic groups where these are the main item of material culture. A notable exception to this is the work of Jeff Walker. Sebastiaan Knippenberg and Benoît Bérard have taken lithic analysis to new heights (I should also mention Reniel Rodríguez Ramos). The investigation of sources for lithic materials and the production sequence, or *chaîne opératoire*, have made significant contributions to our understanding of the relationships between different cultures, and the exchange relations that define interaction spheres. Moreover, despite widespread lapidary arts in the West Indies, few studies have addressed their production. De Mille, Varney, and Turney have devised a unique method for investigating stone-bead drilling techniques. Their results will provide a more comprehensive understanding of both techniques and the time required to produce these objects. The identification of craft specialization and production holds important clues to the organization of production in Saladoid cultures.

In a similar vein, Charlene Hutcheson has developed a technique that also might be described as remote sensing. Casts of bead cavities (De Mille et al. this volume) and basket impressions on ceramics provide superior ways for investigating pre-European technologies. To her credit, Hutcheson already has demonstrated that basket impressions are not simply a by-product of pressing clay on a basket mat as a way of molding pottery forms. There is clear evidence that these impressions convey symbolic meanings. The diversity and distribution of basket impressions on griddles and pots provide an important new avenue for the investigation of cultural affiliations, and provide the opportunity to investigate an element of material culture that typically is not preserved in the archaeological record.

Use-wear analysis, artifact replication, and experimental archaeology rarely have been undertaken in the Caribbean, especially with shell and coral tools. Annelou van Gijn and her students are to be commended for their work. I had the opportunity to help Iris Briels with her experiments using a cassava grater board while we were working in St. Lucia. The problem for me was that the cassava pulp I produced was pink (and my fingertips were shredded). Perhaps I should avoid experimental studies—and all sharp objects. Seriously, their investigations are providing solid evidence for the production and use of objects that traditionally have been weighed, counted, and discarded. In addition, their work recognizes that these people produced and used varied toolkits. Too often it is assumed that shell tools were only used when lithics were not available. Through their work we now recognize that stone, shell, and coral all have unique properties that made them valuable, and that they were used in concert. I would also note for my colleagues working in the Caribbean that, although Harold Kelly focused on *Porites* coral tools, he also demonstrated that staghorn coral (*Acropora cervicornis*) could be used for drilling wood. The result is a coral tip with uniform wear caused by the circular motion of drilling. Thanks to Harold, we have identified many of these at sites in the Turks and Caicos Islands.

Jaime Pagán's investigations of starch grains on lithics and griddles blow me away. We finally have evidence for the wide range of plants described by the Spanish chroniclers. His investigations (with José Oliver) document the use of a variety of plants by so-called Archaic peoples that is far more extensive than previously thought. Nieuwenhuis provides a similar, complementary study, of equal value, for the Plum Piece site on Saba. In addition, Rodríguez and Pagán indicate that griddles were not used only for the baking of cassava bread.

I mentioned Lee Newsom's pioneering role in archaeobotany in my preamble. What more can I say? Plants were a critical component of native lifeways, and her investigations are fleshing out, so to speak, not only the use of cultigens but also changes in local environments caused by the harvesting of fuelwood and land clearance.

The analysis of dental morphological traits by Alfredo Coppa and colleagues presents a unique and promising approach for detecting not only migrations, but also genetic variability among the populations living in the islands. I'm not yet convinced that we can divide the Caribbean into only two migratory waves, but this approach holds exciting possibilities.

Stable carbon and nitrogen isotope analysis already has contributed to our un-

derstanding of prehistoric diet. The addition of strontium isotopes to this repertoire promises significant new insights. Mathijs Booden and colleagues have really
gotten me excited. Recently, I suggested that human burials in a site might reflect
postmortem mobility (Keegan in press). In other words, individuals were buried
in their clan cemetery even if they did not live at the site during their adult life.
Booden and his colleagues obtained strontium isotope signatures that indicate a
significant number of "nonlocal" burials at Anse à la Gourde. This method opens
an important new avenue for investigating both diet and mobility.

All of the contributors deserve credit (kudos even) for describing their methods
in sometimes excruciating detail. This level of detail hopefully will encourage and
enable others to apply these techniques. It is only through the accumulation of evidence from throughout the islands that the important questions can be raised, and
the diversity of cultural expressions, can be addressed.

Conclusions

Caribbean archaeology has entered a new phase. When you depart from a phase
that focused on similarity, and embrace approaches that emphasize differences,
there inevitably is a period of discovery. Investigations must address which things
are similar, which are different, and what do these similarities and differences
mean. The contributors to this volume are asking the right questions. Their results are enhancing significantly our knowledge and understanding of the pre-
European Caribbean. In the end, the diversity they are documenting will create an
entirely new vision of Caribbean archaeology.

References Cited

Abel, T.
1998   Complex Adaptive Systems, Evolutionism, and Ecology within Anthropology: Interdisciplinary Research for Understanding Cultural and Ecological Dynamics. *Georgia Journal of Ecological Anthropology* 2:6–29.

Adovasio, J. M.
1977   *Basketry Technology.* Aldine Press, Chicago.

Adovasio, J. M., R. L. Andrews, D. C. Hyland, and J. S. Illingsworth
2001   Perishable Industries from the Windover Bog: An Unexpected Window into the Florida Archaic. *North American Archaeologist* 22(1):1–90.

Alegría, R. E.
1974   *Discovery, Conquest, and Colonization of Puerto Rico, 1493–1599.* Colección de Estudios Puertorriqueños, San Juan.

1981   El uso de la incrustación en la escultura de los indios antillanos. Centro de Estudios Avanzados de Puerto Rico y el Caribe, San Juan.

1997   An Introduction to Taíno Culture and History. In *Taíno Pre-Columbian Art and Culture from the Caribbean,* edited by F. Bercht, E. Brodsky, J. A. Farmer, D. Taylor, pp. 18–33. El Museo del Barrio and The Monacelli Press, New York.

Alegría, R. E., H. B. Nickolson, and G. R. Willy
1955   The Archaic Tradition of Puerto Rico. *American Antiquity* 21:113–121.

Allaire, L.
1977   *Later Prehistory in Martinique and the Island Carib: Problems in Ethnic Identification.* Ph.D. dissertation, Yale University, New Haven. University Microfilms, Ann Arbor.

1985   Changements lithiques dans l'archéologie de la Martinique. In *Proceedings of the Tenth International Congress for the Study of Pre-Columbian Cultures of the Lesser Antilles,* edited by L. Allaire and F. M. Mayer, pp. 299–310. Centre de Recherches Caraïbes, Université de Montréal, Montreal.

Alley, R. B.
  2000   *Two-Mile Time Machine: Ice Cores, Abrupt Climate Change, and Our Future.*
         Princeton University Press, Princeton, New Jersey.

Andreieff, P., and S. Cottez
  1976   Sur l'âge, la structure et la formation des îles de Grande-Terre et de Marie-Galante,
         Guadeloupe F.W.I. *Bulletin BRGM, 2e série, section IV* (4):329–333.

Antczak, A.
  1998   Late Prehistoric Economy and Society of the Islands off the Coast of Venezuela: A
         Contextual Interpretation of the Non-Ceramic Evidence. Unpublished Ph.D. dis-
         sertation, University College London, London.

Appadurai, A. (editor)
  1986   *The Social Life of Things.* Cambridge University Press, Cambridge.

Ariosa, J.
  1977   Curso de yacimientos minerales metálicos, tipos genéticos. Editorial Pueblo y
         Educación, Havana.

Armstrong, D. V.
  1979   "Scrap" or Tools: A Closer Look at *Strombus gigas* Columella Artifacts. *Journal of
         the Virgin Islands Archaeological Society* 7:27–34

Arts, J.
  1999   Morel I Revisited: A Study of Huecan and Cedrosan Saladoid Ceramics Found at
         the Site of Morel, Guadeloupe, French West Indies. Unpublished master's thesis,
         Leiden University, Leiden.

Atchison, J., and R. Fullagar
  1998   Starch Residues on Pounding Implements from Jinmium Rock-Shelter. In *A Closer
         Look: Recent Australian Studies of Stone Tools*, edited by R. Fullagar, pp. 109–126.
         Sydney University Archaeological Methods Series 6, Sydney.

Baillie, M. G. L.
  1995   *A Slice through Time: Dendrochronology and Precision Dating.* B. T. Batsford,
         London.

Baker, P. E.
  1968   Petrology of Mt. Misery Volcano, St. Kitts, West Indies. *Lithos* 1:124–150.

Balfet, H. (editor)
  1991   *Observer l'action technique: Des chaînes opératoires pour quoi faire?* Éditions du
         C.N.R.S., Paris.

Banks, W., and C. Greenwood
  1975   *Starch and Its Components.* Edinburgh University Press, Edinburgh.

Barbotin, M.
  1970   Les sites archéologiques de Marie-Galante (Guadeloupe). In *Proceedings of the
         Third International Congress for the Study of the Pre-Columbian Cultures of the
         Lesser Antilles* (1969), pp. 27–44. Grenada National Museum, Grenada.
  1973   Tentative d'explication de la forme et du volume des haches Marie-Galante et
         autres pierres. In *Proceedings of the Fourth International Congress for the Study of
         the Pre-Columbian Cultures of the Lesser Antilles* (1971), pp. 140–150. St. Lucia Ar-
         chaeological and Historical Society Castries, St. Lucia.

1974   Archéologie caraïbe et chroniqueurs. *Bulletin de la Société d'Histoire de la Guade-loupe* 21. Basse Terre.

Barton H., and J. P. White

1993   Use of Stone and Shell Artifacts at Balof 2, New Ireland, Papua New Guinea. *Asian Perspectives* 32(2):169–181.

Barton, H., R. Torrence, and R. Fullagar

1998   Clues to Stone Tool Function Re-Examined: Comparing Starch Grain Frequencies on Used and Unused Obsidian Artefacts. *Journal of Archaeological Science* 25:1231–1238.

Bartone, N. R., and J. G. Crock

1991   Flaked Stone Industries at the Early Saladoid Trants Site, Montserrat, West Indies. In *Proceedings of the Fourteenth Congress of the International Association for Caribbean Archaeology,* edited by A. Cummins and P. King, pp. 124–146. Barbados.

Beets, C. J., S. R. Troelstra, P. M. Grootes, M.-J. Nadeau, K. van der Borg, A. F. M. de Jong, C. L. Hofman, and M. L. P. Hoogland

2006   Climate and Pre-Columbian Settlement at Anse à la Gourde, Guadeloupe, North-eastern Caribbean. *Geoarchaeology: An International Journal* 21(3):271–280.

Belhache, P., M. Hubau, N. Platel, C. Ney, R. Chapoulie, and M. Schvoerer

1991   Le dégraissant des céramiques précolombiennes de la Martinique: Méthodologie. In *Proceedings of the Fourteenth Congress of the International Association for Caribbean Archaeology,* edited by A. Cummins and P. King, pp. 1–10. Barbados.

Bello, L.A., and O. Paredes

1999   El almidón: Lo comemos, pero no lo conocemos. *Perspectivas* 50(3):29–33.

Bentley R., T. Alexander, D. Price, and E. Stephan

2004   Determining the "Local" ^{87}Sr/^{86}Sr Range for Archaeological Skeletons: A Case Study from Neolithic Europe. *Journal of Archaeological Science* 31:365–375.

Bérard, B.

1999a Technologie lithique et caractérisation culturelle: L'exemple de l'occupation amérindienne de la Martinique. In *Proceedings of the International Congress for Caribbean Archaeology* (1999), edited by G. Richard, pp. 185–198. Association Internationale d'Archéologie de la Caraïbe, Région Guadeloupe, Mission Archéologique, Guadeloupe St. George's University Campus, True Blue, St. George, Grenada.

1999b Gestión de materias primas silicosas y organización del territorio de los Amerindios de Martinica. Paper presented at "Seminario Regional sobre las Culturas Aborígenes del Caribe, FISS," Santo Domingo.

2001   Technologie lithique et caractérisation culturelle: L'exemple de l'occupation amérindienne de la Martinique. *Actes du XVIIIe Congrès de l'Association Internationale d'Archéologie de la Caraïbe,* idem1999. St. George, Grenada. AIAC, Région Guadeloupe—Mission Archéologique, Basse Terre. Vol. 1, pp. 175–184.

2004   *Les premières occupations agricoles de l'arc antillais, migrations et insularité.* British Archaeological Reports, International Series 1299, Paris Monographs in American Archaeology 15, edited by E. Taladoire. Archaeopress, Oxford.

Bérard B., and J. P. Giraud

2002 Le site de Vivé au Lorrain et les premiers établissements saladoïdes de la Martinique. In *Archéologie précolombienne et coloniale des Caraïbes,* edited by A. Delpuech, J. P. Giraud, and A. Hesse. Actes du 123ème congrès national des sociétés historiques et scientifiques, Antilles-Guyanes 1998, pp, 67-94 CTHS, Paris.

Bérard, B., and G. Vernet

1997 *La savane des pétrifications, Sainte Anne: Opération de fouille programmée, AFAN.* Document final de synthèse. Service Régional de l'Archéologie, Fort de France, Martinique.

Bérard, B., and N. Vidal

2002 Le site précolombien de La Pointe au Marigot en Martinique. In *Archéologie précolombienne et coloniale des Caraïbes,* edited by A. Delpuech, J. P. Giraud, and A. Hesse. Actes du 123ème congrès national des sociétés historiques et scientifiques, Antilles-Guyanes 1998, pp. 68-95. CTHS, Paris.

Bérard, B., G. Kieffer, J. P. Raynal, and G. Vernet

2001 Les éruptions volcaniques de la montagne Pelée et le premier peuplement de la Martinique. In *Proceedings of the Nineteenth International Congress for Caribbean Archaeology,* edited by L. Alofs and R. A. C. F. Dijkhoff, vol. 1, pp. 173-184, Publication Museo Arqueológico Aruba, vol. 9, Aruba.

Berman, M.-J., and C. Dixon Hutcheson

1997 *Basket Impressed Sherds: To Weave and to Eat in the Bahamas.* Paper presented at the 62nd Annual Meeting of the Society for American Archaeology, Nashville, Tennessee.

2000 Impressions of a Lost Technology: A Study of Lucayan-Taíno Basketry. *Journal of Field Archaeology* 27(4):417-35.

2001a Reweaving the Strands: Continued Exploration into Basketry Technology of Prehistoric Bahamians. In *Proceedings of the Eighteenth International Congress for Caribbean Archaeology* (1999), edited by G. Richard, vol. 1, pp. 185-198. Association Internationale d'Archéologie de la Caraïbe, Région Guadeloupe, Mission Archéologique, Guadeloupe St. George's University Campus, True Blue, St. George, Grenada.

2001b Shamanism, Ritual, and Basketry Production in the Prehistoric Caribbean. Paper presented at the 66th Annual Meeting of the Society for American Archaeology, New Orleans.

Berman, M.-J., and D. M. Pearsall

2000 Plants, People, and Culture in the Prehistoric Central Bahamas: A View from the Three Dog site, an Early Lucayan Settlement on San Salvador Island, Bahamas. *Latin American Antiquity* 11(3):219-239.

Berman, M.-J., A. K. Sievert, and T. R. Whyte

1999 Form and Function of Bibolar Lithic Artefacts from the Three Dog Site, San Salvador, Bahamas. *Latin American Antiquity* 10(4):415-432.

Berry, A. C.

1978 Anthropological and Family Studies on Minor Variants of the Dental Crown. In *Development, Function, and Evolution of Teeth,* edited by P. M. Butler and K. A. Joysey, pp. 81-98. Academic Press, New York.

Bertouille, H.

1989　*Théories physiques et mathématiques de la taille des outils préhistoriques.* Cahiers du
　　　Quaternaire 15. C.N.R.S., Paris.

Bishop, R. L., Robert L. Rands, and George R. Holley

1982　Ceramic Compositional Analysis in Archaeological Perspective. In *Advances in
　　　Archaeological Method and Theory,* edited by M. B. Schiffer, vol. 5, pp. 275–330,
　　　Academic Press, New York.

Black, D. E., L. C. Peterson, J. T. Overpeck, A. Kaplan, M. N. Evans, and M. Kashgarian

1999　Eight Centuries of North Atlantic Ocean Atmospheric Variability. *Science*
　　　286:1709–1713.

Bloo, S.

1997　Een morfologische en technologische studie naar de functie van het aardewerk van
　　　Anse à la Gourde, Guadeloupe (F.W.I.). Unpublished master's thesis, Leiden Uni-
　　　versity, Leiden.

Bodu, P.

1984　Deux ateliers de débitage de roches locales en Désirade. Unpublished report,
　　　Guadeloupe.

Bonneton, J. R., and J. M. Vila

1983　Données géologiques à l'île de Saint-Martin (Petites Antilles). *Bulletin de la Société
　　　Géologique de France* 25:867–871.

Bonnissent, D.

1995　Les caractéristiques de la céramique de Hope Estate, Île de Saint Martin. In *Pro-
　　　ceedings of the Sixteenth International Congress for Caribbean Archaeology,* edited
　　　by G. Richard, pp. 333–344. Conseil Régional de la Guadeloupe, Basse Terre.

Bonnissent, D., and T. Romon

2004　Fouilles de la Cathédrale de Basse-Terre, document final de synthèse. I.N.R.A.P,
　　　S.R.A. Guadeloupe.

Booden, M. A., and A. J. D. Isendoorn

2005　Report on the Clay Sampling Survey of 2005 in the Northern Lesser Antilles
　　　on the Islands of Anguilla, St. Maarten, Saba, St. Eustatius, Guadeloupe, and La
　　　Désirade. Leiden University, Leiden.

Boomert, A.

1980　Hertenrits: An Arauquinoid Complex in North West Suriname Archaeology and
　　　Anthropology. *Journal of the Walter Roth Museum* 3(2):68–104.

1986　The Cayo Complex of St. Vincent: Ethnohistorical and Archaeological Aspects of
　　　the Island Carib Problem. *Antropológica* 66:3–68.

1987a　Gifts of the Amazons: "Green Stone" Pendants and Beads as Items of Ceremonial
　　　Exchange in Amazonia and the Caribbean. *Antropológica* 67:33–54.

1987b　Notes on Barbados Prehistory. *Journal of the Barbados Museum and Historical So-
　　　ciety* 38(1):8–43.

2000　Trinidad, Tobago, and the Lower Orinoco Interaction Sphere: An Archaeological/
　　　Ethnohistorical Study. Unpublished Ph.D. dissertation, University of Leiden.
　　　Plantijn Casparie, Heerhugowaard.

Boomert, A., and S. B. Kroonenberg

1977　Manufacture and Trade of Stone Artifacts in Prehistoric Surinam. In *Ex horreo,* edited by B. L. van Beek, R. W. Brandt, and W. Groenman-Van Waateringe, pp. 9–47. University of Amsterdam, Albert Egges van Giffen Instituut voor Prae-en Protohistorie, Amsterdam.

Bourne, E. G.

1906   Columbus, Ramón Pané, and the Beginnings of American Anthropology. *Proceedings of the American Antiquarian Society* 17:310–348.

Bouysse, P., R. Schmidt-Effing, and D. Westercamp

1983   La Désirade Island (Lesser Antilles) Revisited: Lower Cretaceous Radiolarian Cherts and Arguments against an Ophiolitic Origin for the Basalt Complex. *Geology* 11:244–247.

Bray, W.

1993   Techniques of Gilding and Surface Enrichment in Pre-Hispanic American Metallurgy. In *Metal Plating and Patination: Cultural, Technical, and Historical Developments,* edited by S. La Niece and P. T. Craddock, pp. 182–192. Butterworth Heinemann, Oxford.

1997   Metallurgy and Anthropology: Two Studies from Prehispanic America. *Boletín Museo del Oro* 42:37–55.

2003   Gold, Stone, and Ideology: Symbols of Power in the Tairona Tradition of Northern Colombia. In *Gold and Power in Ancient Costa Rica, Panama, and Colombia,* edited by J. Quilter and J. Hoopes, pp. 301–344. Dumbarton Oaks, Washington, D.C.

Briels, I.

2004   Use-Wear Analysis on the Archaic Flint Assemblage of Plum Piece, Saba: A Pilot Study. Unpublished master's thesis, Leiden University, Leiden.

Brokke, A. J.

1999   Anse des Pères: Shell. In *Archaeological Investigations on St. Martin: The Sites of Anse des Pères, Norman Estate, and Hope Estate, with a Contribution to the "La Hueca Problem,"* edited by C. L. Hofman and M. L. P. Hoogland, pp. 105–110. Archaeological Studies, Leiden University, 4, Leiden.

Brooks, T., and M. L. Smith

2001   Caribbean Catastrophes. *Science* 294:1469–1471.

Brownlow, A. H.

1979   *Geochemistry.* Prentice-Hall, Englewood Cliffs, New Jersey.

Brush, S. B.

2004   *Farmer's Bounty: Locating Crop Diversity in the Contemporary World.* Yale University Press, New Haven.

Budd, P., J. Montgomery, B. Barreiro, and R. G. Thomas

2000   Differential Diagenesis of Strontium in Archaeological Human Dental Tissues. *Applied Geochemistry* 15:687–694.

Buléon, A., P. Colonna, V. Planchot, and S. Ball

1998   Starch Granules: Structure and Biosynthesis. *International Journal of Biological Macromolecules* 23:85–112.

Bullen, R. P.

1962   *Ceramic Periods of St. Thomas and St. John Islands, Virgin Islands.* William L. Bryant Foundation, Orlando, Florida.

1964   *The Archaeology of Grenada, West Indies.* Contribution to the Florida State Museum, Social Sciences (11), University of Florida, Gainesville.

Bullen, R. P., and A. K. Bullen

1967   Two Stratigraphic Tests at the Grande Anse Site, St. Lucia. In *The Amerindians in St. Lucia (Ioanalao).* St. Lucia Archaeological and Historical Society, Castries, St. Lucia.

1968   Salvage Archaeology at Caliviny Island, Grenada: A Problem in Typology. In *Proceedings of the Second International Congress for the Study of Pre-Columbian Cultures in the Lesser Antilles,* pp. 31–43. Bridgetown, Barbados.

1970   The Lavoutte Site: A Carib Ceremonial Center. *Proceedings of the Third International Congress for the Study of Pre-Columbian Cultures of the Lesser Antilles,* pp. 61–86. Grenada National Museum, Grenada.

1972   *Archaeological Investigations on St. Vincent and the Grenadines, West Indies.* William L. Bryant Foundation, American Studies, Report No. 8, Orlando, Florida.

Burney, D. A., and L. P. Burney

1994   Holocene Charcoal Stratigraphy from Laguna Tortuguero, Puerto Rico, and the Timing of Human Arrival on the Island. *Journal of Archaeological Science* 21:273–281.

Bush, P. R., and G. de G. Sieveking

1986   Geochemistry and the Provenance of Flint Axes. In *The Scientific Study of Flint and Chert, Proceedings of the Fourth International Flint Symposium,* edited by G. de G. Sieveking and M. B. Hart, pp. 133–140. Cambridge University Press, Cambridge.

Cackler, P. R., M. D. Glascock, H. Neff, H. Iceland, K. A. Pyburn, D. Hudler, T. R. Hester, and B. M. Chiarulli

1999   Chipped Stone Artefacts, Source Areas, and Provenance Studies of the Northern Belize Chert-Bearing Zone. *Journal of Archaeological Science* 26:389–397.

Cárdenas, M.

1981   *Crónicas francesas de los indios caribes.* Editorial Universidad de Puerto Rico y Centro de Estudios Avanzados de Puerto Rico y el Caribe, San Juan.

Carini, S. P.

1991   *Compositional Analysis of West Indian Ceramics and Their Relevance to Puerto Rican Prehistory.* Ph.D. dissertation, University of Connecticut. University Microfilms, Ann Arbor.

Carlson, B.

1995   String of Command: Manufacture and Utilization of Shell Beads among the Taino. In *Proceedings of the Fifteenth Congress of the International Association for Caribbean Archaeology* (1993), edited by R. E. Alegría and M. A. Rodríguez López, pp. 97–109. Centro de Estudios Avanzados de Puerto Rico y el Caribe. Fundación Puertorriqueña de las Humanidades y la Universidad del Turabo, 1991–2000, San Juan.

Carlson, L. A.

1999   Aftermath of a Feast: Human Colonization of the Southern Bahamian Archipelago and Its Effects on the Indigenous Fauna. Unpublished Ph.D. dissertation, Department of Anthropology, University of Florida, Gainesville.

Cartwright, C. P., P. Drewett, and R. Elmer
  2001   Material Culture II—Shell Artifacts. In *Prehistoric Barbados,* edited by P. Drewett, pp. 101–123. University College London, London.

Castellanos, N., M. Pino, R. Sanpedro, and G. Izquierdo
  n.d.   Estudio de la variante cultural Damajayabo. Manuscript on File, Museo Antropológico Luis Montané, Havana.

Castellanos, R.
  1981   La plaza de Chacuey, un instrumento astronómico megalítico. *Boletín del Museo del Hombre Dominicano* 16:31–40.

Chagnon, N. A.
  1997   *Yanomamö,* 5th ed. Stanford University Case Studies in Cultural Anthropology. Harcourt Brace, Orlando, Florida.

Chancerel, A.
  2003   Haches polies en pierre du site Saladoïde tardif de tourlourous à Marie-Galante. In *Proceedings of the Twentieth Congress of the International Association for Caribbean Archaeology,* edited by G. Tavarez María and M. A. García Arévalo, pp. 143–150. International Association for Caribbean Archaeology, Santo Domingo.

Chanlatte Baik, L. A.
  1977   Primer adorno corporal de oro (nariguera) en la arqueología indoantillana. Museo del Hombre Dominicano and Fundación García Arévalo, Santo Domingo.
  1981   La Hueca y Sorcé (Vieques, Puerto Rico): Primeras migraciones agroalfareras antillanas. Published by author, Santo Domingo.
  1984   *Arqueología de Vieques: Catálogo*, 2nd ed., 90 pp. Río Piedras, Puerto Rico. Centro de Investigaciones Arqueológicas, Museo de Antropología, Historia y Arte, Universidad de Puerto Rico, Río Piedras.

Christman, R. A.
  1953   Geology of St. Bartholomew, St. Maarten, and Anguilla. *Bulletin of the Geological Society of America* 64:65–96.

Church, T.
  1994   *Lithic Resource Studies: A Source Book for Archaeologists.* Lithic Technology Special Publication 3. University of Tulsa, Oklahoma.

Clerc, E.
  1974   Travail du coquillage dans les sites précolombiens de la Grande-Terre de Guadeloupe. In *Proceedings of the Fifth International Congress for the Study of Pre-Columbian Cultures of the Lesser Antilles,* edited by R. P. Bullen, pp. 127–132. The Antigua Archaeological Society, Antigua.

Cody, A. K.
  1991   From the Site of Pearls, Grenada: Exotic Lithics and Radiocarbon Dates. In *Proceedings of the Thirteenth International Congress for Caribbean Archaeology* (1989), edited by E. N. Ayubi and J. B. Haviser, part II, pp. 204–226. Reports of the Archaeological-Anthropological Institute of the Netherlands Antilles, No. 9, Curaçao.

Conrad, G. W., J. W. Foster, and C. D. Beeker
  2001   Organic Artifacts from the Manantial de la Aleta, Dominican Republic: Preliminary Observations and Interpretations. *Journal of Caribbean Archaeology* 2:1–20.

Coomans, H. E.
1965   Shells and Shell Objects from an Indian Site on Magueyes Island, Puerto Rico. *Caribbean Journal of Science* 5:15–24.

Coppa, A., B. Chiarelli, A. Cucina, F. Luna Calderón, and D. Mancinelli
1995   Dental Anthropology and Paleodemography of the Pre-Columbian Populations of Hispaniola from the IIIrd Millennium B.C. to the Spanish Conquest. *Human Evolution* 10(2):153–167

Coppa, A., A. Cucina, D. Mancinelli, R. Vargiu, and J. Calcagno
1998   Dental Anthropology of Central-Southern Iron Age Italy: The Evidence of Metric versus Non-Metric Traits. *American Journal of Physical Anthropology* 107: 371–386.

Coppa, A., A. Cucina, R. Vargiu, D. Mancinelli, and M. Lucci
2000   The Pleistocene-Holocene Transition in Italy: The Evidence of Morphological Dental Traits. In *Science and Technology for the Safeguard of Cultural Heritage in the Mediterranean Basin, 1999*, edited by A. Guarino. Proceedings of Second International Congress, C.N.R., C.N.R.S., July 5–9. Vol. 2, pp. 1009–1013. Paris.

Coppa, A., A. Cucina, M. Lucci, F. Luna Calderón, G. Tavarez, and R. Vargiu
2003   El poblamiento del área circum-caribeña: Afinidades biológicas y patrón de migración desde el tercer milenio a.C. hasta la conquista. In *Proceedings of the Twentieth International Congress for Caribbean Archaeology (IACA) June 29th and July 6th, 2003, Santo Domingo, Dominican Republic.* Vol. 2, pp. 493–504.

Coppa, A., B. Chiarelli, A. Cucina, S. M. Damadio, F. Luna Calderón, D. Mancinelli, and R. Vargiu
1992   Il progetto di ricerca "La popolazione di Hispaniola da popolamento dell'isola alla sua estinzione dopo la colonizzazione europea." Analisi antropologica preliminare. *Antropologia Contemporanea* 15:25–38.

Coppa, A., N. Cappello, A. Cucina, M. Lucci, D. Mancinelli, S. Rendine, R. Vargiu, and A. Piazza
1997   Analysis of Phenetic Distances between Living and Ancient Populations through the Study of Non-Metric Dental Traits. Human Evolution Meeting, October 3–6, p. 24. Cold Spring Harbor, New York.

Cornette, A.
1991   La céramique Galibi en Guyane Française, étude morpho-stylistique et technique. In *Proceedings of the Thirteenth Congress of the International Association for Caribbean Archaeology,* edited by E. N. Ayubi and J. B. Haviser, part 2, pp. 509–523. Reports of the Archaeological-Anthropological Institute of the Netherlands Antilles, No. 9, Curaçao.
1992   Étude morpho-stylistique et technique de la céramique galibi en Guyane Française. *Caribena* 2:41–101.

Cortella, A. R., and M. L. Pochettino
1994   Starch Grain Analysis as a Microscopic Diagnostic Feature in the Identification of Plant Material. *Economic Botany* 48(2):171–181.

Cosculluela, J. A.
1946   Prehistoric Cultures of Cuba. *American Antiquity* 12:10–18.

Cowell, M. R.
  1981   The Archaeological and Geochemical Implications of Trace Elements Distributions in Some English, Dutch, and Belgium Flints. In *Third International Symposium on Flint,* edited by F. G. H. Engelsen. *Staringia* 6:81–84.
Cox O'Connor, B.
  1997   Sourcing for Temper and Clay in Ceramics from Selected Sites on the United States Virgin Islands. In *Proceedings of the Nineteenth International Congress for Caribbean Archaeology,* edited by J. H. Winter, pp. 148–156. Bahamas.
Cox O'Connor, B., and M. S. Smith.
  2001   Comparative Petrography of Pottery from St. Croix, United States Virgin Islands: Aklis, Salt River, Prosperity, and Northside Sites. In *Proceedings of the Nineteenth International Congress for Caribbean Archaeology,* edited by L. Alofs and R. A. C. F. Dijkhoff, 1:29–42. Aruba.
  2003   Petrographic Analysis of Ceramic Sherds from the Prehistoric Sites of Peter Bay and Trunk Bay, St. John, United States Virgin Islands. In *Proceedings of the Twentieth Congress of the International Association for Caribbean Archaeology,* edited by G. Tavarez María and M. A. García Arévalo, pp. 383–390. International Association for Caribbean Archaeology, Santo Domingo.
Crabtree, D. E.
  1972   An Introduction to Flintworking. *Occasional Paper of the Idaho State University Museum,* 28:1–98. Idaho State University Museum, Pocatello.
Craddock, P. T., M. R. Cowell, M. N. Leese, and M. J. Hughes
  1983   The Trace Element Composition of Polished Flint Axes as Indicator of Source. *Archaeometry* 25:135–163.
Crock, J. G.
  2000   *Interisland Interaction and Development of Chiefdoms in the Eastern Caribbean.* Ph.D. dissertation. University of Pittsburgh, University Microfilms, Ann Arbor.
Crock, J. G., and R. N. Bartone
  1998   Archaeology of Trants, Montserrat. Part 4: Flaked Stone and Stone Bead Industries. *Annals of the Carnegie Museum* 67(3):197–224.
Crock, J. G., and J. B. Petersen
  2004   Inter-Island Exchange, Settlement Hierarchy, and a Taíno-Related Chiefdom on the Anguilla Bank, Northern Lesser Antilles. In *Late Ceramic Age Societies in the Eastern Caribbean,* edited by A. Delpuech and C. L. Hofman, pp. 139–158. BAR International Series 1273. British Archaeological Reports, Oxford.
Cucina. A., F. Luna Calderón, R. Vargiu, and A. Coppa
  2003   Las poblaciones caribeñas desde el tercer milenio a.C. a la conquista española: Las filiaciones biológicas desde la perspectiva antropológica dental. *Estudios de Antropología Biológica* 11(2):913–927.
Curet, L. A.
  1997   Technological Changes in Prehistoric Ceramics from Eastern Puerto Rico: An Exploratory Study. *Journal of Archaeological Science* 24:497–504.
  2003   Issues on the Diversity and Emergence of Middle Range Societies of the Ancient Caribbean. *Journal of Archaeological Research* 11:1–42.

2005 *Caribbean Paleodemography: Population, Culture History, and Sociopolitical Processes in Ancient Puerto Rico.* University of Alabama Press, Tuscaloosa.

Curet, L. A., and J. R. Oliver

1998 Mortuary Practices, Social Development, and Ideology in Pre-Columbian Puerto Rico. *Latin American Antiquity* 9(3):217–239.

Curet, L. A., S. L. Dawdy, and G. La Rosa (editors)

2005 *Dialogues in Cuban Archaeology.* University of Alabama Press, Tuscaloosa.

Curtis, J. H., and D. A. Hodell

1993 An Isotopic and Trace Element Study of Ostracods from Lake Miragoane, Haiti: A 10,500 Year Record of Paleosalinity and Paleotemperature Changes in the Caribbean. In *Climate Change in Continental Isotopic Records,* edited by P. K. Swart, K. C. Lohmann, J. A. McKenzie, and S. Savin, pp. 135–152. Geophysical Monograph 78. American Geophysical Union, Washington, D.C.

Curtis, J. H., M. Brenner, and D. A. Hodell

2001 Climate Change in the Circum-Caribbean (Late Pleistocene to Present) and Implications for Regional Biogeography. In *Biogeography of the West Indies: Patterns and Perspectives,* edited by C. A. Woods and F. E. Sergile, pp. 35–54. CRC Press, Boca Raton, Florida.

Curtis, J. H., D. A. Hodell, and M. Brenner

1996 Climate Variability on the Yucatán Peninsula (Mexico) during the Past 3,500 Years and Implications for Maya Cultural Evolution. *Quaternary Research* 46:37–47.

Dacal Moure, R.

1978 *Artefactos de conchas en las comunidades aborígenes cubanas.* Publicaciones del Museo Antropológico Montané, No. 5, Universidad de la Habana, Havana.

1989 The Manufacture of Beads from Shell. In *Proceedings of the 1986 Shell Bead Conference,* edited by C. Hayes and L. Ceci, pp. 25–36. Rochester Museum and Science Center, Research Records 20, Rochester.

1997 The Recurrent Forms in Tanki Flip. In *The Archaeology of Aruba: The Tanki Flip Site,* edited by A. H. Versteeg and S. Rostain, pp. 159–188. Archaeological Museum Aruba, Aruba.

Dacal Moure, R., and F. Croes

2001 La industria de concha de Aruba. Paper presented at the Nineteenth International Congress for Caribbean Archaeology, Aruba.

2004 Shell Tools: Recurrent and Elaborated Forms. In *Archaeology of Aruba: The Marine Shell Heritage,* edited by R. A. C. F. Dijkhoff and M. S. Linville, pp. 53–112. Publications of the Archaeological Museum of Aruba, No. 10, Aruba.

Dacal Moure, R., and M. Rivero de la Calle

1984 *Arqueología aborigen de Cuba.* Editorial Gente Nueva, Havana.

1996 *Art and Archaeology of Pre-Columbian Cuba.* University of Pittsburgh Press, Pittsburgh.

Dacal Moure, R., S. Hernandez, and H. J. Kelly

2004 Replication and Microscopy in the Study of Shell Artifacts. In *The Archaeology of Aruba: The Marine Shell Heritage,* edited by R. A. C. F. Dijkhoff and M. S. Linville, pp. 115–123. Publications of the Archaeological Museum of Aruba, No. 10, Aruba.

Dahlberg, A. A.

1945   The Changing Dentition of Man. *Journal of the American Dental Association* 32:676–690.

1949   The Dentition of American Indian. In *The Physical Anthropology of the American Indian,* edited by W. S. Laughlin, pp. 138–176. Viking Fund, New York.

1956   Materials for the Establishment of Standards for Classification of Tooth Characteristics, Attributes, and Techniques in Morphological Studies of Dentition. Zolier Laboratory of Dental Anthropology, University of Chicago, Chicago.

1971   Penetrance and Expressivity of Dental Traits. In *Dental Morphology and Evolution,* edited by A. A. Dahlberg, pp. 257–262. University of Chicago Press, Chicago.

Davis, D. D.

1988   Coastal Biogeography and Human Subsistence: Examples from the West Indies. *Archaeology of Eastern North America* 16:177–185.

2000   Jolly Beach and the Pre-Ceramic Occupation of Antigua, West Indies. Yale University Publications in Anthropology 84, New Haven.

2002   Flaked Stone Artifacts from the Tutu Site. In *The Tutu Archaeological Village Site. A Multidisciplinary Case Study in Human Adaptation,* edited by E. Righter, pp. 274–283. Routledge, London.

Deagan, K. A.

2004   Reconsidering Taíno Social Dynamics after Spanish Conquest: Gender and Class in Culture Contact Studies. *American Antiquity* 69(4):597–626.

De Bruin, M., P. J. M. Korthoven, C. C. Bakels, and F. C. A. Groen

1983   The Use of Non-Destructive Activation Analysis and Pattern Recognition in the Study of Flint Artefacts. *Archaeometry* 14:55–63.

Deetz, J.

1968   The Inference of Residence and Descent Rules from Archaeological Data. In *New Perspectives in Archaeology,* edited by S. R. Binford and L. R. Binford, pp. 41–48. Aldine, Chicago.

De France, S., and L. A. Newsom

2005   The Status of Paleoethnobiological Research on Puerto Rico and Adjacent Islands. In *Ancient Borinquen: Archaeology and Ethnohistory of Native Puerto Rico,* edited by P. E. Siegel, pp. 122–184. University of Alabama Press, Tuscaloosa.

De Jong, H. N.

2003   Strontium Isotope Analysis (^{87}Sr/^{86}Sr) on Enamel and Bone from a Sample ($n = 14$) of the Pre-Columbian Population of Anse à la Gourde, Guadeloupe: A Test for Matrilocality and a Pilot Study in Provenancing Individuals in the Caribbean. Unpublished master's thesis, Leiden University, Leiden.

DeMarrais, E., C. Gosden, and C. Renfrew (editors)

2004   *Rethinking Materiality: The Engagement of Mind with the Material World.* McDonald Institute Monographs, Cambridge.

De Mille, C. N.

1996   Analysis of the Post-Saladoid Lithic Assemblage, Muddy Bay (PH-14), Antigua, 1994. In Archaeological Investigations at Muddy Bay (PH-14), Antigua, West Indies: A Post-Saladoid Settlement, by A. Reginald Murphy, pp. 155–190. Unpublished master's thesis. Trent University, Peterborough, Canada.

De Mille, C. N., and T. L. Varney

2003   A Preliminary Investigation of Saladoid Stone Bead Manufacturing. In *Proceedings of the Nineteenth International Congress for Caribbean Archaeology,* edited by L. Alofs and R. A. C. F. Dijkhoff, vol. 1, pp. 43–55. Aruba.

De Mille, C. N., A. R. Murphy, and P. F. Healy

1999   Preliminary Archaeological Investigations at Winthorpe's Bay, Antigua. In *Proceedings of the Seventeenth Congress of the International Association for Caribbean Archaeology,* edited by J. H. Winter, pp. 105–121. Rockville Centre, New York.

De Waal, M. S.

1999a   Stone Tools from the Hope Estate Excavations, Saint Martin, F.W.I. In *Archaeological Investigations on St. Martin: The Sites of Anse des Pères, Norman Estate, and Hope Estate, with a Contribution to the "La Hueca Problem,"* edited by C. L. Hofman and M. L. P. Hoogland, pp. 203–214. Archaeological Studies, Leiden University, 4, Leiden.

1999b   Occupations amérindiennes dans l'est de l'archipel guadeloupéen: Note intermédiaire des prospections thématiques La Désirade et Petite Terre. Unpublished report, Leiden University, Leiden.

2002   Occupations amérindiennes dans l'est de l'archipel guadeloupéen, tome II, Inventaire du mobilier découvert. Unpublished report, Leiden University, Leiden.

Diamond, J.

2005   *Collapse: How Societies Choose to Fail or Succeed.* Viking Penguin, New York.

Dobkin de Rios, M.

1984   *Hallucinogens: Cross-Cultural Perspectives.* University of New Mexico Press, Albuquerque.

Dobres, M.-A.

2000   *Technology and Social Agency.* Blackwell, Oxford.

Dobres, M.-A., and C. R. Hoffman

1994   Social Agency and the Dynamics of Prehistoric Technology. *Journal of Archaeological Method and Theory* 1(3):211–258.

Domínguez, L.

2005   Historical Archaeology in Cuba. In *Dialogues in Cuban Archaeology,* edited by L. A. Curet, S. L. Dawdy, and G. La Rosa Corzo, pp. 62–71. University of Alabama Press, Tuscaloosa.

Donahue, J., D. R. Watters, and S. Millspaugh

1990   Thin Section Petrography of Northern Lesser Antilles Ceramics. *Geoarchaeology: An International Journal* 5(3):229–254.

Drooker, P. B.

1992   *Mississippian Village Textiles at Wickliffe.* University of Alabama Press, Tuscaloosa.

2001   Approaching Fabric through Impressions on Pottery. In *Approaching Textiles, Varying Viewpoints: Proceedings of the Seventh Biennial Symposium of the Textile Society of America,* edited by the Textile Society of America. Textile Society of America, Earleville, Maryland.

Duarte Silva, A. P., and A. Stam

1995   Discriminant Analysis. In *Reading and Understanding Multivariate Statistics,* edited by L. G. G. Grimm and P. R. Yarnold, pp. 277–318. American Psychological Association, Washington, D.C.

Duin, R. S.

2000/ A Wayana Potter in the Tropical Rain Forest of Surinam/French Guyana. *News-*
2001 *letter of the Department of Pottery Technology* (Leiden University) 18/19:45–58.

Dunn, O., and J. E. Kelley, Jr.

1989 *The Diario of Christopher Columbus's First Voyage to America, 1492–1493, Ab-stracted by Fray Bartolomé de las Casas.* Transcribed and translated into English, with notes and a concordance of the Spanish. University of Oklahoma Press, Norman.

Earle, T. K.

1991 The Evolution of Chiefdoms. In *Chiefdoms: Power, Economy, and Ideology,* edited by T. K. Earle, pp. 1–15. A School of American Research Book. Cambridge University Press, New York.

1997 *How Chiefs Came to Power: The Political Economy in Prehistory.* Stanford University Press, Stanford, California.

Earle, T. K., and A. W. Johnson

2000 *The Evolution of Human Societies: From Foraging Group to Agrarian State.* Stanford University Press, Stanford, California.

Egan, G., and F. Pritchard

1991 *Dress Accessories, c. 1150–c.1450.* H.M.S.O., London.

Ensor, B. E.

2000 Social Formations, *Modo de Vida,* and Conflict in Archaeology. *American Antiquity* 65:15–42.

Espenshade, C. T.

2000 Reconstructing Household Vessel Assemblages and Site Duration at an Early Ostionoid Site from South-Central Puerto Rico. *Journal of Caribbean Archaeology* 1:1–22.

Evans, C., and B. J. Meggers

1960 *Archeological Investigations in British Guiana.* Bureau of American Ethnology Bulletin 177, Smithsonian Institution, Washington, D.C.

Fandrich, J. E.

1991 Stone Implements from Grenada: Were They Trade Items? In *Proceedings of the Thirteenth International Congress for Caribbean Archaeology.* Curaçao.

Farnum, J. F., and M. K. Sandford

2002 Trace Element Analysis of Skeletal Remains with Associated Soils from the Tutu Site. In *The Tutu Archaeological Village Site: A Multidisciplinary Case Study in Human Adaptation,* edited by E. Righter, pp. 250–262. Routledge, London.

Faupl, P.

1986 Mikroskopische Untersuchungen und prähistorischer Keramik von St. Lucia, West Indies. In *Grabungen und Forschungen auf St. Lucia 1984,* edited by H. Friesinger, E. Reuer, F. Steiniger, and P. Faupl. Mitteilungen der prähistorischen Kommission der Österreichischen Akademie der Wissenshaften. Band XXIII. Verlag der Österreichischen Akademie der Wissenschaften, Vienna.

Febles, J., and G. Baena

1995   Aplicación experimental de índices porcentuales y el factor de correlación de una muestra de superficies de piedra en volumen. In *Contribuciones al conocimiento de industrias líticas en comunidades aborigenes de Cuba,* edited by J. Febles, G. Baena, R. Perez, S. Silva, and M. B. Cruz, pp. 52–59, Editorial Academia, Havana.

Febles, J., G. Baena, R. Pérez, S. Silva, and M. B. Cruz (editors)

1995   *Contribuciones al conocimiento de industrias líticas en comunidades aborígenes de Cuba,* pp. 1–3. Editorial Academia, Havana.

Felsenstein, J.

1973   Maximum-Likelihood Estimation of Evolutionary Trees from Continuous Characters. *American Journal of Human Genetics* 25:471–492.

1985   Confidence Limits on Phylogenies: An Approach Using the Bootstrap. *Evolution* 39:783–791.

Fenner, M., and K. Thompson

2005   *The Ecology of Seeds.* Cambridge University Press, Cambridge.

Fernández, P., and J. Garita

2004   La metalurgia del sureste de Costa Rica: Identificación de producciones locales basadas en evidencia tecnología y estilística. In *Tecnología del oro antiguo: Europa y América,* edited by A. Perea, I. Montero, and O. García-Vuelta, pp. 49–61. Anejos del Archivo Español de Arqueología XXXII. Consejo Superior de Investigaciones Científicas, Madrid.

Field, J., and R. Fullagar

1998   Grinding and Pounding Stones from Cuddie Springs and Jinmium. In *A Closer Look: Recent Australian Studies of Stone Tools,* pp. 96–108. Sydney University Archaeological Methods Series 6, Sydney.

Fitzpatrick, S. M.

2004   *Quo vadis* Caribbean Archaeology? The Future of the Discipline in an International Forum. *Caribbean Journal of Science* 40:281–290.

Ford, J. A.

1954   On the Concept of Types, an Article by James A. Ford with Discussion by Julian H. Steward. *American Anthropologist* 56:42–57.

Fortuna, L.

1978   Análisis polínico de Sanate Abajo. *Boletín del Museo del Hombre Dominicano* 10:125–130.

Freeman, M. F., and J. W. Tukey

1950   Transformations Related to the Angular and the Square Root. *Annual Survey of the Mathematical Statistics* 21:607–611.

Fuess, M. T.

2000   Post-Saladoid Age Pottery in the Northern Lesser Antilles: Lessons Learned from Thin Section Petrography. Unpublished master's thesis, Department of Anthropology, University of Pittsburgh, Pittsburgh.

Fuess, M. T., J. Donahue, D. R. Watters, and D. Nicholson

1991   A Report on Thin Section Petrography of the Ceramics from Antigua, Northern Lesser Antilles: Method and Theory. In *Proceedings of the Fourteenth Congress of the International Association for Caribbean Archaeology,* edited by A. Cummins and P. King, pp. 25–39. Barbados.

Fullagar, R. (editor)

1998   *A Closer Look: Recent Australian Studies of Stone Tools.* Sydney University Archaeological Methods Series 6, Sydney.

Fullagar, R., and J. Furby

1997   Pleistocene Seed Grinding Implements from the Australian Arid Zone. *Antiquity* 71:300–307.

Fullagar, R., J. Field, and L. Kealhofer

In press Grinding Stones and Seeds of Change: Starch and Phytoliths as Evidence of Plant Food Processing. In *New Approaches to Old Stones: Recent Studies of Ground Stone Artifacts, part 4,* edited by Y. M. Rowan and J. Ebeling. Equinox, Oakville, Connecticut.

Fullagar, R., T. Loy, and S. Cox

1998   Starch Grains, Sediments, and Stone Tool Function: Evidence from Bitokara, Papua New Guinea. In *A Closer Look: Recent Australian Studies on Stone Tools,* edited by R. Fullagar, pp. 49–60. Sydney University Archaeological Methods Series 6, Sydney.

Gauthier, J.

1974   Étude des pâtes céramiques de la Martinique pré-colombienne. In *Proceedings of the Fifth International Congress for the Study of Pre-Columbian Cultures of the Lesser Antilles,* edited by R. P. Bullen, pp. 133–139. Antigua Archaeological Society, Antigua.

Glascock, M. D., G. E. Braswell, and R. H. Cobean

1998   A Systematic Approach to Obsidian Source Characterisation. In *Archaeological Obsidian Studies: Method and Theory,* edited by M. S. Shackley, pp. 15–65. Advances in Archaeological and Museum Science, vol. 3. Plenum Press, New York.

González, L.

2003   *Flora de la República de Cuba,* Fascículo 8(4): Zamiaceae, pp. 4–22. A. R. Ganter Verlag, Koenigstein, Germany.

Goodwin, R. C.

1979   *The Prehistoric Cultural Ecology of St. Kitts, West Indies: A Case Study in Island Archaeology.* Ph.D. dissertation, Arizona State University. University Microfilms, Ann Arbor.

Goodwin, R. C., and P. Thall

1983   Production Step Measures and Prehistoric Caribbean Ceramics: An Exploratory Study. In *Proceedings of the Ninth International Congress for the Study of Pre-Columbian Cultures of the Lesser Antilles,* pp. 301–323. Santo Domingo.

Goodwin, R. C., and J. B. Walker

1975   The Excavation of an Early Taino Site in Puerto Rico: Villa Taina de Boqueron, pp. 62–88. Unpublished report. Puerto Rico.

Gordus, A. A., and I. Shimada

1995   Neutron Activation Analysis of Microgram Samples from 364 Gold Objects from a Sicán Burial Site in Peru. In *Materials Issues in Art and Archaeology IV,* edited by P. B. Vandiver, J. R. Druzik, and J. L. Galvan, pp. 128–142. Materials Research Society Proceedings, vol. 352. Pittsburgh.

Gorelick, L., and A. J. Gwinnett
1978   Ancient Seals and Modern Science. *Expedition* 20(2):38–47.

Gosden, C., and Y. Marshall
1999   The Cultural Biography of Objects. *World Archaeology* 31(2):169–178.

Granberry, J., and G. S. Vescelius
2004   *Languages of the Pre-Columbian Antilles.* University of Alabama Press, Tuscaloosa.

Granberry, J., and J. H. Winter
1995   Bahamian Ceramics. In *Proceedings of the Fifteenth International Congress for Caribbean Archaeology* (1993), edited by R. E. Alegría and M. A. Rodríguez López, pp. 3–13. Centro de Estudios Avanzados de Puerto Rico y el Caribe, San Juan, Puerto Rico.

Graves-Brown, P. M. (editor)
2000   *Matter, Materiality, and Modern Culture.* Routledge, London.

Green, R., and J. Suchey
1976   The Use of Inverse Sine Transformation in the Analysis of Non-Metrical Data. *American Journal of Physical Anthropology* 45:61–68.

Guarch, J. M.
1978   *El Taino de Cuba: Ensayo de reconstrucción etno-histórica.* Dirección de Publicaciones, Academia de Ciencias de Cuba, Havana.

Guarch, J. M., C. Rodríguez Arce, and R. Pedroso
1987   Investigaciones preliminares en el sitio El Chorro de Maíta. *Revista de Historia Holguín* 3:25–40.

Guo, S. W., and Thompson, E. A.
1992   Performing the Exact Test of Hardy-Weinberg Proportions for Multiple Alleles. *Biometrics* 48:361–372.

Gustave, S., M. Habau, P. Belhache, J. Fabre, C. Ney, and M. Schroever
1991   Composition élémentaire d' une série de tessons recueillis sur les sites préhistoriques de Vivé et du Diamant (Martinique). In *Proceedings of the Fourteenth International Congress for Caribbean Archaeology,* edited by A. Cummins and P. King, pp. 40–48. Barbados.

Gwinnett, A. J., and L. Gorelick
1979   Ancient Lapidary. *Expedition* 21(1):17–32.
1981   Beadmaking in Iran in the Early Bronze Age. *Expedition* 24(1):10–23.

Haag, W. G.
1970   Stone Artifacts in the Lesser Antilles. In *Proceedings of the Third International Congress for the Study of Pre-Columbian Cultures of the Lesser Antilles,* edited by R. P. Bullen, pp. 129–138. Grenada.

Hagen, J. F.
1991   *Orihno Nï-Karè. Sprekend aardewerk.* Unpublished master's thesis, Leiden University, Leiden.

Hamon, C.

2004   Broyage et abrasion au néolithique ancien: Caractérisation fonctionnelle de l'outillage en grés du bassin parisien. Unpublished Ph.D. dissertation, Université de Paris I, Paris.

Hanihara, K.

1992   Dental and Cranial Affinities among Populations of East Asia and the Pacific: The Basic Populations in East Asia, IV. *American Journal of Physical Anthropology* 88:163–182.

Hardman, J. R., D. C. Heuberger, and M. E. Collins

1998   Characterization of Soils at the Coralie Archaeological Site Grand Turk, British West Indies. *Soil Survey Horizons* 39(1):1–15.

Harrington, M. R.

1921   *Cuba before Columbus,* vols. 1 and 2. Indian Notes and Monograph, Museum of the American Indian. Heye Foundation: New York.

Harris, D. R.

1965   *Plants, Animals, and Man in the Outer Leeward Island, West Indies: An Ecological Study of Antigua, Barbuda, and Anguilla.* University of California Press, Berkeley.

Harris, E. F.

1977   Anthropologic and Genetic Aspects of the Dental Morphology of Solomon Islanders, Melanesia. Unpublished Ph.D. dissertation, Arizona State University, Tempe.

Harris, E. F., and H. L. Bailit

1980   The Metaconule: A Morphologic and Familiar Analysis of a Molar Cusp in Humans. *American Journal of Physical Anthropology* 53:349–358.

Harris, P. O'B.

1978   A Revised Chronological Framework for Ceramic Trinidad and Tobago. In *Proceedings of the Seventh International Congress for the Study of the Pre-Columbian Cultures of the Lesser Antilles,* edited by J. Benoist and F. M. Mayer, pp. 47–63. Centre de Recherches Caraïbes, Université de Montréal, Montreal.

1983   Antillean Axes/Adzes: Persistence of an Archaic Tradition. In *Proceedings of the Ninth International Congress for the Study of the Pre-Columbian Cultures of the Lesser Antilles,* edited by L. Allaire and F. M. Mayer, pp. 257–290. Centre de Recherches Caraïbes, Université de Montréal, Montreal.

1991   Biche Point. In *Proceedings of the Fourteenth Congress of the International Association for Caribbean Archaeology,* edited by A. Cummins and P. King, pp. 73–93. Barbados.

1995   Ethnotypology: The Basis for a New Classification of Caribbean Pottery. In *Proceedings of the Sixteenth Congress of the International Association for Caribbean Archaeology,* edited by G. Richard, pp. 345–366. Conseil Régional de la Guadeloupe, Basse Terre.

2001   St. Lucia Vessel Stratigraphy. In *Proceedings of the Nineteenth International Congress for Caribbean Archaeology,* edited by L. Alofs and R. A. C. F. Dijkhoff, pp. 40–54. Aruba.

Haslam, M.

2004　The Decomposition of Starch Grains in Soils: Implications for Archaeological Residue Analyses. *Journal of Archaeological Science* 31(12):1715–1734.

Hastorf, C. A.

1988　The Use of Paleoethnobotanical Data in Prehistoric Studies of Crop Production, Processing, and Consumption. In *Current Paleoethnobotany: Analytical Methods and Cultural Interpretations of Archaeological Plant Remains,* edited by C. A. Hastorf and V. S. Popper, pp. 119–144. University of Chicago Press, Chicago.

Haug, G. H., K. A. Hugen, D. M. Sigman, L. C. Peterson, and U. Rohl

2001　Southward Migration of the Intertropical Convergence Zone through the Holocene. *Science* 293:1304–1308.

Haug, G. H., Gunther, D., L. C. Peterson, D. M. Sigman, K. A. Hughen, and B. Aeschlimann

2003　Climate and Collapse of Maya Civilization. *Science* 299:1731–1735.

Haviser, J. B.

1990a　Perforated Prehistoric Ornaments of Curaçao and Bonaire, Netherlands Antilles. *Beads* 2:85–92.

1990b　Geographic, Economic, and Demographic Aspects of Amerindian Interaction between Anguilla and St. Martin–St. Maarten. 55th Annual Meeting of the Society for American Archaeology, Las Vegas.

1999　Hope Estate: Lithics. In *Archaeological Investigations on St. Martin (Lesser Antilles): The Sites of Norman Estate, Anse des Pères, and Hope Estate, with a Contribution to the "La Hueca Problem,"* edited by C. L. Hofman and M. L. P. Hoogland, pp. 189–202. Archaeological Studies, Leiden University, 4, Leiden.

Hess, J., M. L. Bender, and J. Schilling

1986　Evolution of the Ratio of Strontium-87 to Strontium-86 in Seawater from Cretaceous to Present. *Science* 231(4741):979–984.

Heumann, A., and G. R. Davies

2002　U-Th Disequilibrium and Rb-Sr Age Constraints on the Magmatic Evolution of Peralkaline Rhyolites from Kenya. *Journal of Petrology* 43(3):557–577.

Higuera-Gundy, A.

1991　Antillean Vegetational History and Paleoclimate Reconstructed from the Paleolimnological Record of Lake Miragoane, Haiti. Unpublished Ph.D. dissertation, Botany Department, University of Florida, Gainesville.

Higuera-Gundy, A., M. Brenner, D. A. Hodell, J. H. Curtis, B. W. Leyden, and M. W. Binford

1999　A 10,300 ^{14}C yr Record of Climate and Vegetation Change from Haiti. *Quaternary Research* 52:159–170.

Hill, J. N.

1970　*Broken K Pueblo.* Anthropology Papers of the University of Arizona, No. 18. University of Arizona Press, Tucson.

Hodell, D. A., J. H. Curtis, and M. Brenner

1995　Possible Role of Climate in the Collapse of Classic Maya Civilization. *Nature* 375:391–394.

Hodell, D. A., M. Brenner, J. H. Curtis, and T. Guilderson
  2001   Solar Forcing of Drought Frequency in the Maya Lowlands. *Science* 292:1367–1370.
Hodell, D. A., M. Brenner, J. H. Curtis, R. Medina-González, E. Ildefonso-Chan Can,
A. Albornaz-Pat, and T. P. Guilderson
  2005   Climate Change on the Yucatán Peninsula during the Little Ice Age. *Quaternary Research* 63(2):109–121.
Hodell, D. A., J. H. Curtis, G. A. Jones, A. Higuera-Gundy, M. Brenner, M. W. Binford, and
K. T. Dorsey
  1991   Reconstruction of Caribbean Climate Change over the Past 10,500 Years. *Nature* 352:790–793.
Hoffman, C. A., Jr.
  1967   *Bahama Prehistory: Cultural Adaptation to an Island Environment.* Ph.D. dissertation, Department of Anthropology, University of Arizona, Tucson. University Microfilms, Ann Arbor.
  1970   The Palmetto Grove Site on San Salvador, Bahamas. Contributions of the Florida State Museum. *Social Sciences* 16:1–26.
  1979   The Ceramic Typology of the Mill Reef Site, Antigua, Leeward Islands. *Journal of the Virgin Islands Archaeological Society* 7:35–51.
Hofman, C. L.
  1993   In Search of the Native Population of Pre-Columbian Saba (A.D. 400–1450), Part One: Pottery Styles and Their Interpretations. Unpublished Ph.D. dissertation, Leiden University, Leiden.
Hofman, C. L., and A. J. Bright
  2004   From Suazoid to Folk Pottery: Pottery Manufacturing Traditions in a Changing Social and Cultural Environment on St. Lucia. *Nieuwe West-Indische Gids* 78(1/2):73–104
Hofman, C. L., and M. L. P. Hoogland
  2003   Plum Piece, Evidence for Archaic Seasonal Occupation on Saba, Northern Lesser Antilles around 3300 B.P.. *Journal of Caribbean Archaeology* 4:12–27.
Hofman, C. L., and M. L. P. Hoogland (eds.)
  1999   *Archaeological Investigations on St. Martin (Lesser Antilles). The Sites of Norman Estate, Hope Estate and Anse des Pères with a Contribution to the 'La Hueca Problem'.* Archaeological Studies Leiden University, 4, Leiden.
Hofman, C. L., and L. Jacobs
  2000/   The Dynamics of Technology, Function, and Style: A Study of Early Ceramic Age
  2001   Pottery from the Caribbean. *Newsletter of the Department of Pottery Technology* (Leiden University) 18/19:7–43 (published in 2003).
  2004   Different or Alike? A Technological Comparison between Late-Prehistoric and Modern-Day Folk Pottery on St. Lucia, (W.I.). *Leiden Journal of Pottery Studies* 20:23–52.
Hofman, C. L., A. J. Bright, and M. L. P. Hoogland
  2006   Archipelagic Resource Procurement and Mobility in the Northern Lesser Antilles: The View from a 3,000-Year-Old Tropical Forest Campsite on Saba. *Journal of Island and Coastal Archaeology* 1:145–164.

Hofman, C. L., M. L. P. Hoogland, and A. Delpuech

1999   Guadeloupe, Le Moule: Site Précolombien de Morel. Internal report, Leiden.

Hofman, C. L., M. L. P. Hoogland, and A. Delpuech (editors)

2001   *Le site de l'Anse à la Gourde, St. François, Grande-Terre, Guadeloupe: Fouille pro-grammée pluriannuelle, 1995–2000.* Rapport de synthèse 2000, Direction Régionale des Affaires Culturelles/Université de Leiden, Basse-Terre/Leiden.

2003   Les occupations amérindiennes de l'Anse à la Gourde (Grande-Terre de Gua-deloupe): 400 à 1400 de notre ère. In *Archéologie précolombienne et coloniale des Caraïbes,* edited by A. Delpuech, J.-P. Giraud, and A. Hesse, pp. 123–145. Actes du 123e Congrès national des sociétés historiques et scientifiques, Antilles-Guyane, 1998. Éditions du C.T.H.S., Paris.

Hofman, C. L., A. J. D. Isendoorn, and M. A. Booden

2005   Clays Collected: Towards an Identification of Source Areas for Clays Used in the Production of Pre-Columbian Pottery in the Northern Lesser Antilles. *Leiden Journal of Pottery Studies* 21:9–26.

Hofman, C. L., L. Jacobs, and P. van Olst

1993   Technological Aspects of the Pottery from Saba. In Corinne L. Hofman, In Search of the Native Population of Pre-Columbian Saba (A.D. 400–1450), Part One: Pot-tery Styles and Their Interpretations, pp. 159–196. Unpublished Ph.D. dissertation, Leiden University, Leiden.

Hofman, C. L., A. J. Bright, A. Boomert, and S. Knippenberg

2007   Island Rhythms: The Web of Social Relationships and Interaction Networks in the Lesser Antillean Archipelago between 400 B.C. and A.D. 1492. *American Antiquity* 72.

Holmes, W. H.

1884   Prehistoric Textile Fabrics of the United States Derived from Impressions on Pot-tery. *Annual Report of the Bureau of American Ethnology, 1881–1882,* pp. 393–425. Smithsonian, Institution, Washington, D.C.

Hoogland, M. L. P.

1996   In Search of the Native Population of Pre-Colonial Saba (A.D. 400–1450): Settle-ments in Their Natural and Social Environment. Unpublished Ph.D. dissertation, Leiden University, Leiden.

Hoogland, M. L. P., and C. L. Hofman

In press Island Dynamics: Evidence for Mobility and Exchange at the Site of Anse à la Gourde, Guadeloupe. In *New Perspectives on Prehistoric Settlement of the Ca-ribbean,* edited by S. M. Fitzpatrick and A. H. Ross. University Press of Florida, Gainesville.

Hooijkaas, G. R., and M. A. Booden

2004   Provenance of Pre-Colonial Ceramics on St. Lucia, West Indies. Unpublished master's thesis, Vrije Universiteit Amsterdam (Free University Amsterdam), Amsterdam.

Howarth, R. J., and J. M. McArthur

1997   Statistics for Strontium Isotope Stratigraphy: A Robust LOWESS Fit to the Marine Sr-Isotope Curve for 0 to 206 Ma, with Look-Up Table for Derivation of Numeric Age. *Journal of Geology* (105):441–456.

Hrdlicka, A.
 1920   Shovel-Shaped Teeth. *American Journal of Physical Anthropology* 3:429–465.
Hulme, P., and N. L. Whitehead
 1992   *Wild Majesty: Encounters with Caribs from Columbus to the Present Day, An Anthology.* Clarendon Press, Oxford.
Hutcheson, C. D.
 2001   Reweaving the Strands: Continued Exploration into the Basketry Technology of Prehistoric Bahamians. In *Proceedings of the Eighteenth International Association for Caribbean Archaeology* (1999), edited by L'Association Internationale d'Archéologie de la Caraïbe Région Guadeloupe, pp. 185–198. St. George's University Campus, True Blue, St. George, Grenada.
Hutcheson, C. D., and L. McWeeney
 1999   Reweaving the Strands: The Search for Prehistoric Bahamian Basketry Fibers. Poster presented at the Eighteenth International Congress for Caribbean Archaeology, St. George, Grenada.
Inizan, M. L., M. Reduron, H. Roche, and Tixier J.
 1995   *Technologie de la pierre taillée.* Préhistoire de la pierre taillée, 4. Cercle de recherches et d'études préhistoriques, Meudon.
Irish, J. D.
 1993   Biological Affinities of Late Pleistocene through Modern African Aboriginal Populations: The Dental Evidence. Unpublished Ph.D. dissertation, Arizona State University, Tempe.
 1997   Characteristic High-and-Low-Frequency Dental Traits in Sub-Saharan African Populations. *American Journal of Physical Anthropology* 102:455–467.
 1998a Ancestral Dental Traits in Recent Sub-Saharan Africans and the Origin of Modern Humans. *Journal of Human Evolution* 34:81–98.
 1998b Affinités des populations d'Afrique du Nord et d'Afrique sub-saharienne depuis la fin du Pléistocène jusqu'à l'Actuel, d'après la morphologie dentaire. *Bulletin et Mémoire de la Société d'Anthropologie* 10:237–272.
 2000   The Iberomauresian Enigma: North African Progenitor or Dead End? *Journal of Human Evolution* 39:393–410.
Isendoorn, A. J. D., M. Booden, and C. L. Hofman
 2005   Back to the Source: Provenance Areas of Clays and Temper Materials of Pre-Columbian Caribbean Ceramics. Paper presented at the 71st Meeting of the Society for American Archaeology, San Juan, Puerto Rico.
Izquierdo Diaz, G.
 1988   Ajuares de concha aborígenes, un estudio preliminar. *Reporte de Investigación del Instituto de Ciencias Históricas* 10:1–9. Academia de Ciencias de Cuba, Havana.
 1991   La industria de la concha del sitio arqueológico El Paraíso, Santiago de Cuba. *Estudio Arqueológicos* 141–175. Academia de Ciencias de Cuba, Centro de Antropología, Departamento de Arqueología, Havana.
Jackson, J. B. C., M. X. Kirby, W. H. Berger, K. A. Bjorndal, L. W. Botsford, B. J. Bourque, R. H. Bradbury, R. Cooke, J. Erlandson, J. A. Estes, T. P. Hughes, S. Kidwell, C. B.

Lange, H. S. Lenihan, J. M. Pandolfi, C. H. Peterson, R. S. Steneck, M. J. Tegner, and R. R. Warner

2001　Historical Overfishing and the Recent Collapse of Coastal Ecosystems. *Science* 293:629–638.

Jacobs, L., and M. Van den Bel

1995　Technological Research. In Kamuyune: The Palikur Potters of French Guyana, by M. Van den Bel, pp. 123–130. Unpublished master's thesis, Leiden University, Leiden.

Jacobson, K.

2002　Étude des formes et des décors de la céramique précolombienne du site de L'embouchure de Baillif (Guadeloupe). Unpublished master's thesis, Université Paris I, Pantheon Sorbonne, Paris.

Jérémie, Sylvie

1995　Résultats de l'étude lithique. In *Proceedings of the Sixteenth International Congress for Caribbean Archaeology,* edited by G. Richard, vol. 2, pp. 135–145. Conseil Régional de la Guadeloupe, Basse-Terre.

Jones O'Day, S., and W. F. Keegan

2001　Expedient Tools from the Northern West Indies. *Latin American Antiquity* 12(3):1–17.

Jouravleva, I., and G. La Rosa Corzo

2003　La tecnología del burén y la elaboración final del casaba. *El Caribe Arqueológico* 7:73–78.

Juel Jensen, H.

1988　Functional Analysis of Prehistoric Flint Tools by High-Power Microscopy: A Review of West-European Research. *Journal of World Prehistory* 2:51–88.

Kars, H., J. B. H. Jansen, and S. P. Vriend

1990　Petrography and Geochemistry of Flint from the Lanaye Chalk (Rijkholt-St. Geertruid), and Some Other Neolithic Sources. In *Le silex de sa genèse à l'outil,* edited by M. R. Séronie-Vivien and M. Lenoir, pp. 131–140. Actes du 5e colloque international sur le silex, Bordeaux 1987. Paris.

Kaye, Q.

2001　The Paraphernalia Associated with Intoxicant Use by Prehistoric Caribbean Islanders, with Particular Reference to Spouted Ceramic Bowls. In *Proceedings of the Eighteenth International Congress for Caribbean Archaeology,* edited by G. Richard, vol. 1, pp. 199–213. Conseil Régional de la Guadeloupe, Basse Terre.

Keegan, W. F.

1981　*Artifacts in Archaeology: A Caribbean Case Study.* Master's thesis, Florida Atlantic University. University Microfilms, Ann Arbor.

1984　Pattern and Process in *Strombus gigas* Tool Replication. *Journal of New World Archaeology* 6(2):15–24.

1985　*Dynamic Horticulturalists: Population Expansion in the Prehistoric Bahamas.* Ph.D. dissertation, Department of Anthropology, University of California, Los Angeles. University Microfilms, Ann Arbor.

1986   The Optimal Foraging Analysis of Horticultural Production. *American Anthropologist* 88:92–107.

1992   *The People Who Discovered Columbus: The Prehistory of the Bahamas.* University Press of Florida, Gainesville.

1994   West Indian Archaeology, 1: Overview and Foragers. *Journal of Archaeological Research* 2:255–284.

1996a   West Indian Archaeology, 2: After Columbus. *Journal of Archaeological Research* 4(4):265–294.

1996b   Remote Sensing. In *Encyclopedia of Cultural Anthropology,* edited by D. Levinson, pp. 1109–1111. Henry Holt, New York.

1997a   *Bahamian Archaeology: Life in the Bahamas and Turks and Caicos before Columbus.* Media Publishing Co., Nassau, Bahamas.

1997b   "No Man [or Woman] Is an Island": Elements of Taíno Social Organization. In *The Indigenous People of the Caribbean,* edited by S. M. Wilson, pp. 111–117. University Press of Florida, Gainesville.

2000   West Indian Archaeology, 3: Ceramic Age. *Journal of Archaeological Research* 8:135–167.

2007   *Taino Indian Myth and Practice: The Arrival of the Stranger King.* University Press of Florida, Gainesville.

In press Central Plaza Burials in Saladoid Puerto Rico: An Alternative Perspective. *Latin American Antiquity.*

Keegan, W. F., and M. J. DeNiro

1988   Stable Carbon- and Nitrogen-Isotope Ratios of Bone Collagen Used to Study Coral-Reef and Terrestrial Components of Prehistoric Bahamian Diet. *American Antiquity* 53(2):320–336.

Keegan, W. F., and R. Rodríguez Ramos

2005   Sin rodeos. *El Caribe Arqueológico* 8:8–13.

Keeley, L. H.

1980   *Experimental Determination of Stone Tool Uses: A Microwear Analysis.* University of Chicago Press, Chicago.

Kelly, H. J.

2001   Application of Use-Wear Analysis in the Determination of Coral Tools. Paper presented at the Nineteenth International Congress for Caribbean Archaeology, Aruba.

2003   Amerindian Coral Tools: A Pilot Study in Experimental Archaeology on Coral Artifacts from Anse à la Gourde, Guadeloupe. Unpublished master's thesis, Leiden University, Leiden.

2004   Experimental Archaeology and Use-Wear Analysis: Understanding the Effects of Coral Tools on Shell. In *The Archaeology of Aruba: The Marine Shell Heritage,* edited by R. Dijkhoff and M. S. Linville, pp. 127–131. Publications of the Archaeological Museum of Aruba 10, Aruba.

Kelso, W. M., and B. Straube

2004   *Jamestown Rediscovery, 1994–2004.* Association for the Preservation of Virginia Antiquities, Richmond.

Kennedy, M. J., O. A. Chadwick, P. M. Vitousek, L. A. Derry, and D. M. Hendricks

1998　Replacement of Weathering with Atmospheric Sources of Base Cations during Ecosystem Development, Hawaiian Islands. *Geology* 26:1015–1018.

Kennett, D., and B. Winterhalder (editors)

2006　*Behavioral Ecology and the Transition to Agriculture.* University of California Press, Berkeley.

Kimber, C.T.

1988　*Martinique Revisited: The Changing Plant Geographies of a West Indian Island.* Texas A&M University Press, College Station.

Kjellmark, E.

1996　Late Holocene Climate Change and Human Disturbance on Andros Island, Bahamas. *Journal of Paleoclimatology* 15:133–146.

Klecka, W. R.

1980　*Discriminant Analysis.* Sage University Paper, Series Quantitative Applications in the Social Sciences, No. 07–019. Sage Publications, Beverly Hills.

Knippenberg, S.

1995　Norman Estate and Anse des Pères: Two Pre-Columbian Sites on Saint Martin: Survey and Lithics. Unpublished master's thesis, Faculty of Archaeology, Leiden University, Leiden.

1997　Flint and Chert on Antigua: Characterisation of the Little Cove and Corbison Point Sources. Unpublished report, Amsterdam.

1999a　Provenance of Flint within the Leeward Region, West Indies. In *Proceedings of the Sixteenth International Congress for Caribbean Archaeology* (1995), edited by G. Richard, vol. 1, pp. 261–271. Conseil Régional de la Guadeloupe, Basse Terre.

1999b　Anse des Pères: Lithics. In *Archaeological Investigations on St. Martin (Lesser Antilles): The Sites of Norman Estate, Anse des Pères, and Hope Estate, with a Contribution to the "La Hueca Problem,"* edited by C. L. Hofman and M. L. P. Hoogland, pp. 87–104. Archaeological Studies, Leiden University, 4, Leiden.

1999c　Norman Estate: Lithics. In *Archaeological Investigations on St. Martin (Lesser Antilles): The Sites of Norman Estate, Anse des Pères, and Hope Estate, with a Contribution to the "La Hueca Problem,"* edited by C. L. Hofman and M. L. P. Hoogland, pp. 35–46. Archaeological Studies, Leiden University, 4, Leiden.

2001　Lithic Procurement during the Saladoid Period within the Northern Lesser Antilles. In *Proceedings of the Eighteenth International Congress for Caribbean Archaeology* (1999), edited by Association Internationale d'Archéologie de la Caraïbe, vol. 1, pp. 262–271. Région Guadeloupe, Mission Archéologique, Guadeloupe. Grenada.

2004　Distribution and Exchange of Lithic Materials: Three Pointers and Axes from St. Martin. In *Late Ceramic Age Societies in the Eastern Caribbean,* edited by A. Delpuech and C. L. Hofman, pp. 121–138. BAR International Series 1273. British Archaeological Reports, Oxford.

2006　Stone Artefact Production and Exchange among the Northern Lesser Antilles. Unpublished Ph.D. dissertation, Leiden University, Leiden.

Knippenberg, S., M. Nokkert, A. Brokke, and T. Hamburg

1995   A Late Saladoid Occupation at the Anse des Pères Site, St. Martin. In *Proceedings of the Sixteenth Congress of the International Association for Caribbean Archaeology*, edited by G. Richard, pp. 352–373. Conseil Régional de la Guadeloupe, Basse Terre.

1999   Anse des Pères: Lithics. In *Archaeological Investigations on St. Martin (Lesser Antilles): The Sites of Norman Estate, Anse des Pères, and Hope Estate, with a Contribution to the "La Hueca Problem,"* edited by C. L. Hofman, and M. L. P. Hoogland, pp. 87–104. Archaeological Studies, Leiden University, 4, Leiden.

Krauskopf, K. B.

1956   Dissolution and Precipitation of Silica at Low Temperature. *Geochimica et Cosmochimica Acta* 10(1):1–26.

1959   *The Geochemistry of Silica in Sedimentary Environments.* Society of Economic Paleontologists and Mineralogists, Special Publication No. 7, pp. 4–19. Tulsa.

Krieger, H. W.

1930   The Aborigines of the Ancient Island of Hispaniola. In *Annual Report of the Board of Regents of the Smithsonian Institution for 1929*, pp. 473–506. Government Printing Office, Washington, D.C.

Lalueza-Fox, C., F. Calafell, A. J. Mártinez-Fuentes, and J. Bertranpetit

2003   Secuencia de DNA de restos prehistóricos de Cuba; Reconstrucción del poblamiento del Caribe. In *Biología de poblaciones humanas: Diversidad, tiempo, espacio*. Acts of the 13th SEAB Conference, Oviedo, Spain, 2003, pp. 323–327. Oviedo.

Lalueza-Fox, C., M. T. P. Gilbert, A. J. Martínez-Fuentes, F. Calafell, and J. Bertranpetit

2003   Mitochondrial DNA from Pre-Columbian Ciboneys from Cuba and the Prehistoric Colonization of the Caribbean. *American Journal of Physical Anthropology* 121:97–108.

Lalueza-Fox, C., F. Luna Calderón, F. Calafell, B. Morera, and J. Bertranpetit

2001   MtDNA from Extinct Taínos and the Peopling of the Caribbean. *Annals of Human Genetics* 65(part 2):137–151.

Lammers-Keijsers, Y. M. J.

1999   Excavations on Anse à la Gourde: Use-Wear on Pre-Columbian Shell Artefacts. In *Proceedings of the Eighteenth International Congress for Caribbean Archaeology*, edited by Association Internationale d'Archéologie de la Caraïbe, Région Guadeloupe, Mission Archéologique, Guadeloupe, pp. 185–198. St. George's University Campus, True Blue, St. George, Grenada.

2001   Shell Tools. In *Le site de l'Anse à la Gourde, St. François, Grande-Terre, Guadeloupe: Fouille programmée pluriannuelle, 1995–2000*, edited by C. L. Hofman, M. L. P. Hoogland, and A. Delpuech, pp. 235–265. Rapport de synthèse 2000, Direction Régionale des Affaires Culturelles/Leiden University, Basse-Terre/Leiden.

2007   Tracing Traces from Present to Past: A Functional Analysis of Pre-Columbian Shell and Stone Artifacts from Anse à la Gourde and Morel. Unpublished Ph.D. dissertation, Leiden University, Leiden.

La Niece, S., and N. Meeks

2000   Diversity of Goldsmithing Traditions in the Americas and the Old World. In *Pre-

columbian Gold: Technology, Style, and Iconography, edited by C. McEwan, pp. 220–239. British Museum Press, London.

Larsen, C. S., and M. A. Kelley

1991 Introduction. In *Advances in Dental Anthropology,* edited by M. A. Kelley and L. C. Spencer, pp. 1–5. Wiley Liss, New York.

Las Casas, B.

1909 *Apologetica historia de las Indias.* Nueva Bibliotheca de Autores Españoles 13, Madrid.

1971 *History of the Indies* (European Perspectives). Harper and Row, New York.
[1527–
65]

Lavin, L., and D. R. Prothero

1992 Prehistoric Procurement of Secondary Sources: The Case for Characterisation. *North American Archaeologist* 13:97–113.

Layfield, J.

1995 Relación del viaje a Puerto Rico de la expedición de Sir George Clifford, tercer
[1598] conde de Cumberland, escrita por el Reverendo Doctor John Layfield, capellán de la expedición. (Fragmentos) Año 1598. In *Crónicas de Puerto Rico desde la conquista hasta nuestros días (1493–1955),* compiled and edited by E. Fernández Méndez, pp. 135–156. Editorial Universitaria, San Juan, Puerto Rico.

Lechtman, H.

1988 Traditions and Styles in Central Andean Metalworking. In *The Beginning of the Use of Metals and Alloys,* edited by R. Maddin, pp. 334–378. MIT Press, Cambridge.

Lemonnier, P.

1986 The Study of Material Culture Today: Toward an Anthropology of Technical Systems. *Journal of Anthropological Archaeology* 5:147–186.

1993a Introduction. In *Technological Choices: Transformation in Material Cultures since the Neolithic,* edited by P. Lemonnier, pp. 1–35. Routledge, London.

Lemonnier, P. (editor)

1993b *Technological Choices: Transformation in Material Cultures since the Neolithic.* Routledge, London.

Lepofsky, D., and K. Lertzman

2005 More on Sampling for Richness and Diversity in Archaeobiological Assemblages. *Journal of Ethnobiology* 25(2):175–188.

Leroi-Gourhan, A.

1943 *L'homme et la matière.* Albin Michel, Paris.

1964 *Le geste et la parole I: Techniques et langage.* Albin Michel, Paris.

Levin, D. A.

2001 The Recurrent Origin of Plant Races and Species. *Systematic Botany* 26(2):197–204.

Lewenstein, S. M.

1980 Analyzing Chipped Stone Artifacts: The Study of Lithic Technology, Function, and Exchange. In *Proceedings of the Eighth International Congress for the Study of the Pre-Columbian Cultures of the Lesser Antilles,* edited by S. M. Lewenstein, pp. 406–425. Arizona State University, Anthropological Research Papers No. 22, Tempe.

Linville, M. S.

2004   "Non-Tool" Shell Artifacts in the Collection of the Archaeological Museum of Aruba. In *The Archaeology of Aruba: The Marine Shell Heritage*, edited by R. Dijkhoff and M. S. Linville, pp. 135–177. Publications of the Archaeological Museum of Aruba, No. 10, Aruba

Littman, S. L., and W. F. Keegan

1991   A Shell Bead Manufacturing Centre on Grand Turk, T.C.I. In *Proceedings of the Fourteenth Congress of the International Association for Caribbean Archaeology*, edited by A. Cummins and P. King, pp. 147–156. Barbados.

Longacre, W. A.

1970   *Archaeology as Anthropology: A Case Study.* Anthropology Papers of the University of Arizona, No. 17. University of Arizona Press, Tucson.

Lopez Varela, S., A. L. van Gijn, and L. Jacobs

2002   De-Mystifying Pottery Production in the Maya Lowlands: Detection of Use-Wear Traces on Pottery Sherds through Microscopic Analysis and Experimental Replication, *Journal of Archaeological Science* 29(10):1133–1147.

Lovén, S.

1935   *Origins of the Tainan Culture, West Indies.* Elanders Boktryckeri Aktiebolag, Göteborg, Sweden.

Loy, T., M. Spriggs, and S. Wickler

1992   Direct Evidence for Human Use of Plants 28,000 Years Ago: Starch Residues on Stone Artefacts from the Northern Solomon Islands. *Antiquity* 66:898–912.

Luedtke, B. E.

1978   Chert Sources and Trace Element Analysis. *American Antiquity* 43:413–423.

1979   The Identification of Sources of Chert Artifacts. *American Antiquity* 44:744–757.

1992   *An Archaeologist's Guide to Chert and Flint.* Archaeological Research Tools 7. University of California, Los Angeles.

Lugo, A. E., J. K. Francis, and J. L. Frangi

1998   *Prestoea montana* (R. Graham) Nichols. Sierra Palm. SO-ITF-SM-82, pp. 420–427. Department of Agriculture, Forest Service, Southern Forest Experiment Station, New Orleans.

Luna Calderón, F.

2002   Mitochondrial DNA in the Dominican Republic. *KACIKE: Journal of Caribbean History and Anthropology*, special issue. Electronic document, http://www.kacike.org/CalderonEnglish.pdf, accessed August 18, 2006.

Lundberg, E. M., J. H. Burton, and W. C. Lynn

2002   Investigation of Ceramic Variability at the Tutu Site through Acid-Extraction Elemental Analysis. In *The Tutu Archaeological Village Site: A Multidisciplinary Case Study in Human Adaptation*, edited by E. Righter, pp. 199–229. Routledge, London.

Lundberg, E. R.

1985   Observations on *Strombus* Columella Fragments, Cautionary Notes, and Experimental Microwear Analysis. In *Proceedings of the Tenth International Congress for the Study of Pre-Columbian Cultures of the Lesser Antilles,* edited by L. Allaire and F. M. Mayer, pp. 347–361. Centre de Recherches Caraïbes, Université de Montréal, Montreal.

1989   Preceramic Producement Patterns at Krum Bay, Virgin Islands. Unpublished Ph.D. dissertation, University of Illinois, Urbana.

Lyman, R. L., and M. J. O'Brien

2002   *W. C. McKern and the Midwestern Taxonomic Method.* University of Alabama Press, Tuscaloosa.

Macdonald, R., C. J. Hawkesworth, and E. Heath

2000   The Lesser Antilles Volcanic Chain: A Study in Arc Magmatism. *Earth-Science Reviews* 49:1–76.

Maigrot, Y.

1997   Tracéologie des outils tranchants en os des Ve et IVe millénaire av. J.-C. en bassin parisien: Essai méthodologique et application. *Bulletin de la Société Préhistorique Française* 94:198–2216.

2001   Étude technologique et fonctionnelle de l'outillage en matière dures animales: La station 4 de Chalain (Néolithique final, Jura, France). Unpublished Ph.D. dissertation, University of Paris, Paris.

Mann, C. J.

1986   Composition and Origin of Material I Pre-Columbian Pottery, San Salvador Island, Bahamas, *Geoarchaeology: An International Journal* 1:183–194.

Margeson, S.

1993   *Norwich Households: The Medieval and Post-Medieval Finds from Norwich Survey Excavations, 1971–1978.* East Anglian Archaeology Report No. 58. Norfolk Museums Service, Norwich.

Martínez-Cruzado, J. C., G. Toro-Labrador, V. Ho-Fung, M. A. Estévez-Montero, A. Lobaina-Manzanet, D. A. Padovani-Claudio, H. Sánchez-Cruz, P. Ortiz-Bermúdez, and A. Sánchez-Crespo

2001   Mitochondrial DNA Evidence for a Founder Effect in the Colonization of Puerto Rico by Its Indigenous People. *Human Biology* 73(4):491–511.

Martin-Kaye, P. H. A.

1959   *Reports on the Geology of the Leeward and the British Virgin Islands.* Voice Publishing, St. Lucia.

1969   A Summary of the Geology of the Lesser Antilles. *Overseas Geology and Mineral Resources* 10(2):172–206

Martinón-Torres, M., R. Valcárcel Rojas, J. Cooper, and T. Rehren

2007   Metals, Microanalysis, and Meaning: A Study of Metal Objects Excavated from the Indigenous Cemetery of El Chorro de Maíta, Cuba. *Journal of Archaeological Science,* 34(2):194–204.

Mattioni, M.

1970   Étude théorique des couches archéologiques aux Petites Antilles sur la Base Migrations. In *Proceedings of the Third Congress for the Study of Pre-Columbian Cultures of the Lesser Antilles* (1969) edited by R. P. Bullen, pp. 139–146. Grenada.

1971 L'outillage lithique d'un site du nord-est de la Martinique. In *Proceedings of the Fourth International Congress for the Study of Pre-Columbian Cultures of the Lesser Antilles*, pp. 84–89. St. Lucia Archaeological and Historical Society, Castries, St. Lucia.

1982 Salvage Excavations at the Fond-Brule Site, Martinique: Final Report. University of Manitoba Anthropology Papers, 27. Winnipeg.

1990 Objets de parure issus de la fouille de sondage sur le site de l'Anse Trabaud (Martinique). In *Proceedings of the Eleventh Congress of the International Association for Caribbean Archaeology*, edited by A. G. Pantel Tekakis, I. Vargas Arenas, and M. Sanoja Obediente, pp. 108–111. San Juan, Puerto Rico.

Mattioni, M., and R. P. Bullen

1970 A Chronological Chart for the Lesser Antilles. In *Proceedings of the Third International Congress for the Study of Pre-Columbian Cultures of the Lesser Antilles* (1969) edited by R. P. Bullen, pp. 1–7. St. George, Grenada.

Maury, R. C., G. K. Westbrook, P. E. Baker, P. Bouysse, and D. Westercamp

1990 Geology of the Lesser Antilles, in the Caribbean Region. In *The Geology of North America, Vol. H, The Caribbean Region*, edited by G. Dengo and J. E. Case. Geological Society of America, Boulder, Colorado.

Mauss, M.

1947 *Manuel d'ethnographie.* Payot, Paris.

McKee, J. K.

2003 *Sparing Nature: The Conflict between Human Population Growth and Earth's Biodiversity.* Rutgers University Press, New Brunswick, New Jersey.

McKusick, M. B.

1960 *Distribution of Ceramic Styles in the Lesser Antilles, West Indies.* Ph.D. dissertation, Yale University, New Haven. University Microfilms, Ann Arbor.

Merkel, J. F., A. I. Seruya, D. Griffiths, and I. Shimada

1995 Metallography and Microanalysis of Precious Metal Objects from the Middle Sicán Elite Tombs at Batán Grande, Peru. In *Materials Issues in Art and Archaeology IV,* edited by P. B. Vandiver, J. R. Druzik, and J. L. Galvan, vol. 352, pp. 105–126. Materials Research Society Proceedings, Pittsburgh.

Meyers, F. R. (editor)

2001 *The Empire of Things.* School of American Research Press, Santa Fe.

Miller, D. (editor)

2005 *Materiality.* Duke University Press, Durham, North Carolina.

Minar, C. J., P. B. Drooker, J. M. Hebert, A. G. Henderson, T. M. Johnsen, W. C. Johnson, J. B. Petersen, and C. B. Rieth

1999 Working Group in Impressed Pottery: Problems and Solutions in the Methods of Data Recovery and Analysis of Fabric, Net, Cord, and Basketry Impressed Pottery. Society for American Archaeology Annual Meeting, Chicago.

Minnis, P. E., and W. J. Elisens (editors)

2000 *Biodiversity and Native America.* University of Oklahoma Press, Norman.

Mitchener, M. B., C. Mortimer and A. M. Pollard

1987 Nuremberg and its jetons, c. 1475 to 1888: chemical compositions of the alloys. *Numismatic Chronicle* 147:114–155.

Montgomery, H., E. A. Pessagno, and I. M. Muñoz
1992   Jurassic (Tithonian) Radiolaria from La Désirade (Lesser Antilles): Preliminary
        Paleontological and Tectonic Implications. *Tectonics* 11:1426–1432.
Moore, D. G., R. A. Beck, Jr., and C. B. Rodning
2004   Joara and Fort San Juan: Culture Contact at the Edge of the World. Electronic
        document, http://antiquity.ac.uk/ProjGall/moore/index.html, accessed August 10,
        2006. *Antiquity* 78:299.
Moscoso, F.
1986   *Tribu y clase en el caribe antiguo.* Universidad Central del Este, San Pedro de
        Macorís, Dominican Republic.
Mourre, V.
1996   Le débitage sur enclume au Paléolithique inférieur et moyen: Techniques, mé-
        thodes et schémas conceptuels. Unpublished manuscript, Université de Paris X,
        Nanterre.
Multer, H. G., M. P. Weiss, and D. V. Nicholson
1986   *Antigua: Reefs, Rocks, and Highroads of History.* Leeward Islands Science Associ-
        ates No. 1. Antigua.
Murphy, A. R.
1999   The Prehistory of Antigua, Ceramic Age: Subsistence, Settlement, Culture, and
        Adaptation within an Insular Environment. Unpublished Ph.D. dissertation, Uni-
        versity of Calgary, Calgary.
Murphy, A. R., D. J. Hozjan, C. N. de Mille, and A. A. Levinson
2000   Pre-Columbian Gems and Ornamental Materials from Antigua, West Indies. *Gems
        and Gemology* 3:234–245.
Narganes Storde, Y. M.
1995a   La lapidaria de la Hueca, Vieques, Puerto Rico. In *Proceedings of the Fifteenth
        International Congress for Caribbean Archaeology* (1993), edited by R. E. Alegría
        and M. A. Rodríguez López, pp. 141–51. Centro de Estudios Avanzados de Puerto
        Rico Y el Caribe and Fundación Puertorriqueña de las Humanidades y la Universi-
        dad del Turabo, San Juan. San Juan, Puerto Rico.
1995b   La lapidaria agro 2 de Sorcé e Tecla, Puerto Rico. In *Proceedings of the Sixteenth
        International Congress for Caribbean Archaeology,* edited by G. Richard, vol. 2,
        pp. 17–26. Conseil Régional de la Guadeloupe, Basse-Terre.
Newsom, L. A.
1987   Analysis of Botanical Remains from Hontoon Island (8Vo202), Florida: 1980–1985
        Excavations. *The Florida Anthropologist* 40:47–84.
1993   Native West Indian Plant Use. Unpublished Ph.D. dissertation, Department of An-
        thropology, University of Florida, Gainesville.
1996   Early Historic Plant Remains from Archaeological Deposits at the Bastion de San
        Justo del Muelle, San Juan, Puerto Rico. Report to Louis Berger and Associates,
        U.S. General Services Administration, Region 2, Washington, D.C.
2002   The Paleoethnobotany of the Archaic Mortuary Pond. In *Windover: Multidisci-
        plinary Investigations of an Early Archaic Florida Cemetery,* edited by G. H. Doran,
        pp. 191–210. University Press of Florida, Gainesville.

2006 Caribbean Maize: First Farmers to Columbus. In *Histories of Maize,* edited by R. Blake, J. Staller, and R. Tikot, pp. 325–335. Academic Press, New York.

Newsom, L. A., and K. Deagan

1994 *Zea mays* in the West Indies: The Archaeological and Early Historic Record. In *Corn and Culture in the Prehistoric New World,* edited by S. Johhanesen and C. Hastorf, pp. 203–217. Westview Press, San Francisco.

Newsom, L. A., and D. M. Pearsall

2003 Trends in Caribbean Island Archaeobotany. In *People and Plants in Ancient Eastern North America,* edited by P. Minnis, pp. 347–412. Smithsonian Institution Press, Washington, D.C.

Newsom, L. A., and C. M. Scarry

In press Pineland Cordage and Modified Wood: Material-Technological Aspects of Plant Use. In *The Archaeology of Pineland: A Coastal Southwest Florida Village Complex,* A.D. *100–1600,* edited by K. J. Walker and W. Marquardt, chapter 12. Institute of Archaeology and Paleoenvironmental Studies, Monograph 3. University of Florida, Gainesville.

Newsom, L. A., and E. S. Wing

2004 *On Land and Sea: Native American Uses of Biological Resources in the West Indies.* University of Alabama Press, Tuscaloosa.

Newsom, L. A., R. Brown, and W. Natt.

In press From the Forests: Wood and Fiber Industries at Pineland, Florida. In *The Archaeology of Pineland: A Coastal Southwest Florida Village Complex,* A.D. *100–1600,* edited by K. J. Walker and W. Marquardt, chapter 6. Institute of Archaeology and Paleoenvironmental Studies, Monograph 3. University of Florida, Gainesville.

Nichol, C. R.

1989 Complex Segregation Analysis of Dental Morphological Variants. *American Journal of Physical Anthropology* 78:37–59.

Nieuwenhuis, C. J.

2002 *Traces on Tropical Tools: A Functional Study of Chert Artefact from Preceramics Sites in Colombia.* Archaeological Studies, Leiden University, 9, Leiden.

Nieuwenhuis, C. J., and A. L. van Gijn

2006 Cereal Harvesting and Processing at the Middle Neolithic Site of Schipluiden, a Coastal Site in the Lower-Rhine Basin. In *"Prehistoric Technology" 40 Years Later: Functional Studies and the Russian Legacy.* Proceedings of the Conference Held in Verona, Italy, April 20–23, 2005, edited by L. Longo, M. Dalla Riva, and M. Saracino Verona.

Nieves-Rivera, A. M., J. Muñoz-Vasquez, and C. Betancourt-López

1995 Hallucinogens Used by the Taíno Indians in the West Indies. *Atenea,* Facultad de Artes y Ciencias, Universidad de Puerto Rico, Mayagüez, 15(1–2):125–139.

Niñez, V. K.

1984 *Household Gardens: Theoretical Considerations on an Old Survival Strategy.* Potatoes in Food Systems, Research Series, Report No. 1. International Potato Center (CIP), Lima, Peru.

Norr, L.
2002   Bone Isotopic Analysis and Prehistoric Diet at the Tutu Site. In *The Tutu Archaeo-logical Village Site: A Multidisciplinary Case Study in Human Adaptation,* edited by E. Righter, pp. 264–273. Routledge, London.

Nyberg, J., A. Kuijpers, B. A. Malmgren, and H. Kunzendorf
2001   Late Holocene Changes in Precipitation and Hydrography Recorded in Marine Sediments from the Northeastern Caribbean Sea. *Quaternary Research* 56:87–102.

Oberg, K.
1955   Types of Social Structure among the Lowland Tribes of South and Central America. *American Anthropologist* 57:472–487.

Olazagasti, I.
1997   The Material Culture of the Taino Indians. In *The Indigenous People of the Caribbean,* edited by S. Wilson, pp. 131–139. University Press of Florida, Gaines-ville.

Oliver, J. R.
1998   *El centro ceremonial de Caguana, Puerto Rico: Simbolismo iconográfico, cosmo-visión y el poderío caciquil Taíno de Boriquén.* British Archaeological Reports Inter-national Series 727. Archaeopress, Oxford.
1999   The "La Hueca Problem" in Puerto Rico and the Caribbean: Old Problems, New Perspectives, Possible Solutions. In *Archaeological Investigations on St. Martin: The Sites of Anse des Pères, Norman Estate, and Hope Estate, with a Contribution to the "La Hueca Problem,"* edited by C. L. Hofman, and M. L. P. Hoogland pp. 253–298. Archaeological Studies, Leiden University, 4, Leiden.
2000   Gold Symbolism among Caribbean Chiefdoms: Of Feathers, Çibas, and Guanín Power among Taíno Elites. In *Precolumbian Gold: Technology, Style, and Iconog-raphy,* edited by C. McEwan, pp. 196–219. British Museum Press, London.
2001   The Archaeology of Forest Foraging and Agricultural Production in Amazonia. In *Unknown Amazon,* edited by C. McEwan, C. Barreto, and E. Neves, pp. 50–85. Brit-ish Museum Press, London.
2003   An Interpretative Analysis and Discussion of the Río Cocal-1 Community of Sa-bana Seca, Puerto Rico. In *Archaeological Survey and Evaluation of Sites at NSWC Sabana Seca, Vol. IV (Parts I–II): Evaluation of Prehistoric Site Río Cocal-1 Site,* ed-ited by R. C. Goodwin, J. R. Oliver, D. D. Davis, J. Brown, S. Sanders and M. Sim-mons, pp. 337–402. Submitted to the United States Department of the Navy, At-lantic Division, Naval Facilities Engineering Command, Norfolk.
2004   Soliloquio cubano: An Outsider's Thoughts on Recent Cuban Archaeology. Manu-script on file with the Institute of Archaeology, University College, London.
2005   The Proto-Taíno Monumental Cemís of Caguana: A Political-Religious Manifesto. In *Ancient Borinquen: Archaeology and Ethnohistory of Native Puerto Rico,* edited by P. E. Siegel, pp. 230–284. University of Alabama Press, Tuscaloosa.

Oliver, J. R., and Y. Narganes Storde
2005   The Zooarcheological Remains from Juan Miguel Cave and Finca de Doña Rosa, Barrio Caguana, Puerto Rico: Ritual Edibles or Quotidian Meals? In *Proceedings of the Twentieth International Congress for Caribbean Archaeology,* edited by G. Tava-

rez María and M. García Arévalo, pp. 227–242. Museo del Hombre Dominicano and Fundación García Arévalo, Santo Domingo.

Oliver, J. R., and J. A. Rivera Fontán

2004   *Reconocimiento intensivo del sitio arqueológico "Los Bateyes de Viví" (U-1), Bo, Viví Arriba, Utuado.* Final Technical Report for the 2004 Season. Submitted to the State Preservation Historical Office of Puerto Rico. Unpublished document on file at the Oficina Estatal de Conservación Histórica de Puerto Rico. Cuartel de Ballajá, San Juan.

Oliver, J. R., J. A. Rivera Fontán, and L. A. Newsom

1999   Arqueología del barrio Caguana, Puerto Rico: Resultados preliminares de las temporadas, 1996–1997. In *Trabajos de investigación arqueológica en Puerto Rico: Tercer encuentro de investigadores,* edited by J. Rivera Fontán, pp. 7–26. Occasional Publication of the Division of Archaeology. Instituto de Cultura Puertorriqueña, San Juan.

Olsen, F.

1974   *On the Trail of the Arawaks.* University of Oklahoma Press, Norman.

Ortega, E., and J. Guerrero

1981   *Cuatro nuevos sitios paleoarchaicos en la Isla de Santo Domingo.* Ediciones Museo del Hombre Dominicano, Santo Domingo.

1985   El complejo lítico de la Cordillera, las grandes puntas especializadas y su relación con los modos de vida preagroalfareros en la prehistoria de Santo Domingo. In *Proceedings of the Tenth International Congress for the Study of Pre-Columbian Cultures of the Lesser Antilles,* edited by L. Allaire and F. M. Mayer, pp. 311–334. Centre de Recherches Caraïbes, Université de Montréal, Montreal.

Ortiz, E.

1996   Estudio químicos geológico para identificar fuentes cerámicas precolombinas e impacto en las estradas. Paper presented at the Fifteenth International Congress for Caribbean Archaeology, San Juan, Puerto Rico (1993).

Ortíz Aguilú, J. J., J. Rivera Meléndez, A. Principe Jácome, M. Mélendez Maiz, and M. Lavergne Colberg

1991   Intensive Agriculture in Pre-Columbian West Indies: The Case for Terraces. In *Proceedings of the Fourteenth Congress of the International Association for Caribbean Archaeology,* edited by A. Cummins and P. King, pp. 278–285. Barbados Museum and Historical Society, St. Ann's Garrison.

Oversteegen, J., A. L. van Gijn, and L. P. Louwe Kooijmans

2001   Artefacten van been, gewei en tand. In *Hardinxveld-Giessendam Polderweg. Een mesolithisch jachtkamp in het rivierengebied (5500–5000 v. Chr.),* edited by L. P. Louwe Kooijmans, pp. 285–323. Rapportage Archeologische Monumentenzorg 83, Leiden.

Oviedo y Valdes, G. F. de

1959   *Natural History of the West Indies.* Translated and edited by S. A. Stoudemire.

[1526] University of North Carolina Studies in the Romance Languages and Literature, No. 32. University of North Carolina Press, Chapel Hill.

1851– *Historia general y natural de las Indias y Tierra Ferme de Mar Oceano,* 4 vols, edited

1855   by J. Amador de los Rios. Biblioteca de Autores Espanoles, Madrid.
[1535]

1996   *Sumario de la natural historia de Las Indias.* Fondo de Cultura Económica, Mexico.

Pagán Jiménez, J. R.

2002a   Granos de almidón en arqueología: Métodos y aplicaciones. Unpublished paper
        read at the IV Congreso Centroamericano de Antropología, Universidad Vera-
        cruzana, Xalapa.

2002b   Agricultura precolombina de las Antillas: Retrospección y análisis. *Anales de
        Antropología* IIA, UNAM, 36:43–91.

2003   Reporte de progreso: Estudio de almidones en artefactos líticos de los sitios ar-
        queológicos SR-1 y Utuado-27, Proyecto Utuado-Caguana, Puerto Rico. Report
        submitted to J. Oliver, L. Newsom, and J. Rivera, principal investigators Proyecto
        Arqueológico Utuado-Caguana. Institute of Archaeology, UC-London, Depart-
        ment of Anthropology, Penn State, University Park.

2004   Granos de almidón. Colección de Referencia para los Estudios Paleoetnobotánicos
        de Puerto Rico y Las Antillas (3ra Versión Ampliada). Unpublished manuscript.

2005a   En diálogo con J. R. Oliver y R. Rodríguez Ramos: La emergencia de la temprana
        producción de vegetales en nuestros esquemas investigativos y algunos fundamen-
        tos metodológicos del estudio de almidones. *Diálogo Antropológico* 3(10):49–55.

2005b   Estudio interpretativo de la cultura botánica de dos comunidades precolombinas
        antillanas: La Hueca y Punta Candelero, Puerto Rico. Unpublished Ph.D. disserta-
        tion, Facultad de Filosofía y Letras y Instituto de Investigaciones Antropológi-
        cas, Universidad Nacional Autónoma de México, Mexico City.

Pagán Jiménez, J. R., M. A. Rodríguez López, L. A. Chanlatte Baik, and Y. Narganes Storde

2005   La temprana introducción y uso de algunas plantas domésticas, silvestres y culti-
        vos en Las Antillas precolombinas. Una Primera Revaloración desde la Perspectiva
        del "Arcaico" de Vieques y Puerto Rico. *Diálogo Antropológico* 3(10):7–33.

Pané, Fray R.

2001   *Relación acerca de las antigüedades de los indios* (Nueva Versión con Estudio Pre-
[1505] liminar, Notas y Apéndices por José Juan Arrom). America Nuestra, Siglo Vein-
        tiuno Editores, Mexico City.

Pantel, A. G.

1976   Progress Report and Analysis, Barrera Mordan Complex, Azua, Dominican Re-
        public. In *Proceedings of the Sixth International Congress for the Study of Pre-
        Columbian Cultures of the Lesser Antilles,* edited by R. P. Bullen, pp. 269–271 (1975,
        Guadeloupe). Florida State Museum, University of Florida, Gainesville.

1988   *Precolumbian Flaked Stone Assemblages in the West Indies.* Ph.D. dissertation, Uni-
        versity of Tennessee, Knoxville. University Microfilm International, Ann Arbor.

1991   How Sophisticated Was "The Primitive"? Preceramic Source Materials, Lithic Re-
        duction Processes, Cultural Contexts, and Archaeological Interferences. In *Pro-
        ceedings of the Fourteenth Congress of the International Association for Caribbean
        Archaeology,* edited by A. Cummins and P. King, pp. 157–169. Barbados.

Pearsall, D. M.

1985   Analysis of Soil Phytoliths and Botanical Macroremains from El Bronce Archaeological Site, Ponce, Puerto Rico. Apppendix in Archaeological Data Recovery at El Bronce, Puerto Rico, Final Report Phase 2. Report submitted to the U.S. Army Corps of Engineers, Jacksonville District. U.S. Government Printing Office, Washington, D.C.

1989   Plant Utilization at the Krum Bay Site, St. Thomas U.S.V.I, Appendix C in *Preceramic Procurement Patterns at Krum Bay, Virgin Islands,* by E. R. Lundberg. Ph.D. dissertation, University of Illinois, Urbana. University Microfilms, Ann Arbor.

2000   *Paleoethnobotany: A Handbook of Procedures.* Academic Press, San Diego.

2002a   Analysis of Charred Botanical Remains from the Tutu Site, U.S. Virgin Islands. In *The Tutu Archaeological Village Site: A Multidisciplinary Case Study in Human Adaptation,* edited by E. Righter, pp 109–134. Routledge, New York.

2002b   *Paleoethnobotany: A Handbook of Procedures,* 2nd ed. Academic Press, New York.

Pearsall, D. M., K. Chandler-Ezell, and J. A. Zeidler

2004   Maize in Ancient Ecuador: Results of Residue Analysis of Stone Tools from the Real Alto Site. *Journal of Archaeological Science* 31(4):423–442.

Pelegrin, J.

1995   *Technologie lithique: Le Chatelperronien de Roc de Combe, Lot, et de la Côte, Dordogne.* Cahiers du Quaternaire 20. C.N.R.S., Paris.

Pendergast, D. M., E. Graham, R. Jorge Calvera, and M. J. Jardines

2002   The Houses in Which They Dwelt: The Excavation and Dating of Taíno Wooden Structures at Los Buchillones, Cuba. *Journal of Wetland Archaeology* 2:61–75.

Perry, L.

2002a   Starch Analyses Reveal Multiple Functions of Quartz "Manioc" Grater Flakes from the Orinoco Basin, Venezuela. *Interciencia* 27(11):635–639.

2002b   Starch Granule Size and the Domestication of Manioc (*Manihot esculenta*) and Sweet Potato (*Ipomoea batatas*). *Economic Botany* 56(4):335–349.

2004   Starch Analyses Reveal the Relationship between Tool Type and Function: An Example from the Orinoco Valley of Venezuela. *Journal of Archaeological Science,* 31(8):1069–1081.

Petersen, J. B.

1996   The Study of Fiber Industries from Eastern North America: Resume and Prospect. In *A Most Indispensable Art: Native Fiber Industries from Eastern North America,* edited by J. B. Petersen, pp. 1–29. University of Tennessee Press, Knoxville.

Petersen, J. B., and D. R. Watters

1991a   Archaeological Testing at the Early Saladoid Trants Site, Montserrat, West Indies. In *Proceedings of the Fourteenth Congress of the International Association for Caribbean Archaeology,* edited by A. Cummins and P. King, pp. 131–140. Barbados.

1991b   Amerindian Ceramic Remains from Fountain Cavern, Anguilla, West Indies. *Annals of the Carnegie Museum* 60(4):321–357.

Petersen, J. B., D. R. Watters, and D. V. Nicholson

1999   Prehistoric Basketry from Antigua and Montserrat, Northern Lesser Antilles, West Indies. In *Proceedings of the Seventeenth Congress of the International Association for Caribbean Archaeology,* edited by J. H. Winter, pp. 63–76. Rockville Centre, New York.

Peterson, L. C., and G. H. Haug

2005 Climate and the Collapse of Maya Civilization: A Series of Multi-Year Droughts Helped to Doom an Ancient Culture. *American Scientist* 93:322–329.

Petitjean Roget, H.

1968 Étude d'un horizon Arawak et proto-Arawak à Martinique à partir du niveau II du Diamant. In *Proceedings of the Second International Congress for the Study of the Precolumbian Cultures of the Lesser Antilles* (1967), edited by R. P. Bullen, pp. 61–68. Barbados Museum, Barbados.

1974 La savane des pétrifications (Martinique): Un gisement de l'age lithique. In *Proceedings of the Fifth International Congress for the Study of Pre-Columbian Cultures of the Lesser Antilles* (1973), pp. 82–93. Antigua.

1978 Découverte du site de Gros-Montagne (Guyane). In *Proceedings of the Seventh International Congress for the Study of the Pre-Columbian Cultures of the Lesser Antilles* (1977), pp. 149–155. Centre de Recherches Caraïbes, Université de Montréal, Montreal.

1990 De l'arbre à pierre verte a propos d'une nouvelle acquisition d l'AGAE "une hache emmanchée." In *Proceedings of the Eleventh Congress of the International Association for Caribbean Archaeology,* edited by A. G. Pantel Tekakis, I. Vargas Arenas, and M. Sanoja Obediente, pp. 75–84. San Juan, Puerto Rico.

1995 Les calebasses peintes, la poterie et l'arc en ciel chez les Caraïbes insulaires. In *Proceedings of the Sixteenth Congress of the International Association for Caribbean Archaeology,* edited by G. Richard, vol. 1, pp. 159–175. Conseil Régional de la Guadeloupe, Basse Terre.

Petitjean Roget, J.

1963 The Caribs, as Seen through the Dictionary of the Reverend Father Breton. In *Proceedings of the First International Convention for the Study of Pre-Columbian Culture in the Lesser Antilles,* pp. 43–68. Fort-de-France, Martinique.

1970 Étude des tessons. In *Proceedings of the Third International Congress for the Study of Pre-Columbian Cultures of the Lesser Antilles,* pp. 87–94, Grenada National Museum, Grenada.

1971 Étude de la décoration des vases précolombiens de la Martinique. In *Proceedings of the Fourth International Congress for the Study of Pre-Columbian Cultures of the Lesser Antilles,* pp. 174–180. St. Lucia Archaeological and Historical Society, Castries, St. Lucia.

Pierpont Morgan Library

1996 *Histoire naturelle des Indes: The Drake Manuscript,* preface by C. E. Pierce, Jr., foreword by P. O'Brian, introduction by V. Klinkenborg, translations by R. S. Kraemer. W. W. Norton, New York.

Pike, D. W., and A. G. Pantel

1974 First Flint Worksite Found in Puerto Rico. In *Proceedings of the Fifth International Congress for the Study of Pre-Columbian Cultures of the Lesser Antilles* (1973), edited by R. P. Bullen, pp. 140–142. The Antigua Archaeological Society, Antigua.

Pinchon, R.

1952 Introduction à l'archéologie martiniquaise. *Journal de la Société des Américanistes* n.s. 41:2.

Pinchon, R. (editor)

1961   Description de lisle de Saint-Vincent: Manuscrit anonyme du début du XVIIIème siècle. *Annales des Antilles* 9:35–81.

1964   The Different Forms of Pottery in the Arawak Civilization. In *Proceedings of the First International Congress for the Study of Pre-Columbian Cultures of the Lesser Antilles* (1961), pp. 89–93. Fort de France, Martinique.

Piperno, D. R.

1988   *Phytolith Analysis: An Archaeological and Geological Perspective.* Academic Press, San Diego.

Piperno, D. R., and I. Holst

1998   The Presence of Starch Grain on Prehistoric Stone Tools from the Humid Neotropics: Indications of Early Tuber Use and Agriculture in Panama. *Journal of Archaeological Science* 25:765–776.

Piperno, D. R., and D. M. Pearsall

1998   *The Origins of Agriculture in the Lowland Neotropics.* Academic Press, San Diego.

Piperno, D. R., A. J. Ranere, I. Holst, and P. Hansell

2000   Starch Grains Reveal Early Root Crop Horticulture in the Panamanian Tropical Forest. *Nature* 407:894–897.

Price, T. D., J. H. Burton, and R. A. Bentley

2002   The Characterization of Biologically Available Strontium Isotope Ratios for the Study of Prehistoric Migration. *Archaeometry* 44(1):117–135.

Rachlin, C. K.

1955   The Rubber Mold Technique Used in a Study of Textile Impressed Pottery. *American Antiquity* 20(4):394–396.

Rainey, F. G.

1940   Porto Rican Archaeology. In *Scientific Survey of Porto Rico and the Virgin Islands,* vol. 18, no. 1. New York Academy of Science, New York.

Reber, E.

2005   What did they eat? In *Annual Editions in Archaeology, seventh edition.* 04/05: p. 132–133. McGraw-Hill/Dushkin, Dubuque, IA.

Redman, C. L.

1999   *Human Impact on Ancient Environments.* University of Arizona Press, Tucson.

Redmond, E. M., and C. S. Spencer

1994   The Cacicazgo: An Indigenous Design. In *Caciques and Their People: A Volume in Honor of Ronald Spores,* edited by J. Marcus and J. F. Zeitlin, pp. 189–225. Anthropological Papers No. 89, Museum of Anthropology, University of Michigan, Ann Arbor.

Reichert, E. T.

1913   *The Differentiation and Specificity of Starches in Relation to Genera, Species, Etc.* Carnegie Institution of Washington, Washington, D.C.

Reith, C. B.

2004   Cordage, Fabrics, and Their Use in the Manufacture of Early Late Prehistoric Ceramic Vessels in New York. In *Perishable Material Culture in the Northeast,* edited by P. B. Drooker, chapter 7. New York State Museum Bulletin 500. University of the State of New York, State Education Department, New York State Museum, Albany.

Ricklefs, R. E., and E. Bermingham

2001   Nonequilibrium Diversity Dynamics of the Lesser Antillean Avifauna. *Science* 294:1522–1524.

Rivera Fontán, J. A., and J. R. Oliver

2005   Impactos y patrones de ocupación histórica jíbara sobre componentes Taínos: El sitio "Vega de Nelo Vargas" (Utu-27), Barrio Caguana, Municipio de Utuado, Puerto Rico. In *Proceedings of the Twentieth International Congress for Caribbean Archaeology,* edited by G. Tavares María and M. García Arévalo, pp. 1–14. Museo del Hombre Dominicano and Fundación García Arévalo, Santo Domingo.

Robinson, L. S., E. R. Lunberg, and J. B. Walker

1985   Archaeological Data Recovery at El Bronce, Puerto Rico: Final Report, Phase 2. Report to the U.S. Army Corps of Engineers, Jacksonville, Florida.

Rodríguez López, M. A.

1991a   Arqueología de Punta Candelero, Puerto Rico. In *Proceedings of the Thirteenth International Congress for Caribbean Archaeology 2,* edited by E. N. Ayubi and J. B. Haviser, pp. 605–627. Reports of the Archaeological-Anthropological Institute of the Netherlands Antilles, No. 9, Curaçao.

1991b   Early Trade Networks in the Caribbean. In *Proceedings of the Fourteenth International Congress for Caribbean Archaeology,* edited by A. Cummins and P. King, pp. 306–314. Bridgetown, Barbados.

1997   Maruca, Ponce. In *Ocho trabajos de investigación arqueológica en Puerto Rico: Secundo encuentro de investigadores,* pp. 17–30. Publicación Ocasional de la División de Arqueología. Instituto de Cultura Puertorriqueña, San Juan.

Rodríguez Ramos, R.

1999   Lithic Reduction Trajectories at La Hueca and Punta Candelero Sites (Puerto Rico). In *Proceedings of the Eighteenth International Congress for Caribbean Archaeology 1* (1999), edited by G. Richard, pp. 251–261. International Association for Caribbean Archaeology, Guadeloupe. Grenada.

2001a   Lithic Reduction Trajectories at La Hueca and Punta Candelero Sites, Puerto Rico. Unpublished master's thesis, Texas A&M University.

2001b   Lithic Reduction Trajectories at La Hueca and Punta Candelero Sites (Puerto Rico). In *Proceedings of the Eighteenth International Congress for Caribbean Archaeology* (1999), edited by the Association Internationale d'Archéologie de la Caraïbe, Région Guadeloupe, Mission Archéologique, vol. 1, pp. 251–261. St. George's University Campus, True Blue, St. George, Grenada.

2003   La continuidad tecnológica del Arcaico al post-Saladoide en Puerto Rico: Un vistazo desde la lítica de Paso del Indio. In *Proceedings of the Twentieth Congress of the International Association for Caribbean Archaeology,* edited by G. Tavarez María and M. García Arévalo, pp. 327–331. International Association for Caribbean Archaeology, Santo Domingo.

2005a   La continuidad tecnológica del Arcaico al post-Saladoide en Puerto Rico: Un vistazo desde la lítica de Paso del Indio. In *Actas del XXé congreso internacional de arqueología del Caribe,* 1, pp. 327–330. Museo del Hombre Dominicano and Fundación Garcia Arévalo, Santo Domingo.

2005b The Function of the Edge-Ground Cobble Put to Test: An Initial Assessment. *Journal of Caribbean Archaeology* 6:1–22.

In press From the Guanahatabey to the "Archaic" of Puerto Rico: The Non-Evident Evidence. *Ethnohistory.*

Rodríguez Suárez, R.

1989 ¿Huellas de restos alimenticios en la cerámica precolombina? El caso del sitio Laguna de Limones, Maisí, Guantánamo. Paper presented at the Primer Taller de Investigaciones Arqueológicas, Holguín, Cuba.

2004 Huellas de restos en la cerámica precolombina: El caso del sitio Lagunas de Limonas, Maisí, Cuba. *El Caribe Arqueológico* 8:86–90.

Rodríguez Suárez, R., and J. R. Pagán Jiménez

2006 Primeras evidencias directas del uso de plantas en la dieta de los grupos agroalfareros del Oriente de Cuba. *Catauro: Revista Cubana de Antropología* 8(14): 100–120.

Rodríguez Suárez, R., S. Vidaud, and N. González

2001 "El burén como artefacto multipropósito en la cocina prehispánica de comunidades agroalfareras de Cuba." Paper presented at the Segundo Coloquio Nacional de Arqueometría, IIA, UNAM, Mexico City.

Roe, P. G.

1980 Art and Residence among the Shipibo Indians of Peru: A Study in Microacculturation. *American Anthropologist* 82:42–71.

1989 A Grammatical Analysis of Cedrosan Saladoid Vessel Form Categories and Surface Decoration: Aesthetic and Technical Styles in Early Antillean Ceramics. In *Early Ceramic Population Lifeways and Adaptive Strategies in the Caribbean,* edited by P. E. Siegel, pp. 267–282. BAR International Series 506. British Archaeological Reports, Oxford.

1995 Style, Society, Myth, and Structure. In *Style, Society, and Person,* edited by C. Carr and J. E. Neitzel, pp. 27–76. Plenum Press, New York.

Roe, P. G., A. G. Pantel, and M. B. Hamilton

1990 Monserrate Restudied: The 1978 Centro Field Season at Luquillo Beach: Excavation Overview, Lithics, and Physical Anthropological Remains. In *Proceedings of the Eleventh Congress of the International Association for Caribbean Archaeology,* edited by A. G. Pantel Tekakis, I. Vargas Arenas, and M. Sanoja Obediente, pp. 338–369. San Juan, Puerto Rico.

Rojer, A.

1997 *Biological Inventory of St. Maarten.* KNAP Project 96–10, Carmabi Foundation, Curaçao.

Roobol, M. J., and J. W. Lee

1976 Petrography and Source of Some Arawak Rock Artifacts from Jamaica. In *Proceedings of the Sixth International Congress for the Study of Pre-Columbian Cultures of the Lesser Antilles* (1975), pp. 304–313. Guadeloupe.

Roobol, M. J., and A. L. Smith

2004   *Volcanology of Saba and St. Eustatius, Northern Lesser Antilles.* Royal Netherlands Academy of Arts and Sciences, Amsterdam.

Rose, R.

1987   Lucayan Lifeways at the Time of Columbus. In *Proceedings of the First San Salvador Conference: Columbus and His World,* compiled by D. T. Gerace, pp. 321–339. CCFL Bahamian Field Station, Ft. Lauderdale, Florida.

Rostain, S.

1991   Approche pour une compréhension de l'emmanchement des haches d'Amazonie. In *Proceedings of the Thirteenth Congress of the International Association for Caribbean Archaeology,* edited by E. N. Ayubi and J. B. Haviser, vol. 1, pp. 167–186. Reports of the Archaeological-Anthropological Institute of the Netherlands Antilles, No. 9. Curaçao.

1994   *L'occupation amérindienne ancienne du littoral de Guayane,* 2 vols. Ph.D. dissertation, University of Paris I—Pantheon/Sorbonne, Éditions de l'ORSTROM, Paris.

1995   The Stone Material of Tanki Flip, Aruba. In *Proceedings of the Sixteenth Congress of the International Association for Caribbean Archaeology* (1995), edited by G. Richard, vol. 2, pp. 241–250. Conseil Régional de la Guadeloupe, Basse Terre.

1997   Tanki Flip Coral Material. In *The Archaeology of Aruba: The Tanki Flip Site,* edited by A. H. Versteeg and S. Rostain, pp. 251–256. Archaeological Museum Aruba, Aruba.

2001   Comparative Study of the Tools Made of Various Raw Materials, Tanki Flip Site, Aruba. Paper presented at the Nineteenth International Congress for Caribbean Archaeology, Aruba.

Rostain, S., and R. Dacal Moure

1997   Shape and Function of Tanki Flip Shell, Stone, Coral, and Bone Artifacts on a Comparative Level. In *The Archaeology of Aruba: The Tanki Flip Site,* edited by A. H. Versteeg and S. Rostain, pp. 265–278. Archaeological Museum Aruba, Aruba.

Rostain, S., and Y. Wack

1987   Haches et herminettes de Guyane Française. *Journal de la Société des Américanistes* 73:107–138. Musée de l'Homme, Paris.

Rottländer, R. C. A.

1975a   Some Aspects of the Patination of Flint. In Second International Symposium on Flint. *Staringia* 3:54–56.

1975b   The Formation of Patina on Flint. *Archaeometry* 17:106–110.

1989   Verwitterungserscheinungen an Keramik, Silices und Knochen. Verlag Archaeologica Venatoria. Institut für Urgeschichte der Universität Tübingen, Tübingen.

Rouse, I. B.

1939   *Prehistory in Haiti: A Study in Method.* Yale University Publications in Anthropology, No. 21, New Haven.

1941   An Analysis of the Artifacts of the 1914–1915 Porto Rican Survey. *Scientific Survey of Porto Rico and the Virgin Islands* 18(part 2):336–362, 442–453. New York Academy of Sciences, New York.

1964 Prehistory of the West Indies. *Science* 144:499–514.

1972 *Introduction to Prehistory: A Systematic Approach.* McGraw-Hill, New York.

1982 Ceramic and Religious Development in the Greater Antilles. *Journal of New World Archaeology* 5(2):45–52.

1986 *Migration in Prehistory: Inferring Population Movements from Cultural Remains.* Yale University Press, New Haven.

1989 Peoples and Cultures of the Saladoid Frontier in the Greater Antilles. In *Early Ceramic Population Lifeways and Adaptive Strategies in the Caribbean,* edited by P. E. Siegel, pp. 383–403. BAR International Series 506. British Archaeological Reports, Oxford.

1992 *The Tainos: Rise and Decline of the People Who Greeted Columbus.* Yale University Press, New Haven.

Rouse, I., and L. Allaire

1978 Caribbean. In *Chronologies in New World Archeology,* edited by R. E. Taylor and C. W. Meighan, pp. 431–81. Academic Press, New York.

Rouse, I. B., and J. M. Cruxent

1963 *Venezuelan Archaeology.* Yale University Press, New Haven.

Sanoja Obediente, Mario

1979 Las culturas formativas del oriente de Venezuela: La tradición barrancas del Bajo Orinoco. BANH, Ser, Estud., Monigr. Ensayos 6, Caracas.

Sassaman, K. E.

2003 New AMS Dates on Orange Fiber-Tempered Pottery from the Middle St. Johns Valley and Their Implications for Culture History in Northeast Florida. *The Florida Anthropologist* 56(1):5–13.

Sauer, C. O.

1966 *The Early Spanish Main.* University of California Press, Berkeley.

Scarry, C. M., and E. J. Reitz

2005 Changes in Foodways at the Parkin Site, Arkansas. *Southeastern Archaeology* 24(2):107–120.

Schiffer, M. B. (editor)

2001 *Anthropological Perspectives on Technology.* University of New Mexico Press, Albuquerque.

Schoener, T. W., D. A. Spiller, and J. B. Losos

2001 Natural Restoration of the Species-Area Relation for a Lizard after a Hurricane. *Science* 294:1525–1528.

Schoeninger, M., M. J. DeNiro, and H. Tauber

1993 Stable Nitrogen Isotope Ratios of Bone Collagen Reflect Marine and Terrestrial Components of Prehistoric Diet. *Science* 220:1831–1833.

Schroever, M., P. Guibert, F. Bechtel, M. Mattioni, and J. Evin

1985 Des hommes en Martinique vingt siècles avant Christophe Colomb? In *Proceedings of the Tenth International Congress for the Study of Pre-Colonial Cultures of the Lesser Antilles* (1983), edited by L. Allaire and F. M. Mayer, pp. 369–397. Centre de Recherches Caraïbes, Université de Montréal, Montreal.

Schweingruber, F. H.

1988 *Tree Rings: Basics and Applications of Dendrochronology.* Kluwer Academic Publishers, London.

1996 *Tree Rings and Environment: Dendroecology.* Swiss Federal Institute for Forest, Snow, and Landscape Research, Birmensdorf. Paul Haupt Publishers, Berne.

Scott, D. A.

1991 *Metallography and Microstructure of Ancient and Historic Metals.* Getty Conservation Institute, Marina del Rey, California.

Scott, G. R.

1973 Dental Morphology: A Genetic Study of American White Families and Variation in Living Southwest Indians. Unpublished Ph.D. dissertation. Arizona State University, Tempe.

1977 Classification, Sex Dimorphism, Association, and Population Variation of the Canine Distal Accessory Ridge. *Human Biology* 49:453–469.

Scott, G. R., and C. G. Turner

1997 *The Anthropology of Modern Human Teeth: Dental Anthropology and Its Variation in Recent Human Populations.* Cambridge University Press, Cambridge.

Scott, G. R., R. H. Yap Potter, J. F. Noss, A. A. Dahlberg, and T. Dahlberg

1983 The Dental Morphology of Pima Indians. *American Journal of Physical Anthropology* 61:13–31.

Scott Cummings, L.

2006 Manual for Pollen, Phytolith, Starch, and Macrofloral Sampling. Electronic docu-
(up- ment, www.paleoresearch.com/manuals/manual.html, accessed August 10, 2006.
dated) Paleo Research Institute, Golden, Colorado.

Scudder, S.

2001 Evidence of Sea Level Rise at the Early Ostionan Coralie Site (GT-3), ca. A.D. 700, Grand Turk, Turks and Caicos Islands. *Journal of Archaeological Science* 28:1221–1233.

Sears, W. H., and S. D. Sullivan

1978 Bahamas Archaeology. *American Antiquity* 43:3–25.

Semenov, S. A.

1964 *Prehistoric Technology.* Cory, Adams, and Mackay, London.

Serrand, N.

1995 *Strombus gigas* Parts and Their Utilisation for Artefact Manufacture: Tanki Flip, Aruba. In *Proceedings of the Sixteenth Congress of the International Association for Caribbean Archaeology,* edited by G. Richard, vol. 2, pp. 229–240. Conseil Régional de la Guadeloupe, Basse Terre.

1997 Tanki Flip Shell Artefacts with a Relatively High Modification. In *The Archaeology of Aruba: The Tanki Flip Site,* edited by A. H. Versteeg and S. Rostain, pp. 189–217. Archaeological Museum Aruba, Aruba.

2001 Occurrence of Exogenous Freshwater Bivalves (Unionidae) in the Lesser Antilles during the First Millennium A.D.. In *Proceedings of the Eighteenth International Congress for Caribbean Archaeology* (1999), edited by Association Internationale

d'Archéologie de la Caraïbe, Région Guadeloupe, Mission Archéologique, Guadeloupe, pp. 136–152. St. George's University Campus, True Blue, St. George, Grenada.

2002 Exploitation des invertébrés marins et terrestres par les populations Saladoïdes et
post-Saladoïdes du nord des Petites Antilles (500 B.C.–A.D. 1200), Étude de cas et
comparaisons. Unpublished Ph.D. dissertation, Université de Paris, Paris.

Serrand, N., R. Dacal Moure, and A. Reinink

1997 Conclusions on Tanki Flip Shells. In *The Archaeology of Aruba: The Tanki Flip
Site,* edited by A. H. Versteeg and S. Rostain, pp. 218–221. Archaeological Museum
Aruba, Aruba.

Shackley, M. S. (editor)

1998 *Archaeological Obsidian Studies: Method and Theory.* Advances in Archaeological
and Museum Science, vol. 3. Plenum Press, New York.

Sheets, P.

2006 *The Ceren Site: An Ancient Village Buried by Volcanic Ash in Central America,* 2nd
ed. Case Studies in Archaeology. Thomson Wadsworth, Belmont, California.

Sickler Robinson, L.

1978 Modified *Oliva* Shells from the Virgin Islands—A Morphological Study. In *Proceedings of the Seventh International Congress for the Study of Pre-Columbian Cultures of the Lesser Antilles,* edited by J. Benoist and F. M. Mayer, pp. 169–187. Centre
de Recherches Caraïbes, Université de Montréal, Montreal.

Siegel, P. E.

1989 Site Structure, Demography, and Social Complexity in the Early Ceramic Age of
the Caribbean. In *Early Ceramic Population Lifeways and Adaptive Strategies in the
Caribbean,* edited by P. E. Siegel, pp. 129–144. BAR International series 506. British
Archaeological Reports, Oxford.

1999 Contested Places and Places of Contest: The Evolution of Social Power and Ceremonial Space in Puerto Rico. *Latin American Antiquity* 10(3):209–238.

Siegel, P. E., and K. P. Severin

1993 The First Documented Prehistoric Gold-Copper Alloy Artefact from the West Indies. *Journal of Archaeological Science* 20:67–79.

Sieveking, G. de G., P. Bush, J. Ferguson, P. T. Craddock, M. J. Hughes, and M. R. Cowell

1972 Prehistoric Flint Mines and Their Identification as Sources. *Archaeometry*
14:151–176.

Sil, J. L. R., L. Torres, F. Franco, and E. O. Diaz

2004 Superficies enriquecidas de objetos en oro: Dorado por depleción o corrosión
superficial? Estudio de corrosión y oxidación en aleaciones de oro. In *Tecnología
del oro antiguo: Europa y América,* Anejos del Archivo Español de Arqueología
XXXII, edited by A. Perea, I. Montero, and O. García-Vuelta, pp. 41–47. Consejo
Superior de Investigaciones Científicas, Madrid.

Sipe, E. S., J. P. Collins, A. E. Dittert, and R. C. Goodwin

1980 The Preservation and Study of Prehistoric Coral and Coral Artifacts: A Prelimi-
nary Study from St. Kitts, West Indies. In *Proceedings of the Eighth International
Congress for the Study of Pre-Columbian Cultures of the Lesser Antilles,* pp. 246–263.
Tempe, Arizona.

Sjøvold, T.

1973   Occurrence of Minor Non-Metrical Variants in the Skeleton and Their Quantitative Treatment for Population Comparison. *Homo* 24:204–233.

Skibo, J. M., M. B. Schiffer, and K. C. Reid

1989   Organic Tempered Pottery: An Experimental Study. *American Antiquity* 54:122–146.

Smith, B. D.

2001   Low-Level Food Production. *Journal of Archaeological Research* 9(1):1–43.

2006   Eastern North America as an Independent Center of Plant Domestication. *Proceedings of the National Academy of Sciences* 103(33):12223–12228.

Smith, C. A. B.

1977   A Note on Genetic Distance. *Annals of Human Genetics* 40:463–479.

Stark, M. T. (editor)

1998   *The Archaeology of Social Boundaries.* Smithsonian Institution Press, Washington, D.C.

Steadman, D. W., and A. V. Stokes

2002   Changing Exploitation of Terrestrial Vertebrates during the Past 3,000 Years on Tobago, West Indies. *Human Ecology* 30:339–367.

Steenvoorden, R. I.

1992   Golden Rock Coral. In *The Archaeology of St. Eustatius: The Golden Rock Site,* edited by A. H. Versteeg and K. Schinkel, pp. 119–138. Publications of the St. Eustatius Historical Foundation, No. 2/Publication of the Foundation for Scientific Research in the Caribbean Region, No. 131. St. Eustatius/Amsterdam.

Stevens, F.

2002   Morel Rocks: A Study of Lithics of a La Hueca/Cedros Style Settlement at Morel, Guadeloupe, French West Indies. Unpublished master's thesis, Faculty of Archaeology, Leiden University, Leiden.

Stevens-Arroyo, A. M.

2006   *Cave of the Jagua: The Mythologica World of the Tainos.* University of Scranton Press. Scranton.

Stokes, A. V.

1995   Understanding Prehistoric Subsistence in the West Indies Using Stable Isotope Analysis. In *Proceedings of the Fifteenth International Congress for Caribbean Archaeology* (1993), edited by R. E. Alegría and M. A. Rodríguez López, pp. 191–200. Centro de Estudios Avanzados de Puerto Rico Y el Caribe. Fundación Puertorriqueña de las Humanidades y la Universidad del Turabo, San Juan, Puerto Rico.

1998   A Biogeographic Survey of Prehistoric Human Diet in the West Indies Using Stable Isotopes. Unpublished Ph.D. dissertation, University of Florida, Gainesville.

2005   Ceramic-Age Dietary Patterns in Puerto Rico: Stable Isotopes and Island Biogeography. In *Ancient Borinquen: Archaeology and Ethnohistory of Native Puerto Rico,* edited by P. E. Siegel, pp. 185–201. University of Alabama Press, Tuscaloosa.

Stothert, K. E., K. A. Epstein, T. R. Cummins, and M. Freire

1991   Reconstructing Prehistoric Textile and Ceramic Technology from Impressions of

Cloth in Figurines from Ecuador. In *Materials Issues in Art and Archaeology II,* edited by P. B. Vandiver, J. Druzik, and G. S. Wheeler, pp. 767–776. Materials Research Society Symposium Proceedings, vol. 185. Materials Research Society, Pittsburgh.

Street-Perrott, F. A., P. E. Hales, R. A. Perrott, J. C. Fontes, V. R. Switzsur, and A. Pearson

1993   Late Quaternary Paleolimnology of a Tropical Marl Lake: Wallywash Great Pond, Jamaica. *Journal of Paleolimnology* 9:3–22.

Stringer, G. B., L. T. Humphrey, and T. Compton

1997   Cladistic Analysis of Dental Traits in Recent Humans Using a Fossil Outgroup. *Journal of Human Evolution* 32:389–402.

Sturtevant, W. C.

1961   Taíno Agriculture. In *The Evolution of Horticultural Systems in Native South America: Causes and Consequences,* edited by J. Wilbert, pp. 68–73. Anthropologica Supplement 2.

1969   History and Ethnography of Some West Indian Starches. In *The Domestication and Exploitation of Plants and Animals,* edited by P. J. Ucko, and G. W. Dimbleby, pp. 177–199. Aldine, Chicago.

Sullivan, S. D.

1981   The Colonization and Exploitation of the Turks and Caicos Islands. Unpublished Ph.D. dissertation, University of Illinois, Urbana-Champaign.

Sutty, L.

1978   A Study of Shells and Shelled Object from Six Precolumbian Sites in the Grenades of St. Vincent and Grenada. In *Proceedings of the Seventh International Congress for the Study of Pre-Columbian Cultures of the Lesser Antilles,* pp. 195–209, Universidad Central de Caracas, Caracas.

Szaszdi Nagy, A.

1984   *Un mundo que descubrió Colon: Las rutas del comercio prehispánico de los metales.* Museo de Colon, Cuadernos Colombinos XII, Valladolid.

Ten Brink, U. S., E. L. Geist, and B. D. Andrews

2006   Size Distribution of Submarine Landslides and Its Implication to Tsunami Hazard in Puerto Rico. *Geophysical Research Letters* 33, L11307, June 13.

Therin, M.

1998   The Movement of Starch Grains in Sediments. In *A Closer Look: Recent Australian Studies on Stone Tools,* edited by R. Fullagar, pp. 61–72. Sydney University Archaeological Methods Series 6, Sydney.

Thompson, M., P. R. Bush, and J. Ferguson

1986   The Analysis of Flint by Inductively Coupled Plasma Atomic Emission Spectrometry, as a Method of Source Determination. In *The Scientific Study of Flint and Chert, Proceedings of the Fourth International Flint Symposium,* edited by G. de G. Sieveking and M. B. Hart, 243–247. Cambridge University Press, Cambridge.

Tomblin, J.

1981   Earthquakes, Volcanoes, and Hurricanes: A Review of Natural Hazards and Vulnerability in the West Indies. *Ambio* 10(6):340–345.

Townsend, G. C., and T. Brown

1981   Morphogenetic Fields within the Dentition. *Australian Orthodontic Journal* 7:3–12.

Townsend, G. C., and N. G. Martin

1992   Fitting Genetic Model to Carabelli Trait Data in South Australian Twins. *Journal of Dental Research* 71:403–409.

Townsend, G. C., L. C. Richards, R. Brown, and W. B. Burgess

1988   Twin Zygosity Determination on the Basis of Dental Morphology. *Journal of Forensic Odonto-Stomatology* 6:1–15.

Townsend, G. C., P. Dempsey, T. Braun, G. Kaidonis, and L. Richards

1994   Teeth, Genes, and the Environment. *Perspecives in Human Biology* 4:35–46.

Townsend, G. C., L. C. Richards, T. Brown, V. B. Burgess, G. R. Travan, and J. R. Rogers

1992   Genetic Studies of Dental Morphology in South Australian Twins. In *Structure, Function, and Evolution of Teeth,* edited by P. Smith and E. Techernov, pp. 501–518. Freund Publishing House, London.

Tringham, R., G. Cooper, G. Odell, B. Voytek, and A. Whitman

1974   Experimentation in the Formation of Edge Damage: A New Approach to Lithic Analysis. *Journal of Field Archaeology* 1:171–196.

Turner, C. G.

1967   The Dentition of Arctic Peoples. Unpublished Ph.D. dissertation, University of Wisconsin, Madison.

1969   Microevolutionary Interpretations from the Dentition. *American Journal of Physical Anthropology* 30:421–426.

Turner, C. G., C. R. Nichol, and G. R. Scott

1991   Scoring Procedures for Key Morphological Traits of the Permanent Dentition: The Arizona State University Dental Anthropology System. In *Advances in Dental Anthropology,* edited by M. A. Kelley and C. S. Larsen, pp. 13–31. Wiley Liss, New York.

Ugent, D., S. Pozorski, and T. Pozorski

1986   Archaeological Manioc (*Manihot*) from Coastal Peru. *Economic Botany* 40(1):78–102.

Valcárcel Rojas, R.

2002   Reporte de composición metálica de objetos asociados a entierros en el sitio arqueológico El Chorro de Maíta. Departamento Centro Oriental de Arqueología, CITMA, Holguín, unpublished.

Valcárcel Rojas, R., and C. Rodríguez Arce

2003   Muerte, desigualdad social y jefatura en El Chorro de Maíta. *Catauro: Revista Cubana de Antropología* 5(8):124.

2005   El Chorro de Maíta: Social Inequality and Mortuary Space. In *Dialogues in Cuban Archaeology,* edited by L. A. Curet, S. L. Dawdy, and G. La Rosa, pp. 125–146. University of Alabama Press, Tuscaloosa.

Van As, A., and L. Jacobs

1992   A Technological Study of the Golden Rock Pottery. In *The Archaeology of St. Eustatius: The Golden Rock Site,* edited by A. H. Versteeg and K. Schinkel. pp. 119–138. Publications of the St. Eustatius Historical Foundation, No. 2/Publication of the

Foundation for Scientific Research in the Caribbean Region, No. 131. St. Eustatius/ Amsterdam.

Van de Noort, R., and A. O'Sullivan

2006   *Rethinking Wetland Archaeology.* Duckworth Debates in Archaeology Series. Gerald Duckworth, London.

Van den Bel, Martijn

1995   Kamuyune: The Palikur Potters of French Guyana. Unpublished master's thesis, Leiden University, Leiden.

Van den Bel, M., G. Hamburg, and L. Jacobs

1995   Kwep as a Temper for Clay among the Palikur. *Newsletter of the Department of Pottery Technology* (Leiden University) 13:43–51.

Van den Bos, P.

2006   Reconstructing Archaic Subsistence: Analysis of the Faunal Remains Found at the Plum Piece Site, Saba, Netherlands West Indies. Unpublished master's thesis, Leiden University, Leiden.

Van der Steen, E.

1992   Shell Artefacts of Golden Rock. In *The Archaeology of St. Eustatius. The Golden Rock Site,* edited by A. H. Versteeg and K. Schinkel, pp. 93–118. Publications of the St. Eustatius Historical Foundation, No. 2/Publication of the Foundation for Scientific Research in the Caribbean Region, No. 131. St. Eustatius/Amsterdam.

Van Gijn, A.

1990   The Wear and Tear of Flint: Principles of Functional Analysis Applied to Dutch Neolithic Assemblages. Unpublished Ph.D. dissertation, Leiden University, Leiden. Also appeared in *Analecta Praehistorica Leidensia* 22.

1998   Craft Activities in the Dutch Neolithic: A Lithic Viewpoint. In *Understanding the Neolithic of North-Western Europe,* edited by M. Edmonds and C. Richards, pp. 328–350. Cruithne Press, Glasgow.

2005   A Functional Analysis of Some Late Mesolithic Bone and Antler Implements from the Dutch Coastal Zone. In *From Hooves to Horns, from Mollusc to Mammoth: Manufacture and Use of Bone Artifacts from Prehistoric Times to the Present,* Proceedings of the Fourth Meeting of the ICAZ Worked Bone Research Group at Tallinn, 26th–31st of August 2003, edited by H. Luik, A. M. Choyke, C. E. Batey, and L. Lougas, pp. 47–66. Muinasaja Teadus 15, Tallinn.

In press Toolkits and Technological Choices at the Middle Neolithic Site of Schipluiden, The Netherlands. In *"Prehistoric Technology" 40 Years Later: Functional Studies and the Russian Legacy.* Proceedings of the Conference Held in Verona, Italy, April 20–23, 2005, edited by L. Longo, M. Dalla Riva, and M. Saracino. Verona.

Van Gijn, A. L., and C. L. Hofman

In press Were These Fragments Used as Tools in Pottery Manufacture? An Exploratory Study of Abraded Potsherds from the Sites of Anse à la Gourde and Morel, Guadeloupe. *Caribbean Journal of Science.*

Van Gijn, A. L., V. van Betuw, A. Verbaas, and K. Wentink

2006   Flint: Procurement and Use. In *Schipluiden-Harnaschpolder: A Middle Neolithic*

Site on the Dutch Coast (3800–3500 B.C.), edited by L. P. Louwe Kooijmans and P. F. B. Jongste, *Analecta Praehistorica Leidensia* 37/38:137–176.

Van Klinken, G.-J.

1991   *Dating and Dietary Reconstruction by Isotopic Analyses of Amino Acids in Fossil Bone Collagen—with Special Reference to the Caribbean.* Publications of the Foundation for Scientific Research in the Caribbean Region, 128, Amsterdam.

Van Olst, P., and M. L. P. Hoogland

1996   Physical Setting. In In Search of the Native Population of Pre-Colonial Saba (A.D. 400–1450): Settlements in Their Natural and Social Environment, by M. L. P. Hoogland, pp. 13–40. Unpublished Ph.D. dissertation, Leiden University, Leiden.

Van Soest, M. C.

2000   Sediment Subduction and Crustal Contamination in the Lesser Antilles Island Arc: The Geochemical and Isotopic Imprints on Recent Lavas and Geothermal Fluids. Unpublished Ph.D. dissertation, Vrije Universiteit Amsterdam (Free University Amsterdam), Amsterdam.

Van Tooren, M., and J. B. Haviser

1995   Petrographic Analysis of Lithic Material Recovered from Hope Estate, St. Martin and the Potential Indications of Regional Contact. In *Proceedings of the Sixteenth International Congress for Caribbean Archaeology,* edited by G. Richard, vol. 2, pp. 251–260. Conseil Régional de la Guadeloupe, Basse Terre.

Varela, S. L., A. L. van Gijn, and L. Jacobs

2002   De-Mystifying Pottery Production in the Maya Lowlands: Detection of Traces of Use-Wear on Pottery Sherds through Microscopic Analysis and Experimental Replication. *Journal of Archaeological Sciences* 29:1133–1147.

Vargas Arenas, I.

1997   Puerto Santo: Un nuevo sitio arqueológico en la costa oriental de Venezuela. In *Proceedings of the Seventh International Congress for the Study of Pre-Columbian Cultures of the Lesser Antilles,* edited by J. Benoist and F. M. Mayer, pp. 212–220. Centre de Recherches Caraïbes, Université de Montréal, Montreal.

1979a   Orígenes y filiaciones de la tradición Saladero del Orinoco Medio. *Economía y Ciencias Sociales* 18(4):112–128.

1979b   *La tradición Saladoide del oriente de Venezuela: La fase cuartel.* BANH, Ser. Estud., Monogr. Ensayos 5, Caracas.

Vargas Arenas, I., M. I. Toledo, M. E. Molina, and C. E. Moncourt

1993   Los artefactos de concha. *Contribuciones de la Arqueología Tropical* 1. USDA Forest Service Southern Region, Organización de los Estados Americanos.

Vega, B.

1979   *Los metales y los aborígenes de la Hispaniola.* Museo del Hombre Dominicano and Fundación Garcia Arévalo, Santo Domingo.

Veloz Maggiolo, M.

1980   *Las sociedades arcaicas de Santo Domingo.* Museo del Hombre Dominicano and Fundación García Arévalo, Santo Domingo.

1991   *Panorama histórico del Caribe precolombino.* Edición del Banco Central de la Republica Dominicana, Santo Domingo.

1992 Notas sobre la zamia en la prehistoria del Caribe. *Revista de Arqueología Americana* 6:125–138.

1993 *La isla de Santo Domingo antes de Colón.* Edición Banco Central Republica Dominicana, Quinta Centenario del Descubrimiento de América, Santo Domingo.

1996 *Barril sin fondo: Antropología para los curiosos.* Editora de Colores C. por A., Santo Domingo.

Veloz Maggiolo, M., and E. Ortega

1973 *El precerámico de Santo Domingo, nuevos lugares y su posible relación con otros puntos del área antillana.* Pap. Oc. 1, Museo del Hombre Dominicano, Santo Domingo.

1976 The Preceramic of the Dominican Republic: Some New Finds and Their Possible Relationships. In *Proceedings of the First Puerto Rican Symposium on Archaeology,* edited by L. S. Robinson, pp. 147–201. Fundación Arqueológica e Histórica de Puerto Rico, San Juan.

Veloz Maggiolo, M., E. Ortega, and A. Caba Fuentes

1981 *Los modos de vida Meillacoides y sus posibles orígenes.* Museo del Hombre Dominicano, Santo Domingo.

Vescelius, G. S., and L. S. Robinson

1979 Exotic Items in Archaeological Collections from St. Croix: Prehistorical Imports and Their Complications. Paper presented at the Eighth International Congress for the Study of Precolumbian Cultures of the Lesser Antilles, St. Kitts.

Vialon, A.

2001 L'outillage lithique non taillé: Approche pétrographique et tracéologique. In *Le site de l'Anse à la Gourde, St. François, Grande-Terre, Guadeloupe. Fouille programmée pluriannuelle 1995–2000,* edited by C. L. Hofman, M. L. P. Hoogland, and A. Delpuech, pp 223–233. Rapport de synthèse 2000, Direction Régionale des Affaires Culturelles/Université de Leiden, Basse-Terre/Leiden.

Volckmann, R. P.

1984a *Geologic Map of Cabo Rojo and Parguera Quadrangles, Southwest Puerto Rico.* U.S. Geological Survey Miscellaneous Investigations Series Map I-1557, scale 1:20,000.

1984b *Geologic Map of the Puerto Real Quadrangle, Southwest Puerto Rico.* U.S. Geological Survey Miscellaneous Investigations Series Map I-1559, scale 1:20,000.

Volpato, G., R. Marcucci, N. Tornadore, and M. G. Paoletti

2004 Domestication Process of the Two *Solanum* Section Lasiocarpa Species among Amerindians in the Upper Orinoco, Venezuela, with Special Focus on Piaroa Indians. *Economic Botany* 58(2):184–194.

Vredenbregt, A. H. L.

2002 *Ori:no Ka:nan Wene:po:* Symbolic Content of Kari'na Material Culture. An Ethnoarchaeological Case Study. Unpublished master's thesis, Leiden University, Leiden.

2004 From Myth to Matter: The Ceramic Tradition of the Kari'na of Northeast Suriname. *Leiden Journal of Pottery Studies* 20:75–98.

Wadge, G.

1994 The Lesser Antilles. In *Caribbean Geology: An Introduction,* edited by S. K. Donovan and T. A. Jackson, pp. 167–178. U.W.I. Publishers' Association, Kingston.

Walker, J. B.

1980a Analysis and Replication of Lithic Artifacts from the Sugar Factory Pier Site, St. Kitts. In *Proceedings of the Eighth International Congress for the Study of the Pre-Columbian Cultures of the Lesser Antilles,* edited by S. M. Lewenstein, pp. 69–79. Arizona State University, Anthropological Research Papers No. 22, Tempe.

1980b Analysis and Replication of the Lithic Artifacts from the Sugar Factory Pier Site, St. Kitts, West Indies. Unpublished master's thesis, Washington State University, Pullman.

1983 Use-Wear Analysis of Caribbean Flaked Stone Tools. In *Proceedings of the Ninth International Congress for the Study of the Pre-Columbian Cultures of the Lesser Antilles,* edited by L. Allaire and F. M. Mayer, pp. 239–247. Centre de Recherches Caraïbes, Université de Montréal, Montreal.

Walter, V.

1991 Analyses pétrographiques et minéralogiques de céramiques précolombiennes de Martinique. *Caribena* 1:11–54.

Watters, D. R.

1982 Relating Oceanography to Antillean Archaeology: Implications from Oceania. *Journal of New World Archaeology* 5:3–12.

1997a Ancient Beadmakers of the Caribbean. *Carnegie Magazine* 63:58.

1997b Stone Beads in the Pre-Historic Caribbean. *Bead Study Trust Newsletter* 29:7–8.

1997c Maritime Trade in the Prehistoric Eastern Caribbean. In *The Indigenous People of the Caribbean,* edited by S. M. Wilson, pp. 88–99. University Press of Florida, Gainesville.

Watters, D. R., and I. B. Rouse

1989 Environmental Diversity and Maritime Adaptations in the Caribbean Area. In *Early Ceramic Population Lifeways and Adaptive Strategies in the Caribbean,* edited by P. E. Siegel, pp. 129–144. BAR International series 506. British Archaeological Reports, Oxford.

Watters, D. R., and R. Scaglion

1994 Beads and Pendants from Trants, Montserrat: Implications for the Prehistoric Lapidary Industry of the Caribbean. *Annals of the Carnegie Museum* 63:215–237.

Weiss, M. P.

1994 Oligocene Limestones of Antigua, West Indies: Neptune Succeeds Vulcan. *Caribbean Journal of Science* 30:1–29.

Westermann, J. H., and H. Kiel

1961 *The Geology of Saba and St. Eustatius, with Notes on the Geology of St. Kitts, Nevis, and Montserrat (Lesser Antilles).* Uitgaven Natuurwetenschappelijke Studiekring voor Suriname en de Nederlandse Antillen 24, Utrecht.

Whitehead, N. L.

1990 The Mazaruni Pectoral: A Golden Artefact Discovered in Guyana and the Historical Sources Concerning Native Metallurgy in the Caribbean, Orinoco, and Northern Amazonia. *Journal of Archaeology and Anthropology* 7:19–38.

Willey, G. R., and J. A. Sabloff

1974 *A History of American Archaeology.* W. H. Freeman, San Francisco.

Williams, M. W.

1986   Sub-Surface Patterning at Puerto Real: A 16th Century Town on Haiti's North Coast. *Journal of Field Archaeology* 13:283–296.

Wilson, S. M., H. B. Iceland, and T. R. Hester

1998   Preceramic Connections between Yucatán and the Caribbean. *Latin American Antiquity* 9:342–352.

Wing, E. S., and E. J. Reitz

1982   Prehistoric Fishing Communities of the Caribbean. *Journal of New World Archaeology* 5:13–32.

Winter, J.

1978   A Note on Bahamian Griddles. In *Proceedings of the Seventh International Congress for the Study of Pre-Columbian Cultures of the Lesser Antilles,* edited by J. Benoist and F. M. Mayer, pp. 232–236. Centre de Recherches Caraïbes, Université de Montréal, Montreal.

Winter, J., and M. Gilstrap

1991   Preliminary Results of Ceramic Analysis and the Movement of Populations into the Bahamas. In *Proceedings of the Twelfth International Congress for Caribbean Archaeology,* edited by L. S. Robinson, pp. 371–386, Association Internationale d'Archéologie de la Caraïbe, Martinique.

Wright, L. E.

2005   Identifying Immigrants to Tikal, Guatemala: Defining Local Variability in Strontium Isotope Ratios of Human Tooth Enamel. *Journal of Archaeological Science* 32:555–566.

Yde, J.

1967   *Material Culture of the Wai Wai.* Ethnographic Series 10. National Museum of Copenhagen, Copenhagen.

Zaldivar, M. E., O. J. Rocha, G. Aguilar, L. Castro, E. Castro, and R. Barrantes

2004   Genetic Variation of Cassava (*Manihot esculenta* Cranz) Cultivated by Chibchan Amerindians of Costa Rica. *Economic Botany* 58(2):204–213.

Zeder, M. A., D. G. Bradley, E. Emshwiller, and B. D. Smith, eds.

2006   *Documenting Domestication: New Genetic and Archaeological Paradigms.* University of California Press, Berkeley.

Zijlstra, J. J. P.

1987   Early Diagenetic Silica Precipitation in Relation to Redox Boundaries and Bacterial Metabolism in Late-Cretaceous Chalk of the Maastrichtian Type Locality. *Geologie en Mijnbouw* 66:343–355.

1994   Sedimentology of the Late Cretaceous and Early Tertiary (Tuffaceous) Chalk of Northwest Europe. Geologica Ultraiectina No. 119. Utrecht.

1995   The Sedimentology of Chalk. *Lecture Notes in Earth Sciences* 54.

Zona, S.

2004   Raphides in Palm Embryos and Their Systematic Distribution. *Annals of Botany* 93:415–421.

Contributors

Benoît Bérard is Maître de Conférences (associate professor) of Caribbean archaeology at the Université des Antilles et de la Guyane. He has been conducting archaeological research in Martinique and Dominica. He is currently the director of the French Ministry of Foreign Affairs archaeological mission in Dominica. His research themes center on lithic technology and the first migrations of agroceramist into the Antilles.

Mathijs Booden is pursuing a Ph.D. in geology at the University of Auckland, New Zealand. His current research is on the alteration of volcanic rock by upwelling hydrothermal fluids. He explores the relation between different types of alteration and the formation of precious metal ore deposits.

Iris Briels studied Caribbean archaeology at Leiden University. She graduated in 2004, specializing in use-wear analysis of flint tools. Her research concentrated on the flint assemblage of the Archaic Age Plum Piece site on Saba (Dutch Antilles). She has participated in fieldwork on several islands of the Lesser Antilles and is currently working for RAAP, a Dutch archaeological consulting firm.

Jago Cooper is a Ph.D. student and codirector of the Forum for Island Research and Experience at the Institute of Archaeology, University College London. His main research interests are focused on the changing patterns of cultural interaction in the Caribbean, and he is currently involved with a number of collaborative archaeological projects in Cuba.

Alfredo Coppa is full professor of physical anthropology at the University of Rome "La Sapienza" in Italy. He has conducted studies of human population paleobiology in the Caribbean and circum-Caribbean areas researching in different islands of both the Greater and the Lesser Antilles (Dominican Republic, Cuba, Puerto Rico, U.S. Virgin Islands, Guadeloupe, Martinique, Trinidad, and Curacao). For such studies he has received funding by the University "La Sapienza" of Rome and by the Italian Ministry of Foreign Affairs. Currently his research in the area focuses on the analysis of precontact migratory movements.

Andrea Cucina is a full-time research professor "A" at the Facultad de Ciencias Antropológicas of the Universidad Autónoma de Yucatán in Mérida, Mexico. He received his Ph.D. in paleopathology at the School of Medicine, Catholic University of Rome. His research interests include skeletal biology, with an emphasis on dental anthropology. He is currently investigating the peopling of the Caribbean before the European contact as well as bioarchaeology of the ancient Maya populations.

Gareth Davies is full professor in petrology and chair of the Department of Petrology since 2004 at the Faculty of Earth and Life Sciences, Free University Amsterdam. He is the editor of the *Journal of Petrology.*

Hylke de Jong obtained his master's degree from Leiden University in 2003 specializing in Caribbean archaeology. His thesis was a pilot study applying $^{87}Sr/^{86}Sr$ analysis to the site of Anse à la Gourde, Guadeloupe. Currently, he is doing his Ph.D. (Faculty of Arts Scholarship) at the University of Bristol assessing past human diet and mobility through changes in $^{87}Sr/^{86}Sr$ along tooth enamel using Laser Ablation MC-ICPMS.

Christy de Mille has been involved with the Antigua Archaeological Project for 12 years. She currently codirects an archaeological field school on Antigua run through the Department of Archaeology, University of Calgary. She is also employed as a consulting archaeologist at Bison Historical Services Ltd., Calgary, Alberta, Canada. Her research interests include the Antiguan Preceramic and Saladoid lapidary technology.

Corinne Hofman is full professor of Caribbean archaeology at the Faculty of Archaeology at Leiden University in the Netherlands. She has been conducting archaeological research on several islands of the Lesser Antilles for which she was awarded grants from the Netherlands Foundation for Scientific Research (NWO). Her current research themes center on mobility and exchange and sociopolitical organization in the precolonial Caribbean.

Menno Hoogland is associate professor at the Faculty of Archaeology at Leiden University. In 2004 he was awarded a grant by the Netherlands Foundation for Scientific Research (NWO) for the program "Houses for the Living and the Dead." The project focuses on the organization of Taíno households in the Dominican Republic (A.D. 1000–1500) and is executed in cooperation with the Museo del Hombre Dominicano.

Charlene Dixon Hutcheson is an independent archaeologist in Roanoke, Virginia. She has been working in the Bahamas since 1995 on Lucayan basketry impressed pottery through the Lucayan Ecological Archaeology Project under the direction of Mary Jane Berman and Perry L. Gnivecki. She has also excavated in

Wales, U.K. since 1994, and, since 2002, has worked principally with the Llangynidr History Society on two medieval sites in the Brecon Beacons mountain range.

Daan Isendoorn is a Ph.D. student at the Faculty of Archaeology, Leiden University. His research focus is on the identification of the provenance areas of precolonial exchange items from the Caribbean within the NWO-funded Vidi-project "Mobility and Exchange: Dynamics of Material, Social, and Ideological Relations in the Pre-Columbian Insular Caribbean," directed by Prof. dr. Corinne Hofman.

Loe Jacobs is a ceramist at the Ceramic Laboratory of the Faculty of Archaeology, Leiden University. He has been involved, among others, in the Leiden Caribbean research projects since the 1980s and is coauthor of many publications on pottery technology.

William F. Keegan is curator of Caribbean archaeology at the Florida Museum of Natural History, and professor of anthropology and Latin American Studies at the University of Florida, Gainesville. He has directed research throughout the Caribbean with a focus on social organization and cultural diversity.

Harold J. Kelly obtained his master's degree in archaeology at Leiden University in 2003 and since then has been working at the Archaeological Museum of Aruba in the Scientific Department. He is specialized in experimental archaeology and use-wear analysis on coral artifacts. He publishes on a regular bases in local and international magazines, with rock art and the protection of cultural heritage as special points of interest.

Sebastiaan Knippenberg is currently working for Archol BV, a contract archaeology firm associated with Leiden University. He conducted and participated in many fieldwork projects in the northern Lesser Antilles. Knippenberg recently finished his Ph.D. dissertation about stone artifact production and exchange during the Ceramic Age in the northern Lesser Antilles. During the course of this Ph.D. work he visited many islands and studied collections from many sites.

Yvonne M. J. Lammers-Keijsers is preparing a Ph.D. thesis at Leiden University on the functional analysis of shell tools and flint and stone implements from the pre-Columbian sites of Morel and Anse à la Gourde, Guadeloupe. She is currently working for The Foundation for Dutch Archaeology.

Michaela Lucci, Ph.D., is contract research collaborator of the Department of Human and Animal Biology at the University of Rome "La Sapienza." She has participated in the studies regarding the Caribbean precontact populations examining anthropological remains in the Dominican Republic, the U.S. Virgin Islands, and in Florida. She is a member of the Italian archaeo-anthropological mission in the Dominican Republic.

Fernando Luna Calderón has been director of the Department of Physical Anthropology and director of the Dominican Museo del Hombre, and afterwards director of the Museo Nacional de Historia Natural, a role he held to the day of his premature death in 2005. He has taken part in all of the most important excavations of pre-Columbian sites and cemeteries in the Dominican Republic, as well as in excavations in Martinique, Puerto Rico, and Bolivia. He has been the leading expert of paleopathology of the Taíno populations of the Dominican Republic and has been codirector of the excavation of Loma Candelon in collaboration with the Italian archaeo-anthropological mission in the Dominican Republic.

Marcos Martinón-Torres is lecturer in archaeological science and material culture at the Institute of Archaeology, University College London. He has a special interest in the integration of scientific, archaeological, and textual approaches to materials and technologies, and the way in which these inform about past theories and practices. He has worked primarily on medieval and later metallurgy and alchemy in the Old and New Worlds.

Lee A. Newsom is associate professor of archaeological anthropology at the Pennsylvania State University. Her research is focused in paleoethnobotany with emphasis on human-landscape interactions and the sustainability of biological resources. She has analyzed archaeobotanical assemblages from throughout the Caribbean in collaboration with researchers from several institutions, and is currently involved in projects in the Lesser Antilles islands, Puerto Rico, Hispaniola, and Florida.

Channah Nieuwenhuis is a wear trace and residue specialist working at the Laboratory for Artifact Studies at the Faculty of Archaeology of Leiden University in the Netherlands. She conducted Ph.D. research on chert artifacts from preceramic sites in Colombia. For the past two years she has studied wear traces on artifacts from various sites in the Netherlands and South America and has been engaged in building a reference collection for residue analysis like phytoliths and starch.

José R. Oliver is a lecturer in Latin American archaeology at the Institute of Archaeology, University College London. He has conducted research in Venezuela and the Caribbean, particularly in Puerto Rico, for which he has received grants from the British Academy, the Consejo Para la Protecciòn del Patrimonio Arqueològico de Puerto Rico, and the Puerto Rico State Preservation Historical Office. Research is currently focused on the civic-ceremonial centers (*bateyes*) of the Caguana-Utuado region and on village lifeways and agrarian economies of late (Taíno) societies in Puerto Rico and Dominican Republic.

Jaime R. Pagán Jiménez is a Puerto Rican archaeo-ethnobotanist and independent researcher/consultant in cultural resources management. His main works deal with the early introduction of useful plants into the Caribbean islands and with the interregional dynamics developed around the spread of plants and culinary-cultural traditions of the circum-Caribbean. Other lines of interest are the sociopolitical dimensions of the archaeological practices within Latin America and the Caribbean.

Raphaël G. A. M. Panhuysen is a postdoctoral researcher at the Faculty of Archaeology, Leiden University. He is currently studying the physical anthropology and paleopathology of the buried human remains excavated at Anse à la Gourde, Guadeloupe. His research focuses on developments in health and demography in the Caribbean before the arrival of Columbus.

Roberto Rodríguez Suárez is a Cuban anthropologist and a full-time researcher-professor of the Museo Antropológico Luis Montané, University of Havana. Some of his main research areas are paleonutrition (trace elements of human bones), chemistry and physics of archaeological soils and objects, chronometry, and museum organization. He is now leading a multidisciplinary project at the important Cuban archaeological site Canímar, Provincia de Matanzas.

Glenis Tavarez María is director of the Department of Physical Anthropology of the Dominican Museo del Hombre. She has worked in different archaeological projects in her country, in Martinique and Florida, and in Europe. Her studies focus on the burial practices of the Santo Domingo aborigines and on the first colonial manufactures of the sixteenth century.

Michael Turney is currently employed as a consulting archaeologist by Golder Associates Ltd., in Calgary, Alberta, Canada. His master's thesis was focused on Saladoid period shell artifact assemblages from Antigua, West Indies. He has been involved in archaeological research on both Antigua and St. Vincent, and he maintains an interest in prehistoric artistic expression in the Caribbean.

Roberto Valcárcel Rojas is researcher at the Departamento Centro Oriental de Arqueología del Ministerio de Ciencias, Tecnología y Medio Ambiente de Cuba. He directs the investigations at the site of El Chorro de Maíta and other archaeological sites in Cuba. He is specifically interested in social organization, esthetic expressions, and contacts between the native population and the Europeans.

Annelou van Gijn is associate professor in Material Culture Studies at the Faculty of Archaeology and head of the Laboratory for Artifact Studies at Leiden University, the Netherlands. Her research of technological systems by means of technological and use-wear studies of prehistoric implements focuses on the northwest European late Mesolithic and Neolithic, but her interest also extends to understanding technological choices in Caribbean context.

Rita Vargiu is professor at University of Naples "Federico II," Italy. She has been conducting paleobiological studies on Caribbean human samples dated to the precontact and contact periods. At present, her research is focused on the development of statistical methods useful in reconstructing migratory waves by means of skeletal records.

Tamara Varney is assistant professor of bioanthropology in the Department of Anthropology at Lakehead University in Thunder Bay, Ontario, Canada. For the past nine years she has primarily conducted research on Antigua in conjunction with the Antigua Archaeological Project, and has also worked on projects based on Guadeloupe and Montserrat. In addition, she continues to codirect a field school

through the Department of Archaeology, University of Calgary. Her main research interests focus on diet, health, and population dispersal in the West Indies.

Johannes Zijlstra is chief scientist of a public company that develops methods for treatment for heavy metal pollution with red mud waste of the alumina refinery industry. As a member of the Geochemistry Department of Utrecht University and specialist on the geochemistry and sedimentology of European flint, he was invited by Sebastiaan Knippenberg to help with the investigations of the geology of the chert and flint from Antigua.

Index

.